The Shaping of
Jewish Identity in
Nineteenth-century
France

The Shaping of Jewish Identity in Nineteenth-century France

JAY R. BERKOVITZ

WAYNE STATE UNIVERSITY PRESS   DETROIT

Library of Congress Cataloging-in-Publication Data

Berkovitz, Jay R., 1951–
  The shaping of Jewish identity in nineteenth-century France /
Jay R. Berkovitz.
     p. cm.
  Bibliography: p.
  Includes index.
  ISBN 0-8143-2011-2
  1. Jews—France—Emancipation. 2. Judaism—France—
History—19th century. 3. France—Ethnic relations. I. Title.
DS135.F83B47   1989
  ISBN 0-8143-2012-0(pbk.)   89–16507

To my mother and to the memory of my father

Contents

Acknowledgments

IT IS A PLEASURE for me to express my appreciation to the many individuals who have assisted me in this scholarly endeavor. First, I wish to thank my teachers in the Department of Near Eastern and Judaic Studies at Brandeis University. I am grateful to Professor Ben Halpern for introducing me to the rigors of historical method and to Professor Benjamin Ravid for his patient guidance of my doctoral dissertation. Professor Marvin Fox deserves special mention, not only for helping me learn to appreciate the centrality of classical texts in Jewish history, but also for his unfailing encouragement and sage counsel.

The Memorial Foundation for Jewish Culture and the National Foundation for Jewish Culture provided generous assistance for my dissertation research. I also wish to acknowledge the Graduate Research Council of the University of Massachusetts at Amherst for awarding me a Faculty Research Grant in 1983 to study resistance to modernization, and Professor Murray M. Schwartz, Dean of the Faculty of Humanities and Fine Arts for his support of several research related activities.

I wish to thank the staffs of the numerous archives and libraries which I consulted: Brandeis University Goldfarb Library, and the Rapaporte Treasure Hall which houses the Franco-Judaica Archival Collection; Houghton Library, Harvard University; the Archives of the Jewish Theological Seminary of America, New York; the Archives of the Leo Baeck Institute, New York; the Klau Library and French Jewish Archival Collection, the Hebrew Union College, Cincinnati; the Archives Nationales, Paris; the Bibliothèque Nationale, Paris; the Archives of the Central Consistory and the Paris Consistory; the Library of the *Alliance Israélite Universelle*, Paris; Musee Lorrain, Nancy; the Institute for Microfilmed Hebrew Manuscripts, Jerusalem; the Central Archives for the History of the Jewish People, Jerusalem; Asher Library, Spertus College of Judaica, Chicago; and the University of Massachusetts Library. I also want to express my appreciation to Dr. Bernhard Blumenkranz, director of the *Commission Française des Archives Juives*, for sharing with me sources of the *Nouvelle Gallia Judaica*.

Over the course of the research and writing of this book I have benefited greatly from the generosity of many colleagues and friends. Professors David Ellenson and Aron Rodrigue read the manuscript and offered valuable comments. Professors Shmuel Bolozky, Monford Harris, Jonathan Helfand, and Charles Rearick were kind enough to answer queries and to discuss various difficulties. I am grateful to Professor Moshe Berger for his willingness to discuss some of the broader conceptual issues raised in this study. Professor Charles Raffel has been a loyal friend and a tireless sounding board for many of the ideas in this book and has helped me to clarify my thinking on numerous issues.

The arduous task of producing this volume has been facilitated by the assistance of Peri Tarr and Ellen Seger who typed the manuscript. Betsey Chadwick offered skillful editorial assistance and insightful criticism, all the while prodding me to develop and expand my thinking. I am also grateful to Robert Mandel, director of the Wayne State University Press and to my editors, Laurel Brandt and Anne Adamus.

Finally, I want to express my gratitude to Professor Isadore Twersky, whose own research has illuminated a different era of French and general Jewish intellectual history. He has had a profound and sustaining influence not only on my intellectual growth, but also on my personal vision.

Needless to say, I alone am responsible for the errors and shortcomings in this book.

This book is dedicated to my mother and to the memory of my father. My parents instilled in me a love of learning, took a keen interest in my work, and were selfless in their devotion to me and my brothers. Together they created a home filled with warmth and love, a home where ideas informed our values. Regrettably, my father (d. 5 Tammuz 5742) did not live to see the completion of this work. Nevertheless, the legacy of honesty and kindness which he left behind remains an enriching inspiration for me and our family.

To my dear wife Sharon go the thanks of a frequently preoccupied husband. I am grateful for her many sacrifices that have made it possible for me to complete this book.

10

Introduction

SINCE THE LATE eighteenth century, the Jews of Europe and their descendants have been preoccupied with an ongoing struggle to preserve their identity in a new and rapidly changing world. In this they have not, of course, been unique; like other sectors of European society, Jewish communities were transformed by nineteenth-century economic and social developments. The forces of urbanization, industrialization, and secularization upset the relative stability of a life rooted in tradition. Communal structures were disassembled, the family ceased to function as the basic framework for socialization, and religious authority was undermined by new philosophical, societal, and ideological concerns. Out of these upheavals, the question of identity emerged as a universal problem, marked by an urgent need to justify and define one's existence. Although the modern Jewish experience must be understood in these terms, those factors that distinguished it from the general European pattern must not be ignored. For the Jews—due to the special circumstances of their emancipation from centuries of legal disabilities—the process of modernization has been extraordinarily challenging and unusually intensive, frequently devastating in its consequences. Particularly in western and central Europe, the challenges of modernity have been met with a readiness to conform to the cultural norms of general society, frequently producing an attenuated loyalty to Jewish community and tradition and leading in some instances to the abandonment of

Jewish identity. The legacy of emancipation has been a seemingly irreversible process of alienation and estrangement.

This trend, however, has been neither entirely uniform nor universal. In France, the first country to emancipate the Jews, the Jewish community succeeded in maintaining its own distinct identity despite enormous pressures to become part of the overwhelming Christian majority. Although many Jews assimilated comfortably into French society and culture and lost their connection to the Jewish community, the deterioration of Jewish loyalties was not as severe nor as rapid as might have been expected. Above all, neither the leadership nor the rank and file stood by as the forces of modernization took their toll. The question of how best to define Jewish identity and ensure its continuity was a powerful, evocative issue—an issue that sometimes divided the community, sometimes unified it. How did French Jews respond to the challenges of emancipation, and what enabled French Jewry to withstand the full impact of the forces of attrition?

In evaluating how the forces of revolution and modernization transformed the character of Jewish life in France, we must first consider the degree to which the Jews' own cultural legacy and socio-economic profile influenced larger patterns of integration and ethnic identity in the nineteenth century. Of what importance was the rich intellectual, cultural, and religious heritage of medieval French Jewry to the thinking of modern French Jews? Established since the Roman conquest of Gaul, the Jews of France have a distinguished, if uneven, history. From the year 1000 Franco-Jewish scholarship flourished, achieving its greatest heights in northern France. The most prominent early scholar was Rabbenu Gershom ben Judah (960–1030), known later as the "Light of the Exile." Under his leadership a rabbinic synod met at Worms and issued twenty-five *takkanot*, which ameliorated the legal status of women, promoted community solidarity and authority, and firmly established rules of honesty and morality. With Rabbi Solomon Yizhaki (1040–1105), or Rashi, there emerged a school devoted to biblical commentary, Talmudic study, and halakhah. To this day regarded as the greatest biblical exegete and Talmudic commentator, Rashi combined mastery of the tradition with critical acumen and unparalleled erudition. His use of French to define technical Hebrew terms has enabled modern scholars in their study of medieval French vocabulary and phonetics. The Tosaphists—so named for their "appendices" to Rashi's commentaries on the Talmud—devoted themselves to pointing out and resolving inconsistencies in Talmudic passages dealing with a common theme. Their method advanced the study of rabbinic literature and halakhah significantly.[1] A rival center of Jewish cultural creativity appeared in Provence in the mideleventh century and continued until the beginning of the fourteenth century. Compared to the Talmudists of the north, the Provençal scholars were concerned with a broader range of disciplines, including rabbinics, philosophy, mysticism, ethics, exegesis, and poetry. Their inquiries into metaphysics, medicine, mathematics, and astronomy reveal a concern for the natural sciences as well. R. Moses ha-Darshan of Narbonne, R. Abraham b. David of Posquières, R. David Kimḥi, R. Meshullam b. Jacob of Lunel, and R. Menaḥem ha-Me'iri of Perpignan are the most towering figures of Provençal Jewry. Expulsion of the Jews from France in 1306 and 1394 and the sale of the Comtat Venaissin to Pope Clement VI in 1348, swiftly put an end to Jewish creativity on French soil.[2]

Two centuries later political and economic conditions made it possible for Jews to settle again in France. The different circumstances under which the Sephardim and Ashkenazim were admitted into France account for the vastly different and distinct histories of the two groups. Sephardic Jews were originally admitted to Bordeaux and Bayonne in the midsixteenth century not as Jews but as *nouveaux chrétiens* (new Christians). Owing to their usefulness to the economy of the city, these Portuguese émigrés were accorded royal protection, first in 1550, with the pursuant commercial privileges reconfirmed regularly over the following two centuries. So as not to jeopardize their ever-tenuous status, the Portuguese merchants lived outwardly as Catholics. Only at the end of the seventeenth century, as France became in Arthur Hertzberg's words, "officially indifferent to the religion of those who brought it commercial advantages," did the *nouveaux chrétiens* begin to acknowledge their Judaism openly. They ceased observing public rituals in the church and organized a charity fund, known as *Sedaca*, which quickly developed into a full-scale, autonomous Jewish communal framework.[3] During the same two centuries, but under quite different conditions, communities of Ashkenazic Jews formed in the northeastern provinces of France. Small numbers of Jews were admitted to Metz after the city came under French dominion in 1552. The ordinance of 1567 formalized the status of the Jews by including the following provisions: admission was based on payment of an entrance duty and annual tax; residence was permitted in removed areas, not exceeding four households; permission was granted to lend money at an interest rate of 20–21 percent; they were required to listen to a sermon in church each month. By the end of the century an official Jewish community was organized, and just a few years later, Jewish privileges were confirmed by the *Lettres patentes* of 1603. The Treaty of Westphalia placed Alsace and Lorraine under French control, and France thus acquired an additional Jewish population. As was the case in Metz, the status of the Jews was usually protected by the king, despite efforts by local councils to curtail Jewish privileges. Until the latter part of the eighteenth century, the Jews of the northeast endured severe social, residential, economic, and political restrictions. The Ashkenazic experience of exclusion from French society and culture, as compared with the circumstances under which the Sephardim had come to France and through which they achieved a relatively high degree of acculturation, was clearly a decisive factor in the shaping of modern Jewish identity.[4] The Jews of Alsace faced a much more difficult and traumatic period of adjustment once citizenship was granted because of their social and intellectual isolation. This book is concerned primarily with these Ashkenazic Jews and their encounter with the trauma of emancipation.

Growing criticism of the prevailing class structure of the state in the eighteenth century was accompanied by the assertion that the legal and social segregation of the Jews contradicted the principles of religious tolerance and economic utility. At the same time, it was pointed out that the Jews themselves would need to undergo an extensive transformation in order to take their place in the envisioned new order. Religious rites, moral attitudes, economic patterns, and national sentiments were regarded as impediments to the successful integration of the Jews into general society and therefore needed to be modified in conformity with the prevailing conceptions of the universal brotherhood of man and loyalty to the fatherland. The Jews would need to enter society as new men, fully regenerated from the ill-effects of centuries of social and religious exclusiveness.

The central focus of this book is the ideology of *régénération* as conceived by the enlightened Jewish elite in France during the first two generations of the emancipation period. *Régénération*, a term that was introduced into the vocabulary of the Jewish question several years before the Revolution, became virtually synonymous with modernization.[5] Behind the term, however, lay a novel approach to the Jewish question. According to its general definition, *régénération* was the act of restoring to its original state something that had become corrupted or decadent. With respect to the Jews in the era of the Revolution, the term implied that the prevailing patterns of Jewish existence were socially and morally incompatible with the status of citizenship. Well aware of the compelling nature of the criticism levelled against their coreligionists, Jewish leaders advanced proposals for socio-economic and cultural improvement. After the turn of the nineteenth century, once the civic status of the Jews was firmly established, public discussions of the Jewish question centered on the failure of the Jews to become part of French society. Significantly, the term *régénération* became less popular during the first quarter of that century as gentile observers defined the goal of Jewish modernization as *fusion sociale*. *Fusion* presupposed the abandonment of distinctive Jewish social or religious mores; for Jewish intellectuals in Paris, this constituted a overwhelming challenge to their Jewish identity and would result in nothing short of a redefinition of Jewish existence.

Complicating the challenge of emancipation was the fact that the traditional institutions of communal life had fallen victim to the same revolutionary upheavals that had transformed the ancien régime. In exchange for the rights of citizenship French Jewry was compelled to relinquish its privilege of communal autonomy, exercised within a complex, multidimensional social structure known as the *kehillah*. Throughout the Middle Ages it had been the all-embracing framework for Jewish life and culture; its demise precipitated social, cultural, and religious dislocations of enormous proportions. Upon the dissolution of the communal agencies, educational institutions, and rabbinic authority, the Jews found themselves thrust into a thoroughly new social environment, faced with unprecedented expectations, and with little to rely upon to ease the trauma. No longer a protected member of a corporate community, the individual Jew had become, theoretically at least, a member of general society, now subject directly to the laws of the State. Formerly shielded by the social and political barriers that enveloped the *kehillah*, Jews had rarely needed to address questions concerning the nature of Jewish identity. Now, as the intellectual and communal leadership came under the influence of contemporary social and political philosophy, the traditional assumptions of Jewish life were subjected to critical evaluation according to criteria borrowed from general society.

Only in the third decade of the nineteenth century did a new generation of Jewish intellectuals come of age and formulate a systematic program of *régénération*. The new proponents of *régénération* were committed, as were their predecessors, to Jewish socio-economic modernization. However, in recognizing the unprecedented challenges now posed by emancipation, proponents of *régénération* were distinguished by their efforts to construct an ideology designed to mediate Jewish interaction with French society and culture. Seeking a term for these lay activists and intellectuals, I have chosen not to employ *reformers*, owing to its association with the Reform Movement in Germany. I have decided, instead, to introduce the term *"régénérateurs"* because it calls attention to the distinctive integration of the social, cultural, and religious elements of *régénération* in France. The *régénérateurs* belonged to a generation that had not experienced the disabilities of the preemancipation era. Educated in French secondary schools and universities, these men were profoundly influenced by the currents of the Enlightenment and French liberalism, and succeeded in integrating these cultural and intellectual influences with their own deep commitment to Judaism. Their efforts to modernize Jewish life were directed at the creation of new educational, economic, and religious institutions. Several of these institutions will be examined in some depth. My concern, however, is not with the institutions per se, but with the ideological foundations of institutional activities and the debate or resistance they provoked.

Until approximately 1870 the program of *régénération* remained the major concern of the communal and intellectual leadership. Symbolically and functionally it contributed to what may have been the most enduring feature of nineteenth-century French Jewish history, a single-minded quest for unity. At times nearing an obsession, the drive for unity was marked by efforts to introduce uniform changes in synagogue worship and religious practice and education, and ultimately to create a uniquely Franco-Jewish identity. Such a goal was not at all illogical. The Jewish population, singularly shaped by the government's commitment to the legal equality of its citizens and united in its devotion to the fatherland, was swept up by the idea that a special destiny awaited France and her inhabitants. Having found themselves in a country whose political system and geographical borders were clearly defined, where philosophers and statesmen were continually striving to secure for France a cultural identity of its own, the Jews of France were naturally motivated by these very same forces. Although France fell short of its goal of uniformity, French Jewry realized a measure of success. However, this achievement should not be exaggerated. As much as the "center" sought to unify the whole, local (or regional) forces persisted in their resistance to the imposition of uniformity.

The goal of uniformity was no less a matter of tactical importance than of theoretical significance. Virtually all of the *régénérateurs*, particularly those in Paris together with members of the Central Consistory, regarded uniformity as essential to the success of *régénération*. As policy makers intent on regenerating their less fortunate coreligionists, members of the Paris center naturally tended to define *improvement* in their own terms and dictate specific patterns to distant communities. The *régénérateurs'* concern with the condition of Jews in various parts of France underscores the fact that these reformers regarded themselves as part of a movement. They certainly possessed the essential elements: clearly defined goals, communication among members, and an idealism that transcended their immediate situation.

As French Jewry stood at the threshhold of the modern era, its leaders were forced to reassess the cultural heritage of traditional Judaism. Did it represent an obstacle to the realization of legal equality and social integration? Was it still relevant in an era of swift industrial advances and cultural achievement? Was the collective identity and destiny of the Jewish people, so thoroughly guarded by Jewish tradition, compatible with French citizenship? These questions weighed heavily upon the *régénérateurs*, as they did upon Jewish reformers in Germany. The issues, however, appear to have been approached from quite different perspectives. Whereas many of the same ideological influences were operative in both France and Germany, the French *régénérateurs* displayed a more conservative posture with regard to religious values than the German Jewish reformers. Although the *régénérateurs* often applauded the progress of the Reform movement in Germany, for the most part they did not accept the validity of thoroughgoing ritual reform. Distinct political and legal conditions, institutional forces, and social realities mitigated against the successful implementation of the radical religious reforms that were introduced in Germany. The absence of a prolonged struggle for civic rights in France was the most pronounced difference between the French and German experiences. In Germany, where the political battle for emancipation persisted throughout much of the nineteenth century, Jewish reformers insisted that a reformed religion, divested of its national and social encumbrances, would provide the government with convincing proof that the Jews were indeed worthy of citizenship. French Jews, having achieved enfranchisement relatively soon after the Revolution, did not feel the same urgency to alter their religion. The program of *régénération* was concerned primarily with socio-economic and cultural change and thus could find justification for the circumscription of its activities in the Paris Sanhedrin's decisions. The status of Judaism as a recognized religion and the creation of the consistorial system as its representative organization further reduced the political necessity of ritual modification. Though undeniably influenced by the German model, religious reform in France was without doubt a product of the search for a new Franco-Jewish identity.

No examination of nineteenth century French Jewry is possible without an understanding of the Jewish consistorial system. The imperial decree of 17 March 1808 ordered the formation of a synagogue and consistory in each department with a Jewish population of two thousand or more; departments with fewer Jews would be combined, under one consistory, to reach the required population. The departmental consistories were to be composed of a grand rabbi, one additional rabbi, and three lay members; consistorial officials were to be elected by twenty-five notables, themselves chosen by the government from among the wealthiest and most respected Jews. A central consistory, composed of three grand rabbis and two lay members, was to be established in Paris. Various modifications in the original *règlement* during the first half of the nineteenth century altered the proportion of rabbis to laymen in favor of the latter, resulting in greater lay control of the Central Consistory.[6] The consistories were originally established to administer the Jewish communities, to oversee the moral and socio-economic regeneration of the Jews, and to exercise surveillance over their constituents. The task of regenerating the Jewish masses was taken most seriously. The regenerative activities pursued by the consistories included forming committees to eliminate begging, organizing societies to encourage vocational training, and supervising primary schools.[7] The trend toward lay domination, albeit restrained by certain features of the 1844 *ordonnance*, enabled the consistories and the *régénérateurs* to implement a number of moderate reforms by midcentury: the confirmation ceremony, French sermons, the elimination of selling religious honors, and in some instances the introduction of the organ. Though rather modest achievements, these ceremonial innovations undoubtedly undercut more radical reformers and amounted to co-opting a full-fledged reform movement in France.

Educational reform achieved the greatest degree of uniformity of all areas of *régénération*. Modernizing Jewish education had been regarded since the Revolution as important to successful participation in French society, integrating traditional Jewish values with love of the *patrie*. Religious and secular instruction in Jewish schools followed remarkably uniform patterns throughout France. Instruction adhered to a set of widely accepted principles that could be traced to the Berlin Haskalah, and teaching methods and textbooks were fairly standard. Jewish education in France was, for the most part, free of the bitter controversies that divided communities elsewhere. In no small way, the modernization of Jewish schools contributed to a sense of cohesiveness for French Jewry.

Efforts to create a *rite français* (or *minhag Tsarfat*) inspired the *régénérateurs* to seek a fusion of the Portuguese and German liturgies. Many believed this would dissolve an unnecessary barrier between two segments of the community and enhance the unity of French Jewry. Fusion of the two rites represents French Jewry's search for a distinctive identity. In Paris, the plan was frustrated by the Portuguese, who were intent on preserving their liturgical and ethnic distinctiveness; and in Bordeaux efforts were made to preserve the Sephardic liturgy at the institutional level. The idea of liturgical fusion was never popular in Alsace, and even encountered vigorous opposition.[8] Throughout the century the solution to liturgical diversity remained elusive.

The failure of religious reform and the elusiveness of uniformity may in part be attributed to the continued orthodoxy of Alsatian Jewry and to the character of the French rabbinate. Prior to the Revolution, 80 percent of France's forty thousand Jews lived in Alsace-Lorraine, where they were prohibited from living in nearly all the cities. They resided mostly in small towns and villages scattered throughout the region. After the Revolution, when residence restrictions were removed, Jews throughout Alsace-Lorraine started to move to the cities, beginning a process of urbanization that would ultimately affect their social, cultural, and religious orientation. Although the rate of urbanization among the Jews of France—even within Alsace-Lorraine—was considerably higher that that of the general population, the tendency to remain in rural districts of the northeast predominated throughout the nineteenth century. Even as late as 1871, only 31 percent of the Jewish population of Alsace-Lorraine lived in larger cities as compared to 97 percent of the rest of the Jewish population.[9] Small towns and villages were far removed from the cultural and intellectual centers, insulating the population from the rampant changes affecting urban dwellers—especially residents of Paris. Jews in rural districts remained orthodox in their religious behavior, though laxity in observance was increasing in larger cities such as Metz, Strasbourg, and Nancy. The continued use of Yiddish in sermons until at least midcentury, as compared with the decline of Judaeo-Spanish and Judaeo-Provençal in the south, attests to the slow progress of social integration in northeastern France. Vigorous resistance to various programs for religious reform was the most obvious indication of the tenacity of Alsatian traditionalism.[10]

Unlike their counterparts in Germany, French rabbis remained opposed to all but the most minor innovations. The meager salaries and the lack of prestige associated with rabbinic posts tended to attract men from a lower socio-economic background who never received a classical secondary education. University studies were not available to French rabbis for much of the century. The best minds, those whose Jewish scholarly interests might have attracted them to the rabbinate, were repelled by the six-year course of study at the *école rabbinique*. In the various university positions available to Jews, they found an outlet for their scholarly pursuits as well as greater professional status. Those who chose to enter the rabbinate and train at the *école rabbinique* were usually undistinguished as scholars and leaders and therefore unlikely supporters of religious reform. The hierarchical system in the rabbinate, whereby younger men remained in positions of lesser influence under the tutelage of their older superiors, further impeded the implementation of

19

ritual changes.[11] Both the Central Consistory and the *régénérateurs* recognized the importance of the rabbinate to the success of religious regeneration, and directed much energy toward the modernization of rabbinic training. Although these efforts were somewhat successful, results were not apparent until the latter part of the nineteenth century.

Efforts to introduce more than a handful of innovations in ritual matters were, for the most part, a failure. There are a number of explanations for this. Historian Eugen Weber has shown that the French goal of unity and uniformity could not be realized until advances in communications and transportation provided some measure of physical and symbolic bonds between outlying areas and urban centers such as Paris.[12] With respect to the Jews it may be more important to emphasize the continued strong identity of Alsace throughout most of the nineteenth century. Numerous reactions to various consistorial and regenerative innovations reveal intense feelings of resentment to what was perceived as efforts to impose the views of Paris on Alsatian Jewry. Despite the relative population decline of Alsatian Jewry, regional distinctiveness in relation to religious life and national sentiment continued. This phenomenon was not peculiar to Alsace. Though beyond the scope of the present work, the identity of the Bordeaux Jewish community also appears to have been marked by elements of regional distinctiveness.

It was not simply the technical matter of implementation that distinguished the *régénérateur* movement in France from the Reform movement in Germany. The ideology of the French *régénérateurs,* shaped by forces unique to France, differed fundamentally from the philosophy of the German reformers. The French Revolution, the Napoleonic regime and the Sanhedrin, and the legal recognition accorded to the Jewish religion contributed to the crystallization of a particular Franco-Jewish consciousness shared by various sectors of the Jewish community. Rooted in the ideology of *régénération,* this collective identity was expressed in a variety of ways, among them a reverence for the idea of Jewish peoplehood and a respect for Jewish tradition. Alsatian Jews also were fully committed to Jewish political emancipation and socioeconomic modernization. When missionary activity openly threatened French Jewry and challenged the integrity of the Jewish religion in the 1840s, the *régénérateurs* joined hands with the rabbis in working toward the intensification of religious education in order to thwart the efforts of Christian missionaries.

Though the struggle for uniformity encountered severe obstacles and exacerbated existing tensions, the quest for unity was not completely fruitless. Certainly the consistory brought France's many Jewish communities together in a single administrative unit. Regional, cultural, and religious differences aside, a consensus emerged on a number of issues of common concern. Perhaps the very struggle for uniformity helped sustain the myth of a single community,[13] for the myth was respected and affirmed by a large and diverse assemblage of French Jewry.

PART ONE

Enlightenment, Revolution, and Emancipation

1

The Road to Emancipation

THOUGH HARDLY OF numerical significance in a country as large as France and all but absent from the mainstream of public life, the Jews of the ancien régime had nonetheless become a subject of great public concern among churchmen, intellectuals, and government officials. Countless books, essays, and pamphlets focussed public attention on the anomaly of a people that had remained, and was forced to remain, religiously, culturally, and socially distinct from the larger society in which it lived. Intense criticism of the prevailing class structure of the state was accompanied by the assertion that the legal and social segregation of the Jews contradicted the principles of human decency and religious tolerance. Moreover, the exclusion of the Jews deprived the state of their potentially significant contributions to the national economy. At the same time, it was pointed out that the Jews, for their part, would need to undergo an extensive transformation so that they could take their place in the new order. As Jewish intellectuals became increasingly exposed to the ideas of the Enlightenment and in turn became aware of the cultural limitations imposed by their own communities, they began to reevaluate Jewish life according to external standards. Before long they reached the conclusion that a thorough restructuring of the Jewish community and its leadership and significant changes in social and cultural mores were imperative. All would need to be modified in conformity to the conventional wisdom of the European Enlightenment.

Were it not for the process of emancipation, these ideas would have remained the exclusive province of the Jewish intellectual elite. Emancipation exerted a profound impact on all sectors of the Jewish community and on virtually every aspect of Jewish life; for this reason the era of emancipation may very well represent the most cataclysmic period in the history of the Jews. Modifications in the legal status, occupational distribution, cultural pursuits, and religious behavior of the Jews were part of a larger process of change that took hold of western and central Europe in the eighteenth and nineteenth centuries. This general transformation, the final result of which was the emergence of the modern European nation-state from the corporate order of the ancien régime, was comprised of several features: the centralization of government administration, the levelling down of corporate privileges, the emergence of a free market economy, and the acknowledgment of religious liberty. In the era of the modern state the persistence of a Jewish community, on the one hand endowed with the privilege of autonomous rule and on the other hand deprived of many rights enjoyed by other groups, had become anachronistic and anomalous. Seen from the perspective of general political, economic, and intellectual developments, Jewish emancipation, in the words of Salo W. Baron, "was as much a historic necessity for the modern state as it was for the Jews."[1] In the final analysis, the process of emancipation would involve refashioning the long-established legal, social, and intellectual patterns in both European society and the Jewish community.[2] Before the process of Jewish emancipation can be properly analyzed, it is first necessary to review the status of the Jews during the medieval period.

Throughout the Middle Ages the position of the Jews in Europe was dependent upon the good graces of secular and ecclesiastical authorities. Among the factors that influenced these rulers in their treatment of the Jews, most important of all was the theory that the Jews were blasphemers and Christ killers who had been condemned to eternal wandering and damnation. Nevertheless, although Jews of the early medieval period were never free from overt acts of hostility and violence, attacks and murders were relatively sporadic. Only after the First Crusade of 1096 did the position of the Jews become dangerously precarious. In addition to having been responsible for the destruction of entire Jewish communities, the Crusades initiated a period of deterioration in the economic and legal standing of the Jews, on the one hand, and embittered relations between them and their Christian neighbors, on the other. First, from the time of the Crusades onward, Jews were no longer able to compete with Italian traders backed by mighty fleets, thus making their function as international tradesmen unnecessary. Moreover, for a variety of reasons, it became increasingly difficult and often impossible for Jews to engage in

agriculture, commerce, and the crafts. As the range of available liveli-
hoods narrowed, and encouraged by the Church's intensified campaign
against usury and the increased need for money and credit, the Jews
became dependent upon the only occupation left open to them—granting
consumer loans. Lending money on interest thus emerged as the main
Jewish occupation in the cities of England, France, Germany, and northern Italy.[3]

Determination of the legal status of the Jews was in the domain of
both the ecclesiastical and secular authorities. At the Third (1179) and
Fourth (1215) Lateran Councils the Church introduced several restrictive measures including the Jewish quarter and the Jewish badge. While
it is undeniable that official Church policy sought to protect the Jews
from overt violence, it is equally clear that the main reasons for the
toleration of the Jews, namely economic utility and theological considerations, carried little weight with the Christian masses. Both the Jewish
quarter and badge expressed the alien character of Jewry amidst a hostile Christian society, while the preponderance of the Jews in
moneylending further aggravated this hostility. By the middle of the
thirteenth century the Jews of England, France, and the Holy Roman
Empire had become *servi camerae*, serfs of the royal chamber, a concept
implying their complete subjection to the will of the authorities. Jewish
serfdom consisted of two main elements: economic exploitation and the
protection afforded them as property of the king. The state of serfdom
accorded with the popular view of the degradation of the Jews.[4]

In the final analysis, the Jew's stubborn rejection of Christianity at
once explained his deplorable social conduct and moral inferiority and
provided theological justification for persecuting him. This theological
conception was popularized through the development of a mythology
wherein the Jews were not human at all, but cohorts of the devil.
According to the myth, Jews required Christian blood for ritual use and
murdered Christian children to obtain pure, innocent blood. Another
frequent accusation claimed that the Jews would desecrate the wafer of
the Eucharist sacrament, allegedly to reenact the crucifixion of Jesus.
Like the blood libel and ritual murder charge, the desecration of the host
became an excuse for popular anti-Jewish uprisings. The demonic Jew,
the product of the prevailing demonological mythology previously assigned to witches, was thus believed to be a sorcerer. Like witches, the
Jews were regarded as social deviants, who were contemptuous of humanity, and were therefore often blamed for social ills and physical
disasters.[5] Despite numerous local variations, the treatment of the Jews
in western and central Europe followed a remarkably uniform course. In
fact, by the end of the fifteenth century, due to a process of national

amalgamation that affected newly formed nation-states, the Jews were expelled from England, France, the Low Countries, and the Iberian Peninsula. The frequency and uniformity of these developments led Salo Baron to declare that "they almost seemed to operate along the lines of a 'historical law,' practically without exceptions." Quite clearly, treatment of the Jews rested on a nearly universally accepted heritage.[6]

Only a revolutionary break with this powerful medieval heritage could bring about changes in attitude toward the Jews. The idea of religious liberty ignited such a revolution and, in the political discourse of Europe and the New World, made possible a new consideration of the Jews' legal status. Such able spokesmen as Roger Williams and John Locke insisted that freedom of religion implied a separation of Church and State in order to safeguard the rights of all, and that the Jews were no exception to the theory.[7] By the eighteenth century, the principle of religious tolerance had gained currency among thinkers in the West and had become a new and positive religious force, despite its condemnation by Protestants, who regarded it as tantamount to religious indifference and irresponsibility. The theory of tolerance was based on the notion of natural religion, an idea popularized by the English Deists. In their view, the idea of one God, the Creator of the universe, provided religion with a universal dimension: natural law was regarded as equivalent to morality and therefore independent of divine revelation. It followed that religious rites and dogma were merely external wrappings around the real core, moral teaching. By undermining the claims to exclusive authority held by particular faiths, Deism established the theoretical foundation for launching sharp attacks against institutional religion, especially against the Catholic Church. This was also the crucial basis for religious toler- ance, for it permitted these thinkers to regard differences of religion as secondary to the moral substance that institutional religion hoped to represent, however inadequately. It was left to the Enlightenment to endow religion with an identity of its own, independent of all its various rites and interpretations.[8]

However revolutionary it was, the doctrine of universality would not have been historically significant for the Jews were it not for a transforma- tion in the social consciousness of seventeenth- and eighteenth-century Europe. The violent struggles between Protestant and Catholic factions clearly demonstrated the necessity of religious tolerance for the sake of political and social stability. Members of the late sixteenth century *politiques* school had come to the realization that the very existence of the state would be endangered if attempts by religious groups to destroy one another were allowed to continue. Jean Bodin, the outstanding French political thinker of the era, viewed religious tolerance as indispensable to the doctrine of *raison d'état*. In the case of theorist Charles Gravelle, the social and political implications of this doctrine were understood to apply to Jews as well.[9]

Hand in hand with *raison d'état* went a new conception of society characterized by the application of the "geometric spirit" to both psychological and social problems and the structure of state and society. Following Hobbes, who had first established that the state as a "body" could be the subject of analysis,[10] Condillac regarded society as an "artificial body" composed of parts that exert a reciprocal influence on one another, and that must be designed so that no individual class of citizens (by their special prerogatives) be allowed to upset the equilibrium and harmony of the whole. He thus called for the subordination and contribution of all special interests to the common good of society.[11] The Enlightenment's conception of tolerance attained its most developed form in the writings of Montesquieu (1689–1755), a thinker whose work had a profound impact on the course of French liberal thought.[12] He maintained that freedom is possible only when every individual force is limited by a counterforce. Ties among the various individual forces were considered essential for the preservation of social equilibrium: this would prevent the ascendancy of some forces over others and would provide the widest possible margin of freedom of thought through the counterbalance of these forces.[13] Montesquieu believed that the social utility of all religions rested in their prescription of obedience and submission to authority. Moreover, he affirmed the utilitarian importance of the rivalry of sects because, according to his theory, this stimulates their zeal and thereby promotes better observance of their laws. In this way, he theorized, toleration of religious diversity would rectify abuses in society.[14]

The emphasis on the utility of religious tolerance was strengthened further by developments in the economic sphere. Mercantilism, a doctrine of extensive regulation of economic life in the interest of the general good, became an essential component in the development of the modern, centralized state. It envisioned nothing less than the reconstruction of society and its institutions through the substitution of a national economic policy for local regulation. Moreover, mercantilism placed the interests of the state above those of individuals, thus becoming, in effect, a corollary of *raison d'état*. Through efforts against domestic tolls and inequities in the coinage system, and on behalf of centralized legislation, administration, and taxation, mercantilism served as a powerful unifying agent. Most of all mercantilism was distinguished by its emphasis on a purely secular and materialistic conception of society, thus placing it in confrontation with the Catholic Church, the guilds, and the estates of the realm. The main area of conflict involved the immigration of heretical craftsmen or, more generally, the issue of religious tolerance. Mercantilists held that an increase in population leads to an increase in power, security, wealth, and cultural progress, and that there was no reason to exclude potentially useful contributors to the national economy because of religious misgivings. Arguably the foremost representative of the growing process of secularization in Europe, mercantilism made it possible for some states to ignore traditional residential restrictions on Jewish immigrants. In the case of France, government policy in the century before the Revolution bore the imprint of statesman Jean-Baptiste Colbert (1619–1683), although during his lifetime the conflict between economics and religion was still unresolved. Impressed by the examples of Italy, England, and Holland, eighteenth-century French economists defended Jewish immigration and advocated greater commercial freedom for Jewish merchants.[15]

On the ideological plane, the readmission of the Jews to the countries of Western Europe constituted the first step in the process that would culminate in the bestowal of citizenship. However, neither the economic approach to the Jewish question nor the philosophy of tolerance could have brought, on its own, a significant improvement in the legal status of the Jews. The emergence of enlightened absolutism, a form of government strongly influenced by the political philosophy of the Enlightenment, proved to be the single most important force in the active promotion of religious tolerance and legal equality in continental Europe. In France, as well as in the German states, the appearance of an enlightened bureaucracy became an important factor in the diffusion of enlightenment at the ministerial level. As bureaucrats were exposed increasingly to higher education, there was a noticeably heightened awareness of and concern for issues of freedom and human rights.[16] Many became aware that the exclusion of the Jews from society was a glaring contradiction to the principles upon which the Enlightenment was based. Thus the humanistic dimension, when added to the notion of economic utility, encouraged a reconsideration of the place of Jews in general society. This concern, and the accompanying proposals for "regenerating" the Jews, were taken up seriously in the last two decades of the eighteenth century, and would prove indispensable to the extended discourse of emancipation.[17]

The publication of Christian Wilhelm Dohm's *Über die bürgerliche Verbesserung der Juden*[18] (*Concerning the Amelioration of the Civil Status of the Jews*) in 1781 inaugurated the era of Jewish emancipation in Europe. Dohm (1751–1820), a councillor in the Prussian War Ministry, became involved in Jewish affairs and specifically the affairs of Alsatian Jewry, in an indirect manner. Owing to the fraudulent accusations of Jew-baiter François Hell and to oppressive government legislation, the condition of Alsatian Jewry had deteriorated and urgently demanded intervention. In 1780, communal leader Herz Cerfberr appealed to Moses Mendelssohn to write a *mémoire* to the Council of State defending the Jews and requesting elimination of legal discrimination. Mendelssohn in turn passed the request onto his friend Dohm, who agreed to collaborate in the *mémoire,* which was submitted to the Council of State later in 1780.

Dohm's involvement did not end with the composition of the *mémoire.* Shortly after its completion he was persuaded by Mendelssohn to write a treatise on the desirability of admitting the Jews to citizenship. Published in Berlin in 1781, the *Über die bürgerliche Verbesserung der Juden* exerted an unequalled impact on contemporary and subsequent discussions on Jewish emancipation. A glance at the critical and sympathetic responses that were evoked by the work reveals the degree to which Dohm's book set the terms and parameters of debate on the Jewish question. Its influence upon the French public was assured by the appearance of a translation in 1782 under the title *De la réforme politique des Juifs.* Some years later, Dohm's arguments received further exposure through the efforts of Honoré Gabriel Mirabeau, who wrote *Sur Moses Mendelssohn, sur la réforme politique des Juifs*[19] in 1787. What was the secret to the success of Dohm's work? It was to play a decisive role precisely because its appearance anticipated governmental reconsideration of the Jews' political status in Germany (Joseph II's *Toleranzpatent* [1782]) and France (Louis XVI's *Lettres Patentes* [1784]). However, as important as its timing was, Dohm, while employing the theoretical foundations laid in the preceding two centuries, shifted the discussion to the practical issues surrounding the admission of the Jews to citizenship.[20]

The initiative taken by Dohm, together with the debate that ensued in Germany and the attention that the subject of Jewish civic rights received in France, created an atmosphere favorable to a reconsideration of the Jewish question. In 1785, in response to liberal sentiments in the city, and following new legislation for the Jews of Alsace, the *Société des arts et sciences de Metz* decided to sponsor a competition to determine whether "there are means of making the Jews happy and more useful in France." Though not uncommon for French learned societies to initiate discussion of important scientific, literary, or political questions of the day within the framework of a prize essay contest, the Metz competition was the first to bring the Jewish question before the attention of the public. Nine essays, seven of which viewed the question sympathetically, were submitted. Of the three essays that were finally awarded prizes, Abbé Grégoire's *Essai sur la régénération physique, morale et politique des*

Juifs[21] was the mostly widely acclaimed. Like Dohm and Mirabeau, Grégoire discussed the Jewish question in both utilitarian and humanitarian terms. In arguing for an alleviation of legal disabilities, the three advocates of Jewish rights appealed to the self-interest of the state. They pointed out that a continuation of the status quo would only deprive the state of a potentially valuable resource. In conformity with the tenets of mercantilism, particularly the idea that the wealth of nations depends on a steadily growing population, they asserted that the Jews, with some vocational training, would be of considerable benefit to the national economy.[22] "It is hard to believe," Mirabeau wrote, "that such industrious men cannot be useful to the state because they come from Asia, and are distinguished by the beard, circumcision and a particular manner of worshipping the Supreme Being."[23] The potential usefulness of the Jews was substantiated with numerous historical examples of contributions that they had made to the states in which they lived. Thus it was in the state's own interest to emancipate the Jews.

To be sure, the three were critical of the Jews and their religion. Indeed, the image of a morally deficient Jewry remained unquestioned. However, relying as they did on Montesquieu's theory of environmental influence,[24] they maintained that Jewish shortcomings were not their own fault but the result of circumstances beyond their control. Those who claimed that the Jewish character was so corrupt as to warrant restrictive regimentation had confused cause with effect. Instead, it was necesary to acknowledge the Jews' undeniable humanity, or in Dohm's words, that "the Jew is even more a man than a Jew,"[25] who must be emancipated from legal disabilities. Only then could society look forward to the regeneration of the Jew.

The underlying assumption in these works was that the bestowal of equality upon the Jews was the necessary first step in a process that would lead, ultimately, to their civil and moral improvement. This position was criticized by Göttingen scholar Johann David Michaelis (1717–1791), who argued that the Jews were unfit for eventual citizenship on the basis of their innate character and because their religious prescriptions would hinder their social integration and prevent them from fulfilling civic duties to the state.[26] Dohm, Mirabeau, and Grégoire countered this argument first with the assertion that nothing in Judaism nor in the Jewish character categorically precluded the duties of citizenship. Furthermore, they envisioned a crucial role for the government in cultivating the civil improvement of the Jews and their love for the *patrie*, the fatherland, by granting them legal, economic, and religious equality. Moreover, the government would take an active role in the moral education of the Jews and in their vocational training.[27] They would be encour-

31

aged to abandon commerce and moneylending for agriculture and industry. Finally, it was assumed that any religious practices that stood in the way of social integration and duties to the state would soon be modified as the Jews adjusted to freedom. This would require reforms in Jewish education and religion. Thus, those who supported Jewish rights envisioned the gradual formation of a new type of Jew that would eventually come to replace the existing one.

Significant political developments in France in the late 1780s set the stage for the eventual civil emancipation of the Jews. The *Lettres Patentes* of 1784, for all its ambiguities and inconsistencies had recognized the entire Jewish population of Alsace as a juridical entity. More important was the edict of November 1787 that granted non-Catholics an *état civil*. Though subsequently interpreted to include only Protestants, this legislation effectively removed citizenship from the realm of Catholicism. Ultimately only the collapse of the ancien régime at the hands of the Revolution of 1789 would secure civic equality for the Jews. After debates in the French National Assembly extending over the course of nearly two years (1789–1791), Grégoire, Mirabeau, and other sympathetic voices finally succeeded in convincing the majority of its members that the Jews were worthy of civic equality. The successful achievement of emancipation must not, however, obscure the fact that a large segment of the French National Assembly vehemently opposed the idea of Jewish enfranchisement and indeed only enacted it in two stages. The protracted debate on Jewish citizenship derived from the fact that the Declaration of the Rights of Man, which guaranteed automatic equality to all Frenchmen, was not initially interpreted to include the Jews or even Protestants, for that matter. In January 1790, five months after the Declaration of the Rights of Man was voted into law, the Sephardic Jews living in southern France were granted civic equality. By virtue of their dress, language, moderate religious behavior, social organization, and greater overall involvement in French society and culture, the Sephardim were regarded as an ethnically distinct community, and their condition was considered separately from their coreligionists in the northeast.[28]

The question of emancipating the Ashkenazim was much more complex, and it would be an additional eighteen months before they were finally admitted to citizenship. During the prolonged debate the opposition to Jewish emancipation expressed its views unabashedly. One leading clerical adversary, Abbé Jean Sieflein Maury, argued that the Jewish religion had left a profoundly ruinous impression on the character of its adherents. As a result, the Jewish people had become an alien and morally degenerate nation that could never be expected to sustain genuine attachment to France or its society. Opposing emancipation on slightly different grounds, Jean François Rewbell, the Jacobin deputy from Alsace, asserted that the Jewish religion included political and social principles that conflicted with French civil law. In his view, as long as the Jews remained loyal to their religion, they would be incapable of assuming the duties of citizenship.[29]

Opposition to Jewish emancipation was not easily quieted. Well into the nineteenth century critics continued to voice skepticism concerning the decision to grant citizenship to the Jews. The fact that certain assumptions which underlay these reservations had been shared even by proponents of Jewish emancipation suggests that the Jewish question had never been fully resolved. It is therefore necessary to review the background of the negative evaluation of Judaism in order to understand its continuing impact on the formation of evolving Jewish and gentile attitudes. Criticism of the Jews and their religion during and after the Revolutionary period rested on the convergence of medieval theological conceptions of Judaism with modern secular assessments. In medieval times, attitudes were based on theological assumptions interwoven with socio-economic, political, and psychological factors. According to the view of the Catholic Church, the Jew's stubborn rejection of the truth of Christianity not only explained his deplorable social conduct and moral inferiority but also served as theological justification for persecuting him. Moreover, the Jew's preponderance in the forbidden activity of money-lending appeared to corroborate the theological view that he was wicked and damned; in the socio-economic sphere these activities served to aggravate the already embittered sentiments of the Christian masses.

Two major trends that emerged in early modern Europe altered these views. Since the Renaissance, the concept of rationalism had gathered strength, becoming the dominant way of thinking and the principal instrument of understanding the universe. Paralleling this concept—but not dependent on it—was the process of secularization. Together, rationalism and secularization produced an unmistakable decline in the theological hatred of the Jews among intellectuals. Popular religious hatred, of course, survived among the masses; however, among intellectuals there was a noticeable transformation in the articulation of anti-Jewish sentiment. By the middle of the eighteenth century, anti-Judaism had assumed a variety of secular forms that proved to be as passionate as the theological ones.

The first traces of the secularization of anti-Jewish sentiment can be found in the writings of the English Deists. Deism, the belief in God the Creator whose existence is known exclusively through reason, held that a natural religion of morality antedated the various institutionalized religions. Clericalism and elaborate rituals were regarded as extraneous elements that only obscured the real meaning of religion. Denunciation of Judaism followed a dual path: it was attacked as a revealed religion in its own right and also as the progenitor of Christianity. Christian Hebraists of the late seventeenth century had concluded in their studies of the religious customs of the ancient Hebrews that the latter were but a small, enslaved nation which imitated the rituals of their Egyptian masters. This evaluation of the Jews provided a pseudo-scientific basis for belittling the cultural significance, religious contribution, and moral stature of Judaism. The Deists concluded, on the basis of these and their own studies, that the Jews were a superstitious and barbaric tribe whose religious fanaticism and stubbornness deserved denigration. Although the hostility of the Deists was mostly limited to an academic analysis of the foundations of the Jewish religion, their writings carried much wider implications. Inevitably, invectives against Mosaism and the early Hebrews came to be associated with contemporary Jews and Judaism.[30]

This appraisal of the Jewish religion did not go unnoticed in the eighteenth century. The English Deists exerted a decisive influence on the French *philosophes,* particularly on the most important figure of all, Voltaire.[31] In France, even more than in Germany and England, the struggle against institutional religion was intensified and so, too, the Enlightenment's critique of Judaism. Enlightenment literature brought the Deist pronouncements on the early Hebrew religion to their logical conclusion: the link between the ancient Hebrews and contemporary Jews was established more explicitly, based on the premise of permanent character traits. Furthermore, the French Enlightenment added to its arsenal of criticisms a concerted attack on rabbinic literature, a strategy it had borrowed from orthodox Christian theology. The Talmud was portrayed as a wellspring of superstition and immorality that had inflicted permanent damage to the Jews' character. According to this line of reasoning, allegiance to (or simply association with) the rabbinic tradition cast doubts on the ability of the Jews to undergo successful intellectual, religious, or social improvement.[32]

The overriding concern for toleration that characterized the Enlightenment appears to have been contradicted by the severity of its attacks on the Jewish religion and the Jews. Several theories have been advanced to explain this difficulty. Arthur Hertzberg has argued that many *philosophes* passionately hated the Jews and found no use for them or their religion in enlightened society. According to his interpretation the *philosophes'* denunciation of the Jews was essentially a secularization of the theological contempt without any modification of the basic hatred. For Hertzberg, the Enlightenment's critique of Judaism signified the

34

transition from medieval to modern anti-Semitism. His proof consists in part of a content analysis of the writings of the *philosophes*, but more largely it is of a review of the prominence of these writings in contemporary and later anti-Jewish literature. Other, more sympathetic writers are described as having been imbued with the principles of tolerance and are therefore placed within the philo-Semitic tradition.[33] Jacob Katz, though unwilling to accept Hertzberg's far-reaching conclusions, has also argued that Voltaire, like other *philosophes*, was a prominent figure in the history of anti-Semitism. He contends that in spite of Voltaire's departure from the dogmatic content of the Christian tradition, he was unable to liberate himself from its basic psychological predispositions.[34] Hertzberg and Katz are thus united in their attempt to demonstrate that the attitude of certain *philosophes* was inconsistent with the liberal philosophy of the Enlightenment.

A second school of thought, represented most notably by Peter Gay and Hugh Trevor-Roper, maintains that the clash between the Enlightenment's humanism and anti-Judaism was only an apparent inconsistency. The real enemy of the Enlightenment was Christianity. Because it was impossible to criticize the Church publicly, the same purpose could be served by attacking Judaism. But beyond the "smoke screen" theory lay a more plausible explanation. The *philosophes'* conception of toleration could not coexist with anything that might be perceived to be antithetical to the aims of the Enlightenment. According to the *philosophes*, Judaism represented the moral and intellectual antithesis of enlightenment and toleration and therefore was a deserving target of extensive vilification.[35] Paradoxically, the negative attitude toward the Jews and their religion was logically derived from the same philosophical position that enabled Enlightenment thinkers to address the Jewish problem sympathetically. Secularization and the general critique of institutional religion both exerted a double-edged influence on the course of Jewish history. On the one hand, they were instrumental in breaking down religious prejudice and discrimination and thereby laid a foundation for a fresh approach to the Jewish question. On the other hand, however, by introducing new criteria for the assessment of religions, they lent credence to the notion that Judaism was morally and intellectually bankrupt.

A negative assessment of Jews and Judaism was unquestionably endemic to the Enlightenment tradition. To divide the men of Enlightenment into pro-Jewish and anti-Jewish groups, as Hertzberg has done, fails to satisfactorily explain the numerous difficulties and apparent contradictions in the writings of many Enlightenment thinkers. Baron de Montesquieu, for instance, was a leading spokesman for religious tolerance, having ascribed to religion an indispensable social role. Religion, he asserted, could contribute to the strengthening of social values. Montesquieu was quoted frequently by subsequent advocates and defenders of Jewish emancipation. Even so, his well-known denunciation of religious persecution, especially the Spanish Inquisition, and his praise of biblical Judaism, were offset by his own negative appraisal of rabbinic Judaism. His remarks concerning the "poverty" of rabbinic literature and its adverse effects on the Jewish character are not entirely dissimilar from the attitude of Hertzberg's *bêtes noires*, Voltaire and the Encyclopaedists.[36] The source of this commonality was the Enlightenment tradition itself. The major areas of disagreement revolved around the question of whether the Jews could be redeemed from the corrupting effects of their religious heritage, and if so, what steps would need to be taken to realize this goal.

The clearest proof of the ambivalent nature of the Enlightenment's attitude is the espousal of its harsh criticism of the Jewish religion by even the most ardent supporters of the Jews. Echoing the Enlightenment's critique of Judaism, Dohm and Grégoire admitted that centuries of oppression produced individuals for whom perverse behavior had become normative.[37] Although such remarks were invariably accompanied by an acknowledgment that the Jews were not completely responsible for their lowly status, there could be no denying the reality— whatever its cause. Dohm would go so far as to concede that the Jews were more morally corrupt, criminally inclined, and antisocial than other peoples.[38] What was the cause of this moral degeneration? Using "sophistic artistry," rabbinical exegesis had falsified Mosaic Law and had introduced "narrow-minded and petty regulations" to the Jewish religion.[39] Viewed as the product of rabbinic inventiveness and imagination, the ceremonial laws were an obstacle to true piety[40] and a source of self-degradation, as they included prescriptions to hate others.[41] Rather remarkably, this assessment of the Jews and Judaism was an amalgam of many of the same elements of a long-standing, pervasive anti-Jewish tradition. What distinguishes the end of the eighteenth century from the earlier period was a new willingness to reconsider the political status of the Jews *in spite of* these deeply held prejudices. Consequently, impassioned pleas for Jewish civil equality were accompanied by the expectation that the Jews undergo extensive improvement of their religious and social ethos.[42]

Central to all discussions of the suitability of the Jews for citizenship was the question whether the observance of Jewish law was compatible with the exercise of civic duties. It is important to stress that in those years, as the idea of a contract between the state and its citizens enjoyed increasing acceptance, civic responsibilities became endowed with an importance akin to sacred duty. Owing to this development and to the prevailing negative assessment of the Jewish religion, many were skeptical about the full participation of the Jews in the new order, though rarely was there any explanation of just what responsibilities citizenship entailed. Whether stated explicitly or not, the central issue for discussants of the Jewish question was: Does the Jewish religion contain principles that prevent the Jews from performing the duties of citizenship and from dealing honestly with fellow citizens? [43] Not surprisingly, the status of citizenship was regarded as inconceivable for those whose religion impeded the fulfillment of any duties necessary for the maintenance of the state. This idea was expressed as an undisputed political axiom. Most of the debates on the Jewish question, from the 1780s to the middle of the nineteenth century, sought to determine whether the Jewish religion was, in fact, an impediment to full *régénération*.

Opponents of Jewish emancipation advanced the argument that Jewish religious practices were indeed obstacles to successful participation in the life of the country. The claim, of course, had been made innumerable times before. Among the earliest critics were Graeco-Roman authors, who had assailed Jewish exclusiveness, ridiculed the Sabbath as a day devoted to idleness, and censured its observers for the loss of labor.[44] In the modern period the Sabbath laws were the target of criticism from the standpoint of economic utility and military service. Sabbath restrictions, together with Christian Sunday laws, allegedly made agriculture unfeasible, and the general assumption that Jewish law prohibited fighting on the Sabbath cast doubts on the usefulness of the Jews in time of war.[45] Dohm, Grégoire, and Mirabeau took these arguments seriously, especially the charge that because of the Sabbath Jews were prohibited from serving in the army. Dohm cited a number of historical and legal sources, among them an opinion by Moses Mendelssohn, to demonstrate that military service was fully sanctioned by the Jewish religion.[46] This defense of Jewish law, provoked in part by the critical writings of Orientalist Johann David Michaelis,[47] was repeated by Grégoire and Mirabeau during the revolutionary debate against opponents of emancipation. However, these efforts in defense of the Jewish religion did not go unqualified. Advocates of Jewish rights did admit that Judaism as it existed in their day should undergo some modification, albeit in the spirit of pure Mosaism, so that Jews could become truly good citizens.[48]

Partisans of Jewish rights were thus beset by the same reservations concerning the suitability of Jews for citizenship that troubled their opponents. The difference lay in the significance attached to the recognized difficulties posed by the Jewish religion. Advocates of Jewish emancipation maintained that these difficulties were not of sufficient magnitude to preclude the bestowal of civic rights. They argued that emancipation would make the improvement of the Jews possible. According to Dohm, within several generations after the bestowal of civic rights, Jews would practice an enlightened, purified form of Judaism, not unlike Deism. He believed that as soon as Jews were accepted as members of general society and could make its interests their own, "they will reform their religious laws and regulations according to the demands of society. They will go back to the freer and nobler Mosaic Law, will explain and adapt it according to the changed times and conditions, and will find authorizations to do so alone in their Talmud."[49] Grégoire also expected the Jews to observe a more modern form of Judaism following their emancipation. In fact, he viewed the process of emancipation and *régénération* as a transitional phase that would ultimately end in the Jews' adoption of the Christian religion. Grégoire had faith in change through education, and he hoped that as time went on the Jews would be emancipated from the excessive communal authority and influence of the rabbis.[50] Emancipation, then, was conceived not only as freedom from restrictions imposed by society but also as an internal process of liberation from the traditional Jewish behavior and mores that society found objectionable.

2

The Emergence of the "Jewish Question"

BY VIRTUE OF the special relationship between civic equality and *régénération*, wherein the former was granted with the implicit understanding that the latter be carried out, the progress of Jewish modernization became a matter of ongoing public concern and debate in post-Revolutionary France. To most observers the immediate impact of emancipation on the socio-economic status of the Jews was disappointing. Indeed, the unrestricted freedom that the Jews enjoyed during the fifteen years following their emancipation brought about some changes in their residence patterns, though not as pronounced as anticipated. Increasingly, Jews began settling in regions that formerly had few or no Jewish inhabitants. Strasbourg, for example, became a major center of Jewish population, as did Paris. Some communities such as Metz witnessed a trend into surrounding villages in order to facilitate business transactions. Nevertheless, although these residential shifts resulted in a Jewish presence in forty-four *départements,* as compared to only ten on the eve of the Revolution, the relative size of most new communities remained quite small. The greater tendency was to concentrate in cities with already existing Jewish populations. Migration tended to be in the direction of towns and cities in Alsace-Lorraine as well as in the Bordeaux-Bayonne region. Thus, opportunities for residential mobility were indeed utilized, but the Jews were inclined to move in groups and, therefore, the result was less a dispersion than an even greater concentration.[1]

Residential changes were accompanied, though to a lesser degree, by changes in occupation. Jewish artisans, farmers, and professionals began to appear; however, for the most part, Jews tended to use their new opportunities to vary and extend their traditional occupations. Commercial activities became more diversified with the availability of new markets. Some Jews participated in the purchase of nationalized property, not for agricultural purposes but for speculation. Due to a combination of factors, most prominently the lack of economic motivation to shift occupations and the reluctance of Christian masters to accept Jewish apprentices, the greatest concentration of Jews, those of Alsace, remained firmly entrenched in moneylending, peddling, and petty commerce.[2]

Invariably, the failure to demonstrate concrete progress in residential and economic matters was taken to confirm earlier reservations concerning the advisability of emancipation. It was widely observed that the new type of Jew who was to be fashioned by legal equality and resultant opportunities was not appearing in sufficient numbers. Emancipation seemed to have contributed nothing to the "improvement" of the Jews. Impatience with patterns of Jewish integration in the post-revolutionary era was related, at least in part, to the emergence and growth of nationalism. Already a well-rooted phenomenon whose existence can be traced to the Middle Ages, national consciousness had originally assumed the form of dynastic allegiance that, by the seventeenth century, meant the crystallization of a common consciousness focussed on the monarch. This sentiment was intensified by the emphasis that the mercantilist system placed on national interests over those of other countries, and it acquired a religious character in the aftermath of the Protestant Reformation when religious denominations argued over the "right" faith of the nation, chosen by God for a particular historical destiny.[3] The French Revolution transformed these embryonic forms of national consciousness into a genuine nationalism. It substituted loyalty to the State for allegiance to the monarchy, and faith in the French ideals of liberty and equality for identification with the Church. Furthermore, the revolutionary movement conceived of the nation as the totality of its inhabitants; it was the actualization of Rousseau's conception of the general will. Symbols such as the flag, the national anthem, and the festivals of the Revolution were emblematic of the growing national feeling.[4]

The emergence of strong national sentiment in France added to the uneasiness about the social integration of the Jews. Reservations concerning the alien nature of the Jewish people, an argument heard frequently in the National Assembly, were hardly mitigated in subsequent years. Whereas the French attitude to foreigners certainly did not approach the mounting German aversion to non-Germans, based on their claim to the cultural (and later, racial) superiority of the Teutonic people,[5] the French conception of citizenship envisioned the national amalgamation of diverse sectors of the population not only through social and cultural integration but also through the contribution of each citizen to the national good. Based on the Jews' disappointing record of socioeconomic improvement since the Revolution, some concluded that the bestowal of citizenship may have been premature, whereas others, in upholding emancipation, sought avenues for an acceptable transformation of Jewish life.

An illustration of the complaints lodged against Alsatian Jewry and of the opinions held in this regard by French civil servants is provided by a pamphlet written in 1806 by Louis Poujol, a Parisian lawyer originally from Alsace. The purpose of the work was to provide information enabling the government to determine whether citizenship should be maintained or temporarily withdrawn from the "German" Jews. The "Portuguese" Jews, according to Poujol, were entirely different. Economically, they were honest and productive, and the mores they practiced resembled those of the larger French nation. As far as the Jews of Alsace were concerned, the question depended on the readiness of the Jews to abandon deeply rooted patterns of behavior. Primarily historical in nature, his inquiry devoted itself to a review of Jewish involvement in moneylending from the Middle Ages until his own time. Claiming that popular animosity, discriminatory legislation, and numerous expulsions were nothing more than *responses* to the predominantly Jewish occupation, the author legitimized the actions of governments, the Church, and the masses in giving the Jews their just due. Since the Jews had continued to practice usury even after economic restrictions had been removed, citizenship, Poujol argued, should be temporarily withdrawn so that exceptional legal measures could be justifiably invoked. Beyond its economic implications, usury exemplified symbolically the alien nature of the Jews. Their failure to partake of public ceremonies and military obligations, as well as their unwillingness to participate in agriculture and trades, were taken as proof that they were unwilling to pay their debt to state and society. Their profound hatred of Christians made them dangerous enemies of the state; world domination, as promised to them by their religion, was their only true aspiration.[6]

The Jewish religion, according to Poujol, prescribed a value system and a lifestyle that were in total opposition to the general interest. Consequently, Poujol's recommendations for measures to improve the Jews were not limited to strict regulation of their economic activity, for example, the reduction or dissolution of debts owed to Jews or the encouragement of Jewish industry in the manufacture of those articles lacking in

France, but extended to the realm of religious reform as well. Poujol criticized the Sabbath restrictions because they rendered the Jews absolutely useless to the state, and he therefore appealed for the reconciliation of these laws with demands of various occupations. The dietary laws were, in his estimation, detrimental to the relations between Jews and non-Jews and should therefore be abrogated. Poujol also saw no need for instruction in Jewish subjects. Hebrew and Jewish studies were irrelevant and incompatible with the *moeurs*, customs, and education required by the national interest. The Talmud, especially, was seen as a compendium of precepts that contradicted the principles of simple morality. Divested of all their peculiar customs, activities, and attitudes, the Jews, in the mind of Poujol, would ultimately become assimilated in French society, differing only in their manner of worship. In the final analysis, Poujol's observations, though devastatingly critical, reflect an optimism shared by those in governmental positions and in the civil service for the positive effects of the reform of Judaism.[7]

Such optimism explains Napoleon's dramatic attempt to address the failures of Jewish emancipation and regeneration, first in 1806 with the convocation of an Assembly of Jewish Notables, and in the following year, with the establishment of the Paris Sanhedrin. The emperor had become aware of the urgency of the Jewish question while visiting Strasbourg in January 1806 following his return from Austerlitz. Alsatian farmers complained that their progressive impoverishment was the result of extensive debt to Jewish moneylenders. Over the next several months Napoleon concluded, against the nearly unanimous opposition of the legislative section of the Council of State, that exceptional legal measures should be enacted to put an end to Jewish usury.[8] The emperor believed that the special condition of the Jews justified the sort of government action ordinarily considered illegal. In a report to the Council of State Napoleon argued that "it is necessary to consider the Jews as a nation and not a sect, for they are a nation within a nation."[9] Referring to them as the "vilest of all nations," the emperor declared that they deserve to be judged according to political and not civil law[10] in order to put an end to the humiliation of the French people. In a report to the Emperor, the Minister of Religions, Portalis, asserted that "it was not advisable to proclaim them citizens, without investigating if they could or even wanted sincerely to become so. It follows also that it would not be unreasonable or unjust to submit to particular laws a type of corporation, which, on account of its institutions, principles and customs, remains constantly separated from general society."[11]

Jewish social exclusiveness was allegedly the product of two grave flaws in Judaism's legal system. First, it combined the religious and political-civil realms of life, or as Portalis' put it, Judaism included "the religion, the political and the civil laws, the habits, the manners, and all the customs of life."[12] According to Napoleon, a distinction between religious laws and political laws was essential. Religious provisions were of an eternal character, and were therefore immutable; Judaism's political provisions, on the other hand, were limited to ancient times, when the Jews had resided in the Land of Israel and constituted a nation. Since, according to the emperor, Jewish civil law no longer had any contemporary application, the Sanhedrin, then, had "the mandate to abolish all atrocious laws . . . which could only apply to Jews living in Palestine."[13] Behind this claim lay a theoretical argument concerning a more restricted role for religion in society. Shared habits, customs, and behavior common to all citizens would act as agents of national cohesion and unity, whereas religion would be limited to matters of conscience, and only the manner of worship would distinguish one group from another. The combination and interrelation of the religious and civil domains in Judaism was viewed as fundamentally foreign to France and therefore intolerable. For their part, Jews had traditionally understood religion to have an application toward the regulation of social life. Indeed, compliance with the premise that differentiated between the two types of law would ultimately represent an unprecedented departure from rabbinic Judaism. Second, the Jewish religion was criticized for its alleged particularistic moral doctrine. Foremost among the allegations was the contention that Judaism upheld a dual standard of morality freeing adherents, in their relations with gentiles, from most ethical obligations that were required in their dealings with fellow Jews. The Jewish religion's justification of usurious rates of interest for non-Jews, while no interest at all could be taken from a Jew, was the most frequently cited proof of the double standard. In short, usury, as well as the various examples of Jewish exclusiveness, were taken as evidence of Judaism's professed hatred of the non-Jew.[14]

In an effort to address the Jewish question in its totality, Napoleon embarked on the program announced in the Imperial Decree of 30 May 1806. Seeking to resolve the immediate economic problem in Alsace, the first part of the document declared a moratorium on all debts owed the Jews by noncommercial farmers of the northeast. This, however, was not the emperor's sole concern. Although Jewish economic practices were the main target of criticism, they were understood to be symptomatic of a more fundamental problem: the suitability of the Jews to assume the obligations incumbent upon them as citizens of France. For this reason the decree stated that the economic circumstances in the north made it clear "how urgent it is to revive sentiments of civil morality among those who profess the Jewish religion in the countries under our jurisdiction, sentiments which have, sadly, disappeared among a very great number of them due to the state of degradation in which they have languished, a state which it is not at all among our intentions to maintain nor to renew."[15]

A perceived deficiency in "sentiments of civil morality" was thus regarded as the very core of the problem. Consequently, in the second part of the Imperial Decree, Napoleon ordered the convocation of a Jewish assembly empowered with legislative authority to resolve the question of the incompatibility of Judaism and civic duties once and for all. Whether one accepts the convincing suggestion that Israel Jacobson's proposal for the formation of a Jewish council influenced Napoleon,[16] it stands as a fact that the emperor espoused the idea of convening a rabbinical assembly in order to initiate and implement reforms. Although Napoleon did not acknowledge the Jews as full-fledged Frenchmen and although his opinion of their religion was very low, he evidently felt that the entire project would be seen in a more positive light and his goals would ultimately be achieved if he could first secure Jewish endorsement. Napoleon genuinely believed that the situation of French Jewry bore no resemblance to that of any preceding era in Jewish history and that new conditions demanded reinterpretation and adaptation, albeit in the spirit of the Jewish religion and in accordance with its legislative procedures. He therefore viewed the convocation of an authoritative Jewish assembly with the utmost seriousness and asserted that its decisions would be placed "on equal footing with the Talmud, to be articles of faith and principles of religious legislation."[17]

Ostensibly, the questions placed before the Assembly were designed to clarify the attitude of Jewish law, as interpreted by the delegates, toward the state and its citizens. Such issues as intermarriage, attitudes toward non-Jews, civic duties, rabbinic authority, occupational restrictions, and moneylending were therefore examined closely. A careful look at Napoleon's correspondence, however, reveals that the emperor's real objective was hardly to provide a forum for a discussion of these issues but the total assimilation of French Jewry. This was to be achieved in two ways. First, the government would require that of every three marriages involving Jews, one would be between a Jew and a Frenchman. Second, Napoleon believed that greater insistence on military conscription for Jews would ultimately succeed in imparting upon them French culture and *moeurs*.[18] In fact, a private letter written by Napoleon immediately before the convocation contained after nearly each of the questions the specific answer that he demanded, thus proving that the emperor expected from the Assembly nothing short of an endorsement of intermar-

44

riage, a clear affirmation of the "brotherly" relationship between Jews and other Frenchmen, and an express prohibition of usury.[19] Nevertheless, the assembly was not in a position to satisfy the emperor on all counts, chiefly because the rabbinic members of the body struggled to remain loyal to Jewish tradition. At the same time, the answers reflect a sensitivity to the expectations of the emperor, particularly the demand for social integration that the status of citizenship presupposed.[20]

Ironically, the Sanhedrin appears to have inspired a new genre of criticism on the Jewish question. Despite the delegates' unequivocal declarations of patriotism and brotherhood, and despite the religious reassurances provided by the Sanhedrin itself, the government's faith in the ability of the Jews to undergo self-reform faded quickly. On 17 March 1808 the emperor issued three decrees: the first two decrees established the Consistory system for the organization of French Jewry. The consistories were to enforce the decisions of the Assembly of Notables through education and surveillance. In the third decree, Napoleon evinced a radically different approach to the Jewish question, probably in deference to the intense anti-Jewish sentiment among the Alsatian peasantry. In seeking to put an end to Jewish moneylending in Alsace, the "Infamous Decree," as it was later called, nullified all debts owed to the Jews by soldiers, minors, and women, and cancelled any loan granted at a rate of interest beyond 10 percent. These laws also prohibited any movement of Alsatian Jews to other *départements,* and forbade Jewish immigrants from settling in Alsace. Finally, the decree forbade the Jews from supplying replacements for military service, though this was commonly practiced throughout France. The provisions of the decree were to remain in force for a period of ten years and could be extended further if the conditions that brought it into being persisted.[21] With the 1808 decree, emancipation suffered a major setback. French Jewry was denied the rights constitutionally guaranteed to French citizens, and was once again expected to prove itself worthy of citizenship. Whatever the motivation behind the imperial decree, whatever its goals, the result was the establishment of French Jewry as a separate body, subject directly to the will and authority of the emperor. Special legislation, enacted in a humiliating fashion against this one group, signified the return of the Jews of France to a pre-Revolutionary status.

The remaining years of the Napoleonic regime produced virtually no public discussion of the Jewish question. However, with the restoration of the Bourbon Monarchy in 1815, the debate resumed, initially inspired by the question of the impending renewal of the 1808 decree, and subsequently leading to a more general reevaluation of the Jewish condition in France. Figuring most prominently in the discussions was the

Paris Sanhedrin; the assembly was widely commended for having placed Judaism in line with reason and the laws of the state.[22] However, for many writers the Sanhedrin only accentuated the distance between the theoretical possibilities of improvement and the actual Jewish condition. The Jews were commonly taken to task for failing to conduct themselves according to the "noble sentiments" expressed by the assembly of rabbis.[23] According to critics, failure to live up to the ideology of the Sanhedrin was expressed in the Jews' refusal to regard France as their *patrie*.[24] Perhaps more than ever before, the fatherland had become an object of love and devotion; this new emotional attachment intensified the sentiments of civic obligation to the state and heightened the unity of purpose of its citizens.[25] The Jews, by contrast, were accused of loving only the Land of Israel and therefore of regarding themselves as no more than transient sojourners.[26] The belief in the eventual coming of the Messiah was further proof that the Jews could not have any feeling of permanence in the country where they lived.[27] These attitudes, it was argued, undermined the Jews' sense of duty to the state and society, and rendered the decisions of the Sanhedrin irrelevant to their "unique" situation. Many concluded that virtually no change had taken place from the manner in which the Jews related to the state during the Middle Ages.

Former Jacobin leader Agricole Moureau attributed the failures of French Jewry to the numerous shortcomings inherent in Jewish legislation. His pamphlet, *De l'incompatibilité entre le Judaïsme et l'exercise des droits de cité*,[28] argued that Jewish law was incompatible with the modern state because it was of divine origin, therefore outweighing any temporal obligations to the public. Citing the oft-employed examples of Sabbath and military restrictions, Moureau asserted that the Jews could not be expected to serve the state or society faithfully. As long as it was defined in divine terms, Jewish law would pose an insurmountable obstacle to the fulfillment of civic responsibilities.[29] Moureau also claimed that the mentality of the Jews was adversely affected by a legal system that, historically, had required separation from the mainstream of society. In the case of other nations, the author contended, mores serve to inspire the creation of laws but frequently rise above the law. For Jews the opposite is the case: mores are the consequence of their laws, not the determinant. Implying that the Jews had become enslaved to their legal system, Moureau insisted that they were unable to aspire toward a higher political and social morality. In this way Moureau explained how the Jewish people could remain, amidst other nations, strangers both to the public spirit and to the best interests of society.[30]

For many observers, the problem was that Judaism constituted at once a religious and social system; that is, an all-encompassing ideology originally designed for the administration of a theocratic state. This idea was concretely expressed in the claim that the Jews constituted a "state within a state" at a time when medieval corporations were being dissolved.[31] The conflict between the law of the state and Jewish law was therefore seen as inevitable, and one which could not be tolerated. Moreover, Jewish legislation, inasmuch as its goal was to preserve the social and religious integrity of its adherents, prohibited various degrees of social contact between Jew and non-Jew, ranging from casual encounters to intermarriage. In virtually every aspect of Jewish life and thought—whether dietary laws, ceremonial rites, educational segregation, or alleged aspirations for world domination—critics observed an exclusiveness that violated contemporary notions of brotherhood.[32]

More devastating than the charge of exclusiveness was the view that the Jews were uncivilized. The French conception of civilization was relatively new; the term *civilisation* had replaced the conceptions of *civilité* and *politesse* only at the end of the eighteenth century. *Politesse,* "the means of achieving a more affectionate sort of humanity," presupposed a more intensive culture than *civilité,* "the gentle and polite way of conducting oneself toward others."[33] Although these terms enabled writers to classify people according to a hierarchy ranging from savagery to urbanity, they proved inadequate for the students of humanity who sought to interpret the many facts compiled during the eighteenth century. Investigation of the past, primarily in terms of its relationship to the contemporary world, became a significant preoccupation of writers, royal officers, learned societies, and the academies. The emergence and employment of the term *civilisation* signified an awareness of the need for placing these philosophical, scientific, and literary data in an intelligible historical context.[34]

Civilisation represented, in the first analysis, the progress achieved in human knowledge, the ascent toward reason: "Instructing a nation is the same as civilizing it; stifling learning in it means leading it back to the primitive state of barbarity. . . . Ignorance is the lot of the slave and the savage."[35] Rooted in a deep optimism and faith in the future, the French Revolution inspired an unprecedented receptivity to these ideas. It drew strength from, and lent credence to, the philosophy of progress and the infinite perfectibility of men.[36] François Guizot, French historian and statesman, advanced the concept further with his assertion that *civilisation* involves the perfection of man's external condition and his internal, personal nature. The two elements are linked intimately and act upon one another reciprocally. Social improvements and progress in man's material well-being are precarious and unwarranted when implemented without corresponding intellectual development. Insisting that efficient organization of social relations was essential to social and intellectual progress, Guizot declared that "we are called upon to reform, perfect, and regulate all that is. We feel able to act upon the world and to extend throughout it the glorious empire of reason."[37] Guizot's synthesizing construction, encompassing all aspects of the human spirit (religious beliefs, philosophical ideas, the sciences, letters, and the arts) and material well-being, was thus understood to be a moral imperative for those who had already achieved some measure of civilization.

The question of whether there have been distinct civilizations in existence contemporaneously, or instead "one universal civilization of the human race," was debated throughout the nineteenth century. Until the midcentury, however, Guizot and like-minded thinkers displayed a decided preference for the old concept of a "superior" civilization currently entrusted to the French.[38] Owing to this belief, and given its accompanying mandate for reforming those less civilized, French intellectuals viewed the Jewish question as a case of cultural disparity: inferior cultural patterns of the Jewish people needed reform if the Jews were to become part of general society. In short, full emancipation involved experiencing the processes of civilization, as well as modernization, in a single transformation.[39]

Opinions varied on what ought to be done to accelerate the regeneration of the Jews, and in the 1820s the practical aspects of Jewish regeneration once again became a matter of public concern. In 1824, the *Société des sciences, agriculture et arts* of Strasbourg sponsored an essay contest on the following questions:

1. To determine the most appropriate means to enable the Israelite population of Alsace to enjoy the benefits of civilization.
2. To investigate whether the causes that estrange the members that compose this population from society are at all the product of superstitious practices and of the obstinacy to persevere in the ancient customs that the times and changes in the political situation should have modified.[40]

The société explained that it was motivated by a desire to assist the Jewish people, first by reawakening its dormant seeds of perfection and then by publicizing the various means of assistance that could be provided by the general population.[41] A prize of 300 francs awaited the author of the essay judged most useful in the regeneration of the Jews.

The questions posed by the *société* indicate the focus of concerns associated with the Jewish question. Good intentions aside, one can easily detect an unmistakable tone of condescension from the nature of the questions and their phrasing. The first question was predicated on the assumption that the Jewish people, at least in Alsace, was bereft of civilization. Indeed, the program announcing the competition portrayed the Jews as an uncultured people living amidst European nations who owed their high level of civilization to the influence of Christianity as well as to the impact of the arts and sciences. The sharp contrast between the superior culture of Europe and this primitive "Asian" nation—steadfast in its mores and religious tradition, estranged from all other peoples no matter how entrenched in various countries—left the impression that the work of regeneration was far from complete.[42] Despite the bleak assessment of the Jewish condition, the general outlook was optimistic and confident. Such certainty did not characterize the Metz competition of 1785, when the question was, "Are there means . . . ?" Forty years later, regeneration was a concrete goal; the problem was essentially determining the most direct road to that goal.

By suggesting possible avenues of inquiry into the matter of Jewish estrangement from French society and civilization, the second question contained its own explanation for the failure of regeneration: the nature of the Jewish religion and its impact on the character of the Jews. Characterized as "superstitious," Judaism's religious practices were regarded as having produced a segregative, isolationist social *mentalité*. The Jews themselves were to blame for their social and cultural destitution inasmuch as they obstinately persevered in "the ancient customs that the times and changes in the political situation" should have already modified.[43] Adherence to the ceremonial law was now viewed as out of step with contemporary mores and therefore unacceptable. It is interesting to note that at least one French Jew, Michel Berr, criticized the *société* for the prejudiced phrasing of the second question.[44]

Accompanying the essay questions were several special points that the *société* felt worthy of attention. The first related to whether the Sanhedrin decisions could furnish the Central Consistory with the means necessary for achieving the desired regenerative results. Second, the *société* suggested that ritual improvements introduced elsewhere in France and Europe might be applicable to the Jewish population of Alsace. A third point concerned a recommendation that there be a reconciliation of Jewish holidays with state holidays and asked whether this was possible according to the essential dogmas of Mosaism. Finally, the *société* asked whether it would be useful to establish for France, or for Alsace in particular, an *école normale israélite*, which would be able to "replace the incapable [Jewish] teachers with more educated and enlightened men."[45] Although it is not clear whether these ideas originated among the gentile members of the *société*, or Jewish consultants, the three points guided the contestants in the composition of their essays.

Four *mémoires* were submitted to the evaluation commission, three of which were judged to address the subject in the manner conceived by the *société*. Arthur Beugnot, a French lawyer, senator, and historian, was awarded the first prize, and honorable mention was given to the essays submitted by Louis Blanchard and Prosper Wittersheim, a Jewish member of the *société* and secretary of the *Société d'encouragement des arts et métiers* for the Jews of Metz.[46] The contestants and their contemporaries addressed the practical means of regenerating the Jews: religious reform, economic transformation, and educational changes, among others. Modifications in Jewish life were discussed, however, exclusively within the context of government regulation of alleged Jewish abuses. Thus the question of exceptional legislation (i.e., laws created specifically for the Jewish population) came again to the forefront of French political debate. The more conservative critics of the progress of Jewish regeneration contended that such special legal measures, particularly the regulation of economic life, would force the Jews to become rehabilitated. This, of course, was not a new idea. In 1808 French Jewry, with the exception of the Jews in Bordeaux and the *départements* of Gironde and Landes, had been subjected to special laws in matters relating to commercial activity and freedom of movement. By the end of the ten year period few thought that the discriminatory decree would be extended beyond its original term. Napoleon, the legislator of the decree, was in exile, and the 1815 Charter of the Bourbon monarchy reaffirmed the principle of civil and legal equality for all Frenchmen. Nevertheless, in 1817 a petition was addressed to the two chambers of the royal government by M. le marquis Camille de Lattier (from the *département* of Drôme, where no Jews lived) to renew the 1808 decree. Although de Lattier's efforts were not successful, the subject of exceptional legislation lived on. A number of writers continued to recommend strict supervision of the movement and occupational freedom of Alsatian Jewry in an effort to combat their usurious practices.[47]

Thus both punitive and rehabilitative elements played a role in the appeals for special legislation. Indeed, the very fact that certain rights of citizenship had once been taken away, or that the issue was even a subject of discussion, is evidence of an attitude equating the Jews with social criminals. Many felt that punishment, in the form of legal restrictions, would deter the deviant behavior of the Jews and, in turn, be the first step in the process of rehabilitation. The most prevalent argument in defense of special legislation concerned the alien nature of the Jewish people and their religion, the same argument that had been used in the National Assembly to oppose emancipation. Jews were regarded as people "outside of the population" who "voluntarily remain outside the common law."[48] Because Jewish laws were "contrary to those of the country," special legislation could not be considered intolerant but rather an act of strict justice.[49] For some writers the position of the Jews on the periphery of society explained their failure to exercise reciprocity in their dealings with fellow Frenchmen. Moureau, for example, insisted that the voluntary exclusiveness of the Jews, expressed most blatantly by the incompatibility of their laws with the duties of state and society, called for corresponding legal exclusion from certain privileges. He explained further that as human beings, Jews cannot be denied the *droits de l'humanité*, the rights of humanity. The *droits de cité*, the rights of citizenship, by contrast, are subordinate to conditions sine qua non and available only to those who fulfill the necessary conditions. Thus the right of the Jews to exercise and retain full citizenship was regarded as conditional. Moureau even suggested that every French Jew be required to take a special oath, the traditional medieval *more judaico*, once a year as proof of loyalty to the *patrie* and its laws.[50]

Betting de Lancastel, a *sous-préfèt* in the Haut-Rhin district, connected the issue of exceptional legislation to the refusal of the Jews to abide by the decisions of the Sanhedrin. He argued that the Jews were unjustified in citing in their own defense Article V of the 1815 Charter, which provided freedom of religion and equal protection before the law for members of all religions. Betting insisted that the Jewish religion that had been reinterpreted by the Sanhedrin was protected by the charter and not the "cult of prejudices" that most Jews continued to practice. Only those who accepted the decisions of the Sanhedrin merited the protection of the charter; those who remained opposed would be subjected to special legislation without the charter being violated. In short, exceptional legislation for the Jews was justified on the grounds that the continued special status of the Jews warranted it, while general society required it for its own self-protection.[51]

In contrast with these opinions, the commission that evaluated the 1824 *mémoires* did not fully agree with the insistence upon special legal measures, even though the author of the prize-winning essay, Arthur Beugnot, was an advocate of such legislation. While conceding that the Jews of Alsace were in a deplorable state of moral degeneration, the commission felt that Beugnot had exaggerated the evils he attributed to them. In fact, the commission rejected Beugnot's most basic premise, that the Jews of the day were identical with the Jews of the past. It argued that the Jews had benefitted, at least to some degree, from advances in French law and had made important strides toward civilization, as evidenced by the increasing numbers of enlightened figures, greater participation in agriculture, and improved relations with Christians. In the estimation of the commission, these modest ameliorations put to rest the myth of the hopelessness of the Jewish condition. There was, clearly, a positive relationship between legal equality, on the one hand, and the eradication of Jewish vices, on the other. The goal of civilizing the Jews, according to the commission, would therefore not be served by exclusion from common law but through the work of local institutions.[52]

Proposals for the creation of new institutions that would tend to the regeneration of the Jews occupied the most conspicuous place in the essays written in the 1820s. Despite various efforts to justify exceptional legislation, it would appear that reliance on the repressive powers of the state was no longer regarded as a viable solution. The central thrust was not on punitive measures directed at economic and residential patterns but on more positive plans for economic rehabilitation. A variety of projects aiming at the diversification of Jewish economic life in Alsace appeared in response to the acknowledged need for change. Some dealt with the problem of directing the Jews toward productive occupations, most notably agriculture and industry.[53] Others maintained that the problem of Jewish usury had reached excessive proportions because of the absence of dependable sources of credit. One suggestion, advanced by the secretary of the *société*, Amédée Tourette, centered on the creation of a Jewish communal credit institution that would be supported by affluent Jews and supervised by community officials. This institution would be designed to encourage Jews to save money and would enable others (both Jewish and non-Jewish) to borrow at the same rate of interest (5 percent). The profits could be devoted to various communal projects.[54]

The idea of bringing an end to usury through the establishment of a government-controlled credit institution and mortgage fund attracted numerous supporters in the 1820s. Originally formed in Italian cities by Franciscans monks in the mid-1400s, the *monte di pieta* was designed to provide loans at relatively low rates of interest to the urban poor. Its primary purpose, according to its founders, was to eliminate Jewish moneylenders.[55] Betting de Lancastel, for one, advocated the creation of a similar institution for the protection of the general population of Alsace, where the continued role of the Jews as creditors posed an allegedly grave danger.[56] Tourette, by contrast, regarded the plan for credit reform in an altogether different light. He envisioned Jewish participation in a *monte di pieta* as contributing to an improvement in public attitudes toward the Jews. This institution would provide the Jews with an opportunity to publicly display moral uprightness.[57]

In contrast to these rather unsystematic proposals, an all-embracing plan for Jewish *régénération* was offered by Arthur Beugnot. A lawyer, senator, and delegate to the National Assembly, Beugnot was hardly unacquainted with the Jewish question. In 1821, he had participated in an essay contest sponsored by the Académie des Inscriptions et Belles-Lettres on the status of the Jews in medieval France, Spain, and Italy. Together with J. B. Capefigue and G. B. Depping, Beugnot was accorded honorable mention by the Académie, and his essay was subsequently published under the title *Les Juifs d'Occident.* Conceived as "an appeal to justice, amidst an enlightened century," the work focussed first on the nature of the intolerance suffered by Jews throughout their history. Beugnot challenged the idea that the degradation of the Jews was a theological imperative and concluded that the countless instances of social and religious contempt for the Jewish people simply contradicted Christian teaching.[58] He maintained that the charge of Jewish anti-social behavior was accurate as long as the hope to rebuild Jerusalem existed, but once this hope was, for all practical purposes, shattered, the Jews sought only to live together in their own communities. Furthermore, the "crime" of usury, he insisted, was by modern standards a respectable activity. As for Jewish culture, Beugnot expressed admiration for the social and political genius of Mosaic law, the Jewish contributions to European commerce, and important accomplishments in the field of philology. In this last regard Beugnot asked rhetorically, "To whom does Europe owe its success in the study of Oriental languages, if not to the rabbis?" Nevertheless, the fact that Beugnot's work was a positive evaluation of the historical experience and cultural achievement of the Jews must not obscure the traces of prejudice against rabbinic Judaism that occasionally surface in the course of the author's presentation. For example, the praise heaped upon rabbinic literature, grammars, and lexicons in aiding "the progress of the human spirit" was accompanied by stinging criticisms of the "frivolous" works of the rabbis. Christian scholars, according to Beugnot, needed to separate the "truly useful research" from the "Talmudic rubbish" (*fatras talmudique*).[59] Beugnot's work clearly expressed some misgivings concerning the cultural value of traditional Judaism; not surprisingly, the proposals he put forward in the 1824 essay contest reflect this ambivalent assessment of Jewish civilization.

Beugnot had full confidence in the Jews' capacity to direct their own *régénération,* provided that this was carried out under the aegis of the French government. He proposed the establishment of a *Société israélite d'Alsace,* to be divided into five *comités,* each with its own specific function. A *comité des écoles* would supervise the curriculum of general studies in such areas as French language, linear design (draftsmanship), and girls' education. Working closely with this body would be a *comité des livres* that would publish elementary textbooks, particularly a catechism of the Mosaic religion. The goal would be to modify the religious and moral principles that were contrary to life in modern society and to present these ideas in a form comprehensible to schoolchildren. Beugnot proposed the formation of a *comité d'agriculture* to oversee the development of an experimental farm, to be cosponsored by the Jews themselves and the government. A *comité d'industrie* would supervise the placement of young Jews in artisan shops, procure their admission in schools of *arts et métiers*, and find employment for Jewish laborers. Finally, a *comité de bienfaisance* would collect funds on behalf of needy Jews, facilitate entry into hospitals, and aid and visit prisoners.[60]

The recommendations just enumerated constituted the first part of Beugnot's essay. The second part was devoted to the subject of religious reform and to the modernization of the rabbinate. Like many others, Beugnot argued that French rabbis were poorly trained, opposed to civilization, and therefore incapable of fulfilling the two principal functions assigned to them by the *règlement* of 1808: to provide instruction of the religious doctrines contained in the decisions of the Sanhedrin and to direct the education of Jewish youth. Beugnot therefore proposed the establishment of a rabbinical seminary in Strasbourg[61] to prepare rabbis for their diverse obligations. Admission would be restricted to graduates of French secondary schools where a *bachelier ès lettres* could be obtained. The curriculum would consist of the Pentateuch, rabbinic theology, oratory, and ethics, in addition to Talmud. Through such a distribution of subjects, the author hoped to counterbalance the exaggerated influence that he felt rabbinic interpretations exerted on the training of rabbis. Concurring with Beugnot's view, the evaluation commission noted that the proposed theological studies would provide the future rabbis with much-needed enlightenment and would enable them to cooperate in civilizing their coreligionists.[62]

Beugnot's plan for religious reform included a demand for the convocation of a new Sanhedrin. He envisioned an assembly that would revise religious dogma and moral principles, on the one hand, and prescribe concrete changes, on the other. It should be emphasized here that criticism of Jewish ritual was not based on purely religious motivation but also on the social and economic implications of Jewish exclusiveness, seen to be encouraged and sustained by Jewish laws. As an example, Beugnot cited the great number of religious holidays that constituted both a hindrance to normal business relations with Christians and an obstacle to the employment of Jewish workers in gentile shops. As a partial solution to the problem, Beugnot suggested that the Jewish Sabbath be moved from Saturday to Sunday, in accordance with Christian practice. Inverting the historical reality, he argued that the rabbis had originally fixed the day of the Sabbath not according to chronological considerations but as a counterpart to the Christian day of rest. Because of apparent uncertainties in the astronomical calculations, the Jews could, according to Beugnot, transfer their day of rest to Sunday without fear of actually violating Jewish law.[63]

Beugnot also demanded the abandonment of rituals that allegedly precluded Jewish social integration. Some, such as Tourette, cited the Jews' refusal to intermarry as the greatest obstacle to their integration. Beugnot reserved his most severe criticism for Jewish dietary laws that "impede the *fusion sociale des Juifs.*" In his thinking the elimination of these restrictions was not an unjustified demand since he viewed the dietary laws as an example of the many religious customs and ceremonies that were substituted for Pentateuchal laws. The Talmudic legal addenda thus represented, for Beugnot, instances of religious innovations that, on the one hand, since they added to or modified Biblical proscriptions, helped to legitimize his proposals for reform; on the other hand, because rabbinic laws themselves were nothing but later revisions of Biblical legislation, their status as eternal precepts was, in his estimation, of rather questionable validity. He therefore called on the Consistory to make known to the Jews that the prohibition of certain foods had originally been motivated by political and hygenic considerations, in addition to religious reasons. Insofar as these motives were no longer justified in nineteenth-century France, Beugnot contended, the Consistory was obliged to advise its constituency to abandon these outmoded laws. In short, Beugnot and his contemporaries believed that the Jew had an obligation, as a citizen, to become civilized and "to never isolate his interest from the public interest, nor his destiny . . . from the destiny of the grand family of the state."[64]

Because the prize-winning Beugnot essay was never published, it is difficult to measure the impact of the author's proposals. Nevertheless, the *mémoire* is of special significance. It is representative of the general climate of opinion on the Jewish question in Restoration France, having incorporated many themes that were prevalent among government officials, public figures, and other observers, albeit in a rather original formulation. In effect, Beugnot systematized many of the recommendations and views that had been published in the works of Poujol, Moureau, Tourette, and Betting de Lancastel. Aside from the general tone of condescension, perhaps the most striking element in the entire literature on the Jewish question in this period was the universally shared faith in and commitment to change. Based primarily on dissatisfaction with the state of emancipated French Jewry, writers demanded a complete transformation of

Jewish life in keeping with prevailing social, economic, and cultural views. They therefore offered recommendations for implementing reforms intended to effect economic, social, and cultural regeneration.

At the very base of these demands for change was the assumption that traditional Judaism, its institutions, and the resulting impact on the Jewish people were not only corrupted, but also incompatible with the requirements of modern life and civilization. This indictment was so pervasive that Jewish intellectual and communal leaders came to some of the same conclusions as their gentile counterparts, though certainly not without some reservations. The general negative assessment of Judaism and Jewish life was not, however, merely internalized by the Franco-Jewish leadership, but also evoked a new critical responsiveness to the much-debated issues of Jewish modernization. It is within this context that modifications in the social, cultural, and religious orientation of French Jewry, ultimately to be formulated in the ideology of *régénération*, will be examined.

3

French *Maskilim* and
the Paris Sanhedrin

THE FIRST EVIDENCE of change in the social and religious value system of French Jewry can be traced to the final years of the ancien régime, when several Jewish writers began to participate in and respond to public discussions of the Jewish question. The political and intellectual ferment that climaxed in the French Revolution was accompanied by efforts to reconsider the place of the Jews in the new order. At the heart of the debates between proponents and opponents of Jewish emancipation was the question of the compatibility of the Jewish religion with civic duties. Most striking of all was the universally negative assessment of Judaism that characterized, in varying degrees, the views of both advocates and critics, and that carried implications for far-reaching changes in the religious life and social structure of French Jewry. These gentile observations and criticisms served to articulate unequivocally the terms under which the Jews would ultimately be accepted as citizens of France. As participants in these discussions, Jewish writers assumed the important task of demonstrating that their coreligionists were capable of fulfilling the duties of citizenship and the more loosely defined obligations related to social integration.

In defending Judaism against the litany of social, political, and religious allegations, Jewish writers embarked upon the first stage in the formulation of an ideology of emancipation. Their reactions to both the claim that Judaism was incompatible with modern life and the charge of the Jews' moral inadequacy furnished an opportunity to consider the implications of citizenship and advance various proposals of their own concerning *régénération*. Over the course of approximately twenty years, ending with the convocation of the Napoleonic Sanhedrin in 1807, the participation of Jewish communal leaders and intellectuals in public discussions produced new Jewish conceptions of communal organization and leadership, as well as a clarification of attitudes toward the state and its gentile citizens. It will be suggested below that, contrary to the accustomed view, the Sanhedrin only restated positions formulated by Franco-Jewish leaders in anticipation of, and in immediate reaction to, the achievement of civic equality. In reaffirming French Jewry's commitment to the terms of citizenship, the Sanhedrin brought to a close the first period in modern Franco-Jewish history, the period of emancipation. During this initial phase of its modern history French Jewry displayed the first indications of the particular orientation that lay at the foundation of *le mouvement régénérateur*.

Haskalah in France

French Jewish leaders who addressed the socio-economic, cultural, and political ramifications of emancipation identified closely with the ideology of the Berlin Haskalah.[1] The Haskalah, a Jewish variation of the European Enlightenment, was largely responsible for laying the ideological foundation for the modernization of Jewish life and culture in Western Europe. Jacob Katz has attributed the appearance of the Haskalah movement to a growing feeling of impatience with the restrictions on residence and economic life that had virtually confined the Jew to his own community. This community, the *kehillah*, was a multidimensional institution that provided the framework for nearly all activity, including family life, education, and religious services and rites. Granted complete autonomy by the state, the *kehillah* exercised control over the business, social, and religious conduct of its members. A system of fines, physical punishment, and the *herem*, confirmed by the judicial and executive powers of the *kehillah*, served to regulate any behavior considered deviant. As Jewish intellectuals were increasingly exposed to the ideas of the Enlightenment and thus became aware of the cultural limitations imposed by their own communities, they began to evaluate traditional Jewish society according to the Enlightenment's criteria of usefulness and reason. By the beginning of the 1780s the proponents of the Haskalah, the *maskilim*, had formulated an ideology that challenged several elements of the Jewish religious tradition, the authority of the rabbis, and the economic life of their coreligionists. The *maskilim* concluded that significant changes in Jewish social and cultural life were imperative.[2]

Demographic, intellectual, and political conditions in France precluded the emergence of a strong, independent Haskalah movement as in Germany. At the time of the Revolution the Jews of France numbered approximately forty thousand, with all but a few thousand concentrated in the small towns and villages of Alsace-Lorraine. The northeastern communities were composed of Ashkenazic Jews, most of whom were involved in the traditional Jewish occupations of petty trade and moneylending. Unlike Germany, there were no major urban centers, the likes of Berlin, Koenigsberg, or Hamburg, that had more than a handful of Jews, let alone Jewish intellectuals. Strasbourg, the most important city in Alsace, excluded Jews entirely, and in Paris, the greatest city in Europe, there were only five hundred Jews, predominantly poor shopkeepers, peddlers, and laborers.[3] As a result of legal restrictions on residence and mobility, as well as widespread anti-Jewish hostility, most of France's Jews remained in a state of social and cultural isolation, in many ways insulated from the great changes that were taking place in enlightened Europe.

There were, however, two notable exceptions to this general pattern: the Sephardic Jews of Bordeaux and the Ashkenazic Jews of Metz. The Sephardim, having been granted a wide range of economic and religious privileges, experienced a degree of acculturation unparalleled among their Ashkenazic coreligionists. In their manner of dress, economic pursuits, and language the Sephardim appeared no different than their French neighbors. In the realm of culture, they produced several distinguished men of letters: Jacob Rodrigues Péreire, known for his work with the deaf; Isaac de Pinto, author of important essays on finance; and Louis Francia de Beaufleury, a writer on issues of social welfare.[4] Some scholars have concluded that the acculturation of Sephardic Jewry was accompanied by a considerable decline in the standards of religious observance. The curriculum at the Bordeaux *Talmud Torah* included neither Mishnah nor Talmud, heretical ideas were expressed unabashedly, and public infractions of Jewish law, in such areas as *kashrut*, family purity, and the Sabbath, were common among the wealthy and the educated of the community. According to one scholar, Sephardic Jewry's modernized Judaism incorporated non-Jewish standards and values, particularly the notion of a more restricted role for religion in everyday life. Compartmentalization of this kind originated in the Marrano heritage; it served the Sephardim well, since the clear differentiation between personal religious belief and public conduct would be expected of all citizens.[5] Whatever our assessment of the degree of Sephardic assimilation, it is clear that the emphasis the Bordeaux school placed on Hebrew grammar, the Bible, and orderliness anticipated many of the educational reforms subsequently introduced in enlightened Ashkenazic schools.[6] The cultural enlightenment of the Sephardic Jews of Bordeaux and Bayonne did not, however, produce a Haskalah movement. The Haskalah in the West was the product of the confrontation between traditional Jewish culture and the intellectual trends of modern Europe. The movement emerged from the trauma experienced by Jewish intellectuals during their encounter with modernity. The Sephardic Jews, by virtue of their extensive acculturation and freedom from ghetto restrictions, experienced no such trauma and did not feel the need for a movement of socio-cultural modernization.[7]

Conditions in Metz, the leading Jewish community in northeastern France, were more conducive to the emergence of Haskalah. Among the Jews of Metz was a fairly substantial oligarchy of the rich, comprised of army provisioners, bankers, and merchants, though the vast majority of Jews were involved in petty trade and moneylending.[8] Owing to their wealth and influence, the leaders of the Metz community had greater mobility and opportunities for cultural exchange than most of their Alsatian coreligionists. In addition, the presence of liberal voices in Metz, men such as Pierre Louis Lacretelle and members of the *Société des arts et sciences* who were sympathetic to the plight of the Jews, encouraged the concentration of Jewish intellectuals in the city. Metz became the center for a small circle of *maskilim,* some of whom resided in nearby cities in Alsace. Since conditions in France were not ripe for an indigenous widespread Haskalah movement as in Germany, French communal leaders and intellectuals remained in close personal contact with the Berlin figures, and their publicistic efforts set in motion a French variant of the Berlin Haskalah.[9] First, they did much to publicize the literary works written in Germany, mainly through translation. And second, in their own publications they applied the principles of the ideology of Berlin to the particular needs and status of French Jewry.

Several French Jews were prominent in the literary activity of the Haskalah movement. Lipmann Moses Büschenthal (1784–1818), a son-in-law of Rabbi David Sintzheim, composed a number of Hebrew poems lauding Napoleon and the Paris Sanhedrin. Moses Ensheim (1760–1839), a native of Metz, served as a tutor in the home of Moses Mendelssohn, and was a member of the literary circle that founded *Ha-Meassef,* the Hebrew journal of the Berlin Haskalah. Among Ensheim's published works were two Hebrew poems: one an ode to the French National Assembly and the Declaration of the Rights of Man, and the other a hymn on the occasion of the Metz civic fete of 1792. His interests ranged from mathematics, on which he wrote an important treatise, to Hebrew grammar and biblical exegesis. Ensheim was a friend of Abbé

Grégoire and assisted him in writing his prize-winning essay, submitted to the Metz competition in 1785. Through his association with the German *maskilim*, Ensheim represents an important link between the Berlin Haskalah and the French proponents of *régénération*.[10]

A contemporary of Ensheim, Elijah Halfan Ha-Lévi (Elie Halévy, 1760–1826), made important contributions both to literary and educational affairs. Born in Germany, where he became friendly with Mendelssohn, Halévy settled at an early age in Paris; he was cantor of the leading synagogue in the city and secretary of the Central and Paris Consistories. Halévy's linguistic skills enabled him to serve the consistories as a special translator; he also translated Solomon Ibn Verga's *Shevet Yehudah*. He was editor of the first Jewish journal to appear in French, the weekly *L'Israélite français*, and also wrote a catechism for Jewish youth, *Limudei Dat u-Mussar*. Halévy's fame, however, rests on a poem that he wrote in 1803 in honor of the Peace of Lunéville, called *Ha-Shalom*. The poem's classic Hebrew style, lavishly praised by Graetz, was employed to describe the ravages of the Reign of Terror, the rise of Napoleon, and finally peace.[11] Halévy's poem represented one of the first indications of the attitudinal change that developed in the aftermath of emancipation. His use of phrases normally reserved for the Land of Israel displayed a deep patriotic devotion to France, enthusiastically professed several years before the convocation of the Sanhedrin.[12]

More revealing evidence of shifts in Jewish consciousness may be drawn from the work of several individuals whose intellectual commitment to Haskalah was interwoven with their active participation in the political struggle for emancipation. The literature that emerged from their ranks ranged from apologetic expositions written in defense of Jewish claims to citizenship to programmatic essays advocating changes in Jewish institutions. Perhaps the most enigmatic of the French *maskilim* was Zalkind Hourwitz, a Polish Jew who worked as a secretary and interpreter of Oriental languages at the *Bibliothèque royale* in Paris. Born in Lublin in 1740 Hourwitz went as a youth to Berlin, where he became associated with Moses Mendelssohn and his circle.[13] Before finally settling in Paris in 1786 he lived in Nancy, Strasbourg, and Metz, where he pursued Talmudic studies with the renowned Rabbi Aryeh Loeb ben Asher Günzberg, the *Sha'agat Aryeh*. Toward the end of the eighteenth century, after he was no longer employed at the Paris library, Hourwitz earned his livelihood by teaching foreign languages. He was denied a seat in the 1806 Assembly of Notables, as was Moses Ensheim, more likely because of reformist attitudes than because of his untidy appearance, as some have claimed. Nevertheless, Hourwitz was consulted frequently by the commission that prepared the decisions. Although most of Hourwitz's works dealt with linguistics, he is best known for his 1785 submission to the essay contest of the *Société des arts et sciences de Metz*, for which he shared the prize with the Abbé Grégoire and Adolphe Thiery.[14]

According to a recent study, Hourwitz's essay *Apologie des Juifs*[15] may be considered "one of the most poignant examples of the difficulties inherent in defending the integrity of Judaism and the Jews, and simultaneously, in demanding reforms which would transform Judaism."[16] The work was precisely what its title implied: an apologetic defense against accusations that Judaism rendered its adherents incapable of assuming the duties of state and society. Although the onus of responsibility would therefore be placed upon society and its laws, Hourwitz insisted that the successful *régénération* of the Jews would require profound modifications on the part of the Jews themselves, particularly in their communal structure and economic activities.

In a manner similar to the works of Dohm and Grégoire, Hourwitz began his essay with an attack on the existing discriminatory laws under which the Jews suffered.[17] He argued that such legislation could be neither justified nor tolerated in contemporary society. Furthermore, in the case of the Jews the purported reasons or pretexts for these laws no longer existed and, therefore, no obstacles could logically stand in the way of a more humane treatment. Hourwitz contended that the Jews were among the most peaceful and industrious peoples of the world, far from possessing the alleged characteristics of vice and corruption.[18] Among the recommendations in his ten-point program to bring about the integration of the Jews in French society, he advocated a liberalization of laws regarding land purchase, entrance into liberal professions and mechanical arts, commercial freedom, and public education.[19] Inherent in these proposals was Hourwitz's insistence on the general need to reevaluate the purpose and structure of society and, at the same time, for society to revise its attitude toward the Jews.

Hourwitz asserted that the changes he proposed were not at all incompatible with the religious and political laws of the Jews. On this point he took a firm position against the concerted vilification of the Jews by such figures as Michaelis, Voltaire, and Rousseau. Hourwitz rejected emphatically the implicit moral superiority of Enlightenment philosophy,[20] expressed particularly in its denunciation of the Jewish religion. He claimed that the opinions of these writers were based on ignorance rather than on any knowledge of, or even familiarity with, the Old Testament. The Jews were unjustly regarded as "misanthropes," thought to be incapable of living among other nations. "Unfortunately," Hourwitz wrote, "the celebrity of these writers and their tolerance towards all other nations greatly accredited their assertions concerning the Jews,"[21] while "very few Jews . . . have the talent and the courage to resist them." Asserting emphatically that the Jews can be made happy and useful members of society, Hourwitz challenged three of the foremost allegations commonly levelled against them: chauvinism, immorality, and social exclusiveness.[22]

Against the accusation of Jewish chauvinism Hourwitz argued that every nation claims some religious or political superiority over all others, and therefore to single out the Jews for such a natural and prevalent attitude was grossly unjust.[23] A far more serious charge was the claim that Jews were an immoral people. Hourwitz addressed himself first to the sensational accusations of cruel atrocities allegedly perpetrated by the Israelites in their conquest of Palestine. The description of the ancient Israelites as a barbaric, warlike people was a recurrent theme in the biblical studies conducted by the English Deists and repeated by the French Encyclopaedists. Hourwitz refuted these charges by denying the uniqueness of the conquest in the annals of history; if anything, he asserted, the conquest of Palestine may have been the only one borne of necessity, since it was motivated by the need to "establish his [Moses'] wandering people on some corner of the earth."[24] Of greater significance than this apology, however, was Hourwitz's awareness that the Deist and Enlightenment vilification of the ancient Israelites signified a great deal more than disinterested historical interpretation. He recognized that attempts to describe the low moral stature of biblical Jews were inextricably connected to similar allegations made against contemporary Jews. Hourwitz therefore treated the matter of the conquest as part of the larger issue, a defense of contemporary Jewish moral conduct. He went about this task by employing a method not unlike his adversaries: he would first defend the biblical law of Moses against the philosophic attacks and then apply his conclusions to a revised characterization of contemporary Jewry.

In Hourwitz's portrayal of biblical Judaism, Moses emerged as the most tolerant and charitable of all legislators, and in his description of rabbinic law he stressed humanistic-universal values belonging to the general ethical tradition. As an illustrative example, Hourwitz cited the case of the *ger*, the non-Jewish resident of Palestine, for whom Mosaic law prescribed love and tolerance, provided that the *ger* observe the Noahide laws, that is, natural law. Accordingly, the *ger* was granted complete liberty of conscience and full recognition of his religious integrity.[25] Here was an example of fair treatment given to the alien on the condition that he comply with an accepted socio-ethical contract. Hourwitz proceeded to demonstrate the Bible's positive impact on the moral fiber of the Jews themselves. In a direct refutation of Rousseau and Voltaire, he asserted that Mosaic law had rendered the Jews a philanthropic and sociable people, and that these qualities were documented in even greater detail in the Talmud.[26] Passages by "obscure and unknown Rabbis" aside, Hourwitz concluded that it would be an error to argue that the Talmud is less tolerant than the law of Moses. Rather, the Talmud demanded that charity and loving-kindness be extended to all men, regardless of religious affiliation. Finally, in an effort to silence possible objections from his readers, Hourwitz explained that the well-known political laws of Judaism were no longer operative and exerted no influence whatsoever on the present conduct of the Jews.[27] Far from placing obstacles in the way of patriotic loyalty, the Talmud required Jews to pray for the welfare of the state in which they resided and to respect its laws.[28]

Concerning the charge of social exclusiveness, as reflected in the dietary laws and the prohibition against intermarriage, Hourwitz offered a more blatantly apologetic response. He declared that restrictions on food do not preclude dining with non-Jews, provided the food conform to Jewish dietary prescriptions. Here Hourwitz had to overlook the social dimension of the dietary laws that, though not of a strictly legal character, nonetheless was an undisputed part of the Jewish tradition. For obvious reasons Hourwitz interpreted the dietary laws in the narrow, rather technical sense in order not to offend the sensibilities of his non-Jewish readers. On the question of intermarriage between Jews and non-Jews, Hourwitz's explanation relied on a line of reasoning which was rooted in the Jewish–Christian disputations of the Middle Ages. It was then, for the first time, that rabbinic authorities drew a distinction between Christians and the pagan nations referred to in the Bible. Disparaging references to gentiles and idolators were, therefore, not applicable to members of the Christian religion. While the disputations were, of course, forced upon Jewish communities, they did offer opportunities for a reconsideration of Jewish–Christian relations. The exclusion of Christianity from the category of idolatry became the foundation for a more positive attitude toward Christians in later Jewish thought.[29] Hourwitz applied the medieval distinction between Christians and pagan nations to the subject of intermarriage and concluded that Mosaic law prohibited only unions with the latter. He did admit, however, that the prohibition had been extended subsequently to unions with all gentiles in order to avoid, as he put it, the resulting inconveniences in eating.[30] It is highly unlikely that such an explanation could succeed in persuading his enlightened Jewish or non-Jewish readers that the modern prohibition against intermarriage should be taken seriously.[31] Paradoxically, one could infer from Hourwitz that the traditional censure of intermarriage was an outmoded vestige of ancient times, devoid of any religious or national meaning, whose dubious advantage was limited to the alleviation of domestic inconvenience. In fact many members of the Assembly of Jewish Notables reached just this conclusion and recommended that marriages between Jews and Christians be made lawful.[32] Their final response did not, however, make such an unqualified recommendation, due to rabbinic objections.[33]

Hourwitz's unconvincing remarks on intermarriage typify a tendency evident throughout his work to employ apologetics as an argument for an improvement in the legal status of French Jewry. He made it clear, however, that the successful transformation of the Jews would require measures beyond the removal of existing discriminatory legislation and the creation of new vocational and educational opportunities. The Jews, too, would need to bear responsibility for their degraded and isolated state. However, during the initial stage of transformation, in the absence of Jewish initiatives, it would be necessary for the government to exercise limited control over Jewish affairs. This last argument, which found expression in other Jewish writings of the period,[34] was the basis for Hourwitz's demand that the Jews be prohibited from using the Yiddish language in their communal books and contracts, whether among themselves or in dealings with Christians.[35]

Government regulation of Jewish affairs was necessary, according to Hourwitz, because of abuses in the community's leadership. The rabbinate was the principal target of Hourwitz's acerbic criticism: he viewed the extension of rabbinic authority beyond the realm of the synagogue as a severe obstacle to change. Already visible were tensions between the rabbis and those Jews who "cut the beard, who curl the hair, who dress like Christians, who attend the theatre, or who do not observe some other custom utterly irrelevant for their religion, and introduced by superstition solely for the purpose of distinguishing them from other peoples."[36] These "modern" Jews, relates Hourwitz, were excluded from synagogue honors or even, at times, from actual entrance into the synagogue. Obviously sympathetic to the Enlightenment's anticlerical tendencies, Hourwitz identified with those Jews who sought freedom from rabbinic controls. In fact, Hourwitz went so far as to call for the elimination of the institution of the rabbinate, at least in its existing form. In terms of what they offer the community, he maintained, the rabbis were a financial liability. Their upkeep "costs too much, and they are absolutely useless; . . . they do not officiate at all in the synagogue, and preach only two times a year; their sermons still center around a few obscure passages of the Talmud in which they seek subtleties, as far as the eye can see, although nine-tenths of their audience does not understand a word."[37] Thus, to Hourwitz's impatience with rabbinical intolerance was added a condemnation of the rabbinate for its failure to satisfy the religious needs of the laity as dictated by a new social and intellectual reality. Finally, Hourwitz recommended that the Jews be prohibited from moneylending and that there be closer supervision of their commercial activities. Unlike many who expected the Jews to renounce commerce in favor of *arts et métiers,* Hourwitz maintained that with government supervision the Jews could make a unique contribution to the advancement of both commerce and the arts. Nevertheless, he felt that the Jews would continue to abuse the existing mercantile system until such controls as the requirement that Jews deal exclusively in furnished merchandise were exercised on their economic life.[38]

Although the *Apologie* enjoyed a rather positive reception among enlightened gentiles, it appears to have been the object of contempt among Jewish leaders in Metz and Bordeaux. The reactions from Metz are not extant, but they have been reconstructed from Hourwitz's correspondence with non-Jews.[39] The Metz leaders were no doubt disturbed by Hourwitz's antipathy for rabbinic Judaism, his sarcastic description of religious extremism, and his proposals for acculturation. The Sephardic reaction, exemplified by a letter to Hourwitz from Bordeaux Jewish leader Lopes-Dubec, focussed on the emphasis that Hourwitz placed on Jewish vices and on the commercial restrictions that the author proposed. The absence of criticism concerning Hourwitz's characterization of religious practices reflects the limits of Sephardic concern at that time and its divergence from Ashkenazic interests. Nevertheless, each group found aspects of Hourwitz's program objectionable.[40]

The contrast between the Jewish and non-Jewish evaluation of the *Apologie* underscores the tension inherent in the work. The primary purpose of the essay was to demonstrate to the general reader that, contrary to what uninformed writers had charged, the Jews were indeed capable of participating in the envisioned new order. Toward this goal Hourwitz brought numerous examples to prove that the Jews were the beneficiaries of an unusually moral legal tradition. The importance of this vindication of the Jewish religion to his general argument explains his defense of the Talmud, in spite of his antipathy for rabbinic Judaism. Only within the framework of Hourwitz's observations on the *inner* life of the Jews, and specifically his characterization of the rabbinic leadership, was his critical attitude revealed openly. In doing so, he placed himself among those who argued that fundamental changes in the social, cultural, and economic life of French Jewry were essential. Furthermore, Hourwitz had come to the conclusion that his fellow Jews were unlikely to make these changes on their own and therefore proposed some government supervision and control. Whereas it might be argued that Hourwitz's views were hardly unique, his work exhibited a new tendency, one only beginning to emerge but that would become de rigeur in the following generation: Judaism was presented in terms acceptable to the non-Jewish world, as an "enlightened" religion that showed no signs of incompatibility with prevailing notions of reason, morality, and social integration. With its criticism of Jewish clericalism yet its emphasis on social and cultural modifications only, the *Apologie des Juifs* signifies an adumbration of the framework of concerns that would be addressed later by the *régénérateurs.*

Another leading *maskil* who took up the defense of his coreligionists was Isaiah Berr Bing (1759–1805). By profession the director general of the Salines de l'Est, Bing was an accomplished man of letters with strong connections to the Berlin Haskalah. His translations of Mendelssohn's *Phaedon* into French and Hebrew and Judah Halevi's *Song of Zion* from Hebrew into French were among his more significant works. In addition, he served on the editorial committee of the *Décade philosophique*, which contained many of his literary compositions, including a French translation of Lessing's *Nathan the Wise*. Bing was later appointed to the Malesherbes Commission (1787), a body authorized to study the status of French Jewry and its emancipation.[41] His most important contribution to the public discussion of the Jewish question was a letter refuting an anti-Jewish pamphlet that appeared in Metz in 1787. Praised by Mirabeau in his *Monarchie-prussienne,* Bing's letter[42] provides significant evidence of the substance and limits of changing Jewish attitudes in the pre-Revolutionary period. The pamphlet, *Le cri du citoyen contre les juifs,*[43] published under the name of Foissac, (a pseudonym for Jean Baptiste Annibal Aubert-Dubayet, a captain of cavalry and later the Minister of War under the Directory), appeared during the essay contest sponsored by the *Société royale des arts et sciences de Metz.* Quoting Voltaire to substantiate his anti-Jewish polemic, Dubayet maintained that the Jews were a flawed people whose distinguishing characteristics were leprosy, fanaticism, and usury.[44] The author suggested as a solution to the Jewish problem that the government transport the Jews of Alsace to uncultivated land in France where agricultural work might regenerate them.[45] This and other references to Voltaire[46] establish a clear chain connecting the Enlightenment critique of Judaism with more overt enemies of the Jews.

Although the Jews of Metz succeeded in convincing the city's *parlement* to suppress the pamphlet soon after it appeared, Isaiah Berr Bing felt compelled to answer the charges. *Le cri du citoyen* appeared precisely at a time when the Jewish problem was being discussed publicly; many of its allegations had been drawn from Voltaire and other *philosophes*.[47] Bing first addressed the accusation that the Jewish religion claims for its adherents an exclusive hold on salvation. Judaism, he asserted, teaches that all men will partake of divine bliss, provided they observe the Noahide laws. Bringing proof from biblical and rabbinic sources, Bing declared "that our principles oblige us to love you as brothers, and to perform for you all the acts of humanity that our position permits us."[48] The major part of Bing's defense of Judaism was devoted to the subject of usury, an accusation frequently employed by critics to discredit the ethical foundation of the Jewish religion. Bing conceded that Jewish law permitted Jews to lend on interest to gentiles, while prohibiting the same from their fellow Jews; however, he argued that in light of Judaism's positive attitude toward the non-Jew, this distinction could not be motivated by an aversion to strangers as was commonly asserted.[49] Still, the question of usury, particularly when it was formulated in moral terms, necessitated a carefully articulated interpretation and explanation of the law.

Bing approached the subject of moneylending from two entirely different angles; one blatantly apologetic, the other innovative and interpretive. He argued that lending on interest was a simple reality of life and should be regarded as a valuable service to those in need of credit. Nevertheless, only "normal" lending on interest was, in his view, tolerated by Jewish law, whereas usurious rates were absolutely prohibited. This distinction was based on the contention that the biblical term referring to interest, *neshekh*, had been incorrectly translated as "usury," when the term meant simply "interest."[50] Bing attempted, as the Assembly of Notables would do nearly twenty years later, to mitigate the negative evaluation of the Jewish law of moneylending by claiming that the Bible did not expressly sanction usury.[51] However, the absence of any concrete scriptural references to the rates that may be considered "reasonable" or "usurious" exposes the tendentiousness of the author's approach and reveals the lengths travelled by Bing in order to substantiate his apology. One wonders whether the fact that French jurists were at this time proposing the legalization of moneylending and the regulation of the maximum rate of interest may have motivated his distinction between interest and usury.

Since this explanation did not address the apparent moral problem of the double standard posed by the laws of moneylending, Bing resorted to a more innovative interpretation. His claim that lending on interest was an acceptable profession in view of its economic and human importance only explained the permissibility of taking interest from non-Jews. Consequently, Bing focused on the prohibition of charging interest to fellow Jews and, toward that end, inquired into the original meaning and implications of the injunction. He concluded that it had been legislated out of two paramount considerations. The first aim of the law was to preserve the communal-national identity of the Jews. Differentiation between internal and external ethics was intended to remind them of their common origin and to promote a familial spirit among the people.[52] This same explanation would reemerge in the decisions of the Paris Sanhedrin, where the aim of the lawgiver was described in the following terms: "to draw closer between them the bonds of fraternity, to give them a lesson of reciprocal benevolence."[53] The second reason for the injunction was socio-economic: its goal was to mold the Jews into an agrarian people devoted to the cultivation of the land given to them by their God. The Bible's detailed agricultural laws, especially the legislation governing the cancellation of debts in the Sabbatical Year, were offered as the strongest evidence for the theory. Moreover, according to Bing, the prohibition against taking interest from fellow Jews was motivated by important moral considerations. The "commercial spirit" was a dangerous, corrupting force, leading first to an excessive concern with riches and luxuries, and ultimately to an "austerity of *moeurs.*" Finally, taking into account the widespread skepticism concerning the economic usefulness of the Jews, Bing argued that the ancient aversion to moneylending was proof that Judaism unequivocally preferred productive occupations. "Far from permitting us to engage in usury," he concluded, "our law took all possible precautions to remove the circumstances which could lead to it."[54]

Characteristically, however, Bing's willingness to present a new, somewhat unorthodox interpretation of the Jewish law of moneylending did not extend to the area of ceremonial reform: "If scrupulous observance of the prescriptions of our religion appear to you as superstitious, I admit openly that we are. And we will stay this way in spite of the progress of fashionable philosophy, with its aversion for the ceremonial and for everything which it cannot touch physically and immediately."[55] Bing expressed faith in the ability of the Jews to conform to the laws of the country without throwing off the yoke of Jewish law. He urged his coreligionists to remain loyal to the faith of their fathers, and declared that should an improvement in their condition not materialize, then they must be prepared to "live, suffer, and die as Jews."[56] The Jewish problem was thus viewed exclusively in terms of its social and economic parameters; its solution, according to Bing, would center on the removal of residential and occupational disabilities, ultimately leading to the normalization of French Jews. "Experience will demonstrate that two nations, who live under the same climate, between whom there is a sort of political equality, and whose religion is based on the same moral principles, cannot differ essentially, neither in *capacité* nor in character."[57]

The optimism that characterized the prerevolutionary period was rooted in the belief that once the barriers separating the Jews from general society were lifted, integration would proceed in course. It should be noted nonetheless that, in keeping with the views of the Haskalah, Bing did not consider the Jews entirely blameless for their social segregation. He singled out the use of the Yiddish language as an impediment to the process of integration, claiming that it was representative of the mistrust that the Jews felt toward general society and the fear of being misinterpreted by outsiders. Moreover, this "unintelligible jargon" was an obstacle to Jewish scientific and cultural achievement. Continued use of the "coarse language," he asserted, would only encourage reciprocal mistrust on the part of their neighbors, and would prevent Jews from overcoming their social and cultural estrangement.[58] Any continuation of the status quo was thus clearly unacceptable. Nevertheless, although envisioning a restructuring of Jewish social and cultural mores, Bing provided few details of his view of the future.

Fellow *maskil* Berr Isaac Berr (1744–1828) was more explicit in his vision of Jewish regeneration. A native of Nancy and owner of a tobacco factory, Berr was a leader of Ashkenazic Jewry, following in the footsteps of his father, a wealthy banker. The younger Berr served as the spokesman for a six-member Jewish delegation sent to Paris from Alsace and Lorraine to argue the case for Jewish civic equality at the National Assembly. He later served as a leading delegate to the Assembly of Notables and a member of the Paris Sanhedrin. As a man of letters, Berr made an important contribution to the diffusion of the ideas of the Berlin Haskalah in France with the publication of a French translation of Naphtali Herz Wessely's *Divre Shalom ve'Emet,* a tract advocating educational reforms.[59]

Owing to the continuity and longevity of Berr's leadership, his writings provide a valuable source for assessing how, and to what degree, attitudes were transformed under the impact of the Revolution, the Reign of Terror, and the Napoleonic regime. Ashkenazic leaders, evidently unable to conceive of a Judaism independent of communal controls, sought to maintain the juridical and religious status quo. Therefore, until the actual grant of citizenship on 27 September 1791, Berr ardently opposed the dissolution of the autonomous Jewish communities. Following passage of the Declaration of the Rights of Man, Jewish delegates from the communities of eastern France asked for full citizenship, but endeavored to retain the right to a Jewish communal organization. Shortly thereafter, in a joint petition with the Jews of Paris, the Ashkenazim formally dropped their insistence on the retention of communal autonomy. Nevertheless, in the spring of 1790, in response to an anti-Jewish speech given by the Bishop of Nancy, de la Fare,[60] Berr made one last attempt to retain the old communal structure.[61] He proposed that the Ashkenazim voluntarily concede the right to hold public office[62] in exchange for permission to maintain the continued jurisdiction of rabbinic and communal leaders over the Jewish community. Invested by the royal government with juridical and executive powers, the Jewish leaders would, according to the proposal, adjudicate all religious and civil cases involving Jews.[63]

Aware that the plan had little chance of being accepted, Berr declared adamantly that "if we must no longer remain as a community, if we must sacrifice our civil laws in order to be registered with the national law; if, in the end, the revolution which was so fortunate for all Frenchmen, only increased our misfortune, then we prefer a thousand times death over acquiescence; we will obey, but we will persist in demanding justice from the National Assembly, the *plénitude* of the rights of man."[64] This preference for civil autonomy, even at the expense of full citizenship, was not uniformly endorsed. Several younger men strongly opposed this position. Berr's nephew, Jacob Berr of Nancy, accused his uncle of wanting to perpetuate Jewish estrangement from non-Jews. Echoing the views of Zalkind Hourwitz, the younger Berr assailed the "despotic regime" of the *kehillot,* and demanded their elimination.[65]

Following the admission of the Ashkenazic Jews to citizenship, Berr Isaac Berr was clearly in no position to oppose the terms of emancipation. In fact, it is evident from the debates on the Jewish question in the National Assembly that the retention of their prerevolutionary status at the expense of civic rights would have been incompatible with the philosophy of the new regime. Clermont-Tonnere, a strong advocate of Jewish emancipation, had expressed the situation before the Jews very clearly:

> The Jews should be denied everything as a nation, but granted everything as individuals; they must disown their judges, they must have only ours; they must be refused legal protection for the maintenance of the supposed laws of their Jewish corporation; they must constitute neither a state, nor a political corps, nor an order; they must individually become citizens; if they do not want this, they must inform us and we shall then be compelled to expel them. The existence of a nation within a nation is unacceptable to our country.[66]

This unequivocal statement of the conditions of citizenship, formulated by an ardent proponent of Jewish rights, indicates that the Jews of France could have expected no better terms of emancipation. The Ashkenazim relinquished their claim to autonomy because there was no other alternative; the surrender of autonomy was a precondition to citizenship.

In a letter of congratulation to his coreligionists, written on the morrow of the National Assembly's vote, Berr outlined his views on the nature and obligations of citizenship.[67] Most striking was the author's characterization of the newly won status in religious terms; themes such as divine providence and freedom from slavery were used to describe the enormity of the occasion: "we have not deserved this wonderful change by our repentance, or by the reformation of our manners: we can attribute it to nothing but to the everlasting goodness of God. . . . He has chosen the generous French nation to reinstate us in our rights, and to operate our regeneration, as, in other times, he has chosen Antiochus, Pompey, and others, to humiliate and enslave us."[68] The familiar theme of God's utilization of various nations as tools in the execution of divine will was thus applied to the situation in France. However, in contrast to those instances when the Jewish people received punishment at the hands of the nations, the French people had become instruments in the long-awaited reversal of Israel's arduous past. Exuberant over the Jews' new-found freedom, Berr expressed the gratitude of his coreligionists in vivid language reminiscent of the Passover *Haggadah:* "and what bounds can there be to our gratitude for the happy event! From being vile slaves, mere serfs . . . we are, of a sudden, become the children of the country, to bear its common charges, and share in its comon rights."[69]

Berr's description of the bestowal of citizenship in religious terms was designed to persuade his traditionally minded coreligionists that the new status was worth the surrender of communal autonomy. Religious imagery was also invoked to instill enthusiasm for the central theme of his letter: that inherent in the bestowal of citizenship was a responsibility to prove oneself worthy of the new privileges. If, as Berr claimed, the grant of citizenship was an act of providence, then it was incumbent upon the Jews to show their gratitude to their fellow Frenchmen by carefully assessing their own situation and how it might be improved. "Let us, dear brethren, let us conform to their wishes, let us examine with attention what remains to be done, on our part, to become truly happy, and how we may be able to show, in some measure, our grateful sense for all the favors heaped upon us."[70] Introspection and self-examination thus framed the concept of citizenship in even more compelling terms. And with his admission that "we ourselves know how very deficient we are" in respect to the qualifications of citizens, Berr introduced the language of repentance to underscore the urgency of acquiring those qualities necessary for participation in general society.

Successful fulfillment of the duties of citizenship would, in Berr's mind, require an unprecedented commitment to social and cultural transformation. This had not been possible before, since in former times the Jews had been compelled to amass as much money as would ensure royal protection; through no fault of their own they had abandoned the study of physical and moral sciences in order to devote themselves totally to commerce. Now, with the bestowal of citizenship, it would be possible and, therefore, obligatory for French Jews to sieze new educational opportunities enabling them to "give signal proofs of [their] glowing patriotism" and to win the esteem of their fellow citizens. However, the idea of religious innovation was still foreign to Alsatian leaders. To Berr, those who would introduce religious reforms were no less than unscrupulous "monsters."[71] What needed to be done instead was to forge spiritual and physical bonds to the state. However, it would first be necessary to renounce the corporate mentality that had come to characterize medieval Jewish life, or in Berr's words, "to divest ourselves entirely of that narrow spirit, of Corporation and Congregation, in all civil and political matters not immediately connected with our spiritual laws; in these things we must absolutely appear simply as individuals, as Frenchmen, guided only by a true patriotism and by the general good of the nation."[72]

Genuine patriotism entailed defense of the country, usefulness to society, and aiding in the maintenance of public tranquility. Berr confessed that the Jews were not yet able to fulfill these functions, and that the process of acquiring these skills was just beginning. In the absence of concrete manifestations of patriotism and contributions to the general good of society, he felt that the civic oath could guarantee sincere intentions. The suggestion was therefore made to "do for the present what is within our power; let us take the civic oath of being faithful to the nation, to the law and to the king."[73] With this idea, Berr revealed a sensitivity to the prevailing gentile skepticism concerning the ability of Jews to become loyal citizens, and also to the likelihood of this skepticism intensifying if civil *régénération* was not immediately successful. The oath, then, would allay these fears.

Misgivings among the Jews themselves concerning the transition to citizenship and the accompanying surrender of autonomy also represented a serious threat to *régénération*. Claiming that these fears were largely exaggerated, Berr asserted that the disadvantages of a separate community far outweighed its advantages:

We had the privilege of forming a distinct body of people and a separate community; but this carried with it the exclusion from all other corporations, and the submission to particular taxes, much above our means and our resources, and arbitrarily imposed. If a member of that community was accused of any misdemeanor whatever, the reproaches and the humiliation fell on the whole; we were exempt from militia and from public works, but it was because we were deemed unworthy of it; and to palliate the injustice of such proceedings, we were exempted, on condition of paying in money three times the value of such services, &c. It is certainly no hard matter to give up such privileges.[74]

Social exclusion, arbitrary taxes, collective responsibility and guilt for the actions of individuals, and being deemed unworthy of participation in civic affairs were among the ignominies suffered by the Jews while enjoying autonomy. Berr concluded that the civic oath of allegiance was simply "a renunciation of those pretended privileges and immunities . . . [which] were only relative to our state of slavery." By stressing the connection between the humiliation of noncitizenship and the privileges of autonomy, Berr endeavored to minimize the significance of the dissolution of a separate community.[75]

While attempting to convince his coreligionists that they must accommodate themselves to the new social and political reality, Berr certainly did not concede that their sense of community should be surrendered. The maintenance of a communal structure was essential as it would facilitate the establishment of institutions designed to carry out the proposed *régénération*. A voluntary community would administer new enlightened schools, provide services for the elderly and the poor, and superintend the collection of funds. In addition, while the community would, in his view, continue to maintain its rabbi, rabbinical authority would be limited to the areas of religious custom and ceremony. The rabbi's civil functions of the preemancipation era, of course, had been replaced by the civil institutions of the state.[76]

Among Berr's recommendations for *régénération*, those that dealt with education figured most prominently. In this respect he was in accord ideologically with the changes proposed by the *maskilim* of Berlin. Berr's program closely followed the guidelines set down by Naphtali Herz Wessely, author of the tract *Divre Shalom ve-Emet*, which Berr himself had already translated into French. He agreed with Wessely that existing Jewish education was "defective in many points of view," in secular as well as religious instruction, and that educational reform held the key to Jewish destiny.[77] He emphasized first and foremost the need to improve the teaching of the Bible,[78] in accordance with the position of the Berlin *maskilim*, who had regarded Bible study as centrally important in their educational scheme. Preference for biblical studies over the study of other sacred texts had first been noticeable in the intellectual activities of Christian theologians and scholars following the Protestant

Reformation. The preoccupation with the Bible, particularly with the Old Testament, was a part of the revolution against the Catholic Church, whose authority rested on the books of the New Testament as interpreted by the Church Fathers. The English Deists, and later their French and German spiritual heirs, further intensified this trend with more systematic and critical studies. By the beginning of the nineteenth century numerous biblical societies had appeared, though often in conjunction with Christian missions, in England, Holland, Germany, and France. During the last third of the eighteenth century, when Jewish intellectuals first began to look beyond the cultural limits of their own communities, these Jews became aware of the Bible's status as a universally accepted text, representing the common ground between Judaism and Christianity. Mendelssohn saw Bible study in these terms and consequently embarked upon a project of translating the Pentateuch and Psalms into German. In addition to his hope that Jews would learn German by studying the translation, he believed that the Bible could serve as a cultural bridge between Jews and non-Jews.

As a loyal disciple of Mendelssohn, Berr sought to effect a similar program among his coreligionists in France. He therefore proposed a French translation of the Bible, modelled after Mendelssohn's German version, which would enable the children to learn the principal text of Judaism in the original Hebrew, together with explanations in their native tongue. No less importantly, Berr expected the proposed translation to facilitate the study of the French language.[79] Berr's educational plan also involved the establishment of a Jewish public school similar to the ones already functioning in Berlin and elsewhere. The aim of the school would be to shape "good Jews and good French citizens," and emphasis would be placed both on Jewish learning and on secular studies. Berr, like his Berlin counterparts, pointed to the special need for instruction in the sciences and mechanical arts so that Jewish children could encounter wider career opportunities. This would not only prepare a sounder economic base for French Jews but would also enhance their esteem in the eyes of their fellow citizens; the "mercantile and trafficking spirit" would, once and for all, be expunged from the Jewish psyche.[80]

Primary education alone would be within the province of Jewish communal supervision. Once the children were "thoroughly initiated in the principles and spirit" of the Jewish religion, they could be sent to French public schools "to share the advantages of national education." Berr insisted that there was no reason to fear interference in the religious education of the Jewish children and was confident that, in time, they would enjoy the acceptance and love of their fellow students.[81] This optimism was based on the expectation that citizenship would one day replace religion as the major determinant in the establishment of bonds of friendship and brotherhood:

> By means of that union in schools, our children, like those of our fellow-citizens, will remark from their tender youth that neither opinions, nor difference of religion are a bar to fraternal love; and that everyone naturally embracing and following the religion of his fathers, all may, in fulfilling their religious duties, fulfill also those of citizenship; from that, all aversion, all hatred, all antipathy between them will be done away.[82]

Berr thus envisioned a society whose members were united in "fraternal love" despite the plurality of religious beliefs and practices. Incidentally, it is important to note that he rejected any notion of incompatibility between religious obligations and civic duties. The two spheres, the religious and the civic, were viewed as being complementary, and therefore each was crucial for the full realization of the other. For the Jews this idea was thoroughly novel. It would subsequently emerge as one of the most fundamental premises in the arguments made by the Assembly of Jewish Notables before the Napoleonic commission.

Within the first years of the nineteenth century it had become evident to everyone familiar with the Jewish condition that the pace of regeneration was far behind its expected rate of progress. The spirit of optimism that permeated Jewish writings in the revolutionary years was proven to have been rather misplaced. Berr for example had failed to consider various social and religious forces that were likely to slow the pace of modernization. Fifteen years later, on the eve of the convocation of the Assembly of Jewish Notables in 1806, Berr took a more sober view. In *Réflexions sur la régénération complète des Juifs en France*,[83] he explained that the persistence of anti-Jewish prejudices not only impeded the process of Jewish social integration but also exerted a negative impact on Jewish self-perception. The re-creation of a communal organization under official auspices would serve as much-needed proof of the government's commitment to the principle of equality of religion. Equally important would be the role of such an organization in facilitating the formation of regenerative institutions directed by the Jews themselves. Berr had finally realized that French Jewry had been ill-prepared for modernization, in spite of its political achievements. Only under the watchful eye of an enlightened Jewish leadership whose authority was endorsed by the government would the Jews embark on the road to modernization.

The writings of Hourwitz, Bing, and Berr represent the first French attempts to prove that Judaism was compatible with duties to state and society. Like the gentile partisans of Jewish equality, they appealed for the removal of all discriminatory legislation. At the same time, these writings reflect an acceptance of certain aspects of the contemporary gentile critique. Jewish involvement in moneylending was condemned, rabbinic abuses were criticized, and the cultural limitations of Jews were decried. In short, a new conception of community and leadership had begun to emerge in the debate surrounding the bestowal of citizenship.

At the convocation of the Assembly of Jewish Notables, and at the Paris Sanhedrin, Franco-Jewish attitudes toward the state, citizenship, and the idea of Judaism's compatibility with civic duties crystallized. The Sanhedrin occupies a special place in modern Jewish history, not only because of the substance of its decisions, but also in light of the sensational nature of its convocation. The pomp surrounding Napoleon's revival of the ancient Jewish Supreme Court certainly created a stir in the Jewish and general world, and there is little doubt that the attitudes and behavior of the delegates were, in some ways at least, influenced by the unfolding drama.[84] Interpretations of the significance of the Sanhedrin by subsequent generations have further enhanced its importance in modern Jewish history. The Reform movement in Germany, for example, later viewed the assembly's pronouncements on the validity of rabbinical jurisdiction and its answer on intermarriage as precedents for religious reform. The German reformers also admired the Sanhedrin's unequivocal sentiments of patriotism, compliance with civil law, and its implicit disavowal of an expected return to the Holy Land. With the goal of demonstrating that the Jewish religion was in perfect harmony with citizenship, members of the Brunswick Conference (1844–1846) formally endorsed the doctrinal decisions of the Paris Sanhedrin.[85]

In recent years, several historians have challenged the assumption that the Sanhedrin's decisions constitute a break with the normative Jewish tradition.[86] Careful analysis reveals that the delegates did not yield on any substantive aspects of the Jewish religion. Minor concessions aside, the importance of the Sanhedrin lay in its having been the first public organization of Jews to express a positive attitude toward the state and its gentile citizens. Still, the decision to convene a Sanhedrin in itself represented a direct challenge to the fact of Jewish emancipation; and it must be borne in mind that the notables' responses to Napoleon's questions constituted a formal acceptance of the original terms upon which citizenship had been granted. Virtually all the substantive issues discussed at the Assembly of Jewish Notables had been debated by Franco-Jewish leaders at the time of emancipation—intermarriage, Judaism's attitude toward non-Jews, rabbinic authority, and moneylending—and these public discussions undoubtedly influenced the notables' subsequent formulations. The ideational continuity in pre- and post-revolutionary views, on the one hand, and those expressed by the Assembly of Jewish Notables, on the other, suggests that the issues defining the Jewish question remained virtually unchanged. This suggestion is supported by the fact that the old guard, consisting of French *maskilim*, community leaders, and rabbis, were all well represented at the Napoleonic convocation.[87]

Napoleon's motive for convening the assembly clearly was not to encourage open debate but to gain reassurance that the Jews were committed to the French civil code and to further his goal of broad social integration. The twelve questions placed before the Assembly aimed at "reconciling the belief of the Jews with the duties of Frenchmen, and to turn them into useful citizens, being determined to remedy the evil to which many of them apply themselves to the great detriment of our subjects."[88] The questions were as follows:[89]

1. Is it lawful for Jews to marry more than one wife?
2. Is divorce allowed by the Jewish religion? Is divorce valid, although not pronounced by courts of justice, and by virtue of laws in contradiction with the French code?
3. Can a Jewess marry a Christian, or a Jew a Christian woman? Or has the law ordered that the Jews should only intermarry among themselves?
4. In the eyes of Jews, are Frenchmen considered as brethren or as strangers?
5. In either case, what conduct does their law prescribe towards Frenchmen not of their religion?
6. Do the Jews born in France, and treated by the law as French citizens, acknowledge France as their country? Are they bound to defend it? Are they bound to obey the laws and to follow the directions of the civil code?
7. Who appoints the rabbis?
8. What kind of police jurisdiction have the rabbis among the Jews? What judicial power do they exert among them?
9. Are these forms of election and police jurisdiction regulated by law, or are they only sanctioned by custom?
10. Are there professions from which the Jews are excluded by their law?
11. Does the law forbid the Jews from taking usury from their brethren?
12. Does it forbid or does it allow usury toward strangers?

The two main factions in the assembly, the enlightened Jews, who were influenced by the Mendelssohnian school of thought, and the traditionalists, who were orthodox in their religious orientation, appear to have reached general agreement on just how an attitude of tolerance toward non-Jews should be articulated. This was accomplished in spite of the fact that each group drew from its own sources, ideology, and frame of reference. The enlightened Jews, who held a more universalistic conception of humanity and a less severe view of the world outside the ghetto, defined Judaism past and present in terms of the prevailing European concept of society and politics. Inspired by the ideology of the Haskalah, as personified by Moses Mendelssohn, they regarded Judaism as one of several contemporary creeds, and consequently took a tolerant attitude toward Christians. The traditionalists, adhering to the belief in the fundamental superiority of Judaism, nevertheless followed the teachings of the more tolerant rabbinic authorities of the seventeenth and eighteenth centuries.[90] This tendency enabled the traditionalist faction in the Assembly to take a relatively liberal position with regard to Jewish–gentile relations and, at the same time, to maintain its allegiance to the integrity of halakhah and its methods.

In spite of their differences in outlook, the two camps were affected by the same political realities facing French Jewry in the early nineteenth century. Both recognized the need to make the necessary adjustments to citizenship, including all the duties that that new status entailed. Civic duties, such as military service, were the most obvious and tangible requirements, but in addition to these, there was the need to modify a Jewish world view shaped by centuries of restrictions and alienation. The tendency to view non-Jewish society with contempt was no longer considered a plausible position, given the fact of emancipation and the accompanying demand that Jews become part of the larger social setting. Napoleon, along with his advisers, placed these issues in bold relief and forced the Jews of the empire to announce to the world that, at least on their part, there was no feeling of enmity toward gentiles and no ambivalence regarding the primacy of the state.

Conscious of a fundamental distrust reflected in the questions and fearful that their hard-won citizenship might be revoked, the delegates endeavored to prove that nothing in Jewish law contradicted the legal and moral code of France. Their answers to the first three questions stressed that there was no conflict in the realm of personal status. Though not expressly forbidden in Mosaic and Talmudic Judaism, polygamy had been formally prohibited since the synod of Rabbenu Gershom in the eleventh century. On the matter of divorce, the delegates stated that while "repudiation is permitted by the law of Moses . . . it is not valid if not previously pronounced by the French code." With this answer the Assembly then proceeded to underscore the fundamental principle that Jews had recognized since the Revolution, that the law of the state is undisputed: "In the eyes of every Israelite, without exception, submission to the prince is the first of duties. It is a principle generally acknowledged among them, that, in every thing relating to civil or political interests, the law of the state is the supreme law."[91]

The question concerning marriage between Jews and Christians occasioned a division between the progressive and traditionalist camps. The views of the two groups diverged so widely that no agreement could be reached on a single formulation. Therefore, two answers, representing both of the sides, were joined together. The first opinion, that of the progressives, held that intermarriage with Christians was not expressly forbidden by the Torah, since the prohibition extended only to idolatrous nations. The status of Christianity as a monotheistic religion meant that its adherents were exempt from the biblical prohibition of marriage between Jews and idolaters. The second part of the answer referred explicitly to the opinion of the rabbis. It stated that in spite of the foregoing technical permissiblity of marriage with Christians, the rabbis still could not lend their support to such unions. The rabbis insisted that marriage, according to the Talmud, requires certain religious ceremonies and rites which are indispensible to the religious validity of the union. From the standpoint of Jewish law, marriage uniting a Jew with a Christian was not a recognized union. The rabbis did concede, however, that such marriages were valid in the civil sense and that a couple united in this way could dissolve the union without the need for a religious divorce. Implicit in this statement was an awareness that Jews could now choose to live within the civil sphere, well beyond the authority of the rabbis and of Jewish law. While revealing the chasm separating accommodation to the emperor's wishes and rigorous loyalty to the Jewish tradition, the cumbersome juxtaposition of opposing views in a single answer may have served a wholly unintended purpose. By conceding that intermarriage with Christians was not, strictly speaking, prohibited, and then by opposing such unions on religious grounds only, the answer gave the appearance that the delegates had succeeded in balancing the widely divergent demands encountered in the era of emancipation.[92]

The conception of Christianity enabling the delegates to exclude Christians from the category of idolaters had its roots in the efforts of medieval halakhists to reconcile the Jewish tradition with the prevailing economic reality. The distinction between contemporary Christians and those of antiquity was originally intended for specific cases only; in time, this distinction was extended to the general sphere of Jewish-Christian relations. On the immediate, practical level, this meant that Christians were exempted from many of the segregative laws recorded in the Talmud. More significantly, there evolved a theory of religious tolerance that was not only remarkable for its time, but also highly repercussive.[93] Not surprisingly, the delegates to the Napoleonic assembly had recourse to this liberal tradition, hoping to dispel all notions of religious superiority and social exclusiveness routinely attributed to Judaism. Still lacking, however, was a general principle justifying positive relations with non-

Jews. The assembly arrived at such a formulation first by asserting, particularly in its answers to questions four, five, eleven, and twelve, that loyalty to the state and its citizens superseded religious devotion. Further, the delegates affirmed that "France is our country, all Frenchmen our brothers, and this glorious title, while honoring us in our own eyes, becomes a pledge of which we shall never cease to be worthy."[94] The delegates were thus willing to concede that a redefinition of brotherhood was required in light of the new social and political reality of postrevolutionary France. The bonds of fraternity could no longer be defined solely in terms of religious affiliation; citizenship had become, at least in theory, the principal basis for uniting members of the French nation. Consequently, the Jews of France declared themselves "Frenchmen of the Mosaic persuasion."[95]

The real significance of this declaration, however, must not be exaggerated. Theoretically, these words did indeed signify a revolutionary departure from the assumptions concerning the collective identity and destiny of the Jewish people; however, not all sectors of Western Jewry understood citizenship in these terms nor did they all redefine the nature of their affiliations according to the Assembly's pronouncements. Certainly most French Jews would continue, at least until midcentury, to maintain the strongest attachments of brotherhood to their coreligionists, abroad as well as in France. How may this be explained? Suffice it to say here that as a rule historical, communal, and religious bonds do not dissolve quickly and, furthermore, that general conditions in France outside of the major urban centers tended to preserve traditional associations, particularly on the local level. Moreover, the social and cultural barriers that on a daily basis continued to separate Jew and Christian only confirmed, for the Jews, the soundness of traditional Jewish unity and fraternity. Members of the Assembly were undoubtedly aware of the tenacity of these social realities but also understood the immediate need for a clarification of the role of Jewish law in the modern state. At the apparent expense of traditional Jewish solidarity, they affirmed French Jewry's allegiance to the *patrie* in two ways. First, patriotic loyalty and the obligation to defend France in time of war were affirmed, strengthened by the assertion that French Jews would fight Jews of other countries with which France was at war. Second, the delegates confirmed that rabbinic jurisdiction in matters of civil law had been disallowed since the Revolution. The functions of the rabbis were now limited to preaching morality and to the performance of marriages and divorces. Regard for the rabbis' religious authority had become a matter of personal choice or, as the assembly put it, a matter of custom not law.[96]

The major test confronting the Assembly of Notables was whether its stated position on the compatibility of Judaism with duties toward the state and its citizens could accommodate the troublesome Jewish law of moneylending. Moneylending was the specific issue that moved Napoleon to convene the assembly. Jewish law's alleged double standard, permitting interest from gentiles while prohibiting the same from fellow Jews, had been frequently employed by critics to discredit the ethical foundation of the religion. Napoleon had simply extended the accusation to the specific realm of civil morality and, in so doing, challenged the Jews' right to citizenship.

The assembly addressed the problem on two levels. It first attempted to mitigate the negative evaluation of the Jewish law of moneylending by claiming that the Bible did not expressly sanction usury. On this point the assembly echoed the theory advanced by Isaiah Berr Bing twenty years earlier: the biblical conception of the law was the product of an agricultural barter economy. While other nations became engaged increasingly in trade, the Hebrews were discouraged from doing so by "all the regulations of their lawgiver [which] seemed designed to divert their attention from commerce."[97] Having defended the original intention of the law, the assembly then addressed itself to the issue at hand: the charge of a double standard of morality. The delegates attempted to demonstrate that according to Jewish law there was no differentiation between Jewish and gentile borrowers. This contention rested on the premise that there were two categories of transactions, commercial loans and charitable loans. In discussing the case of commercial loans, where interest was permitted, the delegates based their argument on a technical aspect of medieval Jewish law, the fiction of the *hetter 'isqa*. Through this legal device, designed to circumvent the prohibition of taking interest from a fellow Jew, interest became a share in the profits (or losses) that accrued in the temporary business "partnership."[98] The assembly employed this example in order to demonstrate "that interest, even among Israelites, is lawful in commercial operations."[99] In the case of charitable loans (i.e., when a loan was intended for food, clothing, or shelter), the assembly asserted that interest was forbidden, whether the borrower was a Jew or a gentile. Though admittedly unorthodox, this interpretation, according to the assembly, was consistent with the spirit of the law and with a plain reading of the scriptural verse that traditionally served as the basis for forbidding interest from a fellow Jew. Since the verse states "Thou shalt not lend upon interest to thy brother," making no explicit reference to Jews, the delegates declared that the term *aḥikha* (thy brother) could and should be applied to fellow French citizens.[100] Here the conception of brotherhood in terms of citizenship was tested and affirmed. It represented a new vision of the possibilities of

Jewish–gentile relations, far exceeding those advanced by proponents of the early Haskalah.

Although many of the formulations presented by the Assembly were novel, they did not include any significant deviations from traditional Judaism.[101] Where necessary, halakhic procedures were followed carefully. Certain innovations were introduced, but only in matters of an attempted conciliation of socio-economic and civil patterns of behavior with the demands of citizenship. In most cases the delegates were able to find precedents from medieval times and in the writings of Hourwitz, Bing, Berr, and others; in one instance they were truly innovative. At the same time, nothing in the assembly's responses proposed or even hinted at changes in Jewish theology or modification in ritual law. The assembly appears to have been expected to address only those issues concerning citizenship and brotherhood and therefore limited itself to these matters.

The responses made by the Assembly of Jewish Notables generally satisfied Napoleon and his commission. However, as the assembly could not guarantee that French Jewry would welcome its decisions, the emperor convened a Sanhedrin, composed of seventy-one members, two-thirds of whom were rabbis, in order to provide a religious stamp of approval. On 4 February 1807 the Sanhedrin met for the first time, and in one stroke, its decisions became religiously obligatory, as well as legally binding. With its final session on 9 March 1807, the initial period of the emancipation of French Jewry came to a close. The Sanhedrin had succeeded in defining the relation between Jewish law and the modern state, while no serious consideration was given to the idea of altering any rituals or doctrines of Judasim.

Apart from the ideological issues, the assembly played an important role in shaping a distinct Franco-Jewish identity. While the main intention of the government in convening the Assembly of Jewish Notables and the Paris Sanhedrin may have been to challenge the worthiness of Alsatian Jewry as citizens, these convocations served a much broader though possibly unintended purpose: they forced Jews of varied geographical and cultural origins to come together for the first time to address the issues put before them by Napoleon. Napoleon's initiatives succeeded in overshadowing secular–religious and Sephardic–Ashkenazic differences, thus forging a unity, however tenuous, for French Jewry. Moreover, in the process, local leaders such as Abraham Furtado of Bordeaux and Rabbi David Sintzheim of Strasbourg were transformed into prominent national leaders. Their messages were no longer limited to their former constituencies but were directed at the entire Franco-Jewish population.[102] These developments were but an indication of things to come. The convocation of the assembly and the Sanhedrin served as the initial impetus for the unification and centralization of France's Jews. The subsequent creation of the consistorial system would seek to provide the institutional framework for the unity of French Jewry. Furthermore, in reconfirming French Jewry's acceptance of the terms of citizenship, the Sanhedrin was instrumental in shaping a rudimentary ideology of emancipation. Together, these embryonic transformations were essential to the formulation of the ideology of *régénération* and to the development of regenerative programs.

PART TWO

The Beginnings of
Modernization

4

The Jewish Community:
Continuity and Change

THE DEMISE OF the autonomous Jewish community was undoubtedly the most serious casualty of the emancipation period. The credo of the new era was exemplified by the often repeated words of Clermont-Tonnere at the French National Assembly, "everything should be refused the Jews as a nation, but all should be granted to them as individuals." For many contemporary observers, including some Jews, the continuation of the community was incompatible with loyalty to the state, and therefore in order to prove themselves worthy of the status of citizenship, the Jews would need to dissolve their traditional communal bonds. The conscious perpetuation of "community" thus appeared to contradict the cherished goal of social integration. However, it would be an error to assume that emancipation was the death knell of the community. Jewish communal life did not end abruptly. Despite the potent rhetoric of revolution, patriotism, and national consolidation, and the availability of unprecedented opportunity, the community would endure as the outstanding framework of Jewish identity.

The success of the community in surviving the ravages of late-eighteenth-century France is evidence of a remarkable durability, hardened by the experience of history. In the particular case of France, its continuation may be explained as the product of both Jewish and government interests. The effects of legislation that removed the privileges of communal self-government and restricted the authority of rabbis and rabbinic courts to ritual matters, although undeniably repercussive in the long run, may not have been so obvious to the first generation of emancipated Jews. On the social and religious level communal association remained a fact of life that served the essential needs of the Jews. Prayer, ritual slaughtering, and burial are only some of the religious observances that require or presuppose a community and that serve, at the same time, as important outlets for social interaction. In addition, neither lay nor rabbinic leaders were anxious to relinquish their authority. In the case of the rabbis, in particular, their authority in matters of religion would be upheld as long as the community continued to respect the centrality of Jewish tradition. Based on an entirely different, though no less pragmatic consideration, collective effort was a necessity. The Jews of the northeast were held responsible for communal debts accumulated during the ancien régime. If for no other reason, maintaining their communities was therefore necessary in order to discharge their prerevolutionary accounts.[1]

As time passed, it became increasingly clear to the Jewish leadership that a formal communal organization was indispensable to the continued viability of Jewish life in France. Looking back on the initial phase of emancipation, Berr Isaac Berr wrote in 1806 that the absence of a communal organization was the most serious problem facing French Jewry and the principal obstacle to moral and civil *régénération*. In the initial euphoria of citizenship he had underestimated the importance of a formal organization, but now sobered by fifteen years' experience, he acknowledged his error. First, unlike Catholicism and Protestantism, Judaism did not enjoy the protection and support accorded to the legally recognized religions in the French Empire. Berr argued that the exclusion of the Jewish religion from the general law of the organization of *cultes* (18 Germinal, year X) underscored the perceived inferiority of that religion and served to perpetuate popular prejudices that were widespread and especially visible in the public schools.[2] The totality of Jewish life, including its moral, civil, and religious elements, would be enhanced by the kind of government support already provided to other religions in maintaining their respective institutions. *Régénération* would not proceed without an improvement in the public perception of the Jews, a development with important implications for the envisioned transformation of the Jewish self-image.

Second, and parallel to the importance of government recognition of Judaism, was the role of a formal communal organization in the administration of internal Jewish affairs. It had become clear that social conditions alone would not lead to a containment of the abuses that impeded full *régénération*. Many leaders had undoubtedly believed that begging and idleness would disappear once new opportunities for economic diversification and advancement became available. Nevertheless, beggars and vagabonds continued to seek food and lodging from their coreligionists. Berr charged that the acts of kindness shown to poor Jews by their more fortunate coreligionists, although commendable in the humanitarian sense, were harmful to the interests of the community. Charitable assistance, he claimed, only encouraged idleness. Berr therefore asked his readers to withhold charity from any man capable of work and to refuse the means of travel from poor Jews seeking refuge in neighboring towns. Moreover, in anticipation of some reluctance to comply with these recommendations, due to what he termed an excessive "spirit of fraternity," Berr proposed the enactment of government legislation that would outlaw prevailing welfare practices. In the absence of communal controls to enforce adherence to the program of *régénération*, government intervention was regarded as the only effective remedy to this internal problem.[3] Nevertheless, Berr undoubtedly preferred that such matters be handled internally.

The most serious problem facing Jewish leaders was the continued involvement of Jews in the occupations of peddling and moneylending. In the words of Berr, the root of the problem was an "excessive and culpable ambition to amass . . . a fortune," and he maintained that whereas in earlier years there may have been no alternative to moneylending, there was now no justification for "this disgraceful commerce of money which their religion prohibits, and which good sense rejects." Though essentially characteristic of a preemancipation mentality, the proclivity to finances refused to disappear, despite the opportunities presented by civic equality. Berr saw this obsession as "an invincible barrier to . . . complete *régénération*," and expressed the hope that increased education would enable Jews to act judiciously in their choice of professions.[4]

Although these economic failures could be explained simply as vestiges of the old regime, new difficulties arose during the years following emancipation that severely threatened the success of *régénération*. The turmoil of revolution and the demise of the autonomous community precipitated a major institutional crisis involving the school, the synagogue, and the rabbinate. Widespread Jewish ignorance of the principles of Judaism may have been the most devastating consequence of the decade following emancipation. General intolerance for the Jewish religion, the small number of Jews in areas where they were tolerated, and the severe poverty of Jewish communities were the prime factors preventing the creation of institutions for the education of Jewish youth. As a result, those who had been students in the villages and towns where no Jewish schoolmaster or teachers resided, together with those who had been excluded from public schools, now constituted the majority of heads of families. The years of educational deprivation had produced a generation with no knowledge of religious fundamentals or moral and physical principles, or as Berr put it, a class of "crude, uncivil, and faint-hearted" individuals, totally devoid of culture.[5] Berr was confident that the leadership provided by a recognized communal organization would educate people to the need for humanistic studies, vocational training, and the formalization of Jewish religious instruction.

Like the school, the synagogue had suffered a miserable fate. With the disintegration of the Jewish community during this period came an increasingly negative attitude by Jews toward their own religion. In part, this can be traced to an atmosphere of intolerance toward Judaism at the end of the ancien régime, and its intensification during the Revolution and the Reign of Terror, when public rage against religion reached a climax. Following the establishment of the *décadi* as the national day of rest, opposition to Jewish Sabbath observance assumed numerous forms, ranging from verbal assault to forced labor. This state of affairs compelled Jews to take special precautions in the observance of Jewish ceremonies. At times, in order not to antagonize the clergy or magistrates, prayer-meetings and other rituals would be performed clandestinely. In Haguenau, for example, services were conducted secretly in an oil factory. Where Jews *did* receive permission to meet for prayer and ceremonies, they were granted the most obscure and remote quarters, often in the seclusion of their homes. These conditions created an atmosphere of disquietude, frequently expressed by the disorderly performance of religious ceremonies. According to Berr Isaac Berr, because of their lack of enlightenment worshippers failed to overcome these problems, and therefore proved incapable of giving the ceremonies a form befitting the "naturally simple religion." Religious observance was soon reduced to a matter of routine, thus detracting from the solemnity of Jewish worship. Moreover, public ridicule of beards and sidelocks, the wearing of *zizit* and head coverings, and performance of *shehitah* and circumcision, all contributed to the "moral denigration of the Jewish religion" and challenged the Jews' loyalty to tradition. One Talmudic scholar, Rabbi Uri Phoebus Cahen of Metz, reported in 1793 that out of fear that his scholarship would be lost, he hurried to publish his *novellae*. The cumulative result was, in Berr's words, "religious anarchy."[6]

The fate of the rabbinate was directly related to the decline of the synagogue and Jewish education. The low esteem into which the Jewish religion had fallen detracted from the prestige of the rabbis and prevented them from inspiring respect for themselves and their teachings. Moreover, now that the *kehillah* had become a voluntary association, the rabbi's modest existence was dependent upon the good will and charity of those who chose to contribute to his salary, and he therefore no longer held a position of undisputed authority in the community. Ironically, just when *régénération* demanded strong, moral leadership, the contemporary rabbi had become, in the eyes of many, ineffective.[7] "Far from being able to fulfill the true duties of his position, that is in recalling the obligations of religion and virtue to men who turn away, he is compelled to be silent and close his eyes, for fear of no longer seeing the rich contribute to his salary, especially if he would have the courage to address them directly with the admonishment that they sometimes deserve."[8] Among Jewish leaders there emerged a consensus concerning the role that the government could play in addressing the problems facing the rabbinate, and the Jewish religion as a whole. Berr advanced two recommendations: first, that the government establish the Jewish clergy as salaried employees of the state, thereby enabling them to perform their duties without being financially dependent upon their communities; second, that the Jewish religion be accorded the same powers and prerogatives as other religions established by the *Concordat*.[9] Nearly a quarter of a century would pass before Berr's vision for the Jewish religion was realized.

Forces of Continuity

Although there had emerged a virtual consensus among *maskilim* and French civil servants and political leaders concerning the need to transform the Jewish condition in France, the matter would not be easily resolved. For the vast majority of French Jews who belonged to the two generations following 1789, powerful social, economic, and cultural forces promoted continuity with the legacy of the prerevolutionary era. As compared with the highly urbanized Jewish communities in Paris and southern France, those of rural Alsace remained structurally compact and self-contained. Invariably, the Jewish population in the numerous small towns and villages of the northeast was preoccupied with building and maintaining the essential communal institutions: the school, the synagogue, and various philanthropic and religious societies. This ongoing preoccupation became even more intense in the years following the Terror, when many Jewish communities were ravaged. In those cities and towns where Jews acquired the right to settle only after the Revolution, the concern with the establishment of institutions was even more all-encompassing.

Linguistic and fertility trends, widely viewed as valuable indices of modernization, confirm the persistence of social and religious traditionalism among Alsatian Jews. The continued vitality of Jewish languages is an important indication of a community's achievement of or resistance to integration. As the embodiment of culture, a language may point to such things as group cohesiveness, the awareness of social barriers between the smaller group and the larger society, and a conscious differentiation between life inside the community and the world outside. Owing to their relatively high degree of acculturation and interaction in general society, the Sephardim were predominantly French speaking. By 1820 the use of Spanish and Provencal had disappeared from everyday life. On the other hand, much to the chagrin and embarrassment of enlightened leaders, Yiddish endured as a spoken language well past midcentury. In Alsatian communities sermons continued to be delivered in Yiddish and German, and even the chief rabbi of the Central Consistory in Paris, Emmanuel Deutz (1763–1842), failed to learn French well enough to preach in anything but the "jargon." According to reports of critics, many classes at the *école rabbinique* in Metz were also conducted in Yiddish, as were informal discussions among students, as late as midcentury. In fact, ignorance of French explains the appearance of the 1838 German translation of the most widely used Jewish catechism, Samuel Cahen's *Précis élémentaire*.[10]

Preliminary research conducted by Paula Hyman on Jewish fertility in France reveals that Alsatian Jews continued to have large families at midcentury. This was in marked contrast with Sephardic and Ashkenazic residents of Bordeaux, both of whom had significantly fewer children than the Ashkenazim of Alsace-Lorraine. Hyman concludes that regional patterns were more decisive than ethnic origins. Furthermore, an examination of trends in Paris shows that despite urbanization, fertility patterns remained similar to those in rural Alsace-Lorraine, suggesting to Hyman that neither urbanization nor upward social mobility exerted a discernable impact on fertility. Her explanation of this rather remarkable finding is that the transition from rural to urban life may not have presented "as radical a disruption of familial economic habits as it did for non-Jewish peasant populations formerly engaged in agriculture." Finally, the significantly higher fertility among a sample of rabbis and cantors leads Hyman to conclude that the erosion of strict religious observance may have been the most important factor in the trend toward smaller families.[11]

Movement toward cities and towns where no Jewish community existed was continuous, despite local opposition in the 1790s to Jews settling in Bischeim, Habsheim, Sierentz, and Lingolsheim, for example. New settlements in Colmar, Strasbourg, and Mulhouse would eventually become major centers of Jewish life. Many existing communities in Lorraine experienced significant growth, thus reflecting a clear movement from villages to cities. The number of small Jewish communities in the Bas-Rhin was significantly greater than in the Haut-Rhin. In the Bas-Rhin the Jews tended to be spread out in very small localities, while in the Haut-Rhin they were grouped in large *bourgs*. In fact, few new Jewish communities at all were formed in the Haut-Rhin.[12] In either case, we may assume that due to the small size of most communities, there was considerable involvement of townspeople in the administration of various communal affairs. This was accompanied by the potential for significant cohesiveness, as indicated by the mobilization of entire communities against the Central Consistory's plan to weaken rabbinic authority in 1839 and 1846. The situation in southern France was entirely different. There, communities were fewer in number, much larger in size, and thereby lacking the strong participatory element present in Alsace. Moreover, the number of official religious functionaries in Alsace was very large, as a comparison with Sephardic communities reveals. In the Haut-Rhin Consistory, for example, in addition to the grand rabbi, there were twenty communal rabbis and an additional eleven *ministres officiants*. Likewise, in the Bas-Rhin, there were eighteen communal rabbis and eighteen *ministres officiants*. In Bordeaux, by contrast, there was one rabbi (the grand rabbi himself) and two *ministres officiants*. A similar situation prevailed in Marseille and St. Esprit.[13] Deeply embedded in the social and political fabric of community life, the Alsatian incumbents of the numerous rabbinical, cantorial, ritual, and teaching positions undoubtedly served as constant reminders of religious tradition and authority.

The socio-economic condition of Alsatian Jewry tended to further retard the process of cultural and religious modernization. The chief Jewish occupations, rag dealing, secondhand peddling, and money-lending remained predominant during the First Empire. Only in the July Monarchy were these occupations slowly falling into disuse, and even then, they were most frequently replaced by various mercantile-related occupations, small finance, or artisan trades. The case of Saverne reveals a typical situation: in 1824 there were, of the thirty-five heads of family, sixteen merchants, three *commerçants* (shopkeepers), and one peddler. In Herlisheim in 1850 the picture was not very different: of thirty-seven householders, there were thirteen *commerçants* and eleven secondhand dealers.[14] In the much larger city of Strasbourg, change was considerably more evident. In 1805 those involved in petit commerce represented 53.5 percent of the Jewish population. In 1846 the percentage dropped to 24 percent.[15] And in the Haut-Rhin as late as 1838, nearly one-third of the wealthiest Jews in the *département* (i.e., those considered for admission into the *collège des Notables*) were rejected by the French government due to their involvement in usury.[16] One estimate of the percentage of notables in Colmar and Strasbourg engaged in commercial occupations in the 1840s is 70 percent, and in Paris and Marseille approximately 80 percent.[17] It is important to note that most Jews of the northeast did not live near industrial centers. Metz, Nancy, and Alsace in general were predominantly commercial centers.[18] The opportunities for training in the liberal professions were far fewer, and the desirability of these occupations was probably less pronounced than elsewhere. Widespread poverty was also a factor among the Jews of Alsace. The impression that emerges from the contemporary literature of the midnineteenth century is that raising a family and providing for its needs were the major preoccupations of Jews. These goals were inherently conservative.

Animosity toward the Jews was another factor affecting the pace of modernization. From their earliest days as citizens, they were exposed to continued legal discrimination and threats of deportation. Reports from the press and memoire literature offer evidence of popular hostility that emanated both from the peasantry in the countryside and from lay and religious leaders in cities and towns. On certain occasions, verbal assault gave way to physical violence. Following an already established pattern, the Revolution of 1848, like those of 1789 and 1830, precipitated attacks on the Jews of Alsace. The riots can be attributed to any number of factors, including general economic difficulties resulting from poor harvests in 1846–1847, the political turmoil of 1848, and the peasants' frustration with their debt to Jewish usurers, though this has been shown to be relatively small.[19] Whatever the causes of the riots, we may assume that Jews were careful to preserve an unspoken social distance from their Christian neighbors. At this stage, integration within the larger community was neither possible nor desirable.

Continuity with the legacy of the prerevolutionary era is revealed by a strong tradition of rabbinical scholarship and leadership in the first half of the nineteenth century. In the late Middle Ages and early modern period the region had several important yeshivot such as in Metz, Ribeauvillé, and Bischeim. Distinguished rabbinical figures, such as Joshua Falk, Jacob Reischer, Jonathan Eibeschütz, and Aryeh Loeb Günzberg (the *Sha'agat Aryeh*), all of whom served Metz, were world renowned for their scholarship. Other lesser known figures, such as Wolf Jacob Reichshofen, Samuel Halberstadt, and Meschoullam Sussell Enosch are typical of the outstanding Talmudists who were either brought to Alsace to direct a yeshivah or who were so driven by expulsion or economic hardship in the East. Jungholz, Ettendorf, Bouxwiller, Turkheim, Uffholtz, Mutzig, and Wintzenheim are only some of the smaller towns with yeshivot that dotted the Alsatian terrain.[20]

The political and social turmoil that engulfed France following the Revolution had devastating effects on Jewish institutions, and many yeshivot were either ordered closed or ceased to function. During this difficult period of transition, the most towering rabbinic personality in France was Rabbi David Sintzheim (1745–1812). Best known for his leadership of the Napoleonic Sanhedrin, Sintzheim had come to France in 1778 to direct the yeshivah at Bischeim. A descendant of R. Ḥayim ben Beẓalel, Sintzheim wrote numerous volumes of Talmudic *novellae* and responsa. Only one volume, *Yad David* (Offenbach, 1799), appeared during his lifetime, while a halakhic encyclopedia, *Minḥat Ani,* was completed in 1810 but remained unpublished due to burdensome rabbinic duties. These works and those of Sintzheim's contemporaries attest to the fact that though virtually destroyed by the ravages of the Reign of Terror, traditional Jewish culture did not disappear and, indeed, subsequently endeavored to recapture some of its former glory. After the turn of the century, yeshivot were reopened or established anew in numerous communities such as Metz, Strasbourg, Schirrhoffen, Bergheim, and Wintzenheim. Near Strasbourg a network of academies was designed to produce Talmudic scholars of distinction. A student would begin his studies at Ettendorf; from there he would advance to Bischeim, and finally to the yeshivah of Westhoffen.[21] Though hardly comparable to the level and intensity of earlier days, traditional Talmudic learning had survived the Revolution.

Through the mid-1830s and early 1840s, the old-style rabbi, steeped in learning, still predominated in France. More often than not, he was trained in an established German yeshivah, due to the turmoil in France at the end of the eighteenth century, though in some cases Talmudic studies were pursued privately with a local scholar. Two of the Central Consistory chief rabbis, Emmanuel Deutz and Marchand Ennery, had received their training at the yeshivah of Rabbi Hirtz Scheuer in Mayence, as did a number of other French rabbis. Some, such as Arnaud Aron, who would later become the grand rabbi of Strasbourg, were sent to the yeshivah at Frankfurt am Main. Owing to unusual longevity, it was not all uncommon for rabbis of the ancien régime to still be in office well into the 1820s and 1830s. Many Alsatian rabbis frequently held a single position for thirty or forty years. Adding to the stability and continuity of the Jewish religious tradition was the fact that the rabbinic leadership of numerous northeastern communities remained within the same family for extended periods. The rabbinate of Mutzig, for example, was passed from father to son or son-in-law over a period of nearly one hundred fifty years (1716–1864). Members of the illustrious Katzenellenbogen family occupied the rabbinate in Haguenau and various Haut-Rhin communities for more than eighty years (1755–1828). One of the family's most outstanding scholars was Naphtali Hirsch Katzenellenbogen (d. 1823), who served as rabbi in Frankfurt an die Oder before returning to Wintzenheim to become grand rabbi of the Haut-Rhin Consistory. While in Frankfurt in 1797 he wrote *Sha'ar Naphtali*, a commentary on *Even ha-Ezer* and responsa; he also left other *halakhic* commentaries, juridical decisions, and sermons in manuscript. A member of the Paris Sanhedrin, Katzenellenbogen was an outspoken opponent of religious reform, as his participation in *Eleh Divre ha-Brit* reveals.[22]

The chief rabbinate of Metz bore the imprint of an outstanding rabbinic luminary, Aryeh Loeb Günzberg, for nearly a century. The author of the highly respected collection of Talmudic *novellae, Sha'agat Aryeh*, Günzberg served the Metz community from 1766–1785 but was not succeeded by an official chief rabbi until 1810. During the twenty-five year interregnum, three of Günzberg's rabbinic assistants, Oury Phoebus Cahen, Mayer Charleville, and Joseph Gougenheim, formed a supreme *beit din* and acted jointly as chief rabbi. Cahen, president of the *beit din* and director of the Metz yeshivah, assumed the functions of grand rabbi in 1793, though no title was given to him. Cahen's maternal lineage, the Poppers family, was very distinguished; two of his ancestors had served as heads of the rabbinic courts in Frankfurt am Main and Teplitz. On his paternal line, his father and grandfather had preceded him as members of the rabbinic court of Metz. Cahen himself was the author of several Talmudic *novellae,* including *Halakhah Berurah* (Metz, 1793). Following the death of Cahen in 1806, Aaron Worms, also a disciple of Günzberg, was appointed to the Metz *beit din.* An expert in Jewish law, Worms had been working closely with the *beit din* for some time, as he had returned to Metz upon the passing of Günzberg in order to assist the rabbinic council and to succeed his mentor as head of the Metz yeshivah.[23]

The fact that several local scholars were available to fill the chief rabbinical position of Metz did not deter notables of the Jewish community from attempting to restore the mantle of rabbinic leadership to the Günzberg family. In 1809 Asser Lion, son of the *Sha'agat Aryeh,* and rabbi at Wallerstein (in Bavaria), was elected to fill the new position of consistorial grand rabbi. Lion enthusiastically accepted the offer but was soon offered a position by the Central Consistory and the Grand Duke of Baden. To the dismay and anger of the Metz leaders, Lion decided to accept the Baden position. As a result of this turn of events, the Metz chief rabbinate reverted to local control. Despite their advanced ages, members of the aforementioned *beit din* were called to fill the position:

Mayer Charleville was installed in 1810; he was succeeded by Joseph Gougenheim in 1812. The next in line, Aaron Worms, was bypassed in favor of Samuel Wittersheim, evidently because Worms did not know French. Nevertheless, in spite of this disappointment, Worms occupied the premier position of *posek* during Wittersheim's tenure. Eventually, Worms was appointed grand rabbi of Metz (1831), though his French had not improved. He was succeeded in 1837 by his son-in-law Lion-Mayer Lambert, who held the position for twenty-five years.[24] The general pattern of rabbinic succession was invariably a significant expression of conservatism in the northeast provinces.

Other communities such as Colmar maintained a tradition of hiring prominent personalities who combined outstanding scholarship with political acuity. Grand Rabbis Naphtali Hirsch Katzenellenbogen, Simon Cahen, Séligmann Goudchaux, and Salomon Klein were all men of great learning and erudition who, in addition to their rabbinical duties, served as presidents of the Haut-Rhin Consistory. Their staunch conservatism and unflinching resistance to religious reform were undoubtedly bolstered by their political power. Regulation of ritual slaughtering provides an illustration of this phenomenon. The Haut-Rhin Consistory, hoping to control potential ritual abuses, placed the authorization of *shohatim* squarely in the hands of the grand rabbi, its president. In charge of the examination and certification of the functionaries, the grand rabbi was to serve, as well, as judge in cases of dismissal.[25] The result was a *département* that showed fewer signs of religious modernization. The fact that of all the *départements* of France the least number of subscribers to the *Archives israélites* was in the Haut-Rhin may point to a rather broad-based dissatisfaction with the journal's liberal views. A trend initiated in 1842 by the local consistory and followed by many individuals throughout the *département* to cancel subscriptions is proof of the tensions motivated by regional and religious differences.[26]

Although the output of rabbinic scholarship after the turn of the nineteenth century was hardly prolific, there is evidence of impressive learning. Aaron Worms of Metz wrote a major work, *Me'ore Or*, published in seven volumes over a period of forty years (1790–1831). It contains commentaries on the Talmud and *Shulḥan Arukh*, *novellae* on the origins of religious customs, and responsa. Worms' work evinces much halakhic originality and independence. In this last regard he displayed a critical attitude toward the glosses of R. Moses Isserles, claiming that France was not bound by Polish *minhag*. The career of Rabbi Moses Munius is also worthy of note. A descendant of Judah Loew (the Maharal) of Prague, Munius was born in Mutzig (Bas-Rhin) in 1760. Trained at the Prague yeshivah, Munius subsequently returned to

France to direct a yeshivah in Strasbourg. From 1794 until his death in 1842 he served as rabbi of Rixheim. The various manuscripts Munius has left, including *Ner le-Ragli,* an extensive commentary to *Ethics of the Fathers; Or li-Netivati,* a commentary on the *Haftarot;* and *Darash Moshe,* a collection of sermons and eulogies, and various responsa, reveal outstanding rabbinic scholarship and erudition.[27]

The work of Aaron Worms represents the last example of serious Talmudic scholarship published in France. Munius' writings, like some others of the same period, remained in manuscript. Both the cessation of classical publishing, as well as the appearance of a new genre of rabbinic writings after 1820 suggest that there was no longer an indigenous, learned audience in France and may also signify that the scholarly aspirations and interests of French rabbis had become much more modest. A survey of the works published by the generation of rabbis who held leading positions at midcentury reveals the following: Hebrew grammar textbooks and lexicons, catechisms, compendia of devotional prayers, and numerous translations of Hebrew classics into French. In some instances rabbis published programmatic essays on the nature of the rabbinate, on topics in Jewish theology, or on the future of French Judaism, while a few also assumed the task of defending Judaism against public criticism or defamation. Significantly, Lion-Mayer Lambert and Salomon Klein, two rabbis most obviously identified with religious conservatism and classical learning, also fit this pattern. Lambert, who was the first director of the *école rabbinique* of Metz before becoming the grand rabbi of Metz, wrote a catechism, a Hebrew grammar text, and a history textbook. Klein published numerous expositions on Judaism, critical essays on publications of the *Wissenschaft des Judentums* movement, and a volume defending Judaism against virulent anti-Jewish calumnies. Perhaps the most revealing sign of the times is that in seeking the position of Central Consistory grand rabbi, Klein sent a copy of his newly published Hebrew grammar to the Paris body.[28]

We should not, however, be led to the erroneous conclusion that French rabbis were incapable of more serious scholarship. In private correspondence, sermons, and assorted publications there is still much evidence of great classical erudition. Rather, this state of affairs was the product of forces responsible for the transformation of the modern rabbinate itself. Formerly in the role of yeshivah instructor, *dayyan,* or *posek,* the new type of rabbi was a public figure expected to preach every week, visit the sick, supervise elementary education, and, generally, to minister to his unlettered flock. Moreover, when traditional Judaism and rabbinic authority were openly challenged by the consistorial administration and reformers, the rabbis naturally assumed the role of defenders of the faith. It is not at all unlikely that the struggle over religious reform, a battle conducted for at least two decades, exacted most of the energies that might have been directed, under different conditions, to traditional Talmudic scholarship. Most French rabbis, if not all, concluded that public activism, not preoccupation with classical scholarship and publication, was the need of the hour. This view was characteristic of a generation of rabbis that came of age in the 1830s and 1840s. In these years the older generation, whose service dated from before the turn of the century, was being replaced throughout the country. The deaths of Grand Rabbis Worms of Metz (1836), Gougenheim of Nancy (1842), Deutz of the Central Consistory (1844), and Goudchaux of Colmar (1849), and numerous other distinguished figures occurred precisely during the period when traditional Judaism was under siege.

Finally, an important, though overlooked, mark of Alsatian Jewry's loyalty to religious tradition was its pronounced regional distinctiveness. For a number of reasons, some rooted in long standing historical, political, and religious dynamics, Alsatians viewed Paris with unconcealed suspicion. There emerged among many a feeling of common purpose. Grand Rabbi Salomon Klein, for example, asked that the "entire Haut-Rhin *circonscription* consider itself as a single community."[29] One expression of this consciousness was the pronunciation of Hebrew. Adherence to the Ashkenazic pronunciation despite efforts to introduce the Sephardic accent remained widespread.[30] Another manifestation of Alsatian consciousness was the creation of several types of institutions whose aim was to preserve the traditional lifestyle in the region and, more generally, through the perseverence of independence in outlook and behavior. The most important of these institutions was the yeshivah, although well before midcentury most of the yeshivot of Alsace had become informal academies administered by local Talmudic scholars.[31] In some instances, an effort was made to establish an officially sanctioned institute. In 1834 a preparatory school for students planning to enter the *école rabbinique de Metz* was formed in Haguenau by Mayer Cahun. The school's thorough curriculum plan included classical Bible commentaries, Hebrew language, Talmud and *poskim* (including Maimonides, Alfasi, Rabbenu Asher, and the *Tur*), and Jewish philosophical and *mussar* literature. To this was added a full range of secular instruction: French and German reading; composition and speech; arithmetic; general and French history, geography, cosmography, and natural history. A similar effort was undertaken in 1851 by the Haut-Rhin Consistory at the initiative of Grand Rabbi Klein.[32]

The cumulative effect of these forces was that, in contrast with Jewish communities in the large urban centers in France and abroad,

Alsatian Jewry remained, for the most part, extremely traditional in its religious orientation and behavior. A high proportion of school-aged children attended Jewish schools, the number of communities with rabbinic positions was unmatched, and the deviation from traditional norms was much less pronounced than in other parts of France. What is remarkable about this is the fact that emancipation did not lead directly to the attenuation of Jewish loyalties, as might be expected. The tendency to reside in small towns and villages scattered throughout the region, at least through the first half of the nineteenth century, was immeasurably repercussive. Far removed from the cultural and intellectual influences of the larger cities and protected from their erosive effects on Jewish ceremonial observance, Alsatian Jewry remained loyal to traditional values. While laxity in observance was undeniably increasing in larger cities such as Metz, Strasbourg, and Nancy, it was, nonetheless, considerably less than in Paris.

Forces of Change

Already in 1802, following the creation of the Protestant consistorial system, Jewish leaders began to appeal to the government for authorization and assistance in establishing a similar communal organization. The idea of a formal organization of the Jewish religion accorded with the Napoleonic policy of centralization and control. By the first years of the nineteenth century it had become widely acknowledged that any progress in the envisioned transformation of the Jews would require a network of communal frameworks to facilitate the implementation of government policies vis-à-vis the Jews. The emperor therefore instructed his ministers to cooperate with Jewish leaders in the development of a comprehensive plan. A committee consisting of three government officials and a nine-man council selected from the Assembly of Jewish Notables drafted a plan that was adopted as a *règlement* by the entire Assembly and ratified by Napoleon in 1806.[33]

Not until 1808 did the French government under Napoleon organize the Jews of the empire in consistories, according to the model used for non-Catholic minorities. The *règlement* of 17 March 1808 ordered the formation of a synagogue and consistory in each *département* with a Jewish population of two thousand or more; *départements* with fewer Jews could be combined, under one consistory, to arrive at the required number. Originally there were seven departmental consistories, located in Wintzenheim (later Colmar) in Haut-Rhin; Strasbourg, in Bas-Rhin; Nancy, in Meurthe; Metz, in Moselle; Paris, in Seine; Bordeaux, in Gironde; and Marseille, in Bouches-du-Rhône. In 1846 an eighth consistory was established, in St. Esprit, and in 1857 a ninth consistory was established in Lyon, in Rhône. At the administrative helm sat the Central Consistory in Paris. In the early years the departmental consistories were composed of a grand rabbi, one additional rabbi, and three lay members. According to law, consistorial members were chosen by an electoral college of twenty-five notables, themselves selected by the government from among the wealthiest and most respected Jews. Among the various modifications in the original constitution of the consistories, the most significant were those that reduced the number of rabbis, resulting in greater lay control of the central and departmental consistories.[34]

The consistorial system was reconfirmed by every government regime throughout the century. Appointed as the legal representative of French Jewry, the consistories served as the official liason between the government and the Jewish population. As far as specific responsibilities were concerned, the consistories were charged with the following tasks: to administer the communities, to oversee the moral and socio-economic regeneration of those individuals needing "improvement," and to exercise surveillance over their constituents. Administrative duties were the main preoccupation of the consistories, and included the following functions: fiscal matters, including revenue from special taxes; construction, organization, and supervision of synogogues; supervision of charitable organizations, schools, and *kashrut*. Over and above maintaining order within the scattered communities, the consistories were expected to act as agents of *régénération*. The consistories formed committees to eliminate begging, organized societies to encourage vocational training, and supervised Jewish education. Other initiatives included efforts to modernize the rabbinate and modest attempts at religious reform. As a rule, regenerative efforts that touched on religious matters led to divisions within the community.[35]

Though unstated, the goal of unifying French Jewry was relentlessly pursued by the consistorial leadership. It is clear that in this activity was a distinct echo of government efforts to impose centralization on the general populace. More important, there emerged the idea that if the consistories were to realize their mission, particularly the task of regeneration, then they would need to secure a monopoly over communal agencies. Vigorous efforts were made to establish the consistory's preeminence over "rival" institutions, particularly over mutual aid societies and private *minyanim*. Though largely motivated by financial concerns, the war on independent institutions was an assertion of consistorial authority; the persistence of mutual aid societies and private *minyanim* reflects a deep-seated dissatisfaction with the attempted consistorial monopoly and a decided preference for the fellowship and warmth characteristic of the smaller associations. Efforts at maintaining control over communal institutions, and the resistance frequently encountered, together represent a leitmotif in the history of the consistory. At issue was the question whether Jewish life in France could be expressed only through the consistorial framework.[36]

Consistorial control over Jewish communities was most direct, and in several instances, most complete, in the *chefs-lieu,* the cities where the departmental consistories sat. The Paris Consistory displayed the greatest control over local Jewish institutions. Even so, the independence of the Portuguese synagogue challenged the consistorial monopoly. Outside the *chefs-lieu,* the situation was more extreme. Seeking to impose their aims upon local community affairs, the consistories appointed delegates, called *commissaires surveillants,* as representatives of consistorial authority in outlying towns and villages. Abundant evidence of community–consistory tensions reveals significant misunderstanding and resentment on both sides, at times reflected in a *commissaire surveillant's* refusal to obey consistory orders or the refusal of the local population to respect the authority of the *commissaire surveillant.*[37] In some cases, Jews in the provinces even looked to the Central Consistory to take the initiative in this area. For example, in 1841 several Jews from the Haut-Rhin approached the Central Consistory with a plan to facilitate the implementation of synagogue reforms. They claimed that efforts to introduce decorum in the religious services consistently met with the resistance of the synagogue administrators, the *commissaires surveillants.* The Haut-Rhin petitioners therefore proposed the formation of a *conseil synagogal* in every Jewish community with at least two hundred members. The council would consist of five or seven members who would be named by the notables of the community and by the Jewish municipal electors. While the *commissaire surveillant* would serve as president, his authority would be neutralized by the votes of the council and by the requirement that consistorial approbation be first obtained.[38] There is no record that this plan was ever implemented.

Some proponents of *régénération* were outspoken in their criticism of the Central Consistory's failure to assume a leading role in the promotion of modernization. One Paris critic, David Singer, asserted that the Central Consistory could take no credit for the establishment of modern Jewish schools. Simon Bloch of Strasbourg claimed that the Central Consistory exerted a severely limited influence on Jewish life, particularly with respect to religious instruction. Noé Noé of Bordeaux took the Central Consistory to task for its failure to help centralize Jewish education. According to some critics, the realization of *régénération* would remain elusive, unless uniform objectives and methods were introduced.[39] Others charged that the consistory did not represent the sum total of Jewish communal activity and that it ought to avoid acting intrusively. In several instances various towns and cities with Jewish populations preferred to organize themselves independently of the official consistory. Whatever form was used, there was no doubt that the organization of Jewish life around a community was essential to the creation and implementation of regenerative programs.

Beginning in the 1820s the larger cities of Alsace were most likely to see the emergence of modernizing elites that challenged accepted norms of traditional society. In 1831 a consistorial commission in Strasbourg proposed administrative, liturgical, and religious innovations, many of which would anticipate the reform agenda of the following decades. Although these efforts were largely abortive, they provide valuable insight into the ideological premises of *régénération*. Charged by the Strasbourg Consistory with the mission of "researching the obstacles that continue to oppose the complete regeneration of the Jews of Alsace and to indicate the most appropriate means to eliminate these obstacles," a specially appointed commission concluded that the obstacles were not at all related to the fundamentals of the Jewish religion. In fact, the commission emphatically underscored the relevance of Judaism in an age of liberty, as it embodied the love of fellow man, the *patrie*, and justice, and contained exhortations concerning universal brotherhood. Rather, the failure of *régénération* could be traced to several social shortcomings that the Jews themselves would need to overcome: "foreign customs" that had been added at times of persecution but were now antiquated; the small importance attached by some Jews to the decisions of the Sanhedrin; the lack of enlightenment of the rabbis, their stationary opinions, and their indifference to political rights; the apathy of the consistorial lay leadership, and the defective organization of the notables and the consistories. In plotting its course, the commission's report urged three means of regeneration that were, and would continue to be, regarded as fundamental: primary education, vocational training, and agriculture. Particularly significant, however, is that the commission went well beyond previous discussions of *régénération* by proposing a list of religious reforms that it hoped to introduce in the synagogue.[40]

Four categories of reforms were proposed by the Strasbourg commission: (1) administrative modifications that could be implemented by the lay members of the consistory; (2) ritual reforms requiring the concurrence of the consistorial grand rabbi; (3) ritual reforms requiring the concurrence of the Central Consistory and the seven departmental grand rabbis; and (4) changes in the regulations governing the eligibility of notables, consistory members, and rabbis, all subject to the approval of the government. Included in the first category of reforms were efforts to

enhance the aesthetic component of public religious rituals: the maintenance of decorum at the synagogue and funeral services, the elimination
of the sale of religious honors, the introduction of weekly sermons, the
requirement that a boy pass a public examination on the catechism
before being authorized to read the Torah upon reaching his *majorité
religieuse*, and making the synagogue suitable for girls to attend. Emphasis was also placed upon the importance of the decisions of the Paris
Sanhedrin and on the civil laws of France, particularly on those prohibiting burial before twenty-four hours. Reforms of the second category,
those requiring the concurrence of the grand rabbi, point to a new role
for the synagogue in ritual observance. One proposed regulation declared that the cantor and grand rabbi alone would be authorized to
possess a citron (*etrog*), and that this would suffice for the entire community. Similarly, the *kiddush* recited publicly in the synagogue would discharge the religious obligations of all those present. These proposals
represent a shift away from individual or popular observance in favor of
a representative role for official religious functionaries. Although such
proposals do not, in the strict sense, violate the halakhah, they do reflect
a preference for a mode of religious observance normally associated with
the Christian Church.[41]

The third category of reforms was most extreme and would therefore need to be brought before the Central Consistory and the seven
departmental grand rabbis for their consideration. The following measures were included in this class: a reduction in the number of prayers
and suppression of those that might appear hostile to other religions; the
elimination of the prohibition against *yein nesech;* abolition of the custom that beards must be worn under certain circumstances; suppression
of the second day of festivals; elimination of any observances associated
with Tisha B'Av that may express regret over the loss of a national
homeland; the establishment of communion for girls; and the easing of
restrictions on the minor holidays.[42] The outstanding common characteristic of these reforms was the concern for the relationship between the
Jews, their new *patrie,* and their gentile compatriots. In one respect it is
significant that the Strasbourg commission even felt the need to address
the issue of civic loyalty, since the question had been resolved nearly
twenty-five years earlier by the Paris Sanhedrin. However, the proposals
were obviously not motivated by efforts to obtain or retain civic equality,
nor do they reveal any implicit critique of the Jewish religion. The views
of the Strasbourg commission were consistent with the legacy of the
Sanhedrin, which implicitly denied any link between civic equality and
religious reform. Rather, the proposals reflect a desire to render the Jews
more civil. Some changes were deemed essential because various rituals

were still regarded as the cause of social alienation between Jews and gentiles, a view that had found support among some Jewish leaders. Whatever the motivation behind the reforms, it is important to note the opinion of the commission, voiced perhaps for the first time, that issues of this kind could be resolved only by a national body of communal and religious leaders.[43]

The correspondence of the *comité d'administration de la culte israélite* of Strasbourg reveals growing friction between progressive and traditionalist leaders. Throughout the 1830s members of the *comité* urged the Strasbourg Consistory to assume a more active role in the advancement of modernization. Problems arose when modernization was defined in religious terms. For example, following the appointment of the new departmental grand rabbi in 1831, the *comité* complained to the consitory about the rabbi's two and one-half hour sermon "devoted entirely to a Talmudic discussion, without a single word of morality, nor a word of the duties of citizenship, of the *patrie*." In 1838 the *comité* successfully pressured the consistory to abolish the sale of religious honors; some communities of the Bas-Rhin nevertheless continued to sell synagogue honors well after midcentury. And on the question of early burial, a cause célèbre among *maskilim* and reformers for more than a half century, both the consistory and the *comité* took measures prohibiting Jewish burials until after twenty-four hours had elapsed. Commenting on the traditional practice of immediate burial, the *comité* wrote to the consistory; "Like you, we deplore a custom which clashes with all rules of humanity."[44]

The first priority of Jewish communal leaders was the promotion of economic productivity and occupational diversification among the Jewish lower classes. These efforts reflected the influence of the Enlightenment's exaltation of labor and were modelled after existing plans and institutions in French society. Proposals for the entrance of Jews into agriculture emanated from various quarters, dating from the early Restoration period. In 1831 a specially appointed consistorial commission in Strasbourg proposed the creation of a model farm as the most effective way of achieving *régénération*.[45] In the Haut-Rhin there was a plan to add an agricultural school to the vocational school in Mulhouse. A related concern was the eradication of begging, still a persistent problem in the 1840s. In 1843 the Strasbourg Consistory appointed an investigatory commission to take up the question, and the Colmar Consistory, where the problem was particularly acute, founded a special benevolent society that proposed to solve the problem of begging through the internment of beggars in four industrial schools to be established within the *département*. Another plan envisioned the creation of a Jewish agricultural or industrial establishment to employ beggars.[46] The possibility of a joint venture involving the Haut- and Bas-Rhin *départements* was also considered. In fact a project was submitted to the *comité de l'école du travail pour les Israélites du Bas-Rhin* concerning the establishment of a *maison de refuge* to end begging, and an agricultural school for the Jews of the two *départements*.[47] Mayer Cahun, director of the Haguenau Jewish school, proposed the establishment of a *maison de travail* for Jewish beggars born in Alsace or living there for ten years. He suggested this at a time when the government was preparing new legislation on begging and when the *conseil municipal de Strasbourg* was considering the purchase of property for a compulsory agricultural colony for four hundred beggars and indigents.[48] Despite interest within various consistorial and nonconsistorial circles, nothing significant materialized.

Numerous societies for the encouragement of Jewish vocational training were founded in the principal centers of Jewish population. These societies were the creation of affluent Jews who sought to modify the occupational structure within the Jewish community. Initially, financial support for this enterprise came predominantly from individual subscriptions. The first societies of this kind were established in Metz and Paris in 1823 and Nancy in 1825. The *Société d'encouragement pour les arts et métiers* of Metz assumed responsibility for placing young men in local apprenticeships. By 1839 it had placed 120 young men; between 1840–1844, 45 apprentices were placed. In 1843 the Metz *société* counted 250 members.[49] In Paris the *Société des amis du travail* had very limited success and was dissolved in 1834. More success was achieved by the *Société pour l'établissement de jeunes filles israélites (Hakhnassat Kallah)*, founded in 1843 in Paris. Initially, 5 girls were placed in apprenticeship; by the end of 1845 36 apprentices were working in such fields as sewing, linen-trade (lingerie), painting, music, and polished porcelain. By 1851 the *société* had assisted 156 girls.[50]

In both the Haut- and Bas-Rhin, developments in Jewish vocational instruction followed the general pattern of a gradual transfer of technical training from an apprenticeship system to one where professional skills were acquired in vocational schools. This development was driven by the belief that the goals of vocational training and social reform would be served by boarding schools. The *Société d'encouragement au travail en faveur d'Israélites du Bas-Rhin*, established in Strasbourg in 1825 by a group headed by consistory president Auguste Ratisbonne, devoted itself to the funding of an *école de travail* under Jewish auspices. Many parents, particularly in the *campagnes*, would not send their children to general (non-Jewish) vocational schools as this would necessitate desecration of the Sabbath. These fears were projected onto the Jewish school as well and were also reflected in a general reluctance to be trained in manual labor.[51] Hoping to encourage wider support throughout the *département,* the Strasbourg Consistory became more centrally involved in the affairs of the *société* in 1842. Leaders were alarmed by an imbalance between urban and rural involvement: virtually all of the subscribers were from the *chef-lieu,* though most of the forty apprentices were from the *campagnes.* Convinced that the imbalance was due to the persistence of religious misgivings among the rural populace, the consistory urged rabbis to teach that labor was "the source of eternal and temporal felicity." On the organizational level the consistory appointed the *commissaires surveillants* throughout the *département* as delegates of the *société,* and directed them to collect annual subscriptions in their own communities. The commitment of the Strasbourg Consistory to the growth and fiscal stability of the *école de travail* was the exception to the general pattern. As a result of these efforts, the *société* could report that in 1845 a majority of the Jewish communities in the *département* had come to the aid of the school through annual subscription.[52]

Admission to the school was open to boys who were in possession of a "certificate of indigence," had attended a primary school, and were between the ages of thirteen and fourteen and one-half years. Originally, the apprentices were housed and fed in private homes; however, in 1832 the administrative commission acquired a building where fourteen young men were lodged, fed, and given clothing. Upon admission an apprentice would spend several months in the establishment, where he would receive preliminary training in his profession before being placed in a workshop. Reports indicate that discipline in the *école de travail* was intentionally severe, since one main objective of the school was to eradicate the "vicious" habits that students brought from home. This included a provision that no German could be spoken in the school. The school curriculum included a full range of secular and technical subjects: arithmetic, linear design, French, geography, and history. Though not accorded equal importance, religious instruction and observance were emphasized, particularly on Sabbaths and holidays when students were obliged to attend synagogue and were taught to pray. The term of apprenticeship was three years.[53]

The Strasbourg *école de travail* enjoyed considerable respect in government circles. It was highly regarded by Minister of Public Instruction Guizot who, after visiting the school, allotted 500 francs. In 1842 an *ordonnance royale* formally recognized the school as an establishment of "public utility," in recognition of its promotion of the qualities of order, work, and morality. On the local level, the *conseil municipal de Strasbourg* strengthened its endorsement of the school in 1844 by doubling its 1000 franc annual subsidy. This level of support continued through at least 1850. The school was also supported generously by the *conseil général du Bas-Rhin* with 1000 francs and more modestly by the *Ministre de l'Intérieur* in 1850. Between 1833 and 1845 eighty-five young workers had been trained, and in the early 1850s the school trained an average of thirty-six at a time.[54]

Less urbanized than other *départements* and less receptive to new ideas, the Haut-Rhin tended to advance very slowly on the road to modernization. Some blamed the situation on the lack of cooperation of urban leaders who considered it humiliating to work with smaller communities, whereas others held the consistory responsible. In fact, the failure of the consistory to coordinate the encouragement of *arts et métiers* motivated some communities to act on their own. The Jewish community of Ribeauvillé, for example, established its own society in 1834 to place apprentices. Finally, in 1842, an *école israélite des arts et métiers à Mulhouse* was opened by the *Société philanthropique israélite du Haut-Rhin*, independent of consistory effort and, according to the *Archives israélites*, in spite of its indifference. The *société*, which had been established in Colmar in 1835, supported the school through subscriptions; the school also received an allocation from the Minister of the Interior. From 1844, when the school was placed under the direct patronage of the consistorial administration, there was genuine cooperation between the school and the consistory.[55]

Like the Strasbourg *école de travail* and other vocational schools in French society at large, the Mulhouse school was structured so as to facilitate the realization of social and moral reform. Sharing the belief that separation from family was imperative for the reform of the young, theorists of vocational education envisioned institutions that were isolated from potentially harmful influences. In typical fashion, the Mulhouse vocational school provided, in addition to classrooms, a refectory, dormitories, and workrooms. In the evening students received lessons in religion, mathematics, design, French and German language, and during the day they served in their apprenticeships with masters in the city. Like the Strasbourg school, the term of apprenticeship was three years. Obstacles to religious observance were removed as the young apprentices were given time off on Jewish holidays. Initially, the school was open only to boys from indigent families, and because of the lack of resources, only ten students could enroll. In the second year, when resources were more abundant, sixteen were admitted. Starting with its third year, the school permitted paying students to enter, a decision indicating that the school had gained in public esteem and confidence. The figures in 1845 indicate that the school continued to attract more applications than it could accommodate: twenty-five candidates applied for ten openings.[56]

The school and the work of the *société* were highly regarded in diverse quarters. Théophile Hallez, hardly a friend of the Jews, praised the *Société philanthropique du Haut Rhin* for its success in facilitating apprenticeships for poor Jews.[57] The school was applauded by *l'Industriel alsacien* for achieving remarkable progress in mechanical arts, and for the outstanding instruction in French, German, history, geography, mathematics, and design. The newspaper was particularly struck by the students' fluency in French, so very uncommon in rural Alsace.[58] Enrollments at the Mulhouse school were somewhat erratic: fifteen students in 1849, five in 1851, and twenty-two in 1856.[59] Both the Mulhouse school and the Strasbourg school were sources of pride and hope for the Jewish community of Paris. Concern for the vocational training of Alsatian Jewry led in 1844 to the formation in Paris of a *comité de patronage* to assist workers leaving these two *écoles de travail*. The *comité* hoped to eventually extend its support to other *départements* as well.[60]

Regenerative efforts that touched on religious matters were frequently a source of tension between the modernizing elite and the religiously traditional masses and leaders. Many families were concerned that in apprenticeships the young Jewish men would be required to lodge where no kosher food would be available, study with a Christian master, and violate the Sabbath. Although the vocational schools in Strasbourg and Mulhouse followed religious guidelines, for the most part, there were no guarantees once the boys began to work as apprentices. For this reason there occasionally were delays in placement.[61] Responding to criticism that beggars may be forced to violate the Sabbath, the *Archives israélites* asked, "Is it not better to work on the Sabbath than to beg everyday?" The journal argued that in time, after displaying genuine devotion to their work, beggars would gain the respect of their Christian employers and would undoubtedly be able to observe the Sabbath.[62] In the Haut-Rhin, conflict over whether vocational training should be under religious or civil authorities divided the communal leadership. At the insistence of Rabbi Salomon Klein, the Colmar Consistory requested that the *société philanthropique* be placed under the Ministry of Cultes, and under the direction of the consistory, not the prefect. Moreover, the consistory sought to transfer the vocational school from Mulhouse to Colmar, where Klein planned to establish an *école préparatoire* to the *école rabbinique*. He thus hoped to place the school on a more secure religious foundation. Léon Werth, president of the *société*, objected on the grounds that the *société* had already been recognized as an establishment of public utility, and therefore insisted that it remain under civil authority and that the school stay in Mulhouse. Failing to move the Mulhouse school, Klein established a short-lived vocational school in Colmar alongside his yeshivah.[63]

Tensions were especially in evidence during the months before the 1844 Haut-Rhin consistorial elections, as conservatives challenged the eligibility of progressives to assume positions in the *collège des Notables*. One conservative leader from Mulhouse charged the *parti nouveau* with plans to introduce religious reforms "like those in Germany and in Paris." Calling them "enemies of the religious ceremonies," the leader advised electors to cast ballots only for "pious men."[64] Generally speaking, tensions heightened after 1848, when universal suffrage was introduced in consistorial elections. Proponents of reform feared that in Alsace the new democratic electoral procedures would result in the appointment of rabbis and consistory members who were more orthodox. According to Strasbourg Consistory leader Louis Ratisbonne, universal suffrage resulted in the emergence of "an unintelligent, backward, absurd majority" that would obstruct the process of regeneration.[65] Ratisbonne's concerns over universal suffrage may not have been entirely unfounded. In the Haut-Rhin in 1850 opponents of religious reform received, on the average, 57 percent of the vote in local consistory elections. Conservative candidate Salomon Klein gained an even more overwhelming victory over the moderate Samuel Dreyfus in the election for grand rabbi of the *département*.[66]

All told, the numerical results of the *sociétés* and vocational schools were disappointing. By midcentury the total number of trained manual workers was only several hundred. However, the success of the *sociétés* should not be measured solely by their impact on the occupational structure of the Jewish population. Rather, these associations gave publicity to the *idea* of *régénération* and promoted cohesion throughout the respective *départements*. From every indication it is clear that the community continued to serve as the framework for meeting the demands of emancipation. Regeneration was conducted as a community venture, frequently bringing together various sectors of the population: the Central Consistory, local consistory leaders, rabbis, affluent patrons, indigent recipients of social welfare, and those individuals who received training in vocational schools and in apprenticeships. Participation in, or contributions to, various associations promoting regeneration was the basis for social status. For example, fulfillment of communal obligations was a condition for membership in the *Comité d'administration de la culte israélite* of Strasbourg. In one instance the election of a member was invalidated for failure to subscribe to the *Société d'encouragement pour le travail,* the local school, and the begging fund.[67] Finally, and not least importantly, involvement in the various *sociétés* served an essential function for the elite who found expression for an attenuated Jewish identity in the concept of noblesse oblige.[68]

Undaunted by the limited success of these ventures, communal leaders viewed occupational restructuring as the key to modernization. One enthusiast of vocational training referred to manual labor as the *émancipation industrielle* of Jewish youth, a transformation that must complement civil and political emancipation.[69] According to the President of the Metz *société*, I. Berr, the significance of occupational training extended well beyond the economic sphere:

> If it were a matter of demonstrating that among the Jews are also found elite spirits, [some of whom are] qualified for the highest intellectual destinations, the process would have been achieved a long time ago; the first years of emancipation, even the times of inequality and separation offered [examples of] remarkable intelligence; but to view the question in this way is to view it in a narrow and sterile manner; the adoption into society of a few men of the elite leaving our ranks . . . is a matter of little importance; what must be obtained for the welfare and dignity of the Jewish population is assimilation, the complete *fusion* of this population into the bosom of the population of the country; what must be combatted energetically are the customs which make the proletariat Jews a class apart, among their fellow citizens and their peers, rendering them foreign to their works and their mores, weakening their physical and moral energy, and thus exposing them to these repulsions, blind [and] iniquitous without doubt, but explicable nevertheless, to a certain point; for a long time one has been mistaken on the causes which have cut so deep a separation, and whose last traces are often so difficult to remove.[70]

By the early 1840s a broad consensus concerning the importance of economic transformation had emerged. The consistorial leadership, members of liberal professions, rabbis, and teachers all lent their support to the various public and private initiatives. But the ultimate objective of these regenerative efforts still was not agreed upon. Many undoubtedly considered vocational training vital both to the economic and social stability of the Jewish community as well as to the moral integrity of the Jews. Others, such as I. Berr, viewed economic transformation as having broader implications: it was the first element in a grand plan aiming to bring an end to the social and cultural isolation of the Jews. As shall be seen later, defining the limits of *régénération* would constitute a major preoccupation of the Franco-Jewish leadership.

5

The Flight from
Traditional Identity

FOR THE VAST MAJORITY of Jews living in early nineteenth-century France, emancipation produced few visible signs of change. Only in the urban centers—and especially in Paris—were Jews confronted by the full attraction of French culture. Invariably, they were compelled to reassess the importance traditionally placed on the Jewish social and religious heritage. Whether traditional ties were successfully preserved or overcome by competing claims on individual loyalties, every Jew living in an urban setting was forced to come to terms with a myriad of social and intellectual challenges to his or her Jewishness. The Jews encountered a society that at once demanded of them full integration but displayed much ambivalence over their joining its ranks. Not surprisingly, this encounter with French society and culture would lend itself to a variety of novel interpretations. In many instances the pressures of professional and social advancement led them to indifference, while others resolved the Jewish question for themselves by looking beyond the universe of Judaism and the Jewish community. Still others would conclude that reforming the religion would improve the overall prospects of Jewish social integration.

New manifestations of Jewish identity were directly related to the dynamics of social integration. Despite differences over terminology and semantics, sociologists agree on two fairly distinct phases of interaction between a minority and the host society. In the first phase, the minority adopts the culture of the host society, including its memories, sentiments, and attitudes. Because the process is limited to cultural behavior, it will be referred to as *acculturation*. In the second and more advanced phase, the full adoption of the dominant culture occurs through *social* interaction at the primary group level. This second phase, referred to as *assimilation*, normally leads to the attenuation of loyalties to the former culture and ultimately, to the disappearance of group identity.[1] It is important to note that the success of assimilation will depend not only on the willingness of the minority to adapt, but also on the reception it encounters in the dominant society. Prejudice and discrimination normally impede assimilation, although acculturation may still take place; in some cases prejudice will promote cohesion among members of the minority group. Finally, since assimilation is itself composed of several stages, over the course of time, the minority group may be affected by events that will intensify the desire either to assimilate or to remain apart.[2]

The leadership of nineteenth-century French Jewry consciously endorsed acculturation quite unapologetically. Ranging from the staunchly orthodox to the nonobservant, most Jews did not see any contradiction between the adoption of French culture and the preservation of Jewish identity. Indeed, Judaism and French culture were regarded as complementary. Yet for some there appeared the need to reject Judaism if the goal of full social integration could not be attained. As we shall see, those who aspired to full integration failed to realize their dream, as long as they remained Jews. Throughout most of the century, the vast majority of Jews, although acculturated, did not merge with the French population and were not assimilated.

Acculturation occurred most rapidly in Paris. From a mere five hundred on the eve of the Revolution, the Jewish population in the capital increased to seven thousand nearly thirty years later. By mid-nineteenth century, Paris would be the dominant center of urban Jewish culture. The growing number of young Jews from the south and the northeast found widening professional opportunities and a more liberal atmosphere in this city than in their places of origin, both with respect to Christian attitudes toward Jews and the relations among the Jews themselves. Although most of the newcomers had received a traditional Jewish education in their youth, the acquisition of French culture represented their principal intellectual and spiritual experience. At first rather timidly, "enlightened" parents began sending their children to the public high schools. Among those who attended the *lycée* Charlemagne, for example, were Elie Halévy's sons, Léon and Fromenthal, Isaac Rodrigues-Henriques' son Olinde, Michel Berr's son Isaac, and future Jewish leaders Adolphe Crémieux and Adolphe Franck. The *école polytechnique* also attracted numerous Jewish students, many of whom would enter the military or French public life.[3] According to a contemporary observer in Paris after the turn of the century, one could find Jewish homes that were not at all Jewish in character and a noticeable tendency to entrust the education of Jewish children to non-Jews.[4] As the director of the Paris police observed in 1806, the process of acculturation occurred with great rapidity: "Since the bestowal of civil rights to the Jews by the Revolution, their values have come very close to those of the other classes in society. As they are less attached to their religious activities, they acquire for themselves the same freedom of thought as other Frenchmen. They have sensed the wealth which the *patrie* has granted them, and their devotion to it has loosened the ties to their primitive society."[5] In terms of lifestyle the emerging Jewish bourgeoisie in Paris was rapidly becoming almost indistinguishable from its Christian counterpart. A penchant for luxury was visible in the types of Jewish homes, food, and dress. Those who worked in the textile industry, in banking, or in the liberal professions had little difficulty, in the early years of the century, integrating in general social circles. Upward social mobility, a major concern for the general urban population, was no less so for the Jews.[6]

Nevertheless, the acculturation of Parisian Jews must not be confused with assimilation. For several reasons the process of social integration was extraordinarily complex and problematic. In part this was due to the fact that even the upwardly mobile could not easily abandon their Jewish identity. They remained united by the challenges and problems facing a generation that had only recently experienced emancipation from "slavery to freedom." Moreover, many Jews who looked optimistically upon the prospects of social integration found that French society did not anxiously embrace them. They were frequently reminded of their ethnic origins by the precarious political situation in postrevolutionary France and by ever-present traces of anti-Jewish prejudice. In fact, memoire literature and the contemporary press attest to the pariah status of the Jews in a society that still imputed to them social separatist tendencies. With the restoration of the Bourbon monarchy came a return of Catholic traditions and a resumption of anti-Jewish restrictions and theology. Under the Restoration the Jews lost many of the rights that the Revolution had bestowed upon them. Jews were expelled from the universities and barred from the liberal professions. Drawing the logical social conclusions from an exclusivist religious philosophy, De Maitre, De Bonald, and Chateaubriand articulated an ideology of social isolation—not integration—that came to characterize the experience of many young Jews in Paris and other large cities. Those who endeavored to assimilate despite the public depreciation of the Jewish religion found that the society to which they had aspired was still Christian in character. Although the state had become a secular institution, it had appropriated religious symbols of Christianity in order to invest the aims of the state with religious dignity.[7] And thus, although this generation of Jews had increasingly identified with their French neighbors and with their new *patrie,* most were still outcasts in Catholic France. Despite the growing similarity in education and life-style, the religious chasm separating Jews and gentiles remained unbridged.

Despite these setbacks, the new generation of emancipated Jews remained, for the most part, optimistic. They viewed the French Revolution as having created a new world and sensed that theirs was an era of transition. At the base of this conception was the belief that the Revolution had put an end to Jewish homelessness and exile, and that now it was their responsibility to prove, as French citizens, that they were worthy of the trust placed in them. Concerned that Jewish rituals would continue to obstruct the entrance of Jews into French society, a number of young Parisians called for religious reform. The Jewish problem for them was no longer narrowly defined by the performance of civic duties but by the larger question of social integration. Léon Halévy, son of French *maskil* Elie Halévy, asserted that Jewish ritual was "too Asiatic for the nations of Europe" and that decisive changes were essential. He stressed that the language of public prayer ought to be French, inasmuch as Hebrew "estranges most of the Jews who have received French education; at the same time, it continues its vain tradition of a connection to the Holy Land." Religious reforms were envisioned as the most effective means "to bring to fruition the complete and definitive *fusion* of these men of the Mosaic faith with the French people."[8] *Fusion,* a term introduced mainly by gentile discussants of the Jewish question during the Restoration, denoted extensive social assimilation. Despite the enthusiasm of the young would-be reformers, their struggle found neither an organized forum nor a vehicle of literary expression within the Jewish community. In time most lost faith in the efficacy of reform. A growing disillusionment with traditional Judaism left many Parisian Jews in the throes of profound spiritual crisis. Some became indifferent to Jewish concerns, and an increasing number married Christians.[9]

Théodore Ratisbonne epitomizes the disillusionment which had overcome many of the younger generation. As secretary of the *Sociéte d'encouragement au travail en faveur des israélites due Bas-Rhin,* Ratisbonne obviously shared the Strasbourg leadership's commitment to vocational training. His ultimate goal, though, may have been considerably more ambitious. In a *mémoire* published shortly after the 1824 Strasbourg essay contest, Ratisbonne had advanced recommendations for reform that aimed at realizing the vision of a *"fusion sociale"* long demanded by "the friends of humanity."[10] We can only wonder whether it was profound disappointment and discouragement with the prospects of ever realizing this goal which led him and fellow *Société* activist Isidore Goschler, to undergo baptism. Perhaps he had concluded, as did others, that only through conversion to Christianity could the Jewish people expect to achieve a lasting fusion. Indeed, for Ratisbonne's cousin, Cerfberr de Medelsheim, himself a convert to Catholicism, religious reform was a futile exercise because it failed to address the essential incompatibility of Judaism with the mores of French citizenship. Conversion to Catholicism was, in his estimation, the only real solution to the Jewish problem.[11]

Although there are no reliable statistics on the number of Jewish conversions to Christianity in early nineteenth-century France, the few individuals whose identities are known provide important evidence of the tensions felt by the first generation of emancipated Jews. Conversion, in most cases, was not a sudden change of heart nor a callous decision by individuals with nothing to lose. Rather, it was more likely the result of a long arduous process of unsuccessful social integration coupled with growing alienation from the Jewish tradition. And it usually occurred at the cost of significant, often untold, personal suffering. Théodore and Alphonse Ratisbonne, sons of Strasbourg Consistory leader Auguste Ratisbonne, were among the most celebrated Jewish apostates of the nineteenth century. Théodore, a student of Louis Bautain, professor of philosophy at the University of Strasbourg, was drawn to Christianity and finally converted to Catholicism in 1827. Together with two other Jewish students of Bautain, Goschler and Jules Lewel, Théodore entered a seminary and became a priest. From that point on he devoted his life to the conversion of his former coreligionists. Alphonse, the youngest of Ratisbonne's nine sons, adroitly rejected his brother's conversionist approaches for some years. However, after claiming to have had a vision of the Virgin Mary in the Church of San Andrea in Rome in 1842, he himself converted to Catholicism and joined the Jesuit order. In Paris in 1843 he founded, together with Théodore, the *Notre Dame de Sion*, a convent school devoted to missionary activity.[12] Lévy Gumpel, a native of Mutzig (Bas-Rhin) who was brought to Paris at a young age, converted to Christianity in 1826. By profession a military physician, he became a devout Catholic, changed his name to Ignace Xavier-Morel, and was involved in missionary activity. Morel's close association with David Drach, the converted rabbi, was undoubtedly a decisive factor in his decision to abandon Judaism; in fact it was Drach who actually converted his friend.[13]

The conversion of David Drach illustrates that even those who remained in traditionalist circles were not protected from the incursions on Jewish identity in early nineteenth century France. Born in Strasbourg in 1791, Drach was the son of a rabbi known for his Hebraic and Talmudic learning. Trained at the Alsatian yeshivot of Ettendorf, Bischeim, and Westhoffen, and at the feet of leading French Talmudists, young David gained a reputation throughout Alsace. Two years after receiving rabbinic ordination in 1809, he came to Paris to pursue secular studies. Drach reported that as a private teacher in Paris he had the opportunity to meet several Catholics on a social basis and to discuss matters of religion with them. Impressed by their piety, he became enthralled with Christianity. He began to read the Church Fathers, devoted time to the study of Greek and Latin, and engaged in an ambitious project to "reconstruct" the Hebrew text of the Bible based on the *Septuagint*. He subsequently graduated from the *Université royale* with the degree of Doctor of Law, and taught classical languages at the *Institut des nations étrangères*. In 1818 Drach married a daughter of Central Consistory Grand Rabbi Emmanuel Deutz and was appointed first director of the Jewish primary school in Paris. A logical choice for the position, the young scholar undoubtedly had a bright future and was aware that the post of chief rabbi might one day be within his grasp. The entire French Jewish community was therefore shocked when in 1823 Drach converted to Roman Catholicism, together with his three young children, and subsequently became an *abbé*. While many Jews were convinced that Drach was motivated by his aspiration to the Chair of Oriental languages at the Sorbonne, a position he later occupied, Drach vehemently denied the insinuation of insincerity. He insisted that since the age of seventeen he had been interested in Christianity and that his scholarly research led him to an appreciation of its truth. After regaining control over his three children, who had been taken to London by their mother, Drach wrote several works to justify his conversion and persuade his former coreligionists of the supremacy of Catholicism. In addition to converting his own children and his friend Morel, he was probably instrumental in the conversion of his brother-in-law, Simon Deutz, son of the grand rabbi, and Jacob Libermann (abbé Francis Libermann), son of the rabbi of Saverne.[14]

Although it would be unfair to question the sincerity of converts such as Morel, Drach, and the Ratisbonnes, we may still scrutinize the motivations that may have led them to sever their bonds with the Jewish people and religion. Most conversions in Western Europe were motivated by an irresistable desire to partake of European culture. In the case of Germany and Austria, for instance, as long as the Jews were denied the status of citizenship, baptism served, in Heinrich Heine's words, as an indispensable "ticket of admission." One would assume that in France, where Jews had achieved citizenship without a prolonged struggle, conversion to Christianity would have been unnecessary and therefore virtually unknown. The incidence of conversion, then, especially as it denotes *genuine* conversion, suggests that the relationship between emancipation and integration in France was more complex than was anticipated. The fact that the Jews were invited to join a society that was not religiously neutral, but Christian, exerted a powerful influence on Jewish identity.

The Saint-Simonian movement, though numerically small and of rather questionable significance for French intellectual history, also sheds valuable light on the crisis of Jewish identity in the early nineteenth century. Its founder Claude Henri Saint-Simon (1760–1825) interpreted history as an orderly progression culminating in an industrial society ruled by a scientific elite on the basis of division of labor. Instead of regarding religion as an enemy of science, Saint-Simon came to view it as the essence and philosophy of science; and in his scheme for a new industrial society, he gave religion a prominent role. His "religion of science," or physicism, could dispense with the idea of God, since its main function was to serve as a political instrument for social control. Critical of all forms of revealed religion, Saint-Simon regarded physicism as a synthesis of existing faiths. Toward the end of his life, however, Saint-Simon revised his views. Though remaining a resolute critic of the Catholic Church, he proclaimed his system as the only true Christianity. Saint-Simon's "New Christianity" bore a remarkable similarity to Deism, particularly in its claim that the essence of Christianity was its moral content. His contribution was in emphasizing that the amelioration of the lot of the poor was the main concern of religion and that elusive social reform was within reach if carried out by the industrialists and scientists.[15]

The involvement of several Jewish intellectuals in Saint-Simonism is at once fascinating and instructive. The movement included a disproportionate number of Jewish members; in fact opponents, hoping to discredit it, branded it a "Jewish" movement. Of the approximately one dozen Jews who rose to positions of leadership in the movement, virtually all were members of prominent families. The Rodrigues brothers, Benjamin Olinde and Eugène, their cousins, Emile and Isaac Péreire, and Léon Halévy, for example, were sons of Paris banking families and communal leaders. Saint-Simon regarded these men as his closest associates, and they considered themselves his most authentic disciples. Why were these young men, who were part of a generation that anxiously sought to integrate fully within French society, drawn to a cult that remained strikingly marginal? Logically, one would have expected them to join mainstream organizations. The answer may be found in the ideological and social realms. First, its attraction lay in its utopian ideals and in its deep concern for the issues of the day. Its universalism appealed to a generation of Jews that strove to transcend the parochialism and provincialism of their religion and community. Parisian Judaism simply failed to satisfy their spiritual yearnings. Second, they were outcasts in Catholic France of the Restoration, excluded from many of the civic rights that the Revolution had bestowed upon them. Thus beset by a profound spiritual crisis and the dismal prospects of remaining socially detached, they found in Saint-Simonism an answer to their needs. For these men who had lost their sense of belonging, the movement acted as a framework of primary association that did not make distinctions concerning the religio-ethnic or class origins of its members. And despite the increasing emphasis that Saint-Simonism placed on Christianity, the Jewish members considered the Christian coloration to be of little consequence. Paradoxically, most Jewish Saint-Simonians maintained an identity as Jews; in part, this was fuelled by the growing tensions accompanying discussions within the movement over the place of Judaism in the envisioned new order.[16]

A different response to social and intellectual pressures in the capital came from individuals who sought to arrest the erosion of Jewish identity, even though they themselves manifested some of Paris' deleterious effects. Convinced that modernization was the key to preserving Jewish identity, S. Mayer Dalmbert, Théodore Cerfberr, and Olry Terquem, former students at the *école polytechnique,* demanded that greater emphasis be placed on primary religious instruction and greater attention be paid to occupational training and diversification. Apprenticeships in *arts et métiers* were proposed and, in some instances, created by such men, while agriculture, manufacturing, and the liberal professions were heralded as areas of occupation that would be of greatest benefit. It was also felt that the creation of a modern rabbinical facility was crucial to the entire regeneration program. Intended as a normal school of Jewish theology, the Paris-based institution would provide systematic enlightened training to synagogue rabbis and primary school teachers for communities throughout France.[17] Although this and other proposals were well ahead of their time, nearly all of the early Paris initiatives would eventually become realized in one way or another.

For some Parisian Jews, reform of the Jewish religion would remove obstacles hindering modernization and social integration. Although criticism of traditional Judaism had been occasionally expressed in the earlier years of the Restoration, the first French Jew to address the question of religious reform in a systematic manner was Olry Terquem (1782–1862). He was almost solely responsible for bringing the issues of religious reform to the attention of the public. Terquem was a native of Metz, where he received a Talmudic education and then pursued secular studies at the *école centrale*. Here in Metz Terquem became associated with Moses Ensheim, the French *maskil,* first as a student and later as a friend. Ensheim had been employed as a private tutor of mathematics and probably assisted the young Terquem in preparing for his *école polytechnique* entrance examination. Terquem attended the school for three years, after which he occupied the chair in theoretical mathematics at the *lycée* in French-occupied Mayence until 1814. He then moved to Paris where he became librarian at the *Dépôt d'Artillérie,* a position he held until his death. His position on the faculty of the *école centrale rabbinique* as a teacher of elementary sciences is certainly interesting in light of his radical leanings and the institution's reputation as a mainstream religious institution. A frequent contributor to Franco-Jewish journals and the general press, Terquem was best known for his *Lettres Tsarphatiques,* written under the pseudonym Tsarphati, (Hebrew for "Frenchman").[18] The adoption of this pseudonym no doubt was intended to stress the symbiosis of Jewishness and Frenchness. The *Lettres Tsarphatiques,* a series of twenty-seven pamphlets and letters published over a period of twenty years, brazenly advocated radical changes in Jewish religious life. Terquem was in many respects a man of the Enlightenment: his reverence for the *philosophes* and their world view is evident throughout his writings. He adopted many of the criticisms levelled against the Jews during the Age of Reason and endeavored to convince the Jewish establishment of the validity of these claims. Although Terquem's efforts had yielded few concrete results by 1841, when he withdrew from the arena of religious controversy, there can be little doubt that his writings set the ideological stage for subsequent reforms.[19]

The first of the *Lettres Tsarphatiques* appeared in 1821. Owing to their sensational style, undoubtedly intended to stimulate controversy, and the fact that they were written over the course of two decades, the *Lettres Tsarphatiques* did not offer a cogent philosophy for religious reform. However, it is clear that the assemblage of criticisms, proposals for reform, and outright attacks on Judaism all had a single goal: to accelerate the entrance of Jews into the mainstream of French society. Terquem insisted that the Jewish tradition must not be permitted to stand in the way of what he referred to as *fusion.* Throughout his writings, Terquem revealed his appropriation of the widely held gentile view that traditional Jewish identity had run its course and could no longer function in the modern state.

Central to Terquem's thinking was the conception of *civilisation* that had evolved earlier in the century. He contended, as did other French thinkers, that the *Dictionnaire de l'Académie*'s definition equating civilization with refinement of *moeurs* was outdated, and although refinement, or *civilité*, was certainly a result of civilization, it could not be taken as its essential feature. Rather, *civilisation* was comprised of two principal elements, intellectual spirit and social development, that were inextricably linked together. A civilization, Terquem argued, must be judged not only by its intellectual achievements, but by the extent to which the weak receive support and the oppressed find protection in a particular social order.[20] This definition would enable Terquem to subject the entirety of Jewish civilization—that is, its religious legislation and social institutions—to a thoroughgoing reevaluation.

Iconoclastic in his approach, Terquem challenged the accepted sources of authority of the Jewish religion by subjecting Mosaic and Talmudic law to a reexamination based on contemporary notions of civilization, spirituality, and justice. He hoped that this investigation would encourage a reappraisal of Judaism's role in the nineteenth century and, in turn, provide justification for certain essential ritual reforms. Citing a barrage of historical, legal, and political evidence, Terquem concluded that Judaism was an imperfect religious and social system. As we shall see, many *régénérateurs* would come to the same conclusion. It was their contention, however, that rabbinic Judaism (i.e., the Talmud) had corrupted the former purity and simplicity of Mosaism. Terquem went one step further, challenging the assumption that Mosaic law should be immune from criticism. In his analysis of the early development of the religion, he did, to be sure, praise Moses for having taken the idea of one God as the starting point for his legislation. For this, Terquem wrote, contemporary civilization is eternally indebted. Nevertheless, Mosaism did not free itself entirely from pagan influences. In a description of the origins of Mosaic Law, Terquem's account bears remarkable similarity to Deist writings: "Born in Egypt and raised by priests of that country, he [Moses] borrowed from their *culte*, but rendered it *jéhoviste*. The Mosaic code, for the most part, is only an accommodation to grossly superstitious dispositions, to the idolatrous and astrological tendencies of the Hebrews."[21] The majority of religious, dietary, and political prescriptions contained in the Pentateuch, according to Terquem, were borrowed from Egypt, though not without some modifications. He reserved special contempt for the most troublesome example of appropriation, the creation of the priestly cult and caste.[22] In fact, the administration of the sacrificial order was clearly an embarrassment for this resolute critic of clericalism. Although he did not go so far as to conclude that the Jews were devoid of creative abilities, as did the Deists, he certainly minimized the originality of the Jewish religion.

Terquem sharpened his criticism of Mosaic law by comparing the status of women in the Pentateuch and in the New Testament. He asserted that Mosaic law conceived of women only as "instruments of propagation" and not as persons with religious and spiritual needs. There was no religious ceremony for them at birth corresponding to circumcision, and further, the birth of a daughter rendered the mother ritually unclean for a much longer period than the birth of a boy. In marriage women suffered the greatest indignity and inequality: they were acquired and regarded like property, much the same way as in the Orient. Moreover, the Torah permitted polygamy for men, but prohibited, upon pain of death, the same for women. Christianity, Terquem maintained, recognized these shortcomings and responded accordingly. The New Testament replaced circumcision with baptism and made it obligatory for both sexes. And monogamy, introduced to the world by Christianity, was "the basis of civil equality and, by constituting the rights of the woman, created a veritable European family." Claiming that "baptism and monogamy have been the principal *moteurs* of modern civilization," Terquem conceded that in this area Christianity had surpassed Judaism with its invaluable contribution to moral progress.[23]

In his attitude toward the Talmud Terquem displayed his ideological affinity to the *philosophes,* who blamed rabbinic literature for distorting the plain meaning of the Bible. Although he did not agree with their conclusion that Talmudic study was responsible for the moral degeneration of the Jewish people, he considered it unworthy of so much scholarly attention. He ridiculed the subject matter of the Talmud, especially those sections studied in the *école rabbinique,* by citing examples of passages that would be considered valueless for modern society.[24] Moreover, he asserted that the Talmud's dialectical argumentation and "barbaric" style were an intellectual embarrassment: "The ordinary effect of these clashes is to act upon the mind as liquid on the light, to refract it, to break what is right. Another danger, much graver . . . is that the rabbinic lucubrations have a tendency to soil, to stain . . . the virginal imagination of the students."[25] Making good use of hyperbole and satire, Terquem asked his readers how the *chambres* (of the government) could suport with the taxpayers' money an institution where such studies were pursued.[26]

Terquem's philosophical justification for reform relied on the Deists' distinction between *religion* and *culte.* The former was an immutable moral and spiritual essence; the latter represented the forms of external worship, subject to variable conditions such as climate, *moeurs*, and political status. According to the theory, when any one of these elements varies, the *culte* must undergo corresponding modification and adjustment. Claiming that he had no intention of tampering with the essence of the Jewish religion, Terquem directed his attention to those external manifestations that had already undergone substantial modification throughout the course of history.[27] His concern with the external forms of the *culte* reveals the widening gap between France of the eighteenth and nineteenth centuries. Unlike the Deists and the *philosophes*, Terquem acknowledged that the ethereal ideas of the spiritual world required concrete forms of expression. Although rituals such as prayer, festivals, and commemorative rites may have been nothing more than concessions to human frailty, they were, in his mind, essential to the ultimate purpose of religion: the perfection of moral man.[28] This view explains Terquem's near-obsession with ritual reform, an idea foreign to the Deists and the *philosophes*. In effect, Terquem went one step beyond the Enlightenment by applying its general philosophy of progress and the perfectibility of man to the domain of institutionalized religion. Central to his argument was the claim that the Jewish religion had failed to keep pace with political, social, and economic improvements brought on by the French Revolution. Judaism had somehow escaped the dominant influence of European civilization and remained unscathed in its *"accoutrement asiatique."*[29] Terquem bemoaned the fact that despite advances in the civil and political spheres, "we [Jews] are the most backward in the religious sphere, thanks to our present consistorial organization."[30] The time had come, he maintained, when ritual forms should be placed in harmony with contemporary demands of civilization and citizenship.

One prime target which he considered an affront to modern European society was the traditional practice of circumcision. Terquem's basic aversion to the "Asiatic" ritual, is illustrated by the following remarks:

> If I were to tell you that, in a certain country, there exists a population which attaches a religious importance to mutilating, to slashing, to lacerating the weak creatures as soon as they enter life, to submitting them to so painful an operation that sometimes death follows it . . . with no protest ever being raised in favor of the victims, if I let you guess the country, would not your ideas naturally point to an African country, inhabited by some savage race? Such is not the case. It concerns our *patrie*, France, and a notable segment of its inhabitants.[31]

Cases of syphilis, tuberculosis, and diptheria, occasionally resulting in death, were attributed to circumcision. The danger was ascribed to two aspects of the operation that had been added to the biblical ritual by the

Talmud: *peri'ah* (tearing of the edge of the mucous membrane with the thumbnail) and *meẓiẓah* (sucking the blood). Terquem demanded the elimination of these two practices and urged that *mohelim* be certified by a medical faculty. Anticipating religious opposition to his proposals, he recommended that the government be called upon to enforce these guidelines. Convinced that the conclusions of contemporary medical science far outweighed the narrow views of rabbinic Judaism. Terquem could envision the total eclipse of rabbinic Judaism because it so frequently conflicted with *civilisation*. In his words, "the authority of the Talmud ceases where the rights of humanity begin."[32]

In addition to *civilisation*, citizenship also imposed demands that would affect Jewish religious observance. Many of the arguments claiming incompatibility beween Judaism and civic duties that had dominated discussions of the Jewish question in the Revolutionary period occasionally resurfaced later on, serving as added justification for Terquem's reform proposals. The general thrust of these arguments was that the traditional observance of Judaism encroached upon one's ability to be a good citizen. Terquem accepted this as a fundamental truth and proposed that the main source of conflict, Jewish Sabbath observance, be modified.[33] He claimed that the restrictive Sabbath laws stood as an obstacle to the Jews' economic integration into French life by requiring them to be idle two days of the week. Based on his own interpretation of the Sanhedrin's decisions, Terquem argued that the assembly had provided religious dispensation to Jews entering various types of training (i.e., vocational and military) and occupations that might necessitate the violation of traditional religious restrictions. According to Terquem, observance of the Sabbath was, in any event, rapidly becoming a relic of the past, as evidenced by the large number of Jews in commercial businesses and administrative offices[34] (who, it is assumed, worked on Saturdays).

Terquem asserted that, because of mounting economic and social pressures, both the working and the educated classes of Jews found themselves excluded from public worhsip. He urged that the reality of nonobservance be acknowledged by allowing Jews whose occupations did not permit Saturday observance to celebrate the Sabbath on Sunday, the "national day of rest." An appeal to hold Jewish Sabbath services on Sunday, in French, was meant not to supplant the Saturday service but only to supplement it. Answering his critics, Terquem declared that it was not for him to secularize Saturday, since "this secularization is in operation without me." His avowed purpose was, rather, to salvage Sabbath observance, albeit in an unorthodox fashion, for the emancipated Jew.[35] One of the major points of justification used by Terquem in advocating the transfer of the Jewish Sabbath to Sunday was his concern for the material well-being of the Jewish working class. The Jewish "day of idleness," according to Terquem, when observed in addition to the French national day of rest, was responsible for the impoverishment of many Jews. But economic hardship was only the most immediate problem. More ominous was the relationship that he noticed between poverty and apostasy. Claiming that Christian biblical societies engaged in proselytism made their greatest inroads among Jewish indigents and beggars, Terquem warned that continued maintenance of traditional Sabbath restrictions would lead to the ultimate consequences desired by Christian missionaries: the end of the Jewish religion in any form.[36] However laudable his intentions, it is indeed difficult to imagine how the transfer of the Sabbath to Sunday could bring about such a major economic and religious transformation among Jews.

One ray of hope for Terquem was Article 63 of the 1844 *ordonnance*, stating that any head of family may, with the consent of the departmental consistory, obtain authorization to open an *oratoire* (chapel) at his own home and at his own expense.[37] Seeing in this provision a parallel to the Anglo-American practice, Terquem envisioned growth in non-Orthodox religious observances through a process of development and implementation at the individual, nonestablishment level. The provision would, according to Terquem, enable persons of similar religious views and economic station to establish private prayer assemblies; the form and content of the liturgy, as well as the day and time of meeting, would be in accordance with its particular views and needs. Terquem had correctly understood that the major obstacle to reform was structural. As long as authority was vested solely in official institutions, nothing but cosmetic changes would occur. Decentralization, he concluded, was the solution. Terquem therefore offered to contribute his time, money, and guidance toward the creation of such an *oratoire*, which he claimed could become, within fifty years, *the* premier temple of French Jewry.[38]

Finally, and no less importantly, Terquem believed that a fundamental reorientation of Jews toward their non-Jewish fellow citizens was essential for the successful realization of *fusion* and integration into French society. With social exclusiveness no longer possible or desirable, he advocated *rapprochement* with the Christian population, though several obstacles would have to be removed. For example, prayers such as *Kol Nidre*[39] and *Shefokh Hamatkha*[40] were regarded as offensive to non-Jews and generally representative of hateful, antisocial sentiments. Terquem therefore argued that these prayers, among others, should be expunged from the liturgy as a sign of Judaism's willingness to become a part of general humanity.

Despite the urgency of his proposals for reform, Terquem offered no indication of how he expected them to be implemented. He certainly invested very little trust in the established institutions of the Jewish community. The consistory he regarded as an utterly useless body, by nature incapable of attending to the needs of French Jewry. As justification of his demand for government regulation of circumcision, Terquem wrote: "One will respond to me that it is up to the Central Consistory to take initiative on these measures. But I do not want to occupy myself with this administration. It has sunk so low that it is impossible to speak of it in decent terms . . . I prefer to seek support in sacred publicity, since, thanks to your favorable dispositions, Mr. Editor, we can finally make our just grievances heard."[41] The consistorial system was, in the eyes of Terquem, an institution entirely unconcerned with change. But his criticism did not end here. He claimed that the consistories "embrace antisocial and separatist passions; they protect worm-eaten opinions, the superstitious practices of the ignorant, degenerate class, but they do notning for the enlightened, liberal, industrial class."[42] As it embodied all the old values of pre-Revolution days, the consistory was unmercifully identified with the forces of reaction.

Nearly two decades of relentless advocacy of religious reform had produced no discernible results. Certain of future success, Terquem nonetheless assured his supporters that there was no reason to be discouraged, since religious reform normally passes through three distinct phases of development: the period of education, the literary period, and the period of execution. He maintained that Jewish reform was still in its first phase, the period where individuals begin to abandon the opinions of the masses.[43] Terquem's optimism appears to have been misplaced. In most cases, those who fled traditional identity severed their bond with the Jewish community and could no longer be counted on to participate in discussions on reform. The work of regenerating the religion would be undertaken by a group who defined Jewish identity in altogether different terms. By the end of the 1830s Terquem had succeeded, at the very least, in bringing the issues of reform to the attention of the public, and in generating discussion within the leadership of the Jewish community.

It should be pointed out that new expressions of Jewish identity were, of course, not all the product of a calculated theory of assimilation. Many individuals were unconsciously swept away by the lure of French culture and the prevailing currents of social and political thought. Most prominent of all was the tendency to permit traditional religious mores to slowly fade into the background, while concentrating on professional and social priorities. In the process many became indifferent to Jewish interests; a smaller number, despite the abandonment of religious values, remained active in the Jewish community. The new type of Jew who combined a secular lifestyle with undeterred identification with his Jewish community, is best exemplified by Adolphe Crémieux (1796–1880). A native of Nîmes, Crémieux was a lawyer who frequently represented Jewish clients and, in the course of his statements, took pains to defend the Jewish people against accusations commonly hurled at them in the courtroom. Through several cases of the oath *more judaico* Crémieux became involved in and identified with Jewish causes. Rejecting the idea that an oath was a religious ceremony, he defended the right of Jews to be sworn in as other Frenchmen. He also was an ardent spokesman for the separation of religion and state. Crémieux's reputation in Nîmes would eventually bring him to Paris, where he was admitted to practice before the Court of Cassation (French Supreme Court) in 1830. In the same year he was appointed by the Marseille Consistory to represent it in the Central Consistory; he was subsequently elected vice-president (1834) and president (1843) of the central body. At the same time (1842) Crémieux became a leader of the opposition in the Chamber of Deputies. With the establishment of the Second Republic in February 1848, he and coreligionist Michel Goudchaux were appointed to the new cabinet, as ministers of Justice and Finance respectively. During these years Crémieux was regarded as the leading Jew of France. He was the official representative of French Jewry before the king, and he tirelessly sought royal support for Jews abroad (Switzerland, Russia, Germany, Poland, Morocco, and Damascus). In 1864 he was elected president of the *Alliance israélite universelle*. In internal matters Crémieux was regarded with similar respect: he was chairman of the consistorial committee appointed to revise the constitution of the consistory. If, in the case of Crémieux and others, Judaism lost its religious meaning, it may be that both religious and nonreligious elements in the tradition shaped this powerful, variant Jewish identity. For Jacob Katz this new, unprecedented form of commitment is proof that "the fact of Jewishness derived from one's being born a Jew."[44] Although this existential fact did not translate uniformly into a positive Jewish identity, Crémieux may certainly have been a harbinger of the new secular Jew, whose faith rested on values drawn from the Jewish tradition.

PART THREE

Tradition and Transformation

6

Le Mouvement Régénérateur

Pour nous, Français israélites du XIXᵉ siècle, notre
patrie c'est la France; notre noblesse politique, c'est la
sublime révolution de '89.
—Archives israélites de France, 1843

TRANSFORMING THE JEWS into productive members of modern society was an idea whose development has been traced through two fairly
distinct phases. Initially, the process was associated with *régénération*, a
term introduced into the vocabulary of the Jewish question by Henri
Grégoire in 1785. By *régénération* Grégoire meant improvement, or
"civic betterment," as Christian Dohm put it. The goal was to permit the
Jews to recapture their humanity by freeing them of the various disabilities that had corrupted their physical, social, and religious behavior and
mentality. Clearly, society would need to assume much of the responsibility for what was wrong with the Jews; the Jews, for their part, would
need to cooperate both by abandoning those economic pursuits that
violated the public trust and by removing any obstacles posed by their
religion. In the final analysis, the principal objective of *régénération* was
to form worthy citizens of the state; toward this end, Jewish leaders
enthusiastically endorsed socio-economic modernization. Berr Isaac
Berr, among others, regarded it as inherent in the responsibilities of
citizenship, as was devotion to the *patrie*, the essential lesson that the
Jews as citizens needed to learn. Citizenship, according to Jewish leaders, did not appear to require religious reform, an idea still virtually
unknown in France.

From approximately 1806, the entrance of the Jews into modern
French society was viewed from a new perspective. Although doubts

were expressed by various political leaders concerning the ability of the Jews to fulfill their civic duties, citizenship was, willy nilly, an accomplished fact, and this was reconfirmed by the Assembly of Jewish Notables and the Paris Sanhedrin. Discussion subsequently shifted away from the question of the Jews' suitability for citizenship and toward the far less clear, but no less important, matter of what could be envisioned for the future of Jewish–gentile relations. Beginning with Napoleon, who may be regarded as a key transitional figure in redefining the Jewish question, the idea of assimilating the Jews into French society assumed a position of prominence in public discussions. Encouraging intermarriage was one avenue toward *fusion,* a term that came to describe, as far as gentile observers were concerned, the ultimate goal of emancipation: the incorporation of the Jews within the French nation as indistinguishable elements of a single harmonious entity. Throughout the first two decades of the nineteenth century gentile writers criticized the Jews for failing to avail themselves of the generous invitation offered to them. And in seeking to explain this failure, virtually all competitors in the 1824 Strasbourg essay contest concluded that the Jewish religion was the major obstacle to the *rapprochement* of the Jews with French society and civilization.

For Jewish intellectuals in Paris *fusion* came to describe the dream of social acceptance among the intellectual and affluent of the city. For a few like Terquem, the goal of *fusion* was to be pursued not by abandoning one's Jewish identity, but by first rethinking the fundamental ideas of Judaism, and then by shaping one's identity accordingly. Though undeniably radical in his religious views, Terquem did not advocate the disappearance of Jews qua Jews as other proposals would have it. Thus, he did not endorse intermarriage. Furthermore, he viewed the alienation of Jewish intellectuals in Paris as the symptom of a problem, not as behavior to be emulated, and therefore warned that unless changes were introduced, the situation would continue to deteriorate. Nevertheless, his views were clearly unacceptable to the vast majority of French Jews, and as we shall see, evoked considerable protest.

The middle of the 1830s witnessed a third attempt to examine the social and religious significance of emancipation. With the appearance of a new journal, *La Régénération* (Strasbourg, 1836–1837), new meaning was given to the term. It now came to represent the rebirth of the Jewish people; a rebirth not in the sense of a transformation into something new, but a restoration of the original essence that Judaism had lost. *Wiedergeburt,* the German title of the bilingual journal, encapsulated the new meaning assigned to *régénération.* Moreover, proponents of *ré-*

génération, the *régénérateurs*, rejected the goal of assimilation. Their objective was the preservation of a distinct Jewish identity; civil fusion, not social fusion, would be pursued.[1]

Efforts to redefine *régénération* at this time were linked to the conflation of several important political, legal, and social developments. Most important was the Revolution of July 1830, which inaugurated a period of greater openness and liberalism. A return to the values of 1789 and the reemergence of the democratic ideal were reflected in the establishment of a constitutional monarchy and the containment of the role of the Catholic Church in the political and social arena. With respect to the Jews there were unprecedented efforts to treat them as full-fledged citizens. The law of 8 February 1831 redressed the last major example of inequity by declaring that members of the Jewish clergy were civil servants and therefore eligible for state salaries. Beyond its obvious economic importance for communities that had been specially taxed in order to pay these salaries, the law of 1831 was significant for acknowledging Judaism on equal terms with Catholicism and Protestantism. Out of gratitude to the new regime, Samuel Cahen dedicated his French translation of the Bible to the new king, Louis-Philippe, and L. M. Lambert declared the law to be "the greatest act of justice in favor of the Jews since the destruction of the Second Temple." This new-found sense of security during the July Monarchy may explain the rediscovery of ties with Jews abroad. As we shall see, concern for the plight of Jews in Poland, Syria, and Switzerland were only the earliest indications of the Jews' group consciousness, which transcended the national borders of France.[2]

Improvements in the political and legal climate were accompanied by a development within the Jewish community that provided the ideas of *régénération* with a social and intellectual context. *Le mouvement régénérateur*,[3] as it came to be known, was composed of a generation of Jewish intellectuals who had just come of age in the 1830s. Members of this Jewish elite, in most cases one generation removed from preemancipation restrictions, were influenced largely by the ideas of Haskalah, Enlightenment, and French liberalism. Through their involvement in various institutions and activities, be they administrative, educational, or publicistic, they sought to accelerate the modernization of French Jewry. Born at the end of the eighteenth century or at the beginning of the nineteenth century in northeastern France, these men received a traditional Jewish education either in their native Alsace-Lorraine or, more often, in neighboring Germany. As opportunities opened, though slowly, for entrance into French secondary schools and universities, they obtained general secular education as well as specialized training in the liberal professions. This was accompanied by a fair measure of recognition in general society, as evidenced by their professional accomplishments and membership in respected associations. As this generation came of age and took advantage of the liberal climate of the 1830s and 1840s, many of its members gained entrée into the intellectual circles of France. These ardent students of French life and culture, largely through their scholarly pursuits, began to interact regularly with non-Jews and to collaborate in joint ventures. Invariably, this interaction led to their adoption of enlightened gentile values. When these Jewish intellectuals turned their attention to Jewish issues, their approach bore unmistakable traces of a "French" perspective. Armed with the latest tools of science, they subjected the whole of Jewish life to a thorough reevaluation and concluded that Jewish education, rabbinic training, and the synagogue were most in need of reform.

The *régénérateurs* started from the proposition that the condition of French Jewry was without precedent: the rights of citizenship were accompanied by the demands of a new age, never before experienced by earlier generations living under inequality and persecution. Citizenship implied obligations to the *patrie* and to fellow citizens, and these duties touched all facets of religious and socio-economic life. If the Jews of France were to become productive members of society, it was essential that Jewish education take these civic issues into account. But the *régénérateurs* saw an adjustment to emancipated civic life as only half the challenge. They were concerned that emancipation also signalled a tendency among many Jews to forsake the Jewish ritual observances of their fathers. A growing indifference to the life of tradition, expressed especially in decreasing synagogue attendance, was viewed as an ominous danger to the future of the Jewish people. And the unceasing efforts directed at Jews by Christian missionary groups, enhanced by several celebrated apostasies, constituted a threat both to the continued existence of the Jewish community and to the viability of the Jewish religion. These challenges led the *régénérateurs* to reassert a special destiny for the Jewish people in the unfolding of the history of humankind. As the following biographical sketches of leading *régénérateurs* will show, a collective *mentalité* was born out of their common background, orientation, and responsiveness to issues of grave concern.

Gerson-Lévy (1784–1864), a leading spokesman for moderate religious reform and a proponent of educational modernization, was educated at the *école centrale de la Moselle*. During the French occupation, he served as a teacher of French language and literature in Frankfurt am Main. It was in Germany that Gerson-Lévy met some of the leading Jewish intellectuals of the day, including Heinrich Heine, Isaak Jost,

131

Leopold Zunz, as well as fellow-Frenchman Samuel Cahen. Upon his return to France in 1814, Gerson-Lévy entered the bookselling business in Metz; there he became active in Jewish educational reform, intially by helping to establish one of the first primary schools for Jews in France and later as a school inspector. For thirty years he was attached to the *école centrale rabbinique*, both as professor of French language and literature, and as a member of the school's administrative commission. Gerson-Lévy was also extremely active in the general intellectual life of Metz. He was one of the founders of the *Société des amis des lettres, des sciences, et des arts,* later called the *Académie impériale de Metz,* and in addition, he was editor of the political journal *l'Indépendent* from 1830 to 1855.[4]

A close associate of Gerson-Lévy, though separated by considerable geographical distance, was Samuel Cahen (1796–1862). A Jewish educator, editor, and translator of the Bible, Cahen was born in Metz but was sent to Mayence to pursue rabbinical studies under Rabbi Hirtz Scheuer. At the same time, he studied modern languages and literatures. Upon his return to France Cahen turned his attention to education. In 1820 he wrote what would become the most widely used Jewish catechism in France, and in 1823 he became director of the Jewish consistorial school in Paris. Cahen held this position until 1840, when he became the first editor of the *Archives israélites de France.* As head of this important journal, which though devoted to moderate religious reform opened its pages to exponents of orthodox views, Cahen was in contact with every major figure of French Jewry. Moreover, both the journal and his own scholarly interests enabled him to remain associated with leading German Jewish scholars such as Leopold Zunz. A French translation of the Bible, together with critical notes, was his most important achievement in a life devoted to Jewish scholarship. Beyond his scholarly, educational, and communal activities within the Jewish orbit, Cahen was a respected member of French learned societies. Succeeding his father as editor of the *Archives israélites* was Isidore Cahen. Born in Paris in 1826, he was educated at the *école normale supérieure.* In 1849 Catholic pressure prevented him from assuming a newly appointed teaching position, and following this scandal, he devoted himself to journalism and to teaching at the *séminaire rabbinique.* He would emerge as a founder of the *Alliance israélite universelle.*[5]

Michel Berr (1780–1843) and Charles Oulif (1794–1867) were both prominent in the legal profession and used this prominence to advantage in furthering the interests of the Jewish community. Berr, who continued his father's (Berr Isaac Berr) concern for *régénération,* was the first Jew to practice law in France. As a boy he studied the

Hebrew and German languages with Benjamin (Louis) Wolf, who was recommended to Berr's father by Naphtali Herz Wessely. He received his formal education at the *école centrale* in Nancy and the University of Strasbourg, where he studied law. Berr was a deputy to the Assembly of Jewish Notables and secretary of the Sanhedrin. Later, he was employed by the French government in several official capacities, first as division chief in the Ministry of the Interior in Westphalia and then, upon his return to France in 1809, as head of the office of the prefecture of Meurtre. After returning to Paris in 1813, he devoted himself to literature, journalism, and translation. A member of many learned societies, Berr wrote often on issues of general political and social interest, contributed numerous essays in French journals on subjects of Jewish interest, and translated Hebrew poetry, including Wessely's *Shirei Tifferet,* into German and French. Two elementary school textbooks written by Berr reflect his deep interest in Jewish education. Charles Oulif was educated at the *lycée imperial* of Metz and later at the University of Strasbourg, where he became the first Jew to receive a law degree (December 1815). He subsequently was an officer in the National Guard and later a lawyer at the royal court in Metz. As as member of the *Société pour l'encouragement de l'instruction élémentaire dans le département de la Moselle,* Oulif used his influence to found the Jewish primary school in his native city. He also held a position on the faculty of the *école centrale rabbinique,* where he taught comparative law. In 1834 he accepted an invitation to the Chair of Law at the University of Brussels. After returning to France, Oulif was active in the *Société pour l'encouragement des arts et métiers,* and he later became vice-president of the board of trustees of the rabbinical seminary.[6]

Several of the *régénérateurs* were devoted almost exclusively to Jewish scholarship. Their reputations in academe and their expertise in their respective fields of Jewish studies enabled them to exert influence on Jewish affairs. One leading scholar, Adolphe Franck (1809–1893), studied Talmud under Rabbi Marchand Ennery before pursuing advanced studies in medicine and philosophy. In 1840 he became professor of philosophy at Charlemagne College in Paris, and later was professor of Greek and Latin philosophy at the *Collège de France.* He also held a high office in the Royal Library in the 1840s. In addition to numerous studies on topics of Jewish interest, Franck published the first critical work on Jewish mysticism, *La Kabbala ou Philosophie religieuse,* in 1843. Active in Jewish communal affairs, he was vice-president of the Central Consistory.[7]

Salomon Munk (1803–1867), France's most distinguished Jewish scholar, was a native of Glogau, Germany; he studied at the University of Berlin and at the University of Bonn, concentrating in Semitic and

Oriental languages. In 1828 Munk arrived in Paris and supported himself as a tutor of Alphonse and Gustave Rothschild, among others, until he was appointed cataloguer of Hebrew and Semitic manuscripts at the *Bibliothèque Nationale* in 1838. Despite having lost his eyesight, Munk remained undaunted in his academic and scholarly pursuits. In 1863 he succeeded Ernest Renan in the Chair of Hebrew at the *Collège de France*. Among his numerous contributions to *Wissenschaft des Judentums*, Munk's critical edition of the Arabic text of Maimonides' *Guide to the Perplexed*, with a French translation, was his most respected and celebrated work. In addition to his scholarly work, Munk served the Jewish public as educator and communal servant. He was crucially involved in the Crémieux-Montefiore efforts to resolve the Damascus Affair and also worked as secretary of the Central Consistory.[8] Munk's successor to the Chair of Hebrew, Joseph Derenbourg (1811–1895), was also a distinguished Arabist and scholar of antiquity. He maintained a keen interest in the education of Jewish youth, and was a member of the central committee of the *Alliance israélite universelle*, and later served as its vice-president.[9]

Though not of Munk's scholarly calibre, Albert Cohn (1814–1877) represented another outstanding blend of scholarship and public service. Born in Hungary and educated in Vienna, Cohn settled in Paris in 1836. He worked as a private instructor of Hebrew and Jewish history in the home of Baron James de Rothschild. From 1839 until his death Cohn served as almoner of the Rothschild's charities and in this capacity travelled extensively to Jewish communities in North Africa and the Near East. His numerous visits to the Holy Land accorded Jewish settlements there much-needed moral and financial support and led to the establishment of hospitals and schools. Cohn was also able to secure an improvement in the status of the Jews in the Ottoman Empire, and he assisted the Jews of Algeria in establishing a communal organization. These efforts abroad did not prevent Cohn from remaining deeply involved in Jewish philanthropy and education in France. He helped organize several charities, taught adult classes in Paris, and served without remuneration as professor of Arabic and biblical exegesis at the *séminaire israélite* for nearly two decades.[10]

United initially by common background, education, socio-economic status, and scholarly interests, these Jewish intellectuals were brought together by their collective self-image and shared commitment to the regeneration of Jewish life. They viewed themselves both as heirs to the legacy of the Berlin Haskalah and as the authentic interpreters of the ideology of emancipation.[11] This entitled them to assume a leading role in the French Jewish community. However, the most immediate impetus for the emergence of *le mouvement régénérateur* was the awareness of growing disaffection among urbanized Jews. The *régénérateurs* traced the roots of this trend to the general low esteem accorded the Jews and their religion and the impact that it left on many members of the Jewish community. Ironically, the achievement of legal equality did not, as some had envisioned, fully eradicate prejudices concerning the Jewish religion. The claim that "Judaism is not fertile ground for genuine civilization" was among the most common allegations, implying that one should cease to be a Jew if one aspires to moral dignity and perfection.[12] Not infrequently, articles in the French press displayed an extremely critical, and often contemptuous, attitude toward Judaism and its adherents. In one instance a writer claimed, in *La Revue des Deux Mondes,* that the Jews were morally degenerate, and referred to them as a "parasitic plant with no roots in the soil." The people of Israel, he insisted, were sworn enemies of society: they "have become a sort of rejected Cain, marked in the front as the first murderer of the world . . . and condemned like him to eternal rejection. In killing the son of the carpenter, the apostle of love and liberty, the Jews have placed humanity and God Himself on the cross."[13] Another journal, *Le Courrier du Haut-Rhin,* included an article calling the Jews "the scourge of Alsace"; it maintained that the Jews "are isolated from the rest of society, their flawed faith is often their only means of success, they are outside the movement of civilization, and, in general, without instruction." One Jewish observer added that it was common for Jews to be addressed in the familiar *tu* form. In his estimation the form was used in a condescending manner, confirming his suspicion that the Jews were still viewed as eternally foreign to social virtues and devoid of human dignity.[14]

Although such forms of derision were clearly drawn from a long legacy of anti-Jewish prejudice, they owed their continued fervor partly to the resurgence of Catholicism, dating from the time of the Restoration. Félicité de Lamennais, for example, a liberal Catholic theologian, repeated the traditional church doctrine concerning the spiritual blindness of the Jews.[15] The Jews' failure to recognize Jesus as their savior had brought upon them a fall from divine grace, as evidenced by their history of dispersion and persecution. For theologians such as Lamennais, these facts proved the alien nature of the Jews and the inadequacy of their religious teachings. Furthermore, the accusation that the Jews were guilty of deicide isolated them from the rest of humanity: to have been capable of committing such a heinous crime meant that they were, by nature, capable of any other horror. These theological-moral arguments also found expression in various art forms of the period. The legend of the Wandering Jew, for example, became popular in France at the turn of the nineteenth century and was subsequently popularized in the ballet *Ahasvérus* (1833) by Edgar Quinet and in the novel *Juif érrant* (1844–1845) by Eugène Sue.[16] Other authors such as Victor Hugo, Lamartine, Alfred de Musset, Henri de Balzac, and Alfred de Vigny gave literary expression to the dominant anti-Jewish myths.[17] Whatever the medium, the theological condemnation of the Jews, according to Jacob Katz, "prepared the ground for his moral defamation."[18]

Emanating from a variety of intellectual, religious, and popular sources, condemnation of the Jewish religion bore much of the responsibility for the slow pace of Jewish integration into French society. Only a small number of Jews distinguished themselves in French intellectual life and in service to the state before the 1840s. As is often the case for minorities, the perceived lack of progress, in turn, lent additional support to the popular, stereotypic image. The most serious effect of the conflation of these factors was that many of the Jews who succeeded in acquiring some general education reached similar conclusions about their own religious-cultural heritage. Many had come to believe that Jewish society and its institutions could neither serve as an adequate framework for the full development of their talents and moral dispositions, nor provide the resources necessary for the advancement of their professional careers. Among many educated and upwardly mobile Jews, a growing indifference toward religion became discernible; Jewishness came to be regarded as a liability. Consequently, those few who succeeded in penetrating "the sanctuary of science" did so while dissociating themselves from conspicuous Jewish behavior and characteristics. With unprecedented acceptance and recognition in general society, many of these Jews came to the realization that it was unnecessary to maintain an affiliation with the Jewish community and found that working for the benefit of their coreligionists had become a parochial, potentially embarrassing undertaking.[19] For still others, anti-Jewish criticism and prejudice inspired an increasingly stubborn resistance to *la voix du siècle* and to any innovation whatsoever.

The erosion of religious faith and ethnic identity among Jewish intellectuals represented a problem of enormous proportions and implications, both in its own right and in terms of its impact on the Jewish community. The betrayal of Jewish loyalties communicated to those who still identified themselves as Jews the unmistakable message that Judaism lacked relevance in the modern world and that it might even pose an insurmountable obstacle to social integration and professional advancement. In this respect alone the desertion of intellectuals represented a dangerous pattern of behavior and thinking. Beyond this, according to Simon Bloch, editor of *La Régénération*, it threatened the viability of the entire program of regeneration by depriving the community of its most talented resources.

> If the Jews have obtained the same insights as other Frenchmen and have ardently contributed to the public prosperity, this advantage has turned to the detriment of their *culte;* because in laying down the tribute on the altar of the *patrie commune,* they ceased to work for the amelioration of their coreligionists, and feeling too enclosed in the narrow circle of their nation in order to direct its energies to it, they have preferred to spread them out in a wider sphere . . . where they have obtained greater recognition and more consideration than among their coreligionists.[20]

Those Jews who had acquired higher education, sophistication, and professional success could serve as much-needed role models for their less fortunate coreligionists. Moreover, by remaining within the fold, they could make valuable contributions to the advancement of religious regeneration.

The *régénérateurs* were aware of the difficulties of reinvolving disaffected Jews. The argument heard most often was that the first obligation of the citizen was to employ his intelligence in the service of the state and society at large. Bloch challenged the idea that this represented a more significant contribution to the *patrie* than working on behalf of one's own community: "This is an error which reveals a sentiment of pride and egoism; . . . doesn't the learned Jew contribute to the state when he works zealously to spread his knowledge among the 130,000 [*sic*] Jews who are in France, and to contribute of all his power to raise them to the level which they must occupy in society?"[21] Bloch maintained that to assist in the modernization of fellow French Jews was to contribute to the same sacred work of perfecting humanity, albeit on a more limited scale.[22]

It is highly unlikely that Bloch and his fellow *régénérateurs* expected rhetoric alone to lead estranged Jews back to the community. However, it was possible, in their opinion, to arrest or at least retard the process of alienation by addressing some of the issues raised by the confrontation between Judaism and modernity. Fundamental to their thinking was the assumption that with an improved public image Judaism would become more attractive to the modern, sophisticated French Jew. Toward this end, the *régénérateurs* embarked upon various activities intended to modernize their religion in the following areas: the aesthetics of synagogue prayer, the harmonization of religion with the exigencies of citizenship, and the articulation of the validity of Judaism in intellectually intelligible and morally defensible terms.

In setting out their plan of action, the *régénérateurs* rejected Olry Terquem's diagnosis of the problems facing the Jews as well as his proposed solutions. Terquem's inflammatory style, his anti-consistory position, and the intemperance of his proposals for reform evoked strong denunciation and dissociation by Jewish writers. In responding to the *Lettres Tsarphatiques*, Terquem's critics embarked on an important step in the crystallization of the ideology of *régénération*. Ironically, Terquem's writings encouraged moderates to explore the meaning of emancipation and to define the objectives of their own movement. Responses to the early *Lettres Tsarphatiques* branded the documents as "scandalous," "incendiary," and "divisive." Michel Berr, for one, claimed that Terquem's purpose was to erase an "essential and radical demarcation which must exist between Judaism and Christianity."[23] Later reactions were no less vehement in their criticism. Albert Cohn stated that Terquem's rationale for transferring the Sabbath to Sunday was dangerous. Cohn disputed the idea that Sunday was the "national day of rest." Sunday, he insisted, was consecrated not by France but by Christianity, and therefore, the day had no national significance. Observing the Sabbath on Sunday would only bring Judaism a step closer to Christianity, not to the *patrie*. At the same time, it would represent an explicit denial of the historic validity of Mosaism.[24] Salomon Munk argued that the abolition of the Jewish Sabbath would spell the end of the Jewish religion. Terquem's proposal was, according to Munk, characteristic of the rational Deism that the author wished to substitute for Judaism. Such a philosophy could never suit the Jewish community as a whole nor, for that matter, any society.[25] Samuel Cahen attacked Terquem for ridiculing Jews and Judaism in public instead of bringing his proposals directly to the attention of the Central Consistory or other Jewish leaders. The *Lettres Tsarphatiques*, he maintained, were "dangerous and useless."[26]

It is significant, though not surprising, that Terquem's three major critics (Cohn, Munk, and Cahen) became leaders of the *régénérateur* movement. In fact, the three had cooperated once before in an attempt to modernize religious worship.[27] The appearance of the *Lettres Tsarphatiques* offered an opportunity for these *régénérateurs* to begin articulating their positions on religious reform. In the case of each of the three respondents, sharp criticism of Terquem's radical proposals was accompanied by the acknowledgement that certain changes were absolutely essential. In other words, though they disagreed with Terquem's style and methods, the *régénérateurs* did not dismiss the theoretical soundness of reform; rather, they contrasted the impracticality and dangerous implications in Terquem's system to their own alternative ideas of moderate, well-reasoned change. They regarded the amelioration of Jewish practices as a process that would lend strength to the foundations of the religion and faith. In contradistinction to Terquem, they contended that changes could be achieved through cooperation with traditional Jewish institutions and thus envisioned significant roles for the Central Consistory and for the rabbinate.[28] There can be no denying, however, that Terquem's ideas influenced the path taken by more moderate *régénérateurs*. His proposals for regulation of circumcision, liturgical reform, alternatives to traditional worship, improvement of rabbinic training, and decentralization found expression, albeit in a limited manner, in the writings and activities of moderate *régénérateurs*.

The primary contention of proponents of reform was that the meaning and function of the Jewish religion were no longer easily discernible. Many Jews and non-Jews attributed this obfuscation to a general emptiness and inadequacy in Judaism's religious teachings. However, in contrast with the *fusionist* position of Terquem, the *régénérateurs* sought to portray Judaism in positive terms. In their presentation of the functional relevance of Judaism in modern society, the moral virtues of universal brotherhood and charity emerged as fundamental tenets of the religion. Simon Bloch contended that religion is unacceptable to God and therefore devoid of value if it fails to impel its adherents to fulfill obligations toward society. This understanding of the meaning of religion was based on a distinction between *religion* and *piété* (piety or idealism). He insisted that a religion incapable of inspiring *piété* in the hearts of men or operating without *piété* serves no function. *Piété*, in turn, is the element in religion that evokes greater commitment to law, justice, and service to the state. Bloch explained that

> we are born into the religion which our parents profess, but we must elevate ourselves to *piété* by our own efforts. Religion serves us as the guide in this world; *piété* opens for us the perspective of a life to come. We receive, in the bosom of our mother, our first religious impressions, but we draw *piété* from a celestial source: religion is the raw diamond; *piété* is the polished diamond. Religion teaches us to honor God; *piété* shows us the route which leads us to Him. Religion is an object of faith; *piété* is a sentiment of the heart. Religion gives us convictions; *piété* is replete with good works. Religion is a collection of positive truths; *piété* animates, invigorates these truths and gives a happy direction to the will of man. Religion is the temple; *piété* is the Goddess. We can change religion, but *piété* is inseparable from the life of the soul.[29]

An essential component of *régénération*, this conception of *piété*, though stressed repeatedly in classical and medieval rabbinic literature, took on a sense of urgency in nineteenth-century France. Special emphasis was placed upon the teleological role of ritual observances to lead Jews to lofty spiritual ideals by appealing to the heart and other senses. This ideological formulation, mirrored, typically, in Jewish educational thought,[30] reflects the efforts of the movement to guard against mechanical, routinized performance of religious rituals.[31]

At the center of the ideology of *régénération* was the claim that during "centuries of darkness" and persecution Judaism had degenerated, acquiring foreign elements that obscured its "grand principles." Through "an invincible attachment to minutiae," in the words of Gerson-Lévy, "we became enslaved to ritual practices which for us no longer make any sense. Of the ancient Egyptians it is said that to them everything was god except God Himself. One can say the same of our degenerated cult where everything is religion except religion itself."[32] While conceding that the "whole body had become gangrenous," he insisted that it was not too late to administer the remedy: "It is time to erect a dike against this dissolution, to save the demoralization with which it is threatened." Otherwise, there was a distinct danger that political freedom could result in the abandonment of the religion that generations "had consecrated with precious blood."[33]

In theory, the solution was simple. It had become necessary to reverse the historical process responsible for the degeneration of the Jewish religion. Indeed, the very term *régénération* signified a sensitivity to the forces of historical development and the indispensability of interpreting the past. According to the early nineteenth-century definition, *régénération* was action to reconstitute in its original state that which had undergone decadence and regression.[34] At the same time, *régénération* rested on the premise that human history progresses steadily, forming a continuous movement toward a future far superior to the present or the past. The idea of progress presupposed a connection between scientific, technological, and material advances on the one hand, and social improvement on the other. Vico's vision of progress in the form of a spiral, with each turn higher than the preceding one, was an important image in later thought, as was Condorcet's view of the critical role played by the French Revolution in propelling man forward. Kant's idea of moral development and Comte's conception of intellectual progress further contributed to the belief that the possibility of human perfection was within reach and that it could be achieved through universal enlightenment and rational education. For prominent liberals such as Guizot, Cousin, and Madame de Staël, progress was the undisputed law of history.[35]

Paradoxically, proponents of *régénération* defined progress as a return to an idealized past. In their view, the most urgent goal of all was to restore Judaism to its original purity while adjusting religious custom to the demands of contemporary civilization. Samuel Cahen asserted that the greatest obstacle to progress was ignorance of the history of the *minhagim:* "One would be surprised by the number of customs we have borrowed from foreign nations. Many presume that these date from antiquity, but the majority are very recent. The most useful work that one could undertake will be to do for the entire religion that which [Leopold] Zunz has done for the liturgy." This could be accomplished, it was argued, through the elimination of those laws and ceremonies which had been introduced in response to persecution, while bearing no relation to the true essence of the religion.[36]

This distinction between a religion and its ceremonies represented the common ground shared by critical scholarship and ritual reform. Invariably, members of the small cadre of critical scholars were vocal proponents of religious modernization. In contrast with Germany, few were practicing rabbis; they were employed variously as book publishers, teachers, manuscript curators, editors of journals, and later, as university professors. Most of the studies devoted to Hebrew grammar and philology in the first half of the nineteenth century were, on the other hand, undertaken by rabbis. Primarily intended to instill greater enthusiasm in the study of the Hebrew language, these works do not represent an endorsement of the objectives of *Wissenschaft,* although containing some hints of the new critical spirit. Few rabbis were willing to touch the potentially explosive questions raised by historical research. For lay scholars Hebrew grammar was, typically, a preoccupation early in their careers, in a way serving as a bridge between traditional and critical scholarship.

The renewed concern for Hebrew language mirrored the profusion of Hebraic studies in general French society. Eighteenth-century Christian scholars such as François Masclef, P. Houbigant, and Pierre Guarin directed their efforts at developing theories of Hebrew grammar and at the reconstruction of "corrupted" biblical texts. In 1751, with the support of Louis Orléans, a Chair in Hebrew Scripture was established at the Sorbonne. Interest in Hebrew texts and grammar continued into the nineteenth century, attracting the attention of such prominent Orientalists as Silvestre de Sacy and Auguste Pichard. Despite the chasm that still separated Jews from the mainstream of French society in the first decades of the century, Hebrew language came to be the one academic concern shared by Jewish and Christian scholars alike. The creation of the *société asiatique* in Paris in 1822 marked the first time Jews and Christians were able to participate in joint scholarly ventures, but this opportunity was short-lived. Owing to the Catholic reaction in the latter years of the Restoration, Jews lost much ground in their quest for social acceptance, thus making Jewish-Christian collaboration virtually impossible. Only after the 1830 Revolution was there a revivification of Jewish membership in learned societies and a resumption of scholarly collaboration.[37]

Samuel Cahen's ambitious project of publishing a new French translation of the Hebrew Bible was clearly an outgrowth of the new scholarly tradition in France. Begun in 1831, the project constituted an impressive achievement. Before analyzing this literature, however, we
must first consider the social and political background to the project, as
well as the forces that ultimately shaped its character. Despite the fact
that Jewish-Christian collaboration was again possible after 1830, such
opportunities certainly did not materialize immediately; moreover, we
may assume that the decision to undertake the Bible translation was
made during the period when Jewish scholars were still excluded from
academic circles. The reversal of earlier liberal trends, coupled with the
experience of exclusion may have driven Jewish intellectuals more
tightly together. Also, given the strong Christian orientation in French
biblical studies, it is not unlikely that Cahen's project constituted an
attempt to wrest the Bible from Christian dominance and place it
squarely within the province of Jewish studies. This decision may have
been strengthened by the realization that even liberals such as Alexander Vinet, Benjamin Constant, Duc de Broglie, and Guizot continued to
identify French civilization with Christianity, despite their commitment
to the separation of Church and State.[38]

Although Franco-Jewish scholarship mirrored much of the activity
pioneered by the German *Wissenschaft des Judentums*, the principal focus
of research in the two countries was decidedly different. French scholars
rarely worked in the area of rabbinic literature, the field that was given
the greatest attention by the *Wissenschaft* movement in Germany. While
the French did concur with their German counterparts concerning the
evolution of rabbinic law, the possibility of dialogue and cooperation
between the reformers and the rabbis in France precluded unrestrained
assaults on the Talmud. Energies were directed, instead, at biblical and
philosophical studies. Completed over the course of two decades, the
new Cahen translation represented an amalgam of classical and critical
methodologies. French Jewish scholars admitted to modelling their
work after the Mendelssohn *Biur*, the first modern German translation
produced by Jews. Midrashic interpretation was all but rejected in favor
of the medieval French and Spanish schools of "literalist" exegesis, special attention was paid to Hebrew grammar and comparative semitics,
and preference was given to the contextual approach in explaining difficult words or phrases. Convinced, nonetheless, of the indispensability of
rabbinics for biblical research, Samuel Cahen had begun work on a
volume of rabbinic vocabulary, and planned to translate the Mishnah
and the Talmud. Typically, relevant texts of medieval and modern commentaries were translated and published along with a particular book of

the Bible. The Isaiah volume, for example, included Abarbanel's preface to his commentary, and the Ezekiel volume contained portions of Munk's translation of the *Guide of the Perplexed,* Abarbanel's preface to his commentary, and a chapter from Zunz's opus on sermons. The principal variants of the Septuagint and the Samaritan texts were consulted, as were other ancient and modern translations.[39]

In many respects the French translation project signalled a larger development at work among Jewish intellectuals of the West. Early in the nineteenth century many of them appropriated the methods and tools of modern scholarship and proceeded to subject classical Jewish literature to critical examination. Philology, anthropology, ethnography and archaeology—methods used in the burgeoning science of antiquities—yielded new avenues for a broader study of text and people. In the specific case of the Bible project, scholars relied heavily on the work of Germans such as Eichhorn, Ewald, De Wette, Gesenius, and Rosenmüller. Curiously, although this scholarly project was thoroughly consistent with the new intellectual milieu of nineteenth-century western Europe, no such enterprise was undertaken by Jewish scholars elsewhere, particularly not in Germany. With rare exception, German Jewish scholars shied away from biblical studies, while favoring research in rabbinic literature. Their purported traditionalism, however, hardly explains this scholarly trend. It is more likely that politics, not piety, discouraged German Jewish scholars from engaging in biblical research. Then dominated by Protestant scholars, the school of biblical criticism was believed to be motivated by anti-Jewish prejudice and hostility. German Jewish scholars were therefore especially apprehensive about engaging in biblical studies, possibly fearing that their work might be discredited through its association with harsh critics of Judaism. Moreover, research on the Bible would not prove as valuable as critical studies in the areas of post-biblical history and rabbinics, since the latter fields would enable scholars to lay the foundations for religious reform.[40]

French Jewish scholars were not subject to the same political constraints concerning the critical study of the Bible. Operating well beyond the sphere of the heated controversy (despite opposition from Catholic and Protestant circles), they addressed the issues on which German Jews had remained silent. Salomon Munk, for example, was able to treat the various questions concerning the documentary hypothesis dispassionately, refuting most of the claims while accepting the idea, in principle, of human authorship of certain parts of the Pentateuch.[41] Where the text of the Bible appeared overly supernatural, and therefore beyond belief, scholars strenuously sought ways of remaining within the loosely defined borders of Jewish tradition. Some followed German theologian David Friedrich Strauss, who viewed religion as an expression of the mind's capacity to generate myths and treat them as revealed truths. Samuel Cahen went so far as to assert that young men destined for the rabbinate should be schooled in mythic thinking.[42] Whatever device was used in promoting reverence for the text, Franco-Jewish scholars were unique in their reconciliation of faith and science. It may be no accident that the appearance of the first volume of the translation coincided with the important ordinance which finally accorded the Jewish religion full parity with Catholicism and Protestantism by recognizing Jewish clergy as employees of the state. Though originally conceived in response to social and intellectual exclusion, the substantive character of the Cahen Bible project may be viewed as a concrete expression of French Jewry's new-found sense of political security.[43]

Exerting a powerful influence on the foundations of modern Jewish scholarship was western Europe's noticeably heightened admiration for Sephardic culture. Spanish-Jewish cosmopolitanism and enlightenment were viewed as instructive models for modern, emancipated Jewry; medieval Ashkenazic culture, by contrast, was regarded with disdain. Among Franco-Jewish scholars the Spanish bias found expression in a renewed appreciation for Arabic language and Judaeo-Islamic culture, resulting in extensive research on Arabic manuscripts. This new scholarly preoccupation may be explained, additionally, by the contemporary French political reality. "We hope," wrote Samuel Cahen, "for rapid progress in a branch of literature to which our possessions in Africa give even a political importance." For these reasons, Jewish scholars appealed for the creation of a chair in Arabic and other Semitic languages at the *école rabbinique de Metz,* and, further, supported the transfer of the school to Paris where students would benefit by their proximity to leading centers of Oriental scholarship.[44]

The work of Salomon Munk and other French Jewish scholars in the field of medieval Arabic philosophy represents an inestimable contribution to modern Europe's understanding of Islamic civilization. Munk's French translation, careful annotation, and introduction to Maimonides' *Guide of the Perplexed* is the best known and most important scholarly achievement in this area. Actually, Munk published the first segments of the *Guide* as an attempt to elucidate various problems of the ancient Israelite religion. His *Mélanges de philosophie juive et arabe* (1859) was, and still remains today, a remarkable display of classical erudition and painstaking research. Throughout this work Munk demonstrated the indispensability of studying Jewish thought within its general philosophical context, a theme which underlays all of modern Jewish studies. He also included a major discovery concerning the real identity of Avicebron, the author of *Fons Vitae*. Munk proved conclusively that the author was Solomon Ibn Gabirol, the Spanish Jewish poet and philosopher. This discovery was especially important, since *Fons Vitae* is an example of a philosophical work composed by a Jew that was a major influence on thirteenth-century Christian philosophy, although its influence on Jewish thought was insignificant. Charges of the pariah status of Jews could scarcely withstand such formidable evidence to the contrary.[45]

In their studies of theology and philosophy, Jewish scholars appear to have underscored the centrality of "essence" over "form" in Judaism. Generally, the utilization of historical methods in determining the various layers of development of Judaism was offensive to traditional sensibilities. Adolphe Franck's research on ancient philosophy and on the Kabbalah led him to the conclusion that the spiritual and political elements in Judaism were mutually exclusive and antithetical. He viewed the history of Judaism as a process of progressive spiritualization and refinement that was actually accelerated by the Jewish people's loss of political independence and sovereignty. Franck saw in this development evidence of Judaism's universal character, a trait enabling the religion to adapt itself to varying conditions. It is not surprising that in a system where Judaism was viewed as ultimately free from the shackles of material and space, the significance of the ceremonial law would be minimized.[46]

Salomon Munk was significantly more conservative than Franck in his view of the Jewish tradition. Nevertheless, Munk's studies in the history of the Jews in antiquity also led him to views which diverged from the normative tradition. He was critical of Grand Rabbi Lion-Mayer Lambert's account of the history of the Jewish people, *Précis de l'histoire des Hébreux*. Underlying Lambert's presentation was a fundamental assumption which hardly needed to be articulated explicitly: an organic unity in Jewish history links ancient Hebrews and modern French Jews as members of the same nation, though separated by several millennia. This was what legitimized a retrospective glance into the past and made the study of virtuous historical Jewish figures especially instructive and relevant.[47]

Munk was critical of the view of the historical unity of the Jewish people that prevailed among traditionalists. Jewish history, he argued, was the history of the knowledge of God, beginning with "the patriarch who first . . . proclaimed the existence of God the Creator; it is completed by the Messiah, that is, by the triumph of the monotheistic faith over the polytheism of the nations."[48] For Munk, Jewish history was an ideational continuum that constituted the essential link between past, present, and future. The ancient Hebrews were at once a political and a religious community, united by a common land and legislative system. Modern Jews, by contrast, were members of a communion that included individuals separated by their nationality, interests, mores, and cultural origins. Faith alone unified Jews in different parts of the world. Finally, Munk rejected the idea that the suffering experienced by Jews might be considered a component of national identity and consciousness: "This community of suffering relates to religious principles; it does not constitute a distinct nationality, and it will disappear in proportion to the disappearance of pagan elements from the beliefs adopted by modern nations."[49] Thus, the idea of God, which the Jews contributed to mankind, united Jews throughout history and enabled them to play a special role in the perfection of humanity. Echoing the view of Joseph Salvador, who sought to demonstrate that the institutions of Mosaic law were appropriate models for nineteenth-century French republicanism, Munk emphasized that with monotheism Jews had made a decisive contribution to civilization and this ought to be the essence of Jewish identity. Religious rituals, according to Munk, would serve both as tools in concretizing the monotheistic idea and as a means of lending unity to modern Jews.

In general, the oeuvre of Franco-Jewish scholars provided greater substantiation for the view that *régénération* ought to be conceived in religious as well as social terms. Taking the lead in the active promotion of religious *régénération* was the journal *Archives israélites de France*, founded in Paris in 1840. From its inception the journal was dedicated to providing a forum for the scholarly examination of ceremonial laws and customs. Paving what was essentially a moderate path, editor Samuel Cahen urged scholars to research and describe the times and circumstances which had given birth to certain abuses; change would eventually follow as a matter of course, he believed, since "time and reason . . . are the true reformers."[50] The *régénérateurs* routinely cited rabbinic texts as proof that the idea of reform had been endorsed throughout history by eminent authorities and in an effort to show that the *halakhic* sources themselves revealed a process of development where certain specific rituals had undergone modification. Rooted in an abiding faith in evolutionary change, the *régénérateurs'* concern for responsibly examining the history of laws and customs counterbalanced the drive for radical religious reform. *Réforme graduée* was their objective. Eventually a consensus emerged among *régénérateurs* regarding the specific changes that they envisioned.[51]

Two general factors were critically important in guiding the ideology of *régénération*. The first was an appreciation for medieval Sephardic Judaism that constituted a leading motif in modern Jewish scholarship. This appreciation also played a role in the thinking of educational and

146

religious reformers. One of the earliest expressions of the glorification of Sephardic culture concerned the question of Hebrew pronunciation. Shortly after the Paris Jewish elementary school was established (1818), the *Comité des écoles* decided to adopt the Sephardic pronunciation, claiming that this was in accordance with the consensus of scholarly opinion. The Ashkenazic pronunciation was undoubtedly rejected because it sounded like Yiddish, itself a favorite target of enlightened criticism. The decision of the *comité* met with severe rabbinic opposition. Grand Rabbi Séligmann reprimanded the school director, while Grand Rabbi Deutz went so far as to withdraw his two sons from the establishment. However, the matter did not end here. The question of introducing the Sephardic pronunciation in schools and seminaries would continue to divide the *régénérateurs* and staunch traditionalists throughout the century. By the 1840s the consistorial grand rabbis in Paris had joined progressivists in supporting the linguistic innovation, while in Alsace adherence to the Ashkenazic pronunciation persisted.[52] Most proponents of *régénération* also concluded that the Sephardic practice of Jewish law was more liberal than the Ashkenazic interpretation and therefore more appropriate for life under citizenship. Many laws restricting relations between Jews and gentiles (for example, *yein nesekh* and *ḥukkat ha-goi*) were presumed to be a response to the persecutions experienced by Ashkenazic Jewry. Moreover, reformers frequently pointed to Sephardic synagogues as models of decorum. Most of the *régénérateurs* shared the opinion of Zacharias Frankel, founder of the Positive-Historical movement in Germany, who, upon visiting France in 1852, praised the "magnificent" Bordeaux temple and the "noble melodies" of its cantor. As he put it, the Sephardic communities, and Bordeaux above all, had an "incontestable superiority over the German [Ashkenazic] *kehillot* of the country."[53]

The first effort at establishing a reformed sanctuary reveals a different aspect of the Sephardic mystique. Outlining the principles that would guide his proposed Metz *oratoire,* Gerson-Lévy declared that the *piyyutim* were to be replaced by selections from the poetry of Solomon ibn Gabirol, Moses ibn Ezra, and Judah Halevi. The preference for the Spanish poets over the Ashkenazic authors of the *piyyutim* was explained as linguistically motivated: the Hebrew of the Spanish writers was clear and grammatically correct whereas the Ashkenazic *piyyutim* were virtually incomprehensible because of their grammatical flaws. It is likely that there was more to the issue of *piyyutim* than just language. Innovators viewed medieval Spanish Jewry as the quintessential expression of Jewish civilization; Ashkenazic culture, as exemplified by the *piyyutim,* was regarded as outdated, no longer relevant, and overly particularistic.[54]

A second factor, the goal of unifying the Jews of France, provided the movement with a crucially important conceptual framework. Perhaps the most enduring feature of nineteenth-century French Jewish history, the quest for unity was marked by efforts to introduce uniform changes in synagogue worship, religious practice and education, and ultimately to create a Franco-Jewish identity. The inspiration for this objective derived from the uniquely French experience of emancipation, and was fostered by a devotion to the fatherland. French Jewry was undoubtedly swept up by the idea that a special destiny awaited France and her inhabitants. The goal of uniformity was no less a matter of tactical importance than of theoretical significance. Uniformity was widely regarded as essential to the success of *régénération*. As policymakers intent on regenerating their less fortunate coreligionists, members of the Paris "center" naturally tended to define "improvement" in their own terms and sought to dictate its specific patterns to far-off communities. Tensions over regionalism versus centralization, unity versus diversity, and tradition versus reform were thus the inevitable outgrowth of the search for a new Jewish identity in France.[55]

The ill-fated, but incessant, efforts of reformers to combine the Sephardic and Ashkenazic liturgies into a single rite offers an excellent example of the importance placed on uniformity as well as the persistence of the forces of diversity. In 1831 Sephardic leaders requested of the Paris Consistory an administrative fusion of the Ashkenazic synagogue and their own, and in the following year this became a reality. Though initially motivated by financial and administrative concerns, the notion of "fusion" soon assumed a new significance. Inspired by the coexistence of the two communities in Paris, Ashkenazic proponents of religious modernization introduced the idea of creating a combined liturgy that would signify the distinctive ritual of French Jewry and would thus serve as a much sought after instrument of unity. In time, the concept of fusion became an essential priority of the *régénérateur* movement. In fact, candidates for the position of Chief Rabbi in 1846 were expected to subscribe to the philosophical and practical aspects of the proposed liturgical innovation. Elaborate formulas were devised for the determination of which prayers and melodies should be selected from the two rites. For example the Sephardic melody for the reading of the Torah would be used throughout the year, while the Ashkenazic melody would be used on Rosh Hashanah and Yom Kippur. On the whole, the combined liturgy was to be based mainly on the Sephardic ritual. The idea eventually gained currency among several moderate rabbis, although it was vigorously opposed by Grand Rabbi Salomon Klein of Colmar.[56]

It is especially significant that the principal resistance to fusion came from the Sephardim themselves. The Sephardic community of Paris was unenthused about the prospects of a combined liturgy. In a pamphlet published in Paris in 1866, Sephardic leader Prosper Lunel cited the more obvious objections to fusion: significant differences in the liturgy and pronunciation of each group. Futhermore, he asserted that "the autonomy of the Portuguese synagogue has always existed, and it will [continue to] exist despite the hostile efforts of the consistory that reigns in 1866." This last statement, as well as ongoing efforts to consolidate instruction of the Sephardic rite at the Bordeaux cantorial school,[57] point to an unmistakable pride in the ethnic distinctiveness of the Sephardim. Consequently, the *régénérateurs* were thwarted in their efforts to establish a *rite français*. Inspired by the ambitious goal of unity, undoubtedly an echo of governmental efforts to impose centralization upon the Jewish communities of France, leaders of *le mouvement régénérateur* failed to achieve the much desired religious uniformity or the blurring of ethnic distinctions.

The persistence of regionalism, religious traditionalism, and ethnic loyalty was doubtless more powerful than the *régénérateurs* were aware. In the specific areas involving the transformation of time-honored behavioral patterns, *régénération* failed to attract much enthusiastic support, and indeed encountered stubborn resistance on frequent occasions. Nevertheless, for a growing number of intellectuals whose frame of reference remained the Jewish community, *régénération* was the only viable response to the formidable challenges to Jewish identity posed by nineteenth-century French culture. *Régénération* was understood to be an expression of the uniqueness of the emancipation of French Jewry: emancipation was believed to be unassailable precisely because it was a part of the cherished legacy of the Revolution. Moreover, this implied that the envisioned symbiosis of Judaism and French civilization was by no means merely an accommodation, but a sacred mission entrusted to the first Jewish population to have been shaped by the ideals of 1789. Despite differences over the scope, application, and implementation of reforms, the ideology of *régénération* continued to be viewed as the most reliable path toward the realization of that vision.

7

Schools and Schoolmen

AN ANALYSIS OF EDUCATION at virtually any point in history can serve as an extremely sensitive barometer of the ideological concerns of a particular community or society. The school is the main vehicle through which a society seeks to transmit fundamental social, religious, and political values to its youth, and since there usually are conflicting views on precisely what those values are, or should be, education frequently becomes the public focus of ideological debate. In the case of France, a survey of education lends a special perspective to the history of the first generations of emancipated Jews, especially because education was viewed as the means by which the leaders hoped to enable Jewish youth to integrate successfully into French society. Education thus became the central concern of the *régénérateur* movement, as it was for other circles of enlightened Jews throughout Europe. However, the ultimate aim of educational reform was consistent with the specific goal of *régénération:* the formation of Jewish Frenchmen capable of preserving their religious identity while participating in and contributing to the social, economic, and cultural life of France. The history of Jewish education in France, including both educational reform and the opposition it encountered, illustrates the range of ideological and institutional responses of French Jewry to the challenges of emancipation.

The Establishment of Jewish Schools

The Jewish communities of the northeast were severely damaged by the turmoil of the Reign of Terror. The *ḥadarim* and yeshivot remained open during the first years after the Revolution, but most were forced to close during the Terror and Thermidor. The yeshivah of Metz, for example, was ordered closed in 1793, and the *ḥeder* of Isaac Bamberger in Obernai was closed in 1798 for failure to comply with the republican calendar with its ten-day week; that is, for its refusal to stay open on the Jewish Sabbath. In response to these conditions, some children were sent abroad to study in yeshivot.[1] Limited educational opportunities were seen by some families as sufficient reason to continue, even into the nineteenth century, to send their children to neighboring Germany. The Ratisbonne brothers and Alexandre Weill were among those sent there, as were the sons of Metz rabbi Mayer Charleville. According to Weill, the twelve best students at the yeshivah of Frankfurt-am-Main were from France,[2] an indication that this trend must have been quite extensive.

The need to establish special Jewish schools in France was also underscored by the small number of Jewish students who attended the French public schools. It is true that according to a report made by the prefect of the *département de la Seine* in 1806, since the Revolution Jews of the district had begun to take advantage of the right granted to them as citizens to place their children in public boarding schools as well as other educational establishments. He concluded, however, that education among Jews generally continued to be private rather than public.[3] Statistics taken in the year 1810 corroborate the prefect's view, as they give evidence of a relatively small percentage of Jewish school-aged children in the public schools. In Lorraine no more than 20 percent attended public schools, while in the two *départements* of Alsace the figure was nearer to 10 percent.[4] One major reason for the low public school attendance was the gentile opposition, particularly in the northeast where anti-Jewish sentiments ran high. The Central Consistory reported to the Minister of the Interior in 1810 that Jewish children "are still prevented from entering the public schools, especially in rural communes; it is only with the greatest efforts and innumerable sacrifices that their parents manage to obtain some instruction for them."[5] According to the Minister of the Interior, many Christian parents were annoyed with the presence of Jews in the schools, and consequently, many school directors, especially in Alsace, refused to admit Jewish students.[6] Where this opposition was less overt, that is, in Paris and in southern France, enrollments appear to have been substantially higher. By 1808 nearly two hundred Jewish children in the *département de la Seine* were apprenticed to various artisans; others studied medicine, law, and trades. The prefect of Paris wrote that "enlightened" Jews placed their children in the finest boarding schools, and the *école polytechnique* and the *lycées* contained many Jewish students. In the *arrondissement* of Uzès all Jewish students attended public schools, as was the case in Côte-d'Or. In Bordeaux, where there were three Jewish schools in existence in 1807, many attended the Catholic schools and the *lycées*.[7]

While anti-Jewish discrimination may account for the low public school figures, it should be pointed out that the *idea* of attending public schools met with much apprehensiveness and resistance among the Jews themselves. Distrust of what was regarded, generally, as a religiously and socially hostile environment, and the fear of missionary activity in particular, were among the leading motives that kept parents from sending children to study in the Christian schools. In fact, the rabbis frequently inveighed against attendance at the public schools.[8] Taking notice of these sentiments, the Minister of the Interior, Coquebert-de-Montbret, reported that government officials were disturbed by the failure of Jews to avail themselves of public instruction; therefore, in 1807, he offered two recommendations intended to allay Jewish fears of religious interference in the schools. First, he proposed that the grand rabbis be assured unhindered supervision of the religious instruction of the Jewish children in the public school system. Second, as an alternate recommendation, he suggested that the government itself take greater interest in the education of Jewish youth. Recognizing the forces in the Jewish community that militated against public school attendance, the minister proposed that the government establish special schools for Jews.[9]

Beginning in 1809 the Central Consistory submitted requests to the *Grand-Maître* of the *Université* (the government agency that administered public education) and to the Minister of Cultes that the law of 17 March 1808 be amended to include specific provisions for the establishment of Jewish primary schools in every commune where the number of Jews justified such a measure. Unfortunately for the Jews, the authorities were not enthusiastic about the idea of founding separate Jewish public schools. In fact, the ordinance of 29 February 1816 spoke of organizing Catholic and Protestant schools, but not Jewish ones. Finally, in 1819 permission was granted for the opening of the first Jewish primary school.[10] During these same years the Paris Consistory was active in forming several commissions to set up a school, to find a locale and director, and to establish guidelines for instruction.

Efforts by the Central Consistory and local consistories to convince the government of the need for the creation of Jewish primary schools occasioned an intense debate in the Jewish community. The desirability of separate schools and the function of such institutions were issues which touched the very essence of *régénération*. Some argued that the idea of special schools for Jews signified a contradiction to their political status in France. They feared that such a development would intensify the isolation of Jews and impede their social and intellectual *régénération*. The desired objective of full *régénération* would, according to the view, only be served through the enrollment of Jewish youth in the French public schools.[11] Others, however, recognized that at this stage in their development, the Jews had particular problems that required special educational attention. First, the Jews lived in a state whose character was undeniably Christian and whose educational system was coming under the increasing influence of the Catholic clergy. And even with respect to schools where there was no overt clerical influence, the *régénérateurs* voiced reservations. Gerson-Lévy, for example, argued that although the opening of the public elementary schools in Metz to children of all faiths was certainly a sign of progress, Jewish attendance at these schools was not desirable. The mixture of students of diverse religious backgrounds would undoubtedly result in a confusion of *moeurs*, language, and customs, and would ultimately quash the distinctiveness of the Jewish children. Gerson-Lévy's reluctance to accept the pluralistic interpretation of *régénération* was based on the idea of the indispensability of religion to society and on the correlative notion that it is important to society that all people worship God according to their own religious beliefs. The commitment to preserving Jewish religious identity, then, moved the *régénérateurs* to support a separate system of Jewish educational institutions.[12]

A second motive for establishing special schools concerned the envisioned function of education within the general context of *régénération* objectives. The *régénérateurs* regarded the Jewish schools as prime agents in the socialization of French Jewry. Socialization, the process by which a newcomer learns the culture of a group and finds a place in its social structure, was regarded among the most crucial phases of Jewish *régénération*. This view was based on the assumption that centuries of social isolation and discrimination had given birth to habits and attitudes incompatible with the social and political obligations that accompanied citizenship. Instruction in the behavioral patterns and values of French society would thus facilitate the transition to the social and political reality of emancipation. Significantly, however, the *régénérateurs* insisted that the socialization process take place within the framework of the Jewish community.

The demand for a transformation of values was in harmony with the pervasive critical evaluation of Jewish life. Proponents of this view argued that prevailing social, economic, and cultural norms were in desperate need of reform, and would require nothing less than a total reconstruction of Jewish attitudes and *moeurs*. This task was made especially difficult by the absence of the appropriate supportive family life. Ordinarily, as the child grew, the family provided the framework for the communication of desired feelings and attitudes, of cultural norms and values. In the case of the Jews, it was held, indigent families cultivated bad habits and fostered mores that threatened to forestall the envisioned *régénération*. Seeking to overcome the negative influence of Jewish family life, the *régénérateurs*, in conformity with trends in general educational philosophy, looked to formal instruction as the means by which the new generation would acquire the social and cultural values of enlightened France. One member of the *comité des écoles israélites de Metz* described the relationship between socialization and education in the following manner:

> without doubt, instruction by itself exerts the most powerful influence upon the life of a man, and leads to the amelioration of the human species; to uproot ignorance and idleness from the youth is to divert it from the path of vice to place it on the road of virtue. But, let us say it, we would not be fulfilling our mission, we would not be justifying any utility of our schools, if they [the schools] did not, in other respects, enable us to achieve a more important goal, that of substituting new *moeurs* for those which times of misfortune have formed; to sweep off the tastes, customs, [and] a language hardly compatible with the station where Providence has placed the French *israélites*; to give to souls unnerved by humiliations, this energy, this dignity, which alone can lead man toward that which is great and honorable.[13]

In addition to counteracting the undesirable centuries-old influences of the home, the schools would provide training in the vocational skills necessary for Jewish economic regeneration.

The example of the French Protestants also appears to have been influential in the decision of Jewish educators to create separate schools and in the determination of general educational methods employed there. The Protestant network of schools, which began with the founding of a primary school in Paris in 1817,[14] provided a suitable model for the education of a religious minority. Protestant schools were observed and imitated by the *régénérateurs*. In particular, the method of *enseignement mutuel*, an English innovation introduced to France by the Protestants, was borrowed by Jewish educators who were impressed by its high quality of instruction at an extremely low cost.[15]

Depending on the city, the impetus for the creation of Jewish schools came either from consistorial or private initiative. In Paris, although the consistory was the central force promoting modern Jewish education, several individuals brought the issue before the public. In 1817 a detailed plan for the establishment of a Jewish primary school in Paris was first advanced by S. Mayer Dalmbert. He asserted that the modest achievements on behalf of the amelioration of the Jews would go for naught if religious and civil education were neglected. Dalmbert proposed the establishment of a modern school, presumably as a model for institutions elsewhere, and suggested that it be in Paris, "the center of fine arts, taste, and *urbanité*." The curriculum prospectus reflected the dominant educational philosophy of the Berlin Haskalah. Religious instruction would be geared to explanations of religious duties, taught by "virtuous and enlightened doctors of law." The course of study would include instruction in Hebrew grammar and sacred history (*sainte histoire*), as well as French language and general history. Geography, mechanical arts, and arithmetic rounded out the required subjects. Students inclined toward science and letters would have an opportunity to study the classics, the art of oration, mathematics, philosophy, applied physics, and chemistry. Students who intended to enter the field of commerce could learn German, English, Italian, Spanish, and instruction in bookkeeping and correspondence. Finally, recreational activities and studies such as horsemanship, fencing, swimming, drawing, painting, dance, and music would be offered to those students who so desired. An atmosphere conducive to learning and enjoyment, embodying secular and religious studies, as well as opportunities for the cultivation of special interests, both professional and recreational, was understood by Dalmbert to be essential to the success of the educational venture. He concluded that "all must bring our coreligionists, national and foreign, to respond to our expectations, and to support the wishes of the friends of humanity."[16] Though undoubtedly a reflection of liberal Jewish views in the capital, the project may have been overly ambitious and therefore failed to materialize.

A short time later, in its first concrete action on behalf of Jewish education, the Paris Consistory named a commission to formulate the specific provision for the establishment of a primary school in Paris. The plan was approved by the consistory in January 1819. A second commission, charged with finding a director for the school, chose David Drach, doctor of law, graduate of the *université royale*, and former instructor of classical languages at the *Institut des nations étrangères*. The school was officially opened on 4 May 1819.[17] Finally, a commission of instruction, later named the *Comité de surveillance et d'administration des écoles consistoriales de Paris*, was charged with the "high" supervision of the school. Of special significance is the domination of this commission, by its seven lay members, although it included the two grand rabbis of the consistory. Any special role for the rabbis in the leadership of the commission was rejected.[18]

The commission recommended the appointment of one *maître* per hundred students, in conformity to the Lancaster method prevalent in the Christian schools of France, England, Asia, and Africa. Also known as *enseignement mutuel*, this method was considered to be the most cost-effective means of instruction, as it was employed to teach the principles of reading, writing, and arithmetic to a large number of students under the direction of only one teacher. It rapidly gained acceptance among Jewish educators in France.[19] While conceding that Hebrew instruction might require an additional teacher, the Paris commission decided initially to propose the nomination of one *maître* until such time that it became necessary to appoint a *sousmaître*.[20] The commission established the following requirements for the *maître:* in addition to being of the Jewish religion, he must possess a certificate of exemplary moral and religious conduct and, to the extent possible, be qualified to become a consistorial rabbi; finally, he would need a certificate proving his familiarity with *enseignement mutuel*.[21] As more than enough ready funds existed for the establishment of the school, the commission decided to deal only with the means of meeting the annual maintenance costs. Slightly less than half of the school budget would be provided by a fixed consistorial allocation. The balance would be met through a voluntary subscription system consisting of donations, bequests, and endowments. In fact, this procedure had proven so successful for the primary schools in Metz that plans were already underway to establish a secondary school there.[22] Although the school was intended primarily for children of poor families, children of all classes were admitted. The commission recognized that a number of paying students would both ease the financial burden of the school and be viewed as a sign of the success of the institution. The most intelligent students would be sent to the *école normale* to learn to become monitors.[23] Finally, in order for the school to be legally established, the consistory would need to solicit from the Minister of the Interior the authorization to levy the consistorial tax, and from the *Commission d'instruction publique de l'Université* the authorization necessary to establish a primary school according to the regulations.[24]

In Metz the establishment of an *école publique élémentaire* for Jewish youth was achieved through the initiatives taken by enlightened Jewish members of the *Société pour l'encouragement de l'Instruction élémentaire dans le département de la Moselle*. At the meeting of 20 April 1818, one Jewish member of the administrative council (probably Charles Oulif), in urging the *société* to support the idea of a Jewish primary school, underscored the necessity of "placing all the means of perfection and moral improvement within the reach of this class of our fellow citizens, whom we must seek to bring closer to us." He argued that the Jewish population of Metz was large enough to warrant the creation of special schools for its youth and that the Metz Consistory could find sufficient resources for the maintenance of these schools if initial support by the council were granted. Finally, the speaker proposed the formation of a special commission charged with the task of reporting on the state of Jewish education.[25]

The commission report recommended a complete reorganization of education for the Jews of Metz. Originally, the commission had assumed that there were some forms of gratuitous and nongratuitous public schools and that the teachers were subject to regulations derived, perhaps, from "Mosaic legislation." All of these assumptions were proven false. There were no schools under any direction or supervision; generally, fathers took upon themselves the responsibility of teaching their children basic subjects, and thus there were no trained teachers, only men of other professions who would meet informally with small numbers of children to offer instruction in reading and writing.[26]

In spite of the absence of official schools, there was, according to the commission's report, a higher degree of literacy among Jews than among Christians. French public schools had failed to instill an enthusiasm for learning among the students, most of whom would leave with an imperfect education. The Jews, by contrast, combined a genuine zeal for study with an almost universal proficiency in reading and writing. In the estimation of the commission, however, these observations did not eliminate nor reduce the need for institutions designed for Jewish moral *régénération:* "The education of a people does not consist of teaching it to read and write; it must exert an influence on the behavior and the social virtues of men; it must render them such that they be useful to society, that they therein earn esteem and they reach a state of well-being."[27] Seen as a force of potentially great social impact, education was conceived in the widest possible sense, well beyond the simple skills normally acquired in the school. For the Jews, the promise of public education offered an opportunity to improve deficient social attributes, and thus would contribute to their "moral regeneration . . . and fusion in the nation."[28]

The involvement of the consistory was envisioned as crucial to the success of public education. The consistory had heretofore failed to meet the educational needs of its constituency, chiefly because of the many burdens that had occupied its time and energies. Since, in the final analysis, the success of the educational enterprise would be measured by the elimination of Jewish economic involvement in petty trade, a strong,

157

central body was needed to provide guidance and direction. According to proponents of *régénération*, the consistory alone would be capable of exerting an influence on its coreligionists, not only through its cooperation in the establishment of the schools but also in the placement of students in apprenticeships or in institutions of higher studies. Persuaded by these arguments, the commission declared itself firmly in favor of Jewish public education and squarely behind a supervisory role for the consistory, concluding that "such are the views of the enlightened Jews; such must be ours."[29] The commission therefore recommended that the *société* contribute a sum of 500 francs to the expenses of the first free Jewish school. This motion was carried unanimously at the meeting of 21 May 1818.[30]

In response to these initiatives, the Metz Consistory issued a plea to the Jews of the *département* to accede to the "generous resolution" of the *société*, providing for the "advantages of a perfected method of instruction which the king desires to become standardized among his subjects." Under the direction of Rabbi Lion-Mayer Lambert and following the method of *enseignement mutuel*, the school admitted boys only and was free for indigent children.[31] With strong support from Metz Rabbi Aaron Worms, the Metz school opened on 1 September 1818 with fifty students.[32] Led by the examples of Paris and Metz, a total of twelve Jewish public schools were established between 1819–1821 in the seven departmental consistories.[33] This flurry of activity was no doubt linked to the government's general encouragement of primary education, resulting in a dramatic increase in public schools for Protestants as well. However, the Catholic resurgence, especially in the 1820s, accompanied by clerical domination of the *Université* system, soon slowed the growth of public education in non-Catholic communities.[34]

Important changes in Jewish schooling would occur only after the Revolution of 1830 and the deposition of the Bourbon monarchy. A dramatic increase in the number of Jewish schools, as well as improvements in their moral and fiscal well-being can be traced to any number of social and intellectual factors but most importantly to the unprecedented involvement of the government in public education. The new government of the July Monarchy, under the Orleanist Louis-Philippe, sought to broaden the functions of the state and the uses of the public treasury. Subsidy programs greatly extended the state's sphere of participation in the economic life of the French nation: public funds were used for the development of transportation and communications systems as well as an extensive program of public building. In the field of primary education the state assumed a responsibility previously left in private hands or in the province of the church. The crowning achievement of the new government was the *loi sur l'instruction primaire* of 28 June 1833, proposed by François Guizot, the Minister of Public Instruction. The basic provision of the *loi Guizot,* as it was known, was that every commune was required to maintain at least one public school for primary instruction and to pay teachers a small fixed salary. Though education was not free, all indigent children were admitted at no charge. The law also contained the provision that every *département* would have an institution for training teachers (an *école normale*). Where the existing resources of the commune were insufficient, it was to tax itself modestly, in addition to its ordinary taxation. The *département* would similarly tax itself to provide the necessary funds. If this was still insufficient, then the Minister of Public Instruction was to cover the deficit out of funds voted by the chambers.

Government interest in Jewish education was expressed in a series of laws designed primarily to place Jewish schools under state supervision. The *ordonnance* of 16 October 1830, which provided for the nomination of commissioners to supervise Jewish public schools,[35] contained the first reference to Jewish instruction. This was followed nearly two years later by the more detailed *arrêté* of 17 April 1832, issued by the *Conseil royal de l'instruction publique.* Special committees were to be established in each consistorial *circonscription* and in each *arrondissement* where the Jewish population warranted one, for the purpose of inspecting and encouraging Jewish primary education. Each committee would be composed of the local mayor, the justice of the peace, the president of the consistory, the grand rabbi, and distinguished Jews. Although the government was evidently intent on placing Jewish primary instruction within the framework of the *Université* system, no mention was made of the financial basis of the schools.[36]

Since 1808 revenue obtained through special taxation levied by the Jewish consistories had provided the support for Jewish institutions. Fairly often, however, the necessary budget was not met, and the schools tended to suffer most. Prompted by the optimism that accompanied the new regime, requests for government assistance to support Jewish schools began immediately after Louis-Philippe's ascension to the throne. The situation was further complicated by the law of 8 February 1831, under which the state assumed responsibility for the fiscal maintenance of the Jewish *culte.* Under the law, the salaries of the consistorial grand rabbis and *ministres officiants* as well as those of the faculty of the *école rabbinique* came under the budget of the state. Financial assistance would henceforth be granted to the consistories for the acquisition, construction, and repair of synagogues. Finally, the state assumed responsibility for the fiscal maintenance of the *école rabbinique,* including expenditures for food, rent, heat, and lighting.[37] Although this law has generally been viewed as the final act of emancipation of French Jewry, its impact on Jewish institutions, particularly educational ones, was rather ambiguous. The 1831 law deprived the consistories of a fixed legal revenue by abolishing their right to tax their constitutents, and since only those institutions enumerated in the law were to benefit from state support, all others, including schools, were threatened with fiscal destruction.[38]

The 1831 law, together with the dire condition of Jewish schools, inspired bold attempts to obtain government assistance. Although requests for school support had been advanced since the beginning of the July Monarchy,[39] those efforts generally reflected the urgency of the prevailing economic situation. Following the enactment of the law of 1831, however, requests for allocations were based on the presumption that the Jewish schools deserved support equal to that granted to other schools. For example, the president of the Strasbourg consistory argued in a letter to the rector of the *Académie* that the 1200 franc allocation made by the Minister of Public Instruction would not entirely cover the expenses of the Strasbourg school. He therefore demanded that *départemental* authorities provide the support that, heretofore denied, now rightfully belonged to Jewish primary schools; he based his argument on the French Charter, on the significant number of Jews relative to the general population of the Bas-Rhin, and finally, on the special, retarded, development of his coreligionists.[40] The Paris[41] and Marseille[42] consistories addressed similar requests to the Minister of Cultes and of Public Instruction for government assistance, based on the liberal interpretation of the law of 1831; although in contrast to the *circonscription* of Strasbourg, the schools of Paris and Marseille had already been recipients of local funds. The Marseille Consistory argued that with further support, its school could provide instruction for all Jewish boys in Marseille and for a large number in neighboring cities.[43] In 1843 the Paris Consistory defiantly protested the suggestion of the prefecture that the Jews themselves subsidize the construction of a badly needed new school. This, argued the consistory, would be nothing less than a contradiction to *"la complète émancipation du notre culte."* In the end, however, the consistory quietly agreed to *offer* to contribute to the municipal treasury the sum of 20,000 francs.[44] The appearance of the principle of equality thus remained intact.

Efforts to obtain funding for Jewish schools were aided significantly in this period by the involvement of local and provincial authorities. Correspondence between the Ministry of Public Instruction and various prefects and rectors reveals a willingness on the part of public officials to encourage Jewish primary instruction through the organization of committees for school inspection and through the allocation of state and local funds.[45] Most active among supporters of Jewish schools was Louis Cottard, rector of the *Académie* of Strasbourg between 1829 and 1847. The numerous requests for financial assistance that he addressed to the Minister of Public Instruction show a deep concern for improvements in Jewish education. Cottard argued that since Jewish schools needed to maintain two different kinds of teachers, one for secular subjects and another for Hebrew and Bible instruction, they required more support than other communal schools.[46] The Strasbourg school, he warned, was in danger of closing for lack of funds,[47] and the situation was no better in rural districts. Special financial aid, in his view, would ease the burden through the establishment of additional Jewish schools in the Bas-Rhin,[48] which in 1831 counted only eight such establishments.[49]

Beginning in the mid-1830s, attempts to gain the status of *écoles communales* for the Jewish schools met with increased success. Article 9 of the *loi Guizot* stated that "in the case where local circumstances permit, the Minister of Public Instruction can, after having heard the Municipal Council, authorize as *écoles communales* those schools intended particularly for one of the *cultes* recognized by the State." In Paris, for example, the consistorial schools were transformed in this manner by the *arrêté* of 20 January 1836.[50] According to Rabbi Aron's 1843 inspection report on Jewish schools in the Bas-Rhin, of the twenty-seven communities visited, seven had established *écoles communales*. Nevertheless, roughly half the communities were receiving some form of support from the municipal councils: in most cases an outright allocation, in others the use of a building for the school. Aron asserted that although the number of Jewish *écoles communales* was small, this could not be attributed to any lack of enthusiasm on the part of the Jewish communities.[51] In contrast to the time when Jews of the rural areas had refused to set up public schools, by 1843 the poorest among the communities were prepared to make immense sacrifices for primary instruction, as evidenced by the salaries paid to the teachers.[52] Haut-Rhin communities witnessed about the same measure of success in procuring the standing of *écoles communales* for Jewish schools; by 1845 six of twenty-five schools had attained the recognized status. Gradually, the process of municipalization was undertaken in the large cities. In the villages, success was more dependent upon the good will of the municipal council and the mayors.[53]

The relatively small number of Jewish public schools may be attributed to a variety of problems. Communities with a small Jewish population often could not afford the costs of maintaining a separate school and frequently were denied support by the municipal councils. One observer, Simon Bloch, attributed this to the prejudice still found in rural communities where many municipal council members believed that Jewish children ought to attend Christian schools. This was the situation in Brumath for example.[54] In Schlestadt local authorities feared that the establishment of separate schools "would only encourage the prejudice of [Jewish] parents against the Catholic and Protestant population."[55] In communities where a separate public school could not be established, Jewish children were sent to the French *écoles commmunales,* which were officially opened to Jews by the *loi Guizot.* The communal schools provided instruction in the basic subjects of primary education: French reading and writing, arithmetic, history, and religous-moral instruction. Absenteeism, however, was reportedly very high among Jewish students, partly due to their reluctance to attend on Fridays and Saturdays.[56] It is also likely that many parents were apprehensive about the Christian environment in the schools. According to the report of an inspection of rural schools in the *département de la Moselle,* the young Jews were frequently victims of mockery and banter, and repeated torment made it difficult for them to learn.[57] In addition, the Jewish children were subjected to overt attempts at Christianization in certain schools, where religious images were displayed in the classrooms and where recitation of the Catholic catechism and prayers was required of all students.[58] In other schools, where the religious rights of the Jewish students were respected, separate religious instruction was administered by Jewish teachers.[59] For example, in Dijon Rabbi Mahir Charleville taught a course in religion and Hebrew instruction for the Jewish students who attended the city's public school.[60]

In addition to the fiscal problems and the opposition of local authorities to the idea of separate Jewish education, it appears that the small number of Jewish public schools could be traced to forces that originated among the Jews themselves. Cottard maintained that there was still a dearth of Jews sufficiently educated to serve as teachers. Moreover, he claimed that Jewish parents preferred to send their children to the "little Talmudic schools" scattered throughout the various Jewish communes. These clandestine schools operated outside of the *Université* system of inspection and control. They were run by rabbis who, according to Cottard, offered only religious instruction, although they themselves were ignorant in this area. The Talmud, in his view, encouraged religious fanaticism and fostered contempt for other faiths,[61] and the unauthorized educational institutions only served to preserve "the thousand superstitious prejudices which retard the civilization of this unfortunate youth."[62] Most of all, he asserted, their existence detracted from efforts to establish modern schools. The rector therefore supported the Strasbourg Consistory in its battle against the clandestine schools, and he requested the dismissal of the chief rabbi of the Bas-Rhin, Séligmann Goudchaux, who refused to cooperate in the struggle for enlightened instruction. Also unpopular among consistory leaders for his "orthodox opinions" and behavior, Goudchaux resigned and was replaced in 1834 by Rabbi Arnaud Aron, who tirelessly encouraged the creation of modern schools in his *département*.[63]

Nevertheless, the clandestine schools continued to be widespread in northeastern France in the 1840s. This may be explained, in part, by the ineffectiveness of the *loi Guizot*, which obliged each commune, at least in theory, to maintain a school and to accept all the children of the village, whatever their religion. As already stated, the unauthorized Jewish schools were generally found in areas where the municipality and the local population were hostile to the Jews. It would be a mistake, however, to regard the secret establishments as nothing more than a reflection of French social and religious exclusiveness. Even with the approach of midcentury, much of the local population in the Alsatian countryside (both Jewish and non-Jewish) remained hostile to secular studies.[64] For many, the secret schools provided a protective environment at a time when the walls of tradition had begun to crack. Though not well-defined, the curriculum in the rural schools focussed on learning the Hebrew language in "translation classes," where the students rendered the Hebrew Bible into Yiddish. Reading exercises consisted of the daily prayers, excerpts from the weekly portion of the Pentateuch, the Prophets, and medieval commentaries. Writing skills were taught, but no systematic study of grammar was provided. Yiddish was the general language of instruction, since knowledge of French was very limited, even in the 1840s. Lessons in French were given, but by teachers who did not know the language, grammar, or syntax very well. In some schools near the eastern border, German was taught because of its usefulness in conducting business. The sciences were not included in the curriculum, and arithmetic, which presumably could be learned in the home, was neglected as well.[65]

For these reasons, such establishments evoked considerable criticism among *régénérateurs*. By most modern standards, the quality of instruction in the rural Jewish schools tended to be very low. The schools closely resembled the old-style *ḥeder* that belonged to the era before emancipation. Now rendered obsolete by French Jewry's citizenship and by the cultural and intellectual progress of France, the clandestine schools impeded rather than contributed to *régénération*. In the estimation of the *régénérateurs*, they were incapable of instilling religious and moral values in the youth and consequently could not guarantee the preservation of Judaism. One observer, Simon Bloch, described a typical school setting:

> We breathe the foul and contagious odor of tombs which blight the soul of the young *israélites*. We see the children piled one upon another in a narrow room, dark and dirty, and under the watch of a teacher whose spirit is even more narrow and more slovenly than that of his students.
>
> Study is limited to their learning to read Hebrew, to translate the Bible imperfectly, and after having inculcated these elementary things, he [the teacher] can only give them an example of immorality and licentiousness.[66]

According to Bloch, excessively violent discipline further aggravated the situation by choking the development of the child's intellectual faculties and by repressing the growth of his most elevated feelings.[67] The quality of instruction was limited by the teacher's lack of certification and short-term contract, usually six months at a time. Classes were generally held in the home of the teacher, who collected his students' weekly tuition payment in lieu of a regular salary. Consequently there was little, if any, room for children of the poor.[68]

Although the views of public officials and *régénérateurs* on the establishment of modern Jewish schools appear to have been virtually identical, their respective goals were really quite far apart. As a sharp critic of Jewish tradition, Cottard undoubtedly regarded the promotion of public Jewish education as a transitional stage that would prepare the Jews for entrance into *"la grande famille française."*[69] Few French public officials, including Cottard, could have supported, or anticipated, the continued proliferation of separate Jewish schools, as this would have violated their grand plan for social integration. Among the *régénérateurs* a vastly different philosophy underlay their initiatives. It is quite significant that the *Archives israélites,* which only began to appear in 1840, expressed unqualified support for the establishment of separate Jewish schools. One might have expected that after some fifty years of enfranchisement, support among the *régénérateurs* for separate Jewish education would have eroded. This, however, was not the case. The *régénérateur* movement stubbornly rejected the claim that separate education would impede the ultimate goal of successful integration in French society. Not surprisingly, therefore, the *Archives israélites* took issue with the decision of the Nancy Consistory in 1843 to close its Jewish school and have the students attend the city's public school where special courses in Jewish religion were offered.[70] The journal explained that the resurgence of Catholic influence in the public schools and the accompanying possiblity of renewed missionary activity posed a genuine danger for Jewish students throughout France. In the case of Nancy, the seat of notorious Jew-baiter M. Forbin-Fanson, the decision to close the city's Jewish school was, according to the *Archives israélites*, especially ill-advised.[71]

The real issue, however, was ideological. In response to a Lyonnais opponent of separate Jewish education, the journal, after citing the example of the Protestants, put it this way: "Why should we not have our own schools and an organ to discuss our religious interests? If you want to take the word *fusion* in an absolute sense, close your synagogues, your cemetaries, and your benevolent societies. The *israélite* is part of the French people; but for that which concerns religion, he has his own special interests."[72] From this statement it is clear that the *régénérateurs* were careful to set limits on the scope of *fusion*. In their view, there was no contradiction in being both Jewish and French, though the relationship between the two identities demanded special attention. For this reason the *régénérateurs* insisted that the separate schools must provide a complete curriculum of religious *and* secular studies. Thus the *Archives israélites* advised the Jewish community of Besançon against establishing a school for religious instruction only, while permitting the children to pursue secular studies in local Christian schools.[73] The environment of integrated education was evidently viewed as the most effective method of forming Jewish Frenchmen capable of maintaining loyalties to both Judaism and France.

The general desirability of special elementary schools for Jewish youth was not felt, at least initially, to extend to higher education. It was believed that students who had been educated in the Jewish primary schools were capable of attending the French *lycées* without jeopardizing their Jewish identity. The secondary schools were to serve as the arena where the *embourgeoisement* of the new generation would be achieved. With the exception of Metz, where a Jewish secondary school had been established early in the Restoration and was annexed to the *école mutuelle israélite*, the attempts at establishing Jewish high schools met with strong opposition. For example, beginning in 1820, the *Comité de surveillance et d'administration des écoles consistoriales de Paris* made repeated proposals for the creation of a secondary school.[74] The idea was formally rejected in 1826 by a specially appointed commission, which explained its opposition in the following report:

> The education of the youth can and must be uniform in the well-to-do class of society; it [education] is the principal element of its future destination, whether it be a civil or a military career, and without it, the most opulent man will enjoy no consideration in the civilized world. The same is not true for the indigent class: it is given to the laborious professions, and primary education must be sufficient for it. If it [education] is more extended, then

165

the shoemaker like the tailor, the carpenter like the locksmith, will find themselves placed in an inferior level in their education and will be discontent with their position in the social order.[75]

In addition to being based on the claim that the consistory lacked adequate financial resources, the commission's rejection of separate secondary institutions for Jews rested on the assumption that such education would be of no benefit for either the upper or lower classes of Jewish society.[76] Children of well-to-do families would find *entrée* into the corresponding stratum of general society only through the French high school system. For children of poor families, education beyond the level of primary instruction would only encourage frustration with their position in the prevailing social order. The idea that education has fundamentally different objectives in different classes of society had been prevalent among Enlightenment thinkers.[77] This notion of a highly stratified social order also characterized the general outlook of the first generation of *régénérateurs* and may explain their efforts during the first phase of *régénération* to form primary schools chiefly on behalf of indigent Jews. In fact, the philanthropic character of Jewish education discouraged most affluent families, at least in Paris, from sending their children to Jewish public schools.

By midcentury many had become aware of the urgency of making Jewish secondary education available to the entire community. In 1850 the Paris Consistory succeeded in creating *cours d'instruction religieuse israélite* for Jewish high school students of the capital. As a response to the growing estrangement from Judaism, and modelled after a similar program introduced for Protestant students, the courses were directed by Grand Rabbi Isidore. Classes met four times per week at the *lycée Louis-le-Grand,* which served as the central meeting place for students of four high schools.[78]

Though widely viewed as crucial to the success of Jewish education, the Central Consistory, and in many instances the departmental consistories as well, failed to provide effective leadership in this sphere. Criticism of the role of the Central Consistory in the promotion of Jewish education was expressed consistently, starting with the establishment of the first modern primary schools. David Singer, the first to publicly attack the consistory for general ineffectiveness in bringing about *régénération,* asserted that the Central Consistory could take no credit for the new schools created by 1819. For the most part, schools were formed as a result of the initiative of individuals. Simon Bloch, who claimed that the Central Consistory exerted a very limited impact on Jewish life in France, attributed the consistories' lack of influence on religious instruction to an excessive concern with bureaucratic and fiscal affairs. Collecting funds, administering consistorial elections and rabbinic appointments, and other bureaucratic duties prevented the consistories from dealing directly with religious and civil education.

Noé Noé, a librarian in Bordeaux and frequent contributor to the *Archives israélites*, took the Central Consistory to task for its failure to provide centralized direction in the educational sphere. Departmental consistories, he explained, did not consider themselves obligated to supervise the local schools, as such establishments came under the general authority of the departmental inspectors. Noé argued that the abandonment of the Jewish schools to outside surveillance was unjustifiable. Blaming the employment of diverse methods of instruction on the excessive authority accorded school directors, Noé described the state of Jewish education as "a chaos where intelligence expires, where the most beautiful hopes come to be lost." Proposals for educational reform, he asserted, ought to flow from a single legal authority in possession of exclusive administrative power. Were the Central Consistory to assume this function the situation would improve dramatically: greater direction from a central authority would produce a much-needed uniform system of popular instruction. Without uniformity of purpose and method, Noé cautioned, the goals of regeneration would continue to remain elusive. Grand Rabbi Arnaud Aron confirmed this condemnation of the consistory in his school inspection report. In the case of the Bas-Rhin, the local consistory was relatively uninvolved in educational affairs, leaving these matters to individual or private initiative. Proponents of *régénération*, liberal or conservative, believed that only through the auspices of the consistory could education ultimately promote the goal of *emancipation intérieure*.[79]

Teachers

As in the general history of French education, one of the most important elements in the development of Jewish education in France was the emergence of teaching as a viable independent profession. Over the course of the nineteenth century teachers played an important role in creating a national political culture for French Jewry, primarily through the instruction of French language and history. Teachers helped break down regional parochialism and thus served as instruments of centralization. Although in each of these areas Jewish teachers acted as agents of modernization, this was not necessarily achieved at the expense of tradition.[80]

Religious instruction in the early years, not surprisingly, was largely in the hands of rabbis. The directors of the Paris, Metz, and Nancy schools were rabbis, and the others, if they did not possess rabbinical degrees, had some rabbinic training. Conflicts between enlightened Jewish leaders, mainly those serving on school committees, and leading rabbis over control of instruction occurred almost from the beginning of the Bourbon Restoration. In Paris some challenged the very idea that the teaching of religion should be in the hands of rabbis. Their main objection was based on the absence of any institutional guarantees to the morality and enlightenment of Jewish religious leaders. Religious instruction demanded the highest levels of competence, and toward this goal it was proposed that a normal school of Jewish theology be established in Paris, where an elite corps of primary school teachers and synagogue rabbis would be trained.[81] The lay leaders also challenged the authority of the grand rabbis to preside over the school's commission of instruction. No doubt against the opinion of the laymen, the school director, himself a rabbi, supported the idea of charging the grand rabbis with inspection of all matters related to religion at least once a month.[82] In the early years of modern Jewish schooling, Alsace was relatively free of these tensions.

The two main criteria of professionalism, functional specialization and independence from nonprofessional authority, characterized the manner in which French teachers of all denominations came to redefine the nature of their occupation. The accession to power of the July Monarchy in 1830 signified a turning point in the professional status of teaching. First, as a result of the government's usurpation of education from church control, teachers began to emerge from the shadow of clerical domination. A differentiation in the roles played by teachers and clerics, hardly possible during the Restoration, now became more widespread. Second, the Guizot ministry energetically endeavored to improve teacher competence through the enhancement of teacher training, the introduction of a more stringent licensing examination, and the creation of a school inspection system. Above all, the normal schools, the state's system of teacher training, became the key force in shaping the attitudes of those who entered the teaching profession. In addition to being directed by men and women who were educated in the secular system of secondary schools, the normal schools fostered the notion of the teacher as an independent professional. Perhaps most important, the normal schools placed the prospective teacher's academic achievement and pedagogical skills above spiritual and social preparation.[83]

Although the available information is somewhat fragmentary, it can be assumed that by the early 1840s the majority of directors of Jewish écoles communales were certified teachers; that is, they were trained at the normal schools. Even in the small towns of the Bas-Rhin where most schools did not receive any significant public funding, normal school graduates were not unheard of in the 1840s.[84] In the Metz region where there were far fewer Jewish schools, the status of the teaching profession was quite different. In the thirty-three towns of the region (excluding the city of Metz, where there were three schools), there were four Jewish *écoles communales* and three unofficial private schools in 1851. The *écoles communales* were all headed by normal school graduates, while the small, private schools were directed by noncertified instructors. Although it is not clear precisely what arrangements were made for Jewish education in the remaining twenty-four towns, it appears that religious instruction was typically provided by a private instructor to children who attended French primary schools. Responsibility for religious instruction in these twenty-four towns was divided between thirteen *ministres officiants* and eleven *instituteurs* (noncertified).[85]

We may conclude that for Jewish educators, teaching as a bona fide, viable profession was possible only in urban or semiurban areas where Jewish schools could count on some municipal support. In Haguenau and Strasbourg, for example, the subvention for Jewish teachers had been raised to 1500 francs, and in Paris and Mulhouse the municipal authorities placed Jewish teachers on the same footing as those of other religions.[86] Even in the small towns of the Bas-Rhin salaries were higher than those of French teachers.[87] In villages throughout the Haut-Rhin, municipal councils obstinately refused to allocate funds for Jewish teachers' salaries. To add insult to injury, Haut-Rhin Jewish teachers were denied permission to attend conferences of elementary instructors as late as 1844.[88] Moreover, the situation appears to have been aggravated by rural community priorities. In the Haut-Rhin there was much local competition for the scarce resources available for salaries; to the detriment of the Jewish teachers, their needs were considered, if at all, only after those of the rabbis and *ministres officiants*.[89] The results were predictable. Meager salaries forced teachers to live in desperate conditions and frequently to supplement their income by taking other jobs. In the course of one year, six young teachers left their positions for more secure careers. Not surprisingly, the number of Jewish students at the *école normale primaire* of Colmar was reportedly decreasing, and the decline was expected to continue.[90] In the Metz region, more often than not, teaching was entrusted to religious functionaries, no doubt as supplemental activity and income.

The new Jewish teachers, who were products of the normal schools, were frequently criticized for being deficient in Jewish religious studies. Often, the teachers had only a superficial knowledge of Hebrew language, Biblical exegesis, and Jewish history. In line with their secular training, these teachers were more concerned with improving the general atmosphere of their schools and teaching secular subjects in a more systematic manner. Their laxity in religious observance, no doubt, motivated the Haut-Rhin Consistory to issue an *arrêté* requiring teachers to attend services morning and evening. According to Simon Bloch, careerism and a misplaced emphasis on the worldly needs over spiritual ones had motivated Jewish teachers to devote themselves to the study of secular subjects at the expense of gaining a foundation in religious matters. Consequently, Jewish religious instruction had become reduced to the mechanical recitation of the catechism with no attention given to explaining the meaning of religious precepts. Bloch called for the establishment of a consistorial examination commission to determine the competence of teachers in Jewish matters, and Rabbi Lion-Mayer Lambert recommended that an examination with a rabbi would contain the problem. Samuel Cahen, himself a former school director, proposed the introduction of a course in Hebrew language and religious instruction at the normal schools for prospective Jewish teachers. The idea of creating a Jewish normal school was even considered by the Central Consistory in 1855, but neither it nor the other recommendations materialized.[91]

Toward the end of the 1840s there were clear indications that the Jewish teachers had evolved into a well-defined professional class. First, there had emerged a collective consciousness, chiefly an awareness of a common plight of destitution and exploitation. In 1842 Jewish teachers in the Haut-Rhin protested their unfavorable conditions relative to Catholic and Protestant teachers. More concretely, this dissatisfaction was manifested in the organization of Jewish teachers of the Haut-Rhin in 1847: they established regular conferences for discussion of instructional issues, and created a retirement-sick fund for teachers no longer able to work.[92] In Metz in 1850 Jewish teachers had become part of a municipal society of instructors, which represented their interests before the local and regional government. The position of J. Bloch, director of the Jewish school of Metz, as president of the teacher's organization, points to an active concern for professionalism among Jewish teachers.[93] The teachers also appear to have endeavored to emancipate themselves from excessive subservience to the rabbis in matters of education. Various sources reveal unmistakable tensions between rabbis and teachers. In one town, for example, the rabbi tried to prevent boys from studying secular subjects while bare-headed. The teacher, a graduate of a normal school, complained to the rector of the Strasbourg *Académie* who upheld the teacher's protest against rabbinic interference.[94]

In seeking to establish their professional independence, Jewish teachers struggled to free themselves from various noneducational duties. According to the by-laws of the Strasbourg and Bordeaux schools, the teacher was expected to clean the building, make repairs, and attend to the fire in winter.[95] The most frequent duty, however, was synagogue officiation. Throughout most of the first half of the nineteenth century, many Alsatian towns and villages found that the most practical arrangement was to hire the local *ministre officiant* to teach in the school. Although this may appear to have been perfectly natural, it created several problems. First, there were, inevitably, competing claims on the time of the *ministre officiant*, who usually was the *shoḥet* (ritual slaughterer) as well, and often needed to perform certain duties during school hours.[96] Second, in those towns where instructional duties were divided between certified teachers and *ministres officiants*, the professional teachers sought control of educational matters. Thus, there was resentment of a proposal made at a joint meeting of the Metz, Nancy, and Strasbourg consistories (in 1846) to place the *ministres officiants* in charge of religious instruction. One school director, Benoît Lévy, argued that the cantors had neither the requisite training nor the inclination to pursue further studies, and that there was no justification for taking education from the hands of the *laïcs* in order to restore it to the control of ministers of religion. This, he insisted, would be a sign of regression not progress.[97] The *régénérateurs* were fully in support of an independent teaching profession. Speaking of the noncertified teachers, (probably the *ministres officiants*), Gerson-Lévy described "men without character, without capacity, [who] infest our countryside in order to make a moral massacre of our innocents."[98] Comparing trained teachers with *ministres officiants*, Benoît Lévy asserted that the former were distinguished, if not "by their knowledge, then at least by their exemplary conduct."[99] Finally, there was a noticeable preference among teachers for a more specialized function, consistent with their training. They had come to view themselves as uniquely skilled to teach and therefore wanted to be free of other obligations. Thus, for example, one teacher, commenting on the proposed discussion of the merits of a catechism, said: "This is a matter for the Rabbis; our mission is completely pedagogical."[100] Though perhaps extreme, this statement is an indication of the direction that attitudes had begun to take.

Based on diverse but incomplete sources, it is, nonetheless, possible to speculate intelligently on the role of teachers as agents of modernization. Often the only resident in a village with formal education, the Jewish teacher, like his gentile counterpart, played a significant part in promoting French literacy and in increasing the prestige of learning. In the town of Ober-Bergheim (Haut-Rhin), for example, the school director formed a library that encouraged the speaking of French in the school. And by virtue of his own education, the teacher could voice certain concerns on behalf of the community. For example, the director of the Jewish school of Lille saw fit to protest against the prevalent use of the word *juif* in the newspaper.[101] Finally, teachers frequently succeeded in demonstrating the potential usefulness of schooling, especially in relation to vocational training.

It should be stressed, however, that Jewish teachers were by no means committed unconditionally to modernization; they were agents of conservatism and stability as well. To an extent, the teachers who made their residence in rural Alsace were undoubtedly aware that any changes at all would have to be introduced very slowly. The involvement of rabbis and *ministres officiants* as teachers provides an added perspective to our consideration of the teaching profession and its impact on modernization. Although there are no complete records on the subject, there is documentation of sixteen school directors and teachers during the period who had received the rabbinical degree either from the *école rabbinique de Metz* or from another rabbinical seminary. For at least six of these men, the job of teaching was a temporary position; when the opportunity arose, they left to assume a full-fledged rabbinical post. Nevertheless, rabbi-teachers must have exerted a stabilizing influence on the teaching profession. Some, such as Rabbi Salomon Lévy of Rixheim, actually established the schools they later directed, or at least instituted the course in religious instruction at an existing Jewish school. Others, such as Rabbi Samuel Wittersheim and Rabbi Louis Morhange of Metz, were in charge of the city's religious education. A number of rabbis were also involved in producing textbooks for use in the schools.[102] The fact cannot be overlooked that rabbis, as school directors, teachers, and authors, undoubtedly set a tone of traditionalism. In order to serve as cantor or *shoḥet,* the *ministres officiants* were required to provide assurances of traditional religious conduct. The effect of this requirement on Jewish education was obviously quite conservative. It should also be recalled that the teachers themselves were usually products of the Alsatian countryside and, by remaining in that region, may have been expressing a certain empathy with the traditional environment. Many, in fact, were opponents of extreme modernization. The controversy surrounding the Central Consistory's 1839 project for drafting a new constitution provides useful data for evaluating the religious orientation of Jewish teachers. Among the list of Bas-Rhin petitioners who protested the plan to place laymen in control of religious matters was a significant number of teachers.[103] This, and the role of the rabbinate in the review of textbooks, may explain the aura of traditionalism that characterized the otherwise modern educational establishments.

8

The Ideology of Educational Reform

THE PROLIFERATION OF modern Jewish schools throughout France provided the *régénérateur* movement with an opportunity to realize its goals on a grand scale. In the schools, more than in any other institution, the values of patriotism, social and economic regeneration, and moral uprightness found expression, and for the most part without the bitter controversies that divided reformers and traditionalists in central and eastern Europe. Innovation in the new Jewish schools centered on two distinct areas of curriculum reform: the inclusion of a full range of secular subjects, and the modernization of religious instruction. According to French educational philosophers, the introduction of secular studies into the schools would bring civilization to the inhabitants of rural France; according to Jewish educators, training in these areas was vital if Jewish students were to acquire French culture and master the same skills as other citizens of France. The educational process was highlighted by instruction in the French language, considered by general and Jewish educators alike to be an indispensable tool for the achievement of national unity and socialization. In fact, it has been pointed out that debates on the instruction of the national language made the schools the focus of confrontation between supporters and opponents of French nationalism in the Alsatian provinces.[1] In Paris the consistorial school *comité* convinced the Paris consistory in 1820 to resolve that "the national language is the only one which may be spoken in the primary school."[2]

In contrast to developments in the capital, the use of French in the private Jewish schools of the northeast continued to meet with resistance as late as the 1840s. Louis Cottard ascribed this, at least in part, to the lack of bilingual (German and French) teachers, upon whom the success of such instruction depended.[3] According to the Cheuvreusse report of 1843, Yiddish was the language of instruction in the "clandestine schools."[4] Like the *maskilim* of Berlin, Jewish educators in France claimed that Yiddish was a crude and impure language that only perpetuated the exclusiveness that characterized centuries of ghetto life.[5] Many insisted that the use of Yiddish discouraged Jews from acquiring a thorough knowledge of French and thereby constituted a leading obstacle to social integration. It was therefore necessary, according to one *régénérateur,* "to banish, to extirpate . . . this dialect and to succeed, thus, in cooperating toward the political fusion of the *Israélites;* it is necessary that the child learn immediately that he is French, that France is his *patrie;* that it is she and those who govern her who have the right to his affection and love."[6] Thus, the *régénérateurs* regarded the French language as an essential feature of the entire educational program and as an indispensable tool in the shaping of patriotic loyalties.

Classes in French reading and writing became the mainstay of the school curriculum. In the Strasbourg school, for example, more time was devoted to these subjects than to any other.[7] In addition, it was felt that exercises in the translation of the Pentateuch and the Hebrew prayers into French not only would provide greater understanding of these Hebrew texts but would serve much-desired linguistic goals as well. Several books intended primarily for instruction attest to the emphasis placed on French language and, concomitantly, to the decline in the knowledge and concern for the Hebrew language. In 1819 Michel Berr produced an abridged translation of the Bible[8] that was adopted in many of the Jewish schools.[9] Using as a model texts employed in Catholic and Protestant schools, as well as books of religious instruction published in Berlin, Seesen, and Dessau, Berr's translation included those sections of the Bible that stressed morality. This would be of practical use to Jewish adults with little free time to study the complete Hebrew text. The author himself conceded, however, that his own abridgement would not satisfy an equally urgent need for a complete French translation of the Bible. Such a venture would,, in Berr's estimation, unite the diverse communities of Sephardic and Ashkenazic origin.[10] Some years later, another French abridgement of the Bible, entitled *Le Sentier d'Israël,* was produced by Jonas Ennery, director of the Jewish school in Strasbourg, in 1843. One reviewer maintained that the translation would not only provide greater knowledge of Jewish antiquity but would also be useful in the propagation of the French language among Jewish students in Alsace, where knowledge of French was evidently deficient as late as the early 1840s. Thus, it was argued, the text would strengthen Jewish ties to France and its citizens. The book was subsequently approved by the Central Consistory and the *Conseil royal d'instruction de l'Université* for use in Jewish schools.[11]

Efforts to produce French translations of Hebrew texts extended also to the realm of divine worship. The *régénérateurs* maintained that the preparation of a French translation of the prayer book was essential for the enormous numbers of Jews who did not understand Hebrew. The purpose of the translation related to two general concerns of *régénération*. First, by enabling worshippers to understand the prayers, it would assist in making the public service a meaningful religious experience, a goal frequently emphasized by early German reformers.[12] The second function of the translation was to facilitate the learning of French for those Jews who were not fluent in the language. The appearance of a prayer book translated by Joel Anspach in 1820 was the first concrete implementation of this objective.[13] Anspach, a member of the *comité d'administration des écoles israélites de Metz*, collaborated with two other *régénérateurs*, Charles Oulif and Gerson-Lévy, in the preparation of the French translation. As was intended by the author, the new translation was also employed as a textbook to teach French reading.[14]

Quite apart from its role in language instruction, the translation of the Hebrew liturgy into French was regarded by the *régénérateurs* as a significant milestone in the legitimization of the Jewish religion. It represented the "nationalization" of the prayers, that is, a rendering of the public cult in the national language. Seen in this way, the translation was an important step in the development of a particular Franco-Jewish consciousness, *le judaïsme français*.[15] French Jews now had a prayer book that was distinctly French. Typically, though, not all of French Jewry concurred with this assessment. In the traditional environs of rural Alsace, Anspach's translation created a bit of a stir: it is reported that in one village the *commissaire* of the synagogue found the presence of French in the prayer book offensive and therefore banned its use.[16] Nevertheless, because of its ritual, linguistic, and national significance and due to its very wide appeal, the translation assumed a significant role, both for primary instruction and for the broader education of the masses, and thus became an important component in the program of *régénération*.

Emphasis on French language instruction was related, in part, to a decline in the knowledge and appreciation of Hebrew. Opinions varied on how prominent a place Hebrew should occupy in the school curriculum. In any case, instruction in the Hebrew language constituted a departure from the traditional curriculum of premodern schools. The Haskalah's emphasis on the aesthetic ideal and the reverence for classical languages were significant factors in the renaissance of Hebrew language and literature at the beginning of the modern period. Though more the exception than the rule, attempts were made to provide systematic instruction in Hebrew grammar, not only for its own sake but as an indispensable skill in the study of the Bible and the Jewish religion. Toward this end, Samuel Cahen, while serving as director of the consistorial school in Paris, wrote the first Hebrew reader of its kind in France, *Cours de lecture hebraïque*, in 1824. This textbook, containing graduated readings, prayers with interlinear translation, and a Hebrew-French vocabulary list, was approved by the Central Consistory and, later, by the Ministry of Religions for use in the Jewish schools.[17] In Strasbourg, classes in Hebrew reading and writing were an important part of the school curriculum. For first-grade students, thirteen hours per week were devoted to these subjects, and beginning in the second grade, the school held daily classes in the translation of the Pentateuch as part of its Hebrew language program. To this were added, in the third grade, classes in the translation of Hebrew prayers.[18] In other schools Hebrew instruction was not as greatly emphasized. Even the best schools that taught Hebrew regularly, however, failed to produce students literate in the language. Gerson-Lévy attributed this state of affairs to a failure to use modern techniques in teaching Hebrew.[19]

The most vigorous efforts on behalf of Hebrew language instruction were championed by educator Mayer Cahun, director of the Jewish school in Haguenau. Maintaining that Hebrew was an essential element in Jewish education, Cahun wrote two school textbooks, *Ḥinukh Sefat Eber* (1842), an introductory reader, and *Tholdoth Jeschurune* (1841), which included a more advanced grammatical section and slightly abridged selections from the Pentateuch.[20] Actually, there was no dearth of texts devoted to the Hebrew language. Numerous rabbis and teachers were involved in publishing Hebrew instructional materials as well as textbooks on the Jewish religion. Of particular significance here is the fact that the Hebrew readers, as a rule, included prayers and selections from the Bible (together with French translations).[21] In other words, the Hebrew language was routinely regarded as an appropriate medium for the inculcation of religious values, not only by staunch traditionalists but also by the more liberal *régénérateurs*.[22] In fact, Cahun asserted that Hebrew was indispensable to the study of Torah and therefore insisted on more rigorous efforts to teach the language and its grammar.[23]

The curriculum of the consistorial school in Paris in the early 1820s was representative of the general currents in Jewish educational philosophy that prevailed among the German and French school reformers. Religious instruction included reading Hebrew, translating the most important events in the Bible, and reciting the catechism. The secular curriculum consisted of French language instruction, including reading, writing, spelling, and grammar; arithmetic; natural science; geography; and ancient and modern history. Classes in history were expected to give special attention to French political institutions and the advantages they guaranteed to the Jews. All instruction was to be conducted in French, enforced by the threat of the teacher's dismissal.[24] There were, of course, many local variations in the school curriculum. In Metz, for instance, mechanical drawing (*dessein linéaire*) was offered from the inception of the school,[25] while in Paris it was not officially incorporated into the course of studies until 1825.[26] Instruction in singing and other subjects was introduced according to local needs.[27] Despite the variations, Jewish schools were characterized by a remarkable degree of uniformity.

Reports made by departmental inspectors on the state of the Jewish schools reveal general satisfaction with, and even praise for, the quality of secular instruction. According to the inspector of the *Académie* of Strasbourg (1821), more emphasis was placed on the French language in the Jewish school than in the French schools of the city.[28] An inspection report submitted to the *Académie* of Paris (1832) expressed satisfaction with the abilities of the students at the boys' and girls' schools in French and Hebrew reading, French grammar, arithmetic, and the history of France. School director Samuel Cahen was commended for this excellence and the inspector proposed that Cahen, who had already been honored earlier in 1832 by the Minister of Public Instruction, be given an award.[29] Other reports, some of which were published in the French press, enthusiastically described the excellence of Jewish primary education in the schools established in numerous Alsatian towns and cities. The completeness of the curriculum and the aptitude of the teachers met with much approval among gentile observers of Jewish schools.[30]

The Jewish school in Metz was consistently singled out for accolades for having attained a distinguished place among the French schools of the city. Early in its history a member of the *Conseil d'administration de la société d'encouragement* was sufficiently impressed with the instructional method of the school to assert that "in order to become well acquainted with the spirit of the new method, one must study it in the Jewish schools."[31] Before the establishment of the *école normale* of Metz in 1831, the rector of the *Académie* frequently sent Catholic and Protestant teachers to the Jewish school for a practical course enabling them to obtain the *brévêt de capacité* (certificate of competency). In recognition of the efforts of the school's director, Isaïe Bloch, the *Université* and the *société pour instruction élémentaire* presented him with four medals of honor. Moreover, the large number of students who were reported to have gone on to higher education attests to the esteem in which the school was held. Each year many graduates of the Jewish school continued their studies at the *collège royal* and at the *école supérieure municipale*, and numerous others were placed as apprentices in the city's workshops, at the expense of the *société israélite*.[32]

Efforts in the vocational training of Jewish youth also received unqualified praise in the French press. Actually, the two Jewish vocational schools, in Strasbourg and in Mulhouse, provided extensive secular and religious instruction to boys in their early adolescence. For example, in 1843 the *L'Industriel alsacien* publicized the course of instruction offered at the *école israélite d'arts et métiers* in Mulhouse and lauded the courses in French language, German, history, mathematics, and design. The newspaper was particularly impressed by the students' progess in the mechanical arts and by their fluency in French, and reported that the masters were satisfied with their young apprentices.[33]

As noted earlier, the inclusion of secular subjects in the school curriculum was only one component of educational modernization. Religious instruction in the modern Jewish schools also underwent a thorough transformation, consistent with the ideological and social changes first taking root at the turn of the nineteenth century. In an unprecedented manner, the new schools undertook to offer students a systematic presentation of the Jewish religion. "Religion," it should be noted, is a modern concept, one that assumes implicitly the existence of a sphere of life *beyond* the boundaries of religion. Before the modern era no such boundaries existed in Judaism; Jewishness was an all-encompassing system. The introduction of classes in "religion" thus represents a monumental shift in the way Jews viewed the nature of their existence. The new dichotomy between "Jewish" and "non-Jewish," or "religious" and "secular," signified an unprecedented innovation in the traditional approach to Jewish education of earlier times.[34] Traditional education in the *heder* centered on the study of the Pentateuch, first with the aid of a translation and, at the next level, with the commentary of Rashi (R. Solomon Yiẓḥaki, 1040–1105). Drawing on the major sources of the Oral Law—the Talmud and the Midrash— Rashi's commentary provided the most representative and authoritative traditional Jewish interpretation of Scripture. "*Ḥumash* with Rashi," the standard mode of Jewish Bible study, introduced children to rabbinic law and lore and attested to the organic unity of the Written and Oral Law. By studying the Pentateuch with Rashi, who wrote his commentary with a didactic purpose, traditionally educated students were exposed to "the peculiar position of the Jews as a chosen people, the inherently mythic distinction between them and the nations, an understanding of the fate of the Jewish people in the Diaspora and their faith in their coming redemption."[35]

Excellence in Talmudic study constituted the highest goal of Jewish education in the premodern period. Traditional education was geared to the abilities of the most capable students in the hope that they would become Talmudic scholars, the most esteemed level in the Jewish scale of values. Without a systematic curriculum or graded instruction, students were generally introduced to Talmudic study at a very early age, and four or five year olds might be grouped together with more advanced students. More often than not, students pursued these advanced subjects without any training in the fundamental subjects of Hebrew language and Mishnah. Secular studies, perhaps with the exception of simple arithmetic, were not considered important and in fact might impede the manifest goal of instruction: the inculcation of traditional Jewish values.

The first to subject Jewish education to a thorough reexamination were the Berlin *maskilim*. Although modern criticism of prevailing instruction may be traced to the sixteenth-century thinker and rabbinical authority R. Judah Loew (the Maharal) of Prague, the *maskilim* were the first to question both the methods of traditional Jewish education and its underlying ideological principles. The new educational program of the Haskalah was articulated most fully in 1782 by Naphtali Herz Wessely in his pamphlet, *Divre Shalom ve-Emet* (*Words of Peace and Truth*).[36] Almost immediately after its appearance in Berlin, the Hebrew tract was translated by Berr Isaac Berr and circulated in Alsace. Wessely's central premise was that traditional Jewish education was inadequate both in content and methods. He maintained that there were essentially two sources of teaching, the Law of God (*Torat Ha-Shem*) and the Law of Man (*Torat Ha-Adam*) The former was comprised of the Written and Oral Torah; the latter was made up of ethical teachings, manners, and worldly knowledge. According to Wessely one could attain the level of fear of God only by first gaining familiarity with the Law of Man.[37] The author went so far as to emphasize that one who has studied the Law of God and has not been introduced to science, manners, and vocational training was rightfully considered a burden to his own people and to the rest of humanity.[38] Perhaps even more radical was the suggestion that beyond their utilitarian value, secular studies were valuable in themselves and therefore deserved a place next to traditional Torah studies in the school curriculum. Due to these views, *Divre Shalom ve-Emet* encountered bitter

179

opposition from many prominent central European rabbis. Among French rabbis, however, there was no public criticism, nor is there any record of private comment.[39]

Specific proposals for educational reform in Germany and France were, to a significant degree, modelled after the activities of the Philanthropinists, the educational exponents of rationalism. Influenced by the educational psychology of men such as Johann Bernard Basedow and Johann Heinrich Pestalozzi, Jewish reformers on both sides of the Rhine endeavored to establish schools where instruction would be systematic, cumulative, and attuned to the individual needs of each child.[40] Studies in geography, history, mathematics, German or French, and vocational training were expected to produce a new generation of Jews, capable of assuming their place as productive members of general society. Instruction in Jewish subjects, too, would need to be improved. Pentateuchal study, formerly considered secondary to Talmudic learning, now assumed a central position in the new school curriculum. Use of Mendelssohn's German translation became widely accepted in the enlightened schools of Germany, and the accompanying *Biur* (commentary) supplanted the commentary by Rashi. The new commentary, though it did not contradict the traditional Jewish interpretation, stressed the literal meaning of the Bible, as well as its moral and aesthetic elements. This was a tremendously significant innovation, since the student was no longer exposed to the Oral Law, as had been the case when Rashi's commentary was used.[41] Talmud was eliminated from the modern curriculum, a development that may be attributed to its negative appraisal among proponents of the European Enlightenment and the Haskalah. Although Wessely himself did not eschew the value of Talmudic study, he minimized its importance in the new educational system. Rabbinic literature was not considered germane to the goals of the Haskalah, nor was mastery over the Talmud any longer regarded as the most honored achievement in Jewish religious and intellectual life: "We were not all created to be Talmudic scholars, to delve into the depths of the religion and to give instruction; for God differentiated among men and He gave each man his own abilities at the moment of creation; and each one will attain perfection according to his own interest and ability."[42] Obviously influenced by the prevailing conception of human individuality, Wessely conceded that the reordering of curriculum priorities was a legitimate undertaking. With the establishment of the Berlin *Freischule* in 1781, the educational philosophy of the Haskalah was first put into practice. Thereafter, many enlightened Jewish schools in Germany and Austria were founded according to this model, where the curriculum of secular and religious studies followed the guidelines proposed by Wessely and fellow *maskilim*.[43]

Because of France's unified political character, statesmen and philosophers considered the question of the role of religion in education to be critical to the future of French society and civilization. Based on the principle of secularization, the republican ideal of the *école laïque* held that religious teaching should be excluded from the school curriculum. Nevertheless, educational secularization met with persistent opposition, thus requiring every government beginning with Napoleon to abandon the notion of pure *laïcité*. In fact, it was not fully achieved until the Third Republic. According to the Napoleonic compromise, instruction was first and foremost secular, with religion taught as an independent subject. The idea of religion as a separate entity was further advanced by the *loi Guizot*, which gave moral and religious instruction a preeminent position in the curriculum.[44] Although the inclusion of religious studies in the public school curriculum may seem out of character for bourgeois France, it actually reveals the extent to which traditional religion lay deep in the consciousness of the French nation. Guizot, Cousin, and others succeeded in convincing liberal bureaucrats that in light of this reality, controlling religion was preferable to attacking it. Furthermore, to this rather pragmatic position was added a revised conception of religion. *Religion* for the educators really signified "religious morality," a formulation whose emphasis was on the moral component of religious teachings.[45]

While liberal French educators came to legitimate a significant role for religion in the schools at a relatively late date, apparently as a secondary consideration, the Jewish *régénérateurs* viewed religious instruction from the beginning as a crucial element in the overall education of the child. In his report on behalf of the Metz school *comité* in 1819, Gerson-Lévy explained the importance of religious instruction:

> Instruction is not limited to shaping the spirit; it is essentially the heart which must be molded, since it is good sentiments more than spirit and science which form a sweet, sensible, and elevated character. Philosophic truths do not impress the generality of men; [only] the principles of religion are within reach of the less enlightened. Religion, so closely united with sound morality must, then, constitute the first goal of instruction.[46]

The conception of education expressed in this passage reserved a special place for religion. Although secular studies were considered decisive for the development of the mind, religious studies, and those alone, were capable of molding character.

Several factors explain this subtle divergence from the prevailing philosophy of French education. In the post-Sanhedrin era, when Judaism had been theoretically divested of its national character, religion came to represent the single major unifying force for French Jewry. Jewish educators therefore insisted that religious instruction not simply be preserved but strengthened, albeit in a manner that reflected their own ideological orientation. Furthermore, in a period of tumultuous social and political change, when the social conduct and attitudes of the Jews were criticized from within and without, the Jewish religion provided the sole link with the past and, as such, represented an important source of stability. Judaism was regarded both as a foundation upon which new values could be built and as an authority that could be invoked to justify the political and economic transformation of French Jewry.

With the establishment of modern Jewish schools in France the methods and content of religious instruction underwent substantial modification. Whereas, in the ḥeder, the fundamentals of the religion were acquired through the study of traditional source-texts, with no pretense of systematic instruction, the new schools placed emphasis upon a compressed presentation of religious principles. The relatively large number of hours devoted to secular subjects left little time for the sort of religious study that characterized pre-modern Jewish education. It became necessary to condense the subject matter of the Jewish religion so that religious instruction could conform to the students' crowded schedules. For example, according to the 1818 règlement of the Paris school, 9.5 hours per week were devoted to Hebrew reading, translation of the Bible, and "religious instruction," as compared to 21.5 hours for secular subjects.[47] Though the relative number of hours devoted to Jewish subjects in the Strasbourg school was slightly higher, secular studies predominated there as well.[48]

Invariably, the question of how much emphasis to place on secular learning exacerbated tensions between progressivists and traditionalists. In the rural communities of the Bas-Rhin, much of the local population was hostile to the idea of secular studies and therefore resisted the Strasbourg Consistory's attempts to establish modern elementary schools in the countryside.[49] Even in existing schools, there were difficulties. In one instance, in 1842, the director of the Strasbourg school cautioned parents against permitting the literature and poetry of Racine and Corneille to "seduce" the students. He asserted that the beauties of poetry, as well as the best models of piety, devotion, and modesty, were provided not by French literature but by the Bible.[50] The Archives israélites de France reported that in Blotzheim (Haut-Rhin) the Grand Rabbi of Colmar publicly inveighed against secular study, claiming that it was responsible for the weakening of religion. For this reason, the journal explained, the grand rabbi refused to support the creation of modern Jewish schools.[51]

Both the predominance of secular studies in the new curriculum and the accompanying reduction in the time spent on religious instruction explain the emergence of a new type of textbook, the catechism. Modelled after the Christian prototype, the numerous Jewish catechisms that appeared in Germany and France in the first half of the nineteenth century were designed to suit the requirements of the modern curriculum and were directed at the growing numbers of students unable or unlikely to attain proficiency in classical Jewish texts. Organized in a question-answer format, the new textbook represented an attempt to systematize the most important elements of the faith. Typically, the enumeration of religious principles and ethical duties constituted the overwhelming portion of the textbook. Central to this focus was the inclusion of the Decalogue and Maimonides' Thirteen Articles of Faith. The former was seen as the foundation of ethical monotheism, while the latter included specific articles of the Jewish faith. The inclusion of both the Decalogue and the Maimonidean creed reveals the tension that characterized the first modern attempts at Jewish self-definition. On the one hand, early nineteenth-century Jewish thinkers ceased to regard their faith as outside the general circle of world religions. Emphasis was therefore placed on the Ten Commandments, which were regarded as the foundation of all morality.[52] On the other hand, educators sought a formulation that would preserve Jewish identity in an age of universalism. The general decline of a *halakhah*-centered way of life necessitated the substitution of a creed acceptable to the emancipated Jew.[53] Systems such as Maimonides' Thirteen Articles of Faith promoted a consciousness of the particular value and meaning of Jewish identity at a time when other ties binding the individual to the community had loosened.[54]

Failure to provide substantive explanations of the ceremonial laws constituted the major flaw in the catechistic approach to Jewish education. Doctrine was invariably preferred over practical application, usually resulting in a superficial characterization of the Jewish religion. Consequently, reservations concerning the use of catechisms were occasionally voiced. Simon Bloch, editor of *La Régénération,* insisted that the catechistic technique only encouraged the mechanical recitation of abstract ideas "at the expense of sound religious instruction."[55] Grand Rabbi Salomon Ulmann, himself the author of a catechism,[56] argued that the new method, at best, could only be considered supplementary to traditional textual study.[57] These criticisms notwithstanding, the catechism became the predominant mode of religious instruction in the Jewish schools of France.

Instruction in the Jewish religion drew heavily on the ideological premises of the Paris Sanhedrin. Judaism had been defined as a "confession," not unlike Catholicism and Protestantism, which would qualify but not alter a Jew's primary French identity. Various aspects of the traditional Jewish *mentalité*, particularly those relating to social exclusiveness, were no longer considered operative in the context of the new socio-political reality. The catechistic summation of the Jewish religion reflected these changes. As a rule the Sanhedrin's doctrinal decisions appeared as an appendix to the textbook. This was necessary, according to a review of one early catechism, because "the maxims proclaimed by the Sanhedrin concerning the duties of the Jews towards the state and their relations with other citizens are based on unimpeachable authority but are of such great importance that they must be inculcated in the spirit of the young people."[58] Jewish educators therefore urged schools to incorporate obligations to state and society within the framework of religious instruction, since "these duties are religiously ordained."[59]

Of greater importance than the routine reproduction of the doctrinal decisions was the general tendency employed throughout each of the catechisms to enlist the fundamental doctrines of the Sanhedrin in the teaching of religious ideas. The Sanhedrin's conception of the universal brotherhood of man received the greatest emphasis and elaboration. The most widely used Jewish catechism in France, Samuel Cahen's *Précis élémentaire d'instruction religieuse et morale*,[60] devoted much of its attention to the religious and ethical duties incumbent upon people of all faiths, while the sections concerning the distinctiveness of Judaism were more limited. In the spirit of universalism, the textbook taught that the term *brother* included "all men who recognize God."[61] The section that enumerated the specific obligations of "fraternal charity," such as visiting the sick, burying the dead, redeeming captives, and supporting the poor, was based on the idea that there was no distinction between Jew and non-Jew in the performance of ethical duties.[62] The Halévy catechism was even more elaborate in its application of this doctrine. Halévy explained, in accordance with the Sanhedrin's interpretation, that the prohibition against lending money on interest "to your brother" included non-Jews: "Thus a Jew of today cannot, without both transgressing the law of God and offending justice and humanity, allow himself to engage in this illicit commerce towards individuals whose religious opinions, it is true, differ from his, but who are no less strict observers of these great principles, fundamental bases of all . . . civilized peoples."[63]

184

Later on, as we shall see, the uniqueness of the Jewish religion would be given greater attention.

The primacy of moral instruction in Jewish educational thought echoed the liberal conception of education as outlined by Guizot and his supporters. Liberal French educators held that it would be possible to concretize moral teachings by making use of traditional religious principles and texts. Bible study would provide a framework for the discussion of moral issues in a manner that would clarify and underscore their contemporaneity. Setting as their goal the creation of a society of morally perfected citizens, French educators strove to introduce a curriculum that would emphasize loyalty and selflessness, on the one hand, and attack vanity and egoism, on the other.[64] For Jewish educators, the emphasis on the moral component of religious teaching represented a subtle shift from the past. Although it is undeniable that the teaching of virtue had, historically, been the unquestioned aim of instruction, it is equally clear that the inculcation of good character traits had always been inseparable from the practical aspects of ritual conduct. In reevaluating the Jewish past, the *régénérateurs* concluded that the narrow concerns of traditional education permitted the student "to ignore the grandeur of Judaism's dogmas and the purity of its morality."[65] They contended that such a system was dangerous insofar as it could lead to superstition, multiplication of religious practices, and ultimately, to irreligion. Moral teaching was therefore incorporated within the framework of religious instruction in order to serve as a corrective to the failures of previous generations. Not surprisingly, the goals of strengthening the children's faith and proving to them that virtue was the first condition of piety were frequently pursued in the more modern schools at the expense of ritual instruction.[66]

Nevertheless, neither the *régénérateurs'* growing impatience with traditional instruction, nor their contributions to the public discussions of school policy left quite the expected mark on French Jewish education. Schools remained, for the most part, under the control of directors and teachers who were loyal to Jewish tradition and therefore less inclined to innovation. However, in some instances traditionally-minded schoolmen were themselves influenced by the ideology of educational reform; they subsequently sought to integrate the new methods and concepts with traditional goals and techniques. Possibly the best example of a Jewish educator who was at once traditional and innovative was Mayer Cahun, head teacher at the Jewish school in Haguenau and author of several textbooks. A leading theoretician and practitioner of moral instruction, Cahun followed Niemeyer, the German theologian and educational philosopher, in explaining that the goal of education is to mold character so that it is accustomed to practice social virtues: truth, loyalty, goodness, generosity, zeal, and self-denial. The result, he insisted, would be a natural desire for increased enlightenment and a greater sense of loyalty to civic obligations.[67] Most important, Cahun asserted that moral instruction must be the foundation of the entire school curriculum. Declaring that "we are men before Jews, Christians, and Mohammedans . . . , citizens of the world before citizens of the state," he conceived of moral education in universal terms and emphasized the advantages of a uniform course of study for all children. As for methods of instruction, Cahun relied upon the philosophy of Pestalozzi, a leading Philanthropinist who maintained that the success of moral education depends on the presentation of images that appeal to the child's senses and on the formation of moral, intellectual, and aesthetic impressions. According to Pestalozzi, emphasis must be placed on cultivating feelings and ultimately on *"intuitions morales."* In applying this theory to Jewish education, Cahun stressed the importance of the Hebrew language in developing the *sentiment esthétique.* A knowledge of Hebrew would enable the student to appreciate the poetic beauty of Scripture. True moral education, Cahun cautioned, was not a dispassionate, descriptive account of *moeurs* but a subtle blend of the intellectual and the experiential, successful only when "descending to the heart."[68]

Cahun's understanding of the relationship between morality and religion was also inspired by the philosophy of Pestalozzi. Claiming that moral instruction had been neglected in the traditional curriculum, he urged Jewish educators to make morality the central focus of the school, to the point where even "religious education comes to crown morality."[69] Although moral perfection was consistently viewed within traditional literature as an ultimate goal of Jewish law and ritual, Cahun correctly sensed that, in the secular climate of nineteenth-century France, the modern emphasis on morality might be perceived by Alsatian traditionalists as a radical departure from traditional views. In seeking to assuage these concerns, Cahun asserted that religious values can be developed earlier in a child whose moral sentiments have already been awakened. The very first stage in this educational process was ideally in the hands of the mother who teaches the child about virtue and God.[70] Instruction at the school would build on this foundation, or create it for those in whose homes it had been lacking.

In order to justify both the primacy of moral instruction and the inclusion of secular studies, Cahun introduced the notion that the love of humankind must precede the love of God. Echoing Wessely's *Divre Shalom ve-Emet,* this theoretical orientation was at the heart of Cahun's efforts at curriculum reform. Natural history, geology, geography, and mathematics appeared to him as a means to appreciate "the magnificent works of the Creator," enabling the child to obtain "more pure and complete ideas of God and His revelation."[71] Cahun's stance justified secular studies in religious terms. At the same time, religious instruction was tailored to conform to the demands of progressive educational philosophy. Religion, Cahun wrote, must appeal to reason "if one wants to guard against fanaticism and idolatry," for the essence of religion does not lie in the "adhesion to certain national truths, nor in a great number of prayers, ceremonies, *pénitences,*" or other external practices; rather, the essence of religion lies in striving for the greatest good of humanity, and requires the harmonious development of human spirit, soul, and heart. Religion, then, has a moral aim: to energetically combat egoism and to establish a "holy alliance" between God and men. It must endeavor to inspire people to a noble emulation of God, which will result in conformity to moral precepts.[72]

The theoretical system set down by Cahun included a synthesis of progress and tradition typical of German *maskilim* one generation earlier. The chief elements of Philanthropinism, including instruction geared to the individual student, aesthetic perfection, physical education, and hygiene, in addition to the emphasis on moral virtues, all found their place in his system. It would be incorrect to view Cahun as a liberal with reformist views, however. He was aware that modern educational reform had employed language and introduced concepts that were, in some cases, fundamentally foreign to the Jewish tradition. While Cahun was undoubtedly convinced that Jewish values could be transmitted more effectively by modern techniques, he remained a staunch champion of tradition in the battle against secularization. He cautioned his readers that belief in the existence of God, Providence, and eternity, features of what he called natural religion and reminiscent of Deism, were themselves inadequate for the education of the Jewish child. In his view, the primary objective of Jewish education was to teach students that religion was the embodiment of revealed, superior truths. Cahun, like most *régénérateurs,* believed that this could be carried out successfully through sound instruction in biblical studies.[73]

Whereas Jewish education in France reflected many of the ideological, religious, and methodological issues that divided the community at large, the catechisms themselves were consistently orthodox in their presentation of ceremonial laws. On this point the French textbooks diverged significantly from the German textbooks, which tended to reflect the ideology of religious reform. An obvious lack of regard for Talmudic Judaism was more evident in the German catechisms, as was their common assertion that religious practices must be modified in accordance with the new *zeitgeist*.[74] The traditional character of the Franco-Jewish catechisms may be explained by several factors. First, the official involvement of rabbis in the review of books intended for Jewish schools safeguarded the instructional materials from unorthodox formulations. For example, in 1812 the manuscript of a catechism composed by J. Johlson, *Rudiments d'instruction religieuse et morale pour les jeunes français israélites*, was sent to the Central Consistory by the Minister of Cultes, to whom the book was originally submitted for approval. Upon examining the catechism the Central Consistory concluded that the book's emphasis on the pluralistic nature of religion was dangerous for the young child. Moreover, the author had omitted several articles of faith, including the belief in the resurrection of the dead and the doctrine of the Messiah. Johlson was also criticized for having failed to include practices connected with the festivals, the duty of daily prayer, wearing the prayer shawl and phylacteries, circumcision, and the obligation to study the Torah. Finally, the Central Consistory asserted that the catechism contained a "spirit of reform which is always fatal and pernicious to religious societies which stray from the accepted rules."[75] It was decided that the book could only be adopted on the condition that its tone be modified, that its omissions be rectified, and that "those principles which we have described in our remarks as nonorthodox" be eliminated. When a revised edition of the catechism was resubmitted in 1820, the Central Consistory recommended its adoption as an elementary text for Jewish youth, asserting that the book "offers all the necessary guarantees, both with respect to orthodoxy as well as in moral and social respects."[76]

The Central Consistory expressed similar reservations concerning an abridgement of the Bible by Michel Berr in 1820. A thorough examination of the work led the body to conclude that the abridgement was not only too condensed but, more significantly, had "preserved and even created expressions and interpolations [that are] harmful with respect to orthodoxy."[77] The scrutiny to which a textbook was subjected before it could be adopted for use in the schools became an important consideration for prospective authors. It is not at all unlikely that awareness of the process exerted a moderating influence on textbook composition.

The generally moderate position of the *régénérateurs* on the subject of religious reform and its influence on the character of the catechisms can be seen in the efforts to provide meaningful, contemporary explanations for the Jewish holidays. Holidays such as Passover and Tisha B'Av commemorated specific events in history that no longer appeared relevant to the new era in which French Jews lived. On the surface, the Passover holiday recalling the exodus of the Israelites from Egypt, from slavery to freedom, was out of step with the new conception of history exemplified by both the general progress of the nineteenth century and specifically by the emancipation of the Jews. Characteristically, however, the *régénérateurs* retained the ritual and liturgical symbols, but in a new form in order to render them intelligible to the modern Jew. Samuel Cahen, editor of the *Archives israélites de France,* claimed that the words of the Passover Haggadah, "next year in Jerusalem," could not be taken literally by a people that had already achieved political redemption. "We are not speaking of an actual restoration," Cahen explained, "it is a pipe-dream of ailing minds; the times do not move backwards." He insisted that the phrase be understood in symbolic-historical terms and not as an indication of future aspirations.[78] In a slightly different way Michel Berr interpreted prayers for a return to Zion in the broad sense of the universal strivings for human perfection.[79]

This idea had been developed further by Berr in his catechism, *Nouveau précis élémentaire d'instruction religieuse.*[80] After presenting a traditional accounting of the origin and ritual practices of the Passover holiday, the text continues:

> *Question:* Toward which thoughts must we now devote ourselves concerning the holiday, and what must be, in celebrating it, the object of our prayers and our wishes?
>
> *Answer:* To deliver us from evil, from sin and culpable passion; like our ancestors, from oppression and servitude; to enable our brethren everywhere to enjoy the benefits of justice, and that they will become . . . worthy of it by their virtues and their conduct.[81]

Here the child was offered an explanation of Passover that stressed the contemporaneity of the holiday over its historical reality. The holiday's theme of freedom from spiritual and physical enslavement was firmly integrated with the recent experiences of French Jews and the aspirations of their less fortunate coreligionists elsewhere. Although there is certainly no question that the classical Jewish sources stress the idea of contemporary relevance,[82] it is equally clear that the traditional concept of contemporaneity derives from a close identification with the historical events themselves. The new view, as exemplified by Berr's catechism, reflected a subtle shift in emphasis: focus was directed at the present, and those elements in the past in accord with the contemporary situation were retrieved and reinterpreted accordingly. This was, in essence, a retrospective method of reinterpretation that enabled some to preserve the traditional form of religious rituals.

Tisha B'Av, the fast day that commemorates the destruction of the two Temples, presented a similar challenge to the *régénérateurs.* Once again, Berr described the traditional customs observed on the day, including the recitation of the Book of Lamentations and the general mood of mourning, but added the following remarks: "The ministers of our religion must accompany them [the readings and customs] with exhortations conforming to our obligations, to our beliefs, and to our present hopes."[83] Particular emphasis was placed on observance "by remembrance of the events to which it [the fast] is related, by alms-giving and other acts of humanity." The meaning of the holiday was thus understood to transcend its immediate historical reality in favor of its application to contemporary matters. As was the case with Passover, the idea of historical memory was employed in order to retain the traditional customs, but with a new conceptual focus.[84]

Even among the most radical plans to reinterpret Tisha B'Av, there was no suggestion that it be eliminated. In place of the public expression of mourning for the loss of political and religious independence, one writer advocated a modest ceremony where the significance of the day would be reinterpreted in accordance with the following suggested sermon:

> My brothers, two thousand years ago we had a *patrie*, a temple, a Jewish government; we no longer have one nor the other, but the ways of Providence are just: it has given us after long tribulations, a *patrie*, and with it everything that a free man could want: enjoyment of our rights. The government under which we live knows in all Frenchmen only the children of the same family; let us shed a tear for the horrible past, but let us not be ungrateful toward the present; let us thank God for that which he has done for us. Our coreligionists, in truth, are not yet everywhere as fortunate as us; let us pray for them, and especially let us show by our attachment to our *belle patrie*, that all Jews will be worthy to recover one.[85]

Observance of Tisha B'Av had, according to the proposal, a dual function. For French Jews it was an opportunity both to acknowledge the hand of God in correcting the anomaly of 1800 years of Jewish homelessness, and to pray that Jews elsewhere will attain the same good fortune. Without question, attempts to provide justification for the retention of practices and observances were somewhat strained. Nevertheless, they testify to the determined efforts of the *régénérateurs* to ascribe meaning to seemingly obsolescent ceremonies. Thus, neither Passover nor Tisha B'Av were seen as forms of ritualized identification with the experiences of Jews in ancient times, but as symbols of emancipation, patriotic loyalty, and freedom from persecution. In short, the *régénérateurs* emphasized that Jewish holidays had a propaedeutic function; that is, their purpose was to teach moral lessons to contemporary Jews.

The vigorous efforts made by the *régénérateurs* to create modern Jewish elementary schools underscore the centrality of education in the program of *régénération*. Through education the *régénérateurs* hoped to shape a new generation of French Jews that would take its place in general society while maintaining a strong Jewish identity. The ideology of Jewish educational reform, although nurtured by contemporary trends in liberal educational philosophy, remained traditional in its general orientation. In the final anaysis, however, even these limited cognitive goals were subordinated to affective ones. The new system of religious instruction sought, simply, to inculcate the values of patriotism, Judaism, and morality, and in this regard, took its cue from the Paris Sanhedrin. In addition, the dangers posed by growing indifference to Judaism and by Christian missionary activities served as a reminder of the need to strengthen the commitment to Jewish values. Nevertheless, despite its relatively moderate posture on the question of religious reform, the educational ideology of *régénération* failed to go far beyond the incorporation of the major doctrines and beliefs of Judaism.

9

The Modernization of Rabbinic Training

PERHAPS THE MOST critical element in the general conception of *régénération* was the development of a modern, enlightened rabbinate. The consistorial leadership and the *régénérateurs* maintained that changes in the political status, social organization, and religious orientation of French Jewry demanded corresponding modifications in the functions of the rabbi. Moreover, it was widely believed that the successful implementation of religious reforms depended upon the receptiveness of the rabbinate to the ideology of *régénération,* given the centrality of the rabbis in the religious life of their communities. As we shall see, the modernization of the rabbinate proceeded rather slowly, despite the vigorous efforts of the *régénérateurs.*

Early in the Restoration period the rabbinate had become the target of "enlightened" criticism in Paris. David Singer, the first public critic of the consistorial system, argued that the rabbinate was largely responsible for the consistories' failure to effect *régénération.*[1] The rabbis, according to Singer, were generally unenlightened and unconcerned with issues of importance to French Jewry. In comparison to the ministers of the Christian religions, the rabbis were found to be irresponsible and incompetent. The temple services bore no trace of the "priestly" functions associated with a religious leader, other than the celebration of marriages and a small number of orations and sermons. Singer also charged that the rabbis were ignorant of "any useful science" and of the national language. "Their fanatic attachment to the absurd religious practices," their intolerance for those who think and act differently from themselves, and their excessive presumption of power and conceit combined to impede the process of *régénération*.[2]

Appeals for modification in the scope and nature of rabbinic functions were prevalent in western European countries where Jews had achieved at least some degree of civic equality. In Germany and England, as in France, liberal Jews sought to assign to the rabbis pastoral duties normally associated with the Christian ministry: officiating at marriages and funerals, visiting the sick, and preaching. Historically, these functions had not been within the domain of the rabbi, who traditionally served as head teacher of the yeshiva and as chief of the religious court. In some instances, generally limited to Sephardic communities, he also preached in the synagogue.

The first official mention of new functions for the rabbis appeared in the answers of the Assembly of Jewish Notables to the Napoleonic commission. The assembly confirmed that with the dissolution of Jewish communal autonomy, the Jewish judicial system had been abolished and the rabbis no longer exercised their judicial authority. With the closing of most traditional yeshivot by the end of the eighteenth century, rabbis, for the most part, lost their position as heads of the academy.[3] Upon the creation of the consistorial system, the duties of the French rabbinate were formally established by law. The *règlement* of 1806 specified the following rabbinical functions: to teach religion; to teach the doctrines included in the decisions of the Sanhedrin; to teach obedience to French law; to teach that military service is a sacred duty and that Jewish law offers dispensation from religious observances during such service; to preach in the synagogue and recite prayers for the emperor and his family; and to perform marriages and divorces following the completion of the civil ceremony.[4]

This delineation of rabbinical duties reflected the government's hope that the rabbis would play an important role in the regeneration of French Jewry, primarily as teachers of religious and civil morality. The *régénérateurs* envisioned a similar mission for the rabbinate, one that could be carried out chiefly through preaching. The sermon was believed to have great potential as an educational tool, as an effective method of articulating Jewish values in a contemporary idiom. Furthermore, in its most eloquent form, the sermon could serve as a means of edifying the soul. In these two respects the traditional *derashah*, a homiletical discourse rooted in rabbinic sources and delivered in Yiddish, was considered to be seriously deficient. For the new generation of emancipated French Jews, the *derashah* was stylistically repugnant and materially irrelevant.

The *régénérateurs* therefore insisted that the *derashah* be replaced by a new type of preaching that was better attuned to the manner and needs of nineteenth-century French Jewry. The modern Jewish sermon that developed in Germany under the influence of the Protestant pulpit[5] became the natural model for the French *régénérateurs*. Samuel Cahen, who frequently looked across the Rhine to assess the progress of the *régénérateur* movement, maintained that "if our rabbis . . . will give themselves with zeal to the art of oratory and follow the example of their colleagues in Germany, then perchance there will also be found among them a Solomon or a Mannheimer. Until then we will be correct in saying that preaching does not yet exist in the French synagogue."[6] The *régénérateurs* believed that the new style of preaching, with its emphasis on oratory eloquence and spiritual-moral "edification," would greatly enhance the public service and thereby attract estranged Jews back to the synagogue.[7] It was argued further that, as a mode of public education, rabbinic preaching could help meet the dangers posed by Christian missionaries.[8]

Despite demands that sermons become a regular feature of the Sabbath services, preaching in Alsace, and even in Metz, remained infrequent as late as the middle of the century. Most rabbis continued to preach in Yiddish or German and resisted any departure from the traditional pattern of preaching only twice a year, on the Sabbaths before Passover and Yom Kippur.[9] Even Emmanuel Deutz, grand rabbi of the Central Consistory, preached in Yiddish![10] The failure of the rabbis to preach more frequently and their inability (or unwillingness) to adjust to the new style of preaching only motivated the *régénérateurs* to demand that courses in rhetoric be introduced at the *école rabbinique*.

The failure of the rabbinate to play an active role in the *régénération* of French Jewry was attributed, in part, to the absence of a modern rabbinical training facility. The idea of creating a rabbinical seminary first surfaced immediately before the establishment of the consistorial system. A "plan d'organisation du culte juif en France," prepared by a group of Jewish notables at the insistence of the prefect of Moselle in 1805, offered a set of guidelines for Jewish life in the empire. In addition to including suggestions concerning the functions and duties of the rabbis and a recommendation for the formal establishment of the rabbinate as a state-salaried office, the plan envisioned the creation of two seminaries, one in the north for German Jews and one in the south for the Portuguese communities. The plan proposed a curriculum that would include, in addition to the standard religious studies, instruction in French and other languages.[11]

The Central Consistory did not discuss the establishment of a modern rabbinical school until 1816. The Metz Consistory, however, stood in the forefront of the organizational activities by forming a *Comité de l'enseignement religieux* in 1820 to prepare a program of studies for the proposed institution. Metz was chosen over Paris as the site for the new school, apparently because of the city's location in the most heavily concentrated region of Jewish population, its lower costs, and the presence of families willing to board poor students. Furthermore, the availability of space in the old building of the Metz Yeshivah was a strong argument favoring Metz. However, it should be pointed out that more than convenience was at stake. The decision to place the new *école talmudique* in Metz, in the old yeshivah building, was a clear sign of continuity with the prerevolutionary legacy of tradition. Largely for this reason, the *école talmudique de Metz* failed to live up to the expectations of the *régénérateurs*. According to Olry Terquem, a member of the original *comité*, the school offered no significant improvement in the mode of rabbinic training. Instruction was in the hands of former yeshiva teachers; the course of study was limited to Talmud, with no instruction in religious literature, philosophy, or the sciences. As in the prerevolutionary period, instruction was in Yiddish.[12]

In response to various criticisms and suggestions from both Jewish and gentile observers,[13] the Central Consistory opened a central rabbinical school in 1829. Again Metz was selected over Paris for the reasons cited in 1820. The initial program of study announced by the Central Consistory included French, German, Latin, logic, rhetoric, Jewish and French history, and geography. These subjects were not, however, offered with any regularity, if at all. Moreover, the admission requirements according to the *règlement* of the school (knowledge of French, arithmetic, history, and geography, and ability to read biblical and rabbinic sources) were not enforced.[14]

The failure of the *école rabbinique* to implement the modern curriculum may be explained by the fact that the idea of including secular subjects in the program of studies did not originate with the Central Consistory but rather with the government.[15] Although the consistory certainly did not deny the importance of secular education in the training of rabbis, it vigorously resisted the involvement of the Ministry of the Interior in the curricular affairs of the *école rabbinique*. In response to the recommendation that prospective rabbinical students attend the public schools for three years, the consistory charged that such a measure would be unfair inasmuch as ecclesiastical students of other faiths were exempt from similar requirements.[16] The consistory also objected to the ministry's suggestion that knowledge of Latin be required for all rabbinical students. While conceding that knowledge of Latin was desirable for grand rabbis, the consistory nonetheless claimed that the purpose of the rabbinical school was not to produce distinguished men of letters and accomplished scholars. Rather, the goal was to train communal rabbis who would "combine the theological knowledge indispensable to their ministry with the secular knowledge demanded by the present state of civilization." Emphasis would clearly be placed on religious studies.[17]

The Central Consistory similarly rejected government efforts aimed at influencing the religious curriculum. In one instance the Ministry of the Interior proposed that Moses Mendelssohn's *Phaedon* be added to the list of required texts at the school. The consistory took exception to what it considered to be an implicit demand that it prove its acceptance of the doctrine of the immortality of the soul, the central theme of Mendelssohn's work. There was no need, according to the consistory, to provide "a defense of an article of faith that constitutes the base of all revealed religion," nor was it necessary "to cite the numerous passages of Scripture, sages, and books, ancient as well as modern, that include the dogma of the immortality of the soul." The consistory asserted that the works of Mendelssohn were fully appreciated by his coreligionists, and particularly by the Jews of France, as evidenced by the Hebrew translation of *Phaedon*, which had appeared in Metz nearly forty years earlier.[18] Obviously, the rift between the consistory and the ministry hardly concerned the merits of Mendelssohn's philosophy but related to the issue of the consistory's independence in internal religious affairs. Fear that the government would encroach upon the authority of the consistory was expressed frequently. Protesting the Ministry of Justice and Culte's insistence that the *bachelier ès lettres* be required of rabbinical candidates, the Central Consistory declared that "the spontaneous adoption of this measure appears to us to be the annihilation of the moral authority that the Central Consistory has always exercised over the affairs of the Jewish religion."[19] Not until the late 1830s and early 1840s, however, did the government become more actively involved in the internal affairs of the *école rabbinique*.

On the degree of proficiency in secular studies required of candidates for the rabbinate, there was considerable division among Franco-Jewish leaders. The conditions of appointment to the rabbinate had been established originally in the *règlement* of 1806. Article 20 stated that no rabbi could be elected unless he was a native or naturalized Frenchman, had received an attestation of competency signed by three French rabbis, and spoke French. Furthermore, a candidate who added to his knowledge of Hebrew some knowledge of Greek and Latin would be preferred, all other things being equal. In 1822 members of the Metz Consistory and of the *Comité cantonnal des écoles* addressed a request to the government for an addition to the *règlement*, requiring grand rabbis, beginning in 1830, to possess the degree of *bachelier ès lettres*.[20] Expressing fear that the hours devoted to secular studies would detract from the time available for rabbinic studies, the Central Consistory communicated its displeasure with the proposed change to the Minister of the Interior. The consistory argued that the conditions as stated in the 1806 *règlement* were sufficient.[21] The Central Consistory's opposition to establishing the baccalaureate degree as a condition of admission to the rabbinic title was maintained through the 1830s. Claiming a consensus among the departmental consistories, the central body argued that to impose the requirement of such studies would be to demand the sort of "abstract knowledge most of which is entirely foreign to rabbinic functions."[22]

In contrast to the position taken by the Central Consistory, the Metz *Comité cantonnal des écoles,* composed of the leading *régénérateurs,*[23] demanded modifications in prerabbinic training that would take account of recent educational and cultural advances in French society. They maintained that secular studies were indispensable if rabbis were to effectively serve their increasingly enlightened coreligionists. The degree of *bachelier ès lettres* would provide some certification of competency for the French rabbinate and would enable rabbis to exert greater influence upon large numbers of Jews who had become indifferent to Judaism.[24] Although their early attempts to introduce improvements in the training of rabbis failed, the *régénérateurs* remained resolute in their determination to modernize the French rabbinate throughout the following two decades. In 1837 the Metz *régénérateurs* repeated the 1822 demand that the *bachelier ès lettres* be required of all candidates, added the stipulation that each rabbinical student study five years at the *école rabbinique* or at another recognized institution, and proposed that an examination commission be formed to determine the theological competency of each prospective rabbi. The *régénérateurs* also insisted that the candidates be judged by their ability to deliver sermons in the synagogue.[25]

With the coalescence of the *régénérateur* movement in the 1840s, the organization and structure of the *école rabbinique* were subjected to increased critical examination. In 1841 the school's administrative commission, which included several *régénérateurs,* reported on conditions at the school and concluded that important changes in admissions standards and curriculum were essential. The commission lamented the poor quality of students, many of whom were at a level of competence more appropriate for a primary school than an institution of higher religious instruction. It had become necessary, as a result of this state of affairs, to lower the level of instruction and, on some occasions, to discontinue certain courses. Thus, for example, the course in philosophy was interrupted in 1839 because most of the advanced students had left the school and those who remained were not capable of mastering the subject. The report attributed the poor quality of the student body to the laxity of the departmental consistories in selecting candidates for admission. The commission asserted that strict adherence to the admissions standards set forth in the *règlement organique* was essential if the rabbinical school was to be improved.[26] Although such laxity may indeed have been a factor, there can be little doubt that whatever attraction the rabbinate held could not overcome its low prestige and meager salary.

The curriculum of the *école rabbinique,* according to the commission, was unduly limited by its focus on sacred studies. Whereas instruction in Hebrew language, Scripture, and Talmud was considered satisfactory, other disciplines enumerated in the *règlement* (namely, French, Latin, Greek, history, geography, philosophy, rhetoric, and the sciences) were not, in actuality, part of the program of studies. The commission maintained that in addition to these subjects, courses in biblical exegesis and religious literature would provide a more complete education for prospective rabbis. The need for training in the practical aspects of the ministry was also underscored. Although article 40 of the *règlement* had established that there would be an *oratoire* (chapel) in the school and that the students would officiate there by turn, the practice was never implemented due to the inexperience of the students. The commission argued that the addition of a course in sacred music and religious chanting to the school's curriculum would make it possible for students to gain experience in synagogue officiation. The *oratoire* would also provide a forum for students to deliver sermons before their peers and teachers. Finally, in order to encourage the development of writing skills, the commission proposed that students write a composition in Latin and Greek, as well as in history, within the framework of an essay contest.[27]

Most active of the *régénérateurs* in the attempted modernization of rabbinical training was Adolphe Franck, professor of philosophy in Paris. Franck maintained that what was lacking at the *école rabbinique* was a complete system of religious studies where ancient dogma would be allied with modern science. He attacked the existing curriculum which was concerned with questions of "permissible and forbidden foods" and other minutiae of ritual law, but neglected the "true interests of the soul." Franck asserted that with this limited scope of studies, the school could not produce rabbis capable of addressing the problem of Jews who had fallen victim to religious indifference or to the attraction of proselytism. In accord with the general distinction which his fellow *régénérateurs* saw between dogma and *culte,* Franck argued that theology should replace the ceremonial law as the principle focus of study. The works of Saadiah, Albo, Maimonides, Baḥya, and Philo would offer the finest material for theological studies, inasmuch as the medieval religious thinkers possessed "elevated ideas and ardent faith" and "invoked the testimony of high philosophy." The medievals combined "solid piety" with "scientific achievement," and were consequently the most useful models for modern Jewish theologians. The *école rabbinique*, as envisioned by Franck, should continue the work of the medieval philosophers by providing future rabbis with the opportunity to inquire into the meaning of life, duty, justice, and so on. This sort of inquiry would greatly enhance the training of rabbis and thereby enable prospective ministers to better serve their coreligionists.[28]

Judaism's status as a recognized religion was an additional factor in Franck's evaluation of the *école rabbinique* and in his recommendations for change. No longer a political nation or an outlawed caste but citizens under a regime of liberty and civil equality, the Jews of France acquired a public *culte* worthy of their own new position and the *patrie*. Franck was fully aware that the ultimate implementation of religious reforms, particularly those intended to lend greater dignity and solemnity to the synagogue service, would be dependent upon the cooperation of the rabbis. The centrality of the rabbinate to the success of the *régénérateurs'* general efforts would thus necessitate the cultivation of a new, sympathetic generation of Jewish clergy. Franck explained that "for this reason, it is necessary that our young ministers be educated under the eyes of the central administration, with the assistance of the most enlightened men of our times, amidst all the great literary and scientific institutions that only the capital unites in its midst."[29] Franck thus pronounced himself firmly in favor of transferring the *école rabbinique* to Paris, where rabbinical students would have access to the intellectual and cultural institutions of the city. The idea of transferring the school to Paris became a firm tenet in the *régénérateurs'* program. However, due to divisions among French Jewry on this question, it was not until the 1856 rabbinical conference that the transfer was formally decided, and three more years before it was finally executed.

Franck's critique of the *école rabbinique* in 1841 evoked new interest on the part of the government in the quality of rabbinical training. The law of 1831, which recognized rabbis as salaried public functionaries, provided justification for government participation in the rabbinical school debate. Basing itself on the report issued by the school's administrative commission, the Ministry of Justice and Cultes advanced several proposals of its own. First, it argued that the state now had the right to demand that the students at the *école rabbinique* fulfill certain prerequisites that would enable them to perform their duties competently. The Christian seminaries were viewed as the most appropriate model for evaluating the *école rabbinique* and recommending changes. The minister claimed that Christian clerics were far better prepared for their functions because they were required to pursue preliminary studies before being admitted to institutions of higher learning. The Catholic and Protestant seminaries were thus able to carry out a program of advanced studies, including philosophy and French, Greek, and Latin literature. Students at the *école rabbinique*, by contrast, generally lacked adequate preparation and often arrived at the school with very mediocre skills. The Minister of Justice and Cultes urged that aspirants for the rabbinate be required to pursue the humanities at a *collège* of the *Université* system or some other public institution. It would then be possible to devote maximum time and energy to advanced religious and philosophic disciplines during the five years of instruction at the *école rabbinique*.[30]

The active involvement of the *régénérateurs* and the government in the debate on rabbinical training undoubtedly influenced the Central Consistory in its 1844 decision to send an inspection commission to the *école rabbinique;* in fact, Adolphe Franck suggested the procedure. Franck and Salomon Munk visited the school in 1846, and their inspection confirmed many of the earlier criticisms regarding the admissions policy, curriculum, and the physical plant.[31] In response to the various recommendations made by Franck and Munk, the Central Consistory published a project for the reorganization of the rabbinical school in 1847.[32] The consistory revealed its intention to participate more actively in the supervision of the school and therefore introduce regular inspections and examinations. Candidates for admission would require a level of knowledge equivalent to the completion of the *quatrième* class (eighth grade) at the *collège royal* (public secondary school).[33] Classical studies would include courses in rhetoric, philosophy, and history of literature, and exercises in preaching would be instituted for students of the upper division. With respect to religious studies, the most significant curricular additions included the following: a critical, historical, and literary explication of the Bible; history of Jewish people and their literature; history of the Oral Law, based on Ibn Daud's *Sefer ha-Kabbalah,* Zacuto's *Sefer Yuḥasin,* and Conforte's *Koré ha-Dorot;* Talmudic methodology, based on Joshua ben Joseph Halevi's *Halikhot Olam;* the works of Saadiah, Maimonides, and Albo. In addition to these new courses, the students would be required to submit Hebrew compositions on topics in Jewish theology and to study ritual chant under the direction of a special instructor. All subjects, including Talmud, would be taught in French, while the Sephardic pronunciation was to be employed in reading all Hebrew texts.[34] On this last point there appears to have been continued resistance on the part of the Alsatian students (who constituted the vast majority of the school) throughout much of the century.[35]

Although it is difficult to ascertain precisely the extent to which these improvements were implemented, certain changes were introduced almost immediately. In 1847 two professors at the *collège royal de Metz* were appointed to the school's faculty to teach philosophy, French literature, and rhetoric.[36] Courses in biblical exegesis, German language, and homiletics were added, and a chair in theology and religious history was established in 1851, with Lazare Wogue named to the position.[37]

The long-awaited transfer of the rabbinical school to Paris in 1859 inaugurated a new era in the history of the institution and in the annals of French Jewry, for that matter. Officially transformed into a theological faculty, the *séminaire israélite* became an unmistakably more modern facility than its predecessor in Metz. Its proximity to institutions of higher learning in Paris enabled the school to appoint faculty members of some academic distinction, and its new-found freedom provided opportunities for significant curriculum changes. Possibly of greater importance was the impact of the transfer on the redistribution of regional clout. Signalling a break with the traditions of study and observance in Alsace-Lorraine, the transfer was a turning point in the religious legitimization of Paris. Now that the scales had been tipped, greater strides than ever before were made in pursuit of the much-coveted goals of unity and uniformity. Aware of the implications of all this, opposition to the transfer was voiced by the Metz community and by the leadership of Bordeaux as well, but to no avail.[38]

During the 1860s and 1870s vigorous efforts were made to upgrade the level of instruction, particularly in the areas of languages, science, and literature. The initiative was taken by both the administrative commission of the *séminaire* and the Central and Paris Consistories. Increasingly, the administrative commission assumed an active role in curricular affairs. In one instance, after learning that Lazare Wogue, professor of theology and biblical exegesis, assigned his students two Hebrew compositions per month, the commission decided that before giving sermons in the school's *oratoire*, students must submit them in writing to Wogue for his evaluation; and it recommended that Wogue, himself a respected orator, attend the meeting when the sermons were delivered.[39] This example reveals the deep concern for producing rabbis who would be articulate and eloquent. In another instance, the commission, acting upon an initiative of the Paris Consistory, recommended that a team of experts composed of professors from the *collège de France*, the *école normale*, and the Sorbonne, work on revising the rabbinical school's course of study.[40] Precisely what came of this meeting we cannot say. Nevertheless, the very fact that the commission would turn to a group that was neither traditionally minded nor conversant with the texts central to rabbinic training reveals the impact of secularization on the administration of the rabbinical seminary.

In addition to the core of classes in classical Jewish studies, the school offered instruction in philosophy, history, and literature. In 1862, a chair in mathematics and physics was created by the Paris Consistory.[41] A course in Arabic, first introduced in 1860, became a formal requirement for all students when a chair was established in 1875. Instruction in Arabic language, designed to include elements of Syriac as well, represented a four-year course of study.[42] A course in circumcision was also instituted in the 1870s.[43] By the end of the decade, mathematics and natural sciences were replaced with a course in Jewish history. This change points to a positive development in the high school training of new students. Formerly, in the early 1860s, mathematics and science were introduced because many arrived insufficiently prepared. After two decades in Paris, the school no longer needed to provide this sort of instruction, since the *bachelier ès lettres* had become compulsory for entering students. The time had come, the commission explained to the Paris Consistory, to require of candidates a more solid and well-rounded background so that the curriculum at the *séminaire* could concentrate on truly advanced rabbinical studies.[44]

Toward the end of the nineteenth century, as admission requirements stiffened and academic standards were raised as various curricular changes were introduced, the stature of the school and the French rabbinate improved significantly. In the process, the *séminaire israélite* became an important center for *Wissenschaft des Judentums*. Rabbis Israel Lévi, Isidore Loeb, and Zadoc Kahn, to name only the seminary's most illustrious graduates, became actively engaged in modern research, producing scholarly studies in the fields of Jewish history, philosophy, and rabbinical literature.[45] Thus, in the period following the transfer of the rabbinical school from Metz to Paris, virtually all of the *régénérateurs'* efforts to modernize rabbinical training came to fruition.

10

The Struggle over
Religious Reform

THE STRUGGLE OVER religious reform in France reflected and gave expression to the ambiguities inherent in the emancipation of western European Jewry. Divisions between reformers and orthodox, and debates within the orthodox camp itself, centered on determining which elements of the Jewish tradition were in harmony with the status of the Jew as a citizen of the modern state and as a member of general society. Only in the late 1830s, when a major legislative initiative was undertaken by the Central Consistory, did the question of religious reform occupy the attention of community leaders. Before then, with the exception of Terquem's *Lettres Tsarphatiques,* criticism of traditional Judaism was rarely voiced in France. However, as the *régénérateur* movement came of age and the question of Jewish identity assumed greater prominence, thinkers sought to modify religious ceremonies in accordance with the social, cultural, and political changes that had begun to transform Jewish life in France. These efforts rested on many of the ideological and philosophical premises then prevalent in Germany. Nevertheless, in contrast with neighboring Germany where reforms tended to be more radical and found extensive institutional expression, the demands of the *régénérateurs* remained relatively restrained and, for the most part, unrealized.

Among all but the most conservative sectors of the Franco-Jewish leadership, there had emerged a consensus concerning the legitimacy and necessity of ritual reform on the one hand, and concerning the reform agenda on the other. Appeals for religious reform were usually directed at the aesthetics of synagogue worship, as an 1838 report by the Paris *comité de secours et d'encouragement* reveals. "The forms of the *culte*, in order to fulfill their goal and in order not to be a vain comedy which profanes that which is most sacred, must be in harmony with our *moeurs* and our education, and the *israélite* of our day should not be obliged to turn away from the synagogue for fear of rediscovering there a semblance of the Middle Ages."[1] The *comité*'s report emphasized that its goal was not to recommend "reform of the *culte*," but only to render order and dignity to the religious ceremonies. The *régénérateurs* directed virtually all of their attention to reforming the synagogue, the institution considered most central to French Jewish life. Synagogue services, they argued, were disorderly, in some instances repulsive, and incapable of satisfying the spiritual needs of French Jewry. The *piyyutim, yoẓrot, seliḥot,* and *askarot* were incomprehensible to the worshippers, were inconsistent with French mores, and only served to prolong the service and disrupt concentration. It would be necessary to eliminate these prayers, and to institute simple and solemn chanting of the liturgy by a cantor and choir with the accompaniment of an organ, if the synagogue was to function as a vehicle for the edification of the soul. They also urged that preaching become a regular part of the service, and that the auctioning of *miẓvot,* a traditional method of raising funds, be discontinued on the grounds that it was inappropriate for a place of sanctity. Finally, the Paris *comité,* as distinct from partisans of religious modernization elsewhere in France, proposed the fusion of the Portuguese and German liturgies.[2]

Other recommendations for the enhancement of the *culte* included the establishment of the *initiation religieuse* (confirmation ceremony) for both boys and girls and the modernization of funeral ceremonies. Regulation of the circumcision rite, including the elimination of *peri'ah* and *meẓiẓah,* the introduction of new surgical procedures, and the licensing of *mohalim,* was strongly urged by the *régénérateurs.*[3] In addition to these proposals were other recommendations that appeared to be mandated by the emancipation of French Jewry. The laws that restricted Jews in their relations with non-Jews were considered by the *régénérateurs* to be incompatible with the social implications of citizenship. The prohibition of drinking gentile wine, *yein nesekh* (or *stam yeinam*), for example, appeared outmoded in an age of free and open social intercourse.[4]

Both the *régénérateurs'* conception of religious reform and the limitations they placed on the scope of their endeavors are particularly evident in the first French attempt to introduce concrete liturgical and synagogue innovations. In 1841, before an assembly of twenty-six residents of Metz, Gerson-Lévy proposed the formation of a society whose goal was to open a small sanctuary (an *oratoire*) where worship would be conducted with more fervor and contemplation. The initiative taken by the Metz group rested on the claim that during centuries of persecution Judaism had become obsessed with ritual and lost sight of the essential principles of the religion. A pervasive lack of concern for synagogue music, solemnity, and majestic ceremonies was blamed for the indifference of many affluent Jews toward their religion. Accordingly, the remedy would require restoring Judaism's former dignity to the prayer service. All conversation would be prohibited, only the officiant and choir would be authorized to recite prayers aloud, and to enhance concentration, the duration of the services would be shortened.[5] In defending this last innovation, the society accorded legitimacy only to prayers composed by the Men of the Great Assembly and subsequently adopted by the three major rites, the Portuguese, German, and Polish. Although later additions to the liturgy, such as the *piyyutim*, were to be omitted, the society reserved the right to make additions where necessary and stated that it would draw on the poetry of Solomon Ibn Gabirol, Moses Ibn Ezra, and Judah Halevi, among others. These poems would be set to choral music, like the psalms for each holiday. Again, in the mention of these poets, one may note a decided preference among reformers, both in France and Germany, for Spanish culture over the Ashkenazic tradition. The most innovative proposal concerned the establishment of two services: one exclusively in Hebrew, the other would follow in French. The sermon would take place at the end of the French service.[6]

While these proposals clearly constituted a departure from accepted halakhic norms, there is ample evidence that the founders of the *oratoire* envisioned a synagogue that was traditional in character. Men and women would not sit together but were to be separated by a middle aisle, and no organ was mentioned in the proposal. The ark would be placed at the east end of the sanctuary, in its traditional position, facing Jerusalem. In defense of the most radical innovation, the French language service, Gerson-Lévy argued that such methods were intended to lead the irreligious into the fold. Furthermore, he insisted that there were solid halakhic grounds for the recitation of prayers in the vernacular. Quoting the Mishnah (*Sotah* 7:1) and Tosafot (*Berakhot* 3a), Gerson-Lévy charged that certain biblical texts, such as the *Shema*, could be recited in any language and that others, such as the *Kaddish*, had been written in Aramaic just so the unlettered masses could understand it. What is most unique about the entire enterprise of religious reform in France, as compared with Germany, are the limits that the *régénérateurs* placed on their own aspirations. Gerson-Lévy and the Metz group were opposed to the idea of forming a *reform* society for fear that this would

sow dissension in families. Here the group differentiated sharply between public and private aspects of the religion. The domestic ritual,
described as "full of gentleness and consolation," was considered to be
beyond the purview of reform. The sole concern of the group was the
improvement of *le culte publique*. Despite the restrained character of
these proposals, the Metz *oratoire* never opened.[7]

Why did the Metz project fail to materialize? The proposed reforms
encountered opposition from both the left and the right. Radical reformers failed to support the project because they regarded it as overly conciliatory to orthodox practice, and they therefore felt that the plan left
obstacles in the way of *fusion*. Conservatives accused the members of the
society of wanting to destroy the Jewish religion by deviating from
traditional norms.[8] Between the two extremes few appear to have occupied the middle ground; in fact, the project may not have come into
being simply because it failed to attract the thirty heads of families
originally declared necessary for commencement of the society's activities. It is also likely that the Metz Consistory's denunciation of this
unofficial attempt at reform severely undermined its credibility in the
community. Throughout most of the nineteenth century, efforts such as
these were unsuccessful in sustaining a chapel devoted to "reformed" or
"enlightened" services. One exception was the chapel in the Metz
school, where since 1838 a service embodying several of the innovations
proposed by the group headed by Gerson-Lévy was held each Sabbath
morning. The *Shema* was recited in both Hebrew and French, and the
service included an invocation, a sermon, and a prayer for the king—all
in French. Since singing had not yet been introduced in the school's
curriculum, there was no choir. Though certainly ahead of its time, the
school service was regarded as a step toward an *oratoire*, much in the
same way that Israel Jacobson introduced reforms in his school in
Seesen, eventually establishing a reform temple in Hamburg.[9] Nevertheless, because these innovative services were held in schools, they were
not perceived by the religious leadership as a threat to the status quo.

French efforts to modernize the Jewish religion were clearly influenced by the reform program developed in Germany. Most of the *régénérateurs* had long associations with leading German reformers and scholars, and they tended to admire the progressive thinking there. In fact,
virtually all of the issues debated in Germany evoked serious discussion
in France. The Franco-Jewish press reported regularly on the general
progress of the movement, lent its pages to leading German reform
theorists, and provided detailed accounts of the various rabbinical conferences. In one article on the Reform Rabbinical Conference in Frankfort
(1845), the *Archives israélites* deplored the silence of the French rabbinate

as compared to the activism of liberal German rabbis. Despite "certain exaggerations," the journal declared, the Frankfurt synod "responded with enlightenment to the question of how the Messiah, messianic restoration, must be understood." Confident that reform activity in Germany would ultimately leave its mark in the West, the *Archives israélites* expressed deep regret that France would not be represented at the conference. The journal repeatedly denounced the unwillingness of the French rabbis to discuss proposals for reform, in one instance asserting that unless there was cooperation, "France alone would remain in the dark with the rabbis of Bavaria," despite its political achievements.[10]

Though guided by many of the same principles and despite numerous areas of agreement, the *régénérateurs* and the German reformers remained apart on several important ritual and liturgical issues. The differences in approach can be seen in their respective positions on the doctrine of Jewish messianism. The belief in a personal Messiah, a descendant of the house of David who will lead the Jews back to their ancient land and restore the Temple order, appeared to conflict with the social views and political status (or aspirations) of western European Jewry. Traditional messianism, with its emphasis on the centrality of Eretz Israel and the national redemption of the Jewish people, was viewed as too particularistic and overly political in light of the overwhelming prevalence of universalist ideals in Europe and the acceptance of the authority of the state by the Jews.[11]

The first steps toward a reinterpretation of the traditional messianic idea were pursued within the framework of liturgical reform. The Reform movement in Germany regarded divine worship as the official, public expression of the religious convictions of the Jewish community and maintained that it must therefore be tailored to conform to the social, cultural, and political changes that had taken place in the nineteenth century. Leaders argued that the growing sense of German patriotism among Jews, accompanied by the need to define Judaism in universal terms, required, at the very least, a reinterpretation of the prayers related to the coming of the Messiah, the reestablishment of the Temple cult, and the restoration of Zion. For the early reformers, the traditional doctrines of the personal Messiah and the restoration of the sacrificial cult were an embarrassment because of their particularistic and national character. Their approach, however, was not to eliminate these prayers entirely—rather, they argued apologetically that the prayers were essentially universal in character and, therefore, were of no political consequence. Reformers such as Eduard Kley and E. S. Günsburg did remove, although not completely, many of the references in question from their new prayerbook (1817). They aspired to a synthesis between the continuation of the special existence of Judaism as a religion and the transformation of Judaism into a German-patriotic faith. This synthesis, achieved through the universalization of the messianic idea, permitted the retention of some, though not all, of the traditional references in the early Reform prayerbooks. However, the Reform Rabbinical Conferences of the 1840s, which took place during the period of intense struggle for full civil emancipation, finally deleted from the liturgy all such petitions that did not express the universal and spiritual interpretation of the messianic doctrine.[12]

Reassessment of Jewish messianism followed an entirely different course in France. Proposals for liturgical reform were limited to relatively minor issues, unlike those of the German Reform movement. Moreover, it appears that for French Jews prayers for the coming of the Messiah and the restoration of the Temple presented no problem, in part because the question of messianism had been theoretically resolved by the Paris Sanhedrin. Nevertheless, precisely at the height of the raging controversy in Germany, Joel Anspach, author of the first French translation of the prayerbook according to the Ashkenazic rite (1820), addressed the question of deleting those prayers that referred to the Messiah and the Temple. He argued against liturgical modification, claiming that Judaism's doctrine of the Messiah had been misunderstood by would-be reformers. Belief in and prayers for the appearance of the Messiah neither contradicted the contemporary spirit of universal benevolence nor impeded French Jewry's capacity to serve as patriotic citizens. Prayers for the Messiah and the restoration of the Temple order were related, instead, to "the edification and the prosperity of the entire world;" by envisioning the eventual attachment of humankind to a single, true faith and united by inalterable peace, the prophetic doctrine of the Messiah could only strengthen the bonds of fraternity among peoples presently divided by religious opinions.[13] As in many other instances, this interpretation was echoed in Jewish textbooks.[14] Anspach's characterization of the function and significance of prayers which had come under attack by radical reformers reflects an attempt to frame the traditional liturgy in new terms. Nevertheless, though unquestionably liberal in his views, he, like other *régénérateurs*, was genuinely convinced of the resiliency of old forms.

The question of Hebrew in the liturgy also reveals a chasm between German and French reformers. The dispensability of Hebrew was officially endorsed at the Frankfurt Rabbinical Conference, where it was decided that each congregation could determine for itself how much Hebrew to retain in the liturgy. In protest over this decision, Zacharias Frankel dramatically left the conference and formed his own movement.

Out of sympathy for Frankel's views, the *Archives israélites* reevaluated its own position on this issue. The *régénérateurs* had long advocated the use of the vernacular, that is, French, in religious services, in order to enhance synagogue worship for those ignorant of the Hebrew language. Now, in proclaiming its agreement with Frankel, the journal took a more conservative position. The *régénérateurs* urged that Hebrew be preserved in the public service, although certain prayers in Aramaic (*Kaddish, Kol Nidre,* and *Akdamut,* for example) should be recited in French. In justifying their strong attachment to Hebrew, the *régénérateurs* came to the same conclusion as Frankel: for Jews all over the world, Hebrew was, at least in theory, a universal language; suppressing it would ultimately disrupt the unity of the Jewish people.[15] Moreover, it was argued that the maintenance of the Hebrew language and the adoption of the Sephardic pronunciation would enhance the internal unity of French Jewry. In other words, Hebrew would be a definitive mark of identification for the Jews of France.[16] In general, French thinkers were motivated by a concern to retain ritual ceremonies that were fundamental to their conception of Jewish identity. Thus they adamantly rejected the demands by radical reformers, specifically members of the Frankfurt *Reformfreunde,* to abolish the practice of circumcision.[17]

The moderate character of the French reform program can be attributed to a combination of political, social, and intellectual factors peculiar to France. French Jewry's political status, particularly in comparison with the situation in Germany, may hold the key to the matter. In Germany, where the political struggle for civic rights was frustrated by repeated setbacks, liberal Jewish thinkers concluded that a reformed religion, divested of its particularistic features, would ultimately strengthen the case for emancipation. French Jews felt no such urgency to introduce religious reforms, though certain modifications were considered essential. Even so, according to one leading *régénérateur,* Samuel Cahen, it was wrong to blame French Jewry for its apparent apathy, since "liberty is not favorable to religious discussions." "Is it surprising," he continued, "that in the absence of civic . . . and political rights [in Germany], more importance is attached to religious discussions?" To account for the differences between French and German Jewry on the questions of religious reform, Cahen suggested that the timing of emancipation relative to the cultural development of a population was a crucial factor. In the case of Germany, Jewish cultural and intellectual achievement was of a very high order, while the Jews' legal status lagged behind. Cahen concluded that progress in the realm of religious reform owed an enormous debt, ironically, to government intolerance. For French Jewry the situation was reversed. The Jews had been granted citizenship well *before* they had achieved a level of cultural sophistication that would have enabled them to identify problematic religious issues and resolve them.[18] Calls for religious reform would be directed at an entirely different set of issues.

The Napoleonic Sanhedrin contributed decisively to this orientation by virtue of the role it played in shaping a distinctive Franco-Jewish ideology of emancipation. By defining the relation between Judaism and the modern state so that it [the assembly] was able to remain loyal to the Jewish tradition, the Sanhedrin appears to have removed the question of religious reform from French Jewry's political agenda. Accorded the status of law by the Napoleonic regime, the Sanhedrin's decisions were transformed into a powerful legacy whose impact could still be felt, or at least invoked, at midcentury. Government recognition implicitly confirmed the legitimacy of the Sanhedrin's relatively conservative character. For subsequent generations of *régénérateurs*, the Sanhedrin's decisions served as a blueprint for future changes and, given its conservative nature, ultimately exerted a moderating influence on the process of Jewish *régénération*. Although it is undeniable that the decisions were subject to wide interpretation, the general consensus of *régénérateurs* held that the concrete implementation of the assembly's views was all that was needed for the successful modernization of French Jewry. It was assumed that, since emancipation was an accomplished fact, only social and cultural improvements were essential, whereas attaining or maintaining citizenship did not require thoroughgoing religious reform.

The organization of French Jewry within the consistorial system also precluded the emergence of a radical reform ideology. As the official representative of all geographical, ethnic, and religious sectors of the Jewish population, the consistorial system discouraged measures that might fragment the unity, whether imagined or real, of French Jewry. It could ill-afford to alienate the orthodox masses or the rabbinate. Though dominated by men who shared the *régénérateurs'* concern for reconciling religious practice with contemporary French mores, and therefore indisputably a supporter of reform, the consistory chose to mediate in the struggle between traditionalists and reformers. Moreover, the fact that the consistory itself introduced several minor reforms appears to have weakened a would-be reform movement. As we shall see, the implementation of religious reforms would depend on a host of factors, including the views of the local grand rabbi, his influence in his community, and local support for, or resistance to, innovations.

In the hope of discovering a mechanism to facilitate the introduction of improvements in *"le culte publique,"* the Central Consistory submitted a plan in 1839 for a thorough reorganization of its administrative constitution. The Crémieux Project, so called after the chairman of the consistorial commission, Adolphe Crémieux, marked the first overt challenge to traditional Judaism in France. The draft proposal included several articles that granted to lay members of the consistories ultimate authority in religious matters. Article 24, for example, proposed to grant the consistory power to determine which prayerbooks and textbooks would be used and to modify rituals and shorten the length of the prayers. Invited to comment on the draft proposal, the departmental consistories were nearly unanimous in their criticism. Their major objection was that the authors of the project had failed to recognize that the authority to decide religious issues rightfully belonged in the hands of the rabbis, not the consistory. Most of the consistories argued that any proposed ritual change would require the approval of the majority of the grand rabbis of France. While the initial opposition gradually waned, the Metz, Strasbourg, Nancy, and Colmar consistories continued to criticize the project's plan for lay domination of the rabbinate, centralizaton of power in the Central Consistory, and rabbinic hierarchy.[19]

It is worthy of note that in several areas, the Bordeaux Consistory was even more insistent than the Ashkenazic consistories to preserve the autonomy and dignity of the rabbinate. Thus the Bordeaux Consistory alone objected to granting tenure only to grand rabbis (Article 46); communal rabbis, it insisted, should be eligible as well. Similarly, the Bordeaux Consistory stood out as the only consistory not to agree that the right to suspend grand rabbis ought to be accorded to the Central Consistory (Article 45). Fearful of potential abuses at the hands of the lay-dominated Central Consistory, and resistant to the growing, excessive power of the central administration, Bordeaux preferred that this power be limited to the Minister of Religion. In fact, throughout the 1850s, under the leadership of staunch conservative Benjamin Gradis, the Bordeaux Consistory continued to frustrate the Central Consistory's efforts at tighter control of the provinces. One suggestion, that communal rabbis trained at the *école centrale rabbinique* should replace the *ministres officiants,* encountered stiff resistance in Bordeaux. It is not unlikely that the Bordeaux Consistory's decision in 1853 to establish a school for the training of *ministres officiants* in the Sephardic rite was in direct response to these unwanted pressures of centralization. The Bordeaux school was the only institution of its kind in all of France; no formal program was available for Ashkenazic cantors. By 1857 the Bordeaux Consistory had emerged as the leader among the departmental consistories against the Central Consistory on the issue of grand and communal rabbis. And along with Metz, Bordeaux was the only consistory to oppose the transfer of the *école rabbinique* from Metz to Paris.[20]

The reaction of rabbis and orthodox laymen was considerably more vehement. The grand rabbis recognized the threat that the 1839 project posed and therefore employed every strategy available, including refutations published in the Jewish press, a formal protest to a government ministry, and public petitions. Virtually every major rabbinical figure in France, and a host of communal rabbis, voiced criticism of the plan. Not only the rabbis of the eastern provinces (Nancy, Strasbourg, Colmar, and Metz), but also those of Bordeaux and Marseille, opposed the consistory's attempt to wrest religious authority from its accepted practitioners.[21] In the Bas-Rhin a major effort to overturn the Crémieux Project was directed at the Ministry of Cultes. Joining the Strasbourg initiative were petitioners from eighty-two Bas-Rhin communities, totalling more than 2300 head of families.[22] In many cases, with the exception of the largest cities, it appears that opposition to the project was nearly unanimous. Smaller communities were either less prepared to permit a compromise of rabbinic authority or were easier to organize in such a protest. However successful the campaign may have been, the petition was a remarkable display of solidarity with the rabbis. Its message was at once staunchly resistant to religious reform and decidedly anticonsistory.

The project also encountered vigorous resistance in the Metz region, where similar tactics were employed. Information concerning the opposition comes from the Metz Consistory, which, in its letter of resignation to the Central Consistory in 1841, described the massive popular campaign:

> Since its appearance in Metz, [this project] has provoked the most violent fermentation. Secret societies have formed, petitions have been drafted and passed from house to house in order to obtain as many signatures as possible. An individual subscription was established to collect a considerable sum [of money], serving to combat, by all legal and illegal means, any attempt at religious or administrative innovation. In addition, the *campagnes* were provoked to protest against the intentions which they could hardly appreciate. Emissaries were even sent to neighboring districts to incite resistance. Not only the authors of the project, but also the members of the Central Consistory, and even we, who only followed the instructions of our superiors, were reputed to be enemies of religion, of wanting to reverse the most sacred dogmas, eliminate circumcision, substitute Sunday for Saturday, and other accusations equally as absurd.[23]

Community and religious leaders worked diligently to persuade the simple Jews of the Moselle that the new bill was a serious threat to the Jewish tradition, needing only to assemble some of the proposals advanced by radical reformers in France and Germany in order to expose the "real" intentions of the Central Consistory leadership. In the city of Metz and in the outlying towns and villages "secret societies" formed to collect signatures and funds. Spearheading the resistance was the community's religious leader, Grand Rabbi Lion-Mayer Lambert. First director of the *école rabbinique de Metz,* and chief rabbi of the *département,* Lambert enjoyed great prestige and had a large following. An outspoken critic of religious reform, he refused to participate either in the department consistory meetings convened to discuss the 1839 project or, later, in a special committee of three rabbis and two laymen. This refusal to consider any aspect of the plan, along with his own public refutation of the project and his energetic efforts in holding meetings to persuade community members to sign letters of protest, which were subsequently sent to the Minister of Cultes, undoubtedly set the tone for a formidable display of resistance.[24]

The protest seems to have achieved its goal. After five years and six drafts the proposal finally became the *ordonnance* of 1844, but not until some of its more controversial provisions were modified. Article 24, which proposed to grant the Central Consistory the authority to make ritual reforms as it saw fit, was qualified by a concession to the rabbinic opposition: communal rabbis were to be included in the *notabilité* (the consistory's electoral college) and would, as a result, be enabled to influence the selection of Central Consistory members. Although this was a relatively minor change and fell short of an earlier provision that would have required the concurrence of the majority of the grand rabbis before the consistory could institute ritual reforms,[25] it balanced the potentially unchecked drive for reforms among lay members. In addition, the 1844 *ordonnance* required the approbation of the grand rabbi of the Central Consistory before the latter could approve any textbook for Jewish schools, whereas the original project mentioned no such role for the grand rabbi.[26] The *ordonnance* also confirmed the authority of the grand rabbi in specifically religious matters, stating that "no deliberation can be taken by the Central Consistory concerning religious matters . . . without the approbation of the grand rabbi." Powers of censure, suspension, and dismissal of consistorial rabbis were also qualified by the 1844 *ordonnance.* Whereas the 1839 draft proposed that these powers be granted exclusively and without qualification to the Central Consistory, the *ordonnance* stipulated that the Central Consistory could censure consistorial rabbis only after they were addressed with complaints by their respective consistories. Communal rabbis could be censured only according to the opinion of both the local consistory and the grand rabbi.[27]

Although the *ordonnance* of 1844 did contain provisions for the increased participation of lay members in the Central Consistory, the law fell short of its goal of investing the laity with unchecked powers to institute ritual reforms. The most striking aspect of the *ordonnance,* which would remain the legal basis of the consistorial system throughout the nineteenth century, was its concession to the continued dominance of the rabbinic establishment in the areas of religion and education. There can be little doubt that the public resistance of Alsatian Jewry and its leaders to the Crémieux Project of 1839 was an important factor in shaping the final draft of the bill. As a result, the authority of the rabbinate was preserved, and the hands of would-be radical reformers were tied.

A second major display of force by traditionalists took place in 1846, when the Central Consistory, in its efforts to find a successor to Grand Rabbi Emmanuel Deutz, attempted to control the election of France's chief rabbi. The rabbinic candidates were asked to state their position on nine reforms enumerated in the consistory's questionnaire: the fusion of the Ashkenazic and Sephardic rites; the enhancement of the dignity of synagogue ceremonies; the suppression of *piyyutim* and several other prayers; the introduction of the organ; the role of women in the synagogue; the regulation of circumcision; the adoption of the definition of a Jew as one born of either a Jewish mother *or* father; improvements in the *école rabbinique;* and the expansion of rabbinic duties to include pastoral activities.[28] Of the nine reforms, all except the one dealing with the identity of a child of a mixed marriage had been discussed repeatedly, some since 1839 and others since the appearance of the *Lettres Tsarphatiques.* It may be of some significance that, although the consistorial commission that drafted the questionnaire consulted several reform rabbis in Germany, the document contained none of the more radical ideological themes typical of the Reform movement across the Rhine. Candidates were asked to disclose their views on both the religious needs of Judaism and the duties of the chief rabbi. The circular made it clear that the enumerated reforms were important desiderata and that the respondants should indicate their willingness to implement these measures.[29]

Shortly after the appearance of the circular, Grand Rabbis Lambert and Goudchaux, of Metz and Colmar respectively, issued a manifesto warning against the dangers of religious reform. They emphasized the immutability of the Written and Oral Law, as well as those institutions and regulations that had been introduced to protect the law, and asserted that no assembly of rabbis has the authority to modify any aspect of Jewish law. The two grand rabbis warned that "every reformatory attempt to change these constitutes rebellion against the religion . . . and leads to the way of destruction."[30] In Colmar, rabbis of both the Bas- and Haut-Rhin assembled to denounce what they perceived as the consistory's reform initiative and to refute each of the nine recommendations.[31] On the popular level, as was the case in 1839, opposition to the circular was vigorous, well organized, and numerically well represented. For example, petitions to the Central Consistory from at least twenty-eight Haut-Rhin communities assailed the fundamental premise of the questionnaire; namely, that religious reform was a legitimate procedure. The petitioners claimed that by making adhesion to the nine points the *sine qua non* of the nomination, the consistory had violated the freedom of conscience of the rabbinical candidates and, in so doing, unjustly arrogated to itself the authority to introduce ritual reform.[32]

During these years of turbulence, however, modest success was achieved in the implementation of religious reforms. With few exceptions, only the most moderate innovations were introduced by midcentury, and more often in the *chefs-lieu* of the departmental consistory than in smaller towns and villages. Revision of burial customs and regulation of the circumcision procedure were formally enacted in the 1840s, the sale of religious honors in the synagogues was abolished, and legislation requiring rabbis to preach regularly was introduced. These innovations owed their success to the ascendency of modernizing elites in each of the *chefs-lieu.* Committed to all aspects of *régénération,* members of these elites sat on various communal and consistorial committees and exerted influence on religious policy. The *régénérateurs,* though often critical of the communal establishment, consciously supported the consistories in the promotion of religious reforms.[33]

New developments within the French rabbinate also contributed significantly to the modernization of the Jewish religion. Although no sector of French Jewry, including the orthodox, remained unreconciled to emancipation, differences over religious issues split the rabbinic leadership into two main camps. The two groups disagreed specifically on what constituted religious reform and, more generally, on their assessment of the problems facing French Jewry. The older, conservative rabbis employed a variety of arguments in their efforts to discredit religious modernization. Reformers were portrayed as having abandoned the authentic doctrinal principles of the Jewish tradition. To this was added a political argument: that religious reform threatened to disrupt the unity of French Jewry and to sever it from world Jewry. Precisely at the height of conservative opposition and protest to the consistory's proposals, there emerged within the French rabbinate a cadre of progressives, or moderates, who believed that religious modernization was both ideologically correct and politically expedient. Like the *régénérateurs,* the moderate rabbis regarded the modernization of Judaism as the sole solution to the problem of Jewish alienation; in their estimation, disaffected Jews would find a modernized Judaism attractive and would thus be drawn back to the community. On the ideological plane, having arrived at a synthesis of tradition and reform, they defended the idea of moderate reform with their assertion that Jewish law was historically conditioned and therefore open to careful reassessment.

The rabbinic career of Salomon Ulmann (1806–1865), the leading exponent of progressive orthodoxy, coincided with the critical period of religious controversy in France, the *régénération* of French Jewry, and the shaping of the rabbinate into a modern institution. Born in Saverne where his father had served as rabbi, Ulmann studied with Rabbi Moïse Bloch (known as Moshe Utenheim) of Strasbourg, before enrolling at the *école rabbinique*. He began his rabbinic career as a communal rabbi in the Alsatian town of Lauterbourg; he was subsequently appointed consistorial grand rabbi of Nancy, and in 1853 he rose to the position of grand rabbi of the Central Consistory, succeeding Marchand Ennery.[34] Ulmann and like-minded moderates may very well be viewed as the critical link between the ideological and the concrete elements in the religious modernization of Judaism. Responsibility for initially conceptualizing the issues of religious reform and for placing them on the agenda of French Jewry undeniably rests with the *régénérateurs*. By virtue of their close contact with German reformers, their view of history, and their commitment to critical scholarship, they were predisposed to this role. But they were well aware that the rabbis were the key players in the struggle for reform. Vested with authority by the consistory, the rabbis alone were in a position to implement reforms—either on their own authority or by convening a rabbinic assembly. Progressive rabbis who occupied positions of power and influence were able to provide certain innovations with a religious stamp of approval, thus succeeding where the *régénérateurs* had failed.

The most widely implemented innovation in France, the *initiation religieuse*, illustrates the indispensability of the rabbinate to the success of reform. Endorsed by progressive rabbis, this confirmation ceremony was conducted for boys and girls who had passed examinations in Hebrew reading and mastery of the catechism. In the case of Ulmann, one of his first actions as grand rabbi of Nancy was the introduction of the ceremony throughout his consistorial district;[35] in the Bas-Rhin the consistory, undoubtedly with the support of Grand Rabbi Aron, decided to organize the ceremony in all the synagogues under its administration.[36] Usually held on two separate occasions each year, the *initiation religieuse* was an important and celebrated reform because it represented a public display of the new Franco-Jewish spirit. It included virtually all the reform elements that the *régénérateurs* had advocated but did not always achieve: a dignified service, equality for girls, a choir, an organ, and a sacred declaration of patriotic loyalty and love for the king and the royal family. What is more, the *initiation religieuse* provided an opportunity for Jews to prove to the gentile public that genuine progress had been achieved in the realization of *régénération*. Municipal leaders, members of the local public school committee, and special dignitaries were normally in attendance, thus enhancing the self-congratulatory character of the ceremony. Although the *initiation religieuse* was the result of initiatives taken by the *régénérateurs* and some consistory activists, progressive rabbis were centrally involved in designing the program and in officiating at the ceremony. From the early 1840s the *initiation religieuse* was adopted by numerous communities throughout France.[37]

Not all communities, however, were equally enthusiastic about the innovation. At Puttelange the *commissaire surveillant* was opposed to holding the ceremony in the synagogue; the local teacher, though, succeeded in transferring it to the Jewish school building.[38] Metz and Colmar, each under the authority of traditionalist rabbis, failed to implement the *initiation religieuse* until the 1850s.[39] When the ceremony was finally instituted in Metz (in 1852), it was not before Grand Rabbi Lambert had redesigned it by establishing more rigorous academic requirements. He saw to it that students were examined not only on the catechism but also on "sacred history" and Hebrew reading, and he stipulated that the ceremony be conducted in two stages over a two-year period.[40] When Colmar introduced the ceremony in 1851, it was modified to include only the appropriate examinations. Moreover, Rabbi Klein objected to using the expression *initiation*, claiming that "initiation" into Jewish life began at birth, not at age thirteen. In its report on the adoption of the ceremony, the *Archives israélites* criticized this example of Alsatian independence.[41] Such independence was also evident in the area of Hebrew pronunciation. For example, a book published in Metz in 1850 introduced a method for learning to read Hebrew that followed the Ashkenazic pronunciation, though most authorities in Paris had endorsed the Sephardic pronunciation.[42]

The rapid proliferation of the *initiation religieuse* explains the intensification of efforts to introduce the organ into French synagogues. Although the question of the organ had been debated in Germany since the Hamburg Temple introduced it several decades earlier, it was not discussed in France before 1840. The organ made its debut in the Marseille synagogue in 1841 at the first *initation religieuse* ceremony conducted in France. Strasbourg, Nancy, and Lyon, quickly followed the Marseille example.[43] The leading opponent of the organ was Metz Grand Rabbi Lambert, who denounced it as a violation of specific and general proscriptions. He asserted that it was prohibited for a Jew to play a musical instrument on the Sabbath; that it would be inappropriate for a member of another religion to play the organ and thereby participate in the services; and that the use of the organ would create discord within the French Jewish community. Citing *Or Noga* and *Noga Zedek*, the German Reform movement's two leading works on halakhic issues, the *Archives israélites* claimed that the prohibition against playing the organ on the Sabbath was groundless, as it rested only on the fear that one might be tempted to repair it (and thereby perform a prohibited action) if it broke down. The prohibition was no longer applicable, it was argued, because the organ could be repaired only by a trained expert. Furthermore, since, in the words of the journal, "our synagogues are considered as *mikdash me'at* (a miniature Temple)," a preventative prohibition (*shvut*) would not apply there, as it did not in the Jerusalem Temple. This last argument, though unacceptable from the standpoint of traditional Jewish law, was an effort to introduce greater latitude in religious observance by claiming that modern synagogues were a renewal of the ancient sanctuary. Consequently, there was no need to employ a gentile organist.[44]

Beyond the technical issues, however, was the question of *ḥukkat ha-goi*, a restrictive law invoked by Lambert and other traditionalists to discredit reforms that appeared to imitate Christian practices. The law proscribes the emulation of idolatrous customs, as well as customs connected to non-Jewish ritual, including religious garb and gentile folk customs that derive from superstitious beliefs or that promote immoral conduct. *Ḥukkat ha-goi* compelled reformers and traditionalists alike to define for themselves the limits of cultural integration. The *régénérateurs* insisted that the status of the Jews in postrevolutionary and post-Sanhedrin France necessitated a revision of the prohibitions normally connected to *ḥukkat ha-goi*, although they conceded that there were limits to the appropriation of foreign rituals. In the words of Samuel Cahen, the law simply did not apply "to the nation which has adopted us and has recovered for us a *patrie*, [that is], to the most civilized nation whose masterpieces our children study and whose *moeurs* they emulate."[45] The use of the organ in the synagogue did not, according to the *régénérateurs*, fall into the category of *ḥukkat ha-goi*. The organ was regarded simply as a musical instrument devoid of any intrinsic religious significance and, it was therefore argued, the synagogue should not be denied its many positive effects simply because it was used in the Church.

Ulmann publicly endorsed the adoption of the organ for use at Sabbath services. He asserted that there was no technical reason to forbid the use of the organ in the synagogue, provided it was played by a non-Jew. Furthermore, he argued that the organ did not fall under the prohibition of *ḥukkat ha-goi*, since the instrument did not belong exclusively to Christianity.[46] In a private letter to Marchand Ennery, Ulmann elaborated on his decision. There, he could not dismiss the objection of *ḥukkat ha-goi* as facilely as the *régénérateurs*. Rather, Ulmann argued that in this specific case *ḥukkat ha-goi* did not apply. Citing the view of the *Bayyit Ḥadash* (R. Joel Sirkes) that the use of Christian melodies in the synagogue was theoretically permissible, Ulmann concluded that it was possible to borrow other customs from the church, as long as they were not peculiar to Christian ritual observance. The fact that the organ was played in the church did not, in Ulmann's mind, invalidate the instrument for Jewish use:

> In my opinion, since only the public *culte* remains, and the state of faith declines daily, and the Torah is being forgotten from the heart, the rabbinate has the obligation to think of methods to prevent further losses, and to seek in whatever manner to draw the House of Israel to the Lord, to elevate the house of God, and at the very least, to add greater dignity to the service, in order to close the mouths of those who speak with arrogance and disdain. . . . And in my opinion it is not proper what some rabbis are doing by saying that even for a shoestring one must give up one's life; for today the battle of the Lord should not be waged with poison and obstinancy, but rather with gentleness . . . not with the stringency of Shamai, but with the humility of Hillel.[47]

Ulmann had clearly come to the conclusion that certain innovations were justified, and that his opponents could not continue rejecting every innovation categorically. His position on reform can be summarized as follows: as long as no clear, explicit prohibition exists, reforms should be introduced according to the demands of Jewish life. With pride he declared that there was no opposition to the introduction of the organ in his synagogue: "Not that I like music, or see the organ as an index of progress; I congratulate myself in seeing the gradual disappearance of the deplorable habit of rising up against the most innocent innovations."[48] For Ulmann, the tradition of liberally interpreting the halakhah was in need of sustained efforts against conservative rejectionists.

In truth, even a willingness to interpret the halakhah liberally did not always translate easily into implementation. Marchand Ennery was apparently persuaded by Ulmann's arguments concerning the permissibility of the organ and, in presenting his views on the nine-point 1846 questionnaire for the position of Central Consistory Grand Rabbi, supported the innovation. The *régénérateurs* and other partisans of reform were therefore disappointed both by Ennery's personal failure to follow through and by his expression of displeasure with those who instituted the reform. For example, he chided the *commissaire surveillant* of the Lille temple for introducing an organ without the authorization of the grand rabbi. Still, when Ennery's daughter was married in the Paris temple in 1846, the organ was played, though only two years before Ennery opposed its use at the *initiation religieuse* ceremony.[49] By the end of the 1840s the organ had been introduced in numerous consistorial synagogues as musical accompaniment on national holidays, at confirmation ceremonies, at funeral rites, and in several cases, at regular Sabbath services. Even the Colmar synagogue, to the surprise of the *Archives israélites,* introduced the organ for limited purposes.[50]

Ulmann was typical of a small number of rabbis in Germany and France who were sympathetic to moderate reforms, despite their firm commitment to halakhah and rabbinic authority. By mounting attacks on the authority of the Talmud and the Oral Law, the Reform rabbinical conferences in Germany constituted, in Ulmann's words, a modern form of "Karaism" and could not be resisted in silence. The time had come, he wrote to Arnaud Aron, grand rabbi of Strasbourg, for the French rabbinate to declare its position on matters of faith, and he agreed with the idea of Séligmann Goudchaux, grand rabbi of Colmar, that the publication of a manifesto affirming the authority of the Talmud would be best, provided there were no recriminations against German rabbis. Thus Ulmann rejected the appeal made by Hirsch Lehren of Amsterdam after the Brunswick conference to undertake an open battle with several leading German rabbis. A moderately toned declaration, he asserted, would make it known to the Jews of France that French rabbis do not fear taking a public stand.[51] Such a declaration, however, was never issued.

The conciliatory approach to heterodoxy was characteristic of the moderate wing. Among progressive rabbis such as Mahir Charleville, Samuel Dreyfus, and Ulmann, a conception of Jewish law had emerged that allowed for some measure of ritual modification. Their view rested on the assumption that the system consisted of several well-defined categories of law, representing varying levels of immutability. Ulmann himself differentiated between (1) prescriptions included in the Pentateuch; (2) synodal decisions adopted unanimously at various epochs; and (3) customs and usages introduced without any formal sanction. To this class belonged a large number of prescriptions concerning the public service. Reforms of the third category were, in Ulmann's opinion, not only possible but desirable and necessary. These reforms could be introduced without synodal authority. In the case of the second category, those that were incompatible with the present condition of Jews (that is, political and moral) could be changed by synodal assemblies, according to established legal procedures.[52] Theoretical support for a rabbinic synod was a distinguishing characteristic of progressive rabbis, who believed that such a convocation would enable the rabbinate to control the pace of religious modernization.[53]

The impetus for change derived from the view that the function of the public service was to serve as an instrument of *moralisation*. Its objective was to respond to human needs, and to awaken forgotten or unknown moral instincts and responsibilities. Accordingly, Ulmann stressed that the purpose of the *culte* was not so much the adoration of God as the perfection of man, and that to achieve this goal, religion must succeed in edifying and instructing the worshipper. Under existing circumstances, neither edification nor instruction were possible, he claimed, since few could understand the Hebrew prayers, and the services were too long and lacking in dignity. Ulmann's proposals therefore centered on abridging the duration of the services. This had long been regarded as an obstacle to retaining or attracting the growing numbers of people who were unfamiliar with the traditional liturgy. He suggested that the *piyyutim* be abolished; that the Torah reading be shortened, thus making it possible to read the text in French and to discuss the moral lessons contained in the reading; and that a simple recitation of the liturgy be adopted. The time gained from these reforms would permit the introduction of prayer in French, itself an unprecedented innovation, and the adoption of preaching, still resisted in most Alsatian synagogues. A firm proponent of the educational function of sermons, Ulmann prodded his colleagues to draw on Jewish sources, rather than on foreign writings.[54]

Through the Jewish press in Alsace progressive rabbis gained increased opportunities to express their points of view and to emphasize aspects of Jewish thought that existing journals did not address. Although no single journal endured more than a few years, collectively they represent an ongoing attempt to create a forum for public discussion, and their pages reveal both a deep concern for regional issues and a genuine feeling of pride about Alsace. The first Alsatian Jewish journals were published in Strasbourg. Nearly a decade passed before the pioneer, *La Régénération* (1836–1837), was emulated by *La Pure vérité* (1846–1847) and *L'ami des israélites* (1847). Perhaps the most successful regional journal was *Le Lien d'Israël* (1855–1861), founded and edited by Rabbi Samuel Dreyfus. Like its predecessors, *Le Lien d'Israël* was firmly committed to socio-economic *régénération*, while articulating the moderate orthodox view on religious reform. The journal's avowed goal was to strengthen Jewish solidarity by working to renew the former sentiments of *cofraternité israélite* as expressed by their world unity, traditions, and *moeurs*. To achieve these goals, wrote Dreyfus, "the periodical press must become one of the principal tools in the hands of rabbis to direct public opinion according to the true spirit of traditional and historical Judaism."[55] This statement clearly reveals both an awareness on the part of the rabbis of the methods that were now available to them to make their voice heard and an emerging activism to define and meet the challenges facing the Jewish community as it entered an open society.

One mark of its moderation was the similarity in views that Ulmann's following shared with the *régénérateur* movement. Ennery, actually a centrist, saw as his mission the reconciliation of partisans of traditionalism and reform. Ennery's openness to change is exemplified by his willingness to modify the circumcision ceremony. After consulting a medical commission in 1844, Ennery went on record as supporting the suppression of *meẓiẓah*. This opinion was not shared by all of his fellow grand rabbis, and Ennery encountered much criticism on this.[56] Nevertheless, Ennery did not feel that this was the type of question that warranted consideration by a rabbinical synod. *Meẓiẓah* was a *medical* question and therefore could be resolved without recourse to rabbinic analysis.[57] For the moderate orthodox, the conflict between Judaism and contemporary science was apparent, not real.

Ulmann himself had cordial relations with some *régénérateurs*, particularly with Gerson-Lévy, a moderate critic of religious orthodoxy. In one letter he thanked Gerson-Lévy for having referred to his view as "la juste milieu;" in a second letter he expressed support for the Bible translation undertaken by the *régénérateurs*, lamented the fact that more copies had not sold, and proudly described the progress made in his own synagogue with respect to decorum.[58] Characteristically, Ulmann envisioned an important role for the consistories in the reformation process. A proposed meeting of four consistories to discuss the amelioration of the *culte* was in his opinion an excellent idea, despite the fact that this was a lay body. Such an assembly, though not competent to examine the details of the rituals, and certainly not capable of introducing changes, could, he argued, dramatize the need before the Central Consistory and the rabbis: "It is yours to protest against the evil; it is up to the rabbis to find the remedy."[59]

Not surprisingly, Ulmann's liberal views encountered opposition and criticism. In one instance, an article published in 1846 on the permissibility of certain reforms, including the organ, evoked sharp criticism by the editor of *L'Univers israélite*, Simon Bloch.[60] Bloch attacked Ulmann for allegedly denying the authority of the Oral Law. In a letter to Samuel Dreyfus in May 1846, Ulmann modestly resisted the suggestion that he become the leader of a new party of moderates. By the end of 1846, in another letter to Dreyfus, Ulmann was much less hopeful about the prospects for prompt, uniform changes. The Central Consistory could not be counted upon to take a public stand, and the grand rabbis were unwilling to participate in a synod. In the absence of strong support and leadership, Ulmann considered attending the forthcoming rabbinic assembly in Dresden under the leadership of Rabbi Zacharias Frankel, founder of the Positive-Historical movement. It is highly significant that Ulmann regarded Frankel's views as consistent with his own. Even more important, however, are the implications of his suggestion to look across the Rhine for religious guidance. He had concluded that because the French rabbinate was composed of so many heterogeneous elements, its power had been neutralized and its influence virtually nullified. Moreover, he feared that if progressive rabbis were to take a public stand in France, the appearance of unity would be destroyed and the rabbis would be divided by schism, leaving disastrous consequences.[61] Ulmann evidently felt that intercommunal unity, even if only imagined, should not be tampered with. For now, local reforms must suffice.

By the mid-1850s, after assuming the office of chief rabbi, Ulmann modified his position. Like the reformers, he was disturbed both by the growing trend toward religious indifference and the lack of continuity and uniformity in the implementation of religious reforms. In 1855 he issued a call for a conference of all the grand rabbis of France. Owing to its self-defined role as mediator in the religious controversy between traditionalists and reformers, the consistory agreed to authorize a rabbinical conference, not a synod, to discuss the issues and to offer remedies for the problems facing French Jewry. Officially, the goal of the conference was to exchange views on "the most appropriate means of furthering the religious and moral progress" of French Jewry.[62]

At the instruction of Ulmann, two preliminary rabbinic conferences, one in Colmar, the other in Strasbourg, were held several months before the Paris conference. The official objective of these meetings was for communal rabbis to voice their opinions on the matters to be taken up in Paris and thereby guide the grand rabbis in their deliberations. It is not likely that this was Ulmann's real goal. Indeed, neither of the preliminary meetings endorsed the proposed modifications. At Colmar, sixteen Haut-Rhin communal rabbis voted to retain the *piyyutim,* while six supported elimination. At Strasbourg the majority of Bas-Rhin rabbis also voted to retain the liturgical selections. After attending the Colmar conference, Samuel Dreyfus reported on the proceedings in *Le Lien d'Israël.* Commenting on the question of liturgical reform, he asserted that "it is a mistake to attribute the cause of the disorder that reigns in our synagogues to the multiplicity of *piyyutim.*" Dreyfus endorsed the position of later authorities, who prohibited the removal of a *minhag* in prayer. When a particular *minhag* had not been introduced universally, it could be overturned only by a competent *beit din*. Did Ulmann pretend, Dreyfus asked, that the Paris Conference possessed such authority? The meeting of the grand rabbis was meant to be consultative not legislative. Finally, Dreyfus argued that even if there were good reason to eliminate the *piyyutim*, "the fear of provoking divisions is a sufficient motive for maintaining even erroneous customs."[63]

At the meeting of the grand rabbis in Paris the traditionalists were clearly outnumbered by moderates. This imbalance was hardly significant with respect to most issues discussed: The rabbinic assembly endorsed the wider implementation of *initiation religieuse*, more frequent sermons, more courses in religious instruction for youth, and the standardization of marriage and burial ceremonies without much debate. On the question of transferring the *école rabbinique* from Metz to Paris and the adoption of clerical garb for rabbis and *ministres officiants*, there were issues to resolve but no real divisions. However, three innovations—the reduction or elimination of *piyyutim*, the use of the organ on the Sabbath, and the adoption of a new ceremony for blessing newborn children—represented, in the opinion of the traditionalists, a departure from normative halakhah. This opinion notwithstanding, the conference decided to authorize these reforms.

Heading the traditionalists at the conference was Grand Rabbi Salomon Klein (1814–1867) of Colmar, the acknowledged leader of traditionalist orthodoxy in France at midcentury. A native of Bischeim, Klein attended yeshivot in Germany and France and also received a classical secular education. An eminent halakhist, Klein was an outspoken opponent of religious reform on the practical level and a sharp critic of theoreticians whose scholarship was damaging to orthodox belief. He took issue with the work of several scholars of *Wissenschaft des Judentums*, including Zacharias Frankel's *Darkhei ha-Mishnah*. Frankel had attributed to the Men of the Great Assembly a decisive role in the development of the Oral Law, claiming that they invented many substantive laws and devised their own system of interpretive and exegetical procedures. Frankel's historical method and unorthodox conclusions evoked deep concern in Central and Western Europe, including France. Many traditionalists feared that Frankel's reputation as an opponent of reform was a source of confusion to orthodox believers. Klein himself was approached by French traditionalists seeking his opinion on the controversial subject; he responded with the publication of *Mippnei Koshet* (1861), a detailed critique of Frankel's work. Armed with impressive evidence from Talmudic sources and displaying the acumen of a logician, Klein attacked Frankel's fundamental premise that the *gezerot* and the hermeneutical *midot* were the product of human ingenuity. Klein believed, as did Samson Raphael Hirsch and

other defenders of orthodoxy, that should Frankel's views stand uncon-
tested, the damaging effects of heterodoxy would inevitably be felt among
the religiously faithful.[64]

Apart from the substantive issues, but of no less concern to Klein,
was the question of the aim of modern scholarship. The avowed purpose
of *Wissenschaft* was the application of scientific method to study various
historical, philosophical, and literary phenomena. While conceding that
scientific scholarship had become a powerful tool capable of either
strengthening Jewish faith or weakening it, Klein took issue with the
emphasis now placed on objectivity. He insisted that, to the contrary,
"the purpose of writing books is to direct the light outward, to provide
men with light, to place them on the [correct] path and not to lead them
in darkness." However, because of disturbing trends that had been set in
motion by their emancipation

> the Jews have become dangerously vulnerable to the misrepresentation of
> the Jewish tradition written by incompetent scholars. The disappearance of
> houses of study has produced a state of affairs where the ignorant are now
> overwhelming in number, . . . while those who thirst for the knowledge of
> the Lord are few. . . . [Worse still], secular knowledge has assumed [a posi-
> tion] of primary importance, and our holy Torah [has become] marginal,
> left in the corner.[65]

Perhaps the most dreadful consequence was that even those for whom
"the Torah is practically a closed book" become rabbis, and they proceed
to teach Talmud using an abbreviated introductory approach. For them
"its doors [of the Talmud] are locked . . . and they stand at its gates, not
knowing whether to go right or left." The real danger, according to
Klein, was that modern rabbis, innocently seeking to broaden their
knowledge of Talmud, might very well turn to books such as Frankel's.
It was to these rabbis, Klein insisted, that he felt an obligation to declare
that the faith described in *Darkhei ha-Mishnah* was far from the accepted
faith and that the book was therefore unsuitable for study. Finally, making use of the Karaite analogy, Klein claimed that the definition of the
Oral Law as it appeared in *Darkhei ha-Mishnah* belonged to a faith other
than normative Judaism, and he therefore warned of the possibility of a
religious schism.[66]

The causal connection between religious reform and schism was a
fundamental assumption in traditionalist thinking. Some pointed to the
communal divisions in Germany as an example of the bitter consequences of religious reform. This line of reasoning was an important
motivation in Klein's response to the Paris meetings. In an open attack
on the conference following his return to Colmar, he claimed that the
decisions concluded in Paris were illegal because they violated the princi-

ple of majority rule. For Klein, the preliminary meetings in Colmar and Strasbourg proved that the vast majority of French rabbis were opposed to the introduction of religious reforms, and he insisted that the opinions of the communal rabbis ought to carry the same weight as the grand rabbis. Further, he argued that the Jewish religion was not circumscribed by geographical boundaries, and therefore against an overwhelming consensus in other countries, a majority in one country was not decisive. This last point led Klein to conclude that dissident rabbis would therefore not be bound by decisions reached by the *alleged* majority.[67]

In addition to considering both the deleterious effects of reform and the procedural flaws that undermined the integrity of the conference, Klein carefully explained that three of the decisions (*piyyutim,* organ, ceremony for newborns) were unacceptable from the standpoint of Jewish law. In setting down these arguments, the dissenting Klein provided a basis from which his anti-reform ideology emerges. First, he held that, in order for a revision to warrant consideration, it must be demonstrated that the proposed modification is demanded by a real need and that it will, in fact, remedy the problem. The *piyyutim,* he explained, were originally intended as sources of religious inspiration and intellectual stimulation. If, as critics charged, this was rarely achieved, Klein asked, was it the fault of the *piyyutim?* Reform was unwarranted in this case and therefore unacceptable. Second, nothing may be changed without some historical or halakhic precedent. In writing against the use of the organ, Klein asserted that there was no evidence of musical instruments ever having been played during the Temple sacrifices or prayers. Moreover, the use of the organ violated the spirit of Jewish prayer (i.e., solemn concentration), and in a more technical-halahkic sense, the objection against employing a gentile to perform an act prohibited of Jews on the Sabbath was still valid. Interestingly, the argument of *ḥukkat hagoi,* so prominent a decade earlier, was now rejected by Klein in reference to the organ, although he employed it to discredit the ceremony for the newborn. Such a ceremony was foreign to Judaism, and in the particular case of boys, might be wrongly understood to take the place of circumcision. Finally, Klein maintained that any religious innovation is a violation of the status quo established by the Paris Sanhedrin (of 1807). It is important to note that in building his case against the 1856 conference, Klein masterfully invoked rhetoric normally associated with the era of the French Revolution. Ironically, liberty, democracy, and the Sanhedrin came to the defense of religious conservatism. Further, the image of communal and religious division in Germany evoked considerable fears among French traditionalists. In order to avoid a similar catastrophe in France, Klein concluded, in contradistinction to Ulmann, that halakhic permissibility must not be interpreted as necessarily pointing to the advisability of reform.[68]

Klein's denunciation of the conference ignited a bitter controversy involving him, the Central Consistory, the Colmar Consistory, government ministries, and various lay groups. Initially, public support for Klein's position was expressed by the *Commission des conservateurs du judaïsme* of Paris and numerous northeastern communities, which sent petitions to the Ministre de l'instruction publique et des cultes. The Central Consistory reprimanded Klein and demanded of him a public apology. Klein's refusal to apologize was based on several arguments: that the convocation of the rabbinic conference was a violation of various aspects of the 1844 *ordonnance;* that he, or any other rabbi or theologian, had the right to express himself on religious matters; and that there was no rabbinic hierarchy in Judaism, as the Assembly of Jewish Notables had affirmed in 1806, so that the grand rabbi of the Central Consistory had no greater authority than any other rabbi. Relations between Klein and the Central Consistory deteriorated dramatically over the following two years. The Central Consistory obviously viewed Klein as a severe threat to its own authority, and therefore sought to undermine his power within the Haut-Rhin by intervening in the departmental consistorial elections. It also attempted to curtail his independence by demanding that he place his yeshivah under the direct authority of the Colmar Consistory and that he follow consistorial policy on the authorization of religious functionaries. Although the minister admitted privately to the Central Consistory that Klein's sundry criticisms of the conference may have been justified, he nevertheless supported the central administration in its battle against the recalcitrant rabbi. Only the threat of dismissal succeeded in regaining Klein's cooperation in consistorial affairs.[69]

While the battle between Klein and the Central Consistory was clearly political, the rift between traditionalists and moderates may be viewed as a controversy over what constituted the authentic *minhag* of France. Klein and his followers appear to have demanded, implicitly, that French Judaism align itself with its medieval Ashkenazic heritage. France's distinguished tradition of liturgical creativity, as exemplified by the numerous compendia of *piyyutim,* attested to the irrepressible Ashkenazic commitment to *minhag,* and bore witness to the unparalleled historical and religious experience of Ashkenazic martyrdom. Traditionalists insisted that this was a legacy too precious to be discarded;[70] in Klein's view, it was this heritage that was affirmed by the Paris Sanhedrin. The Ulmann camp, by contrast, concluded, in much the same way as had the *régénérateurs,* that *le judaïsme français* first and foremost must be an agent of national unity. Adopting the Sephardic pronunciation of Hebrew, working toward the fusion of the Sephardic and Ashkenazic liturgies, eliminating the Ashkenazic *piyyutim*, recognizing the centrality of the consistory in Jewish life—all these would promote unity through uniformity, thus establishing a veritable *minhag Tsarfat*. The position of the moderate wing of the rabbinate rested on an assumption it shared with the *régénérateurs:* that the cultural and national forces that fashioned a unified polity under the civilization of France must be mirrored by developments within the Jewish religion.[71]

This goal, Ulmann believed, would be served by the 1856 conference. The purpose of the conference evidently was not to break new halakhic ground. Sources indicate that most of the innovations discussed at the conference had been implemented earlier in various localities. The organ had made its debut in several urban synagogues; some communities had modified or eliminated the *piyyutim, selihot,* and *kinot;* and clerical garb was worn by several rabbis.[72] Rather, the aim of the rabbinic conference was to ratify halakhically acceptable reforms, in this way encouraging their adoption throughout France. Perhaps unprepared for the reaction of traditionalists well before the grand rabbis met, Ulmann modified his expectation. By requiring the approval of the departmental grand rabbi *before* any innovation could be adopted, the Ulmann conference retreated slightly from its quest for modernization and uniformity. Paradoxically, in order to avert the ravages of schism, Ulmann and his colleagues came to terms with the powerful forces of religious conservatism and diversity. Traditionalists, for their part, were willing to cooperate and to compromise on certain innovations, however minor, for the sake of communal unity, in contrast with the Hirschian position that split German Orthodoxy. In France, the Revolution and the particular character of emancipation produced a set of values shared by moderates and traditionalists alike. Strong patriotic devotion, an unequivocally positive attitude toward general culture, and a deep commitment to socio-economic *régénération* far outweighed differences over ritual and liturgical issues. The conflation of these values with the institutional predominance of the Consistory and the political climate in France after midcentury explain the preference for pluralism over schism.

PART FOUR

Jewish Identity in
the Second Republic and
Second Empire

11

Unity and Solidarity

NOT UNTIL THE 1840s can the full impact of emancipation on Jewish identity first be discerned. The enormous challenge that emancipation posed for traditional Jewish beliefs had not been completely evident to the generation of the Napoleonic Sanhedrin and the Bourbon Restoration. During those years, the idea of devotion to the *patrie* was still new and relatively unproblematic. Emancipation appeared to make few demands, while its principal significance was felt in the removal of various legal disabilities. Members of the Sanhedrin and their contemporaries therefore engaged in efforts to reconcile Judaism and citizenship without giving serious consideration to the idea of altering any substantive ritual or conceptual elements of their faith. For the generations that followed, the impact of emancipation was much more profound. Adjustments in the demographic and socio-economic profile of French Jewry were accompanied by transformations in the consciousness of Jews who attended universities and had come under the influence of intellectual forces in France. Many found it necessary to reinterpret Judaism's fundamental concepts in light of French Jewry's new political status. The process whereby the *régénérateurs* reinterpreted the theoretical underpinnings of certain religious practices has already been noted, although these efforts rarely led to proposals for the elimination of rituals. With respect to the significance of Jewish peoplehood in the post-emancipation era, the problem was more acute. Jewish intellectuals came to the realization that traditional concepts that had previously explained the Jewish experience

230

were no longer viable; it appeared that neither "exile" nor "redemption" were intelligible within the context of emancipation. They therefore sought to redefine the basis of Jewish national identity by finding a national raison d'être compatible with contemporary conceptions of patriotic loyalty, national brotherhood, and universalism.

It is, nevertheless, necessary to bear in mind that the various transformations resulting from emancipation did not preclude retaining a strong sense of group consciousness and solidarity. As we have seen, collective action was an idea shared by most Jews in northeastern France, as evidenced by their intensive communal life. Social status was measured largely by the degree of participation in, and support for, the community's institutions. Even in Paris and other urban centers where Jewishness came to be expressed in ways that frequently departed from the norms of the classical Jewish tradition, many subscribed to the idea of collective action, even though their involvement, at times, was of a different genre and not limited to local communal affairs. Jews in the upper echelons of banking, brokerage, and commerce as well as those in the liberal professions found that defending Jewish rights or gaining fiscal support for Jewish institutions were legitimate expressions of Jewish identity. As in the case of general society, the notion of noblesse oblige came to define the relationship between the affluent elite and their less fortunate fellow citizens. In the case of the Jewish elite, wealth and stature were oftentimes used to lend prestige to Jewish philanthropic endeavors and to intercede with government authorities. In a quite unconventional and unexpected manner, the urgency of *régénération* enhanced the responsibility felt by the elite toward their coreligionists.

Concern for the plight of Jews outside of France was expressed almost from the start of the July Monarchy. In one instance this was the outgrowth of a more universal issue: the movement for Poland's freedom attracted significant support within France, including noted Jewish figures such as Adolphe Crémieux and Alphonse-Théodore Cerfberr. At the same time, the struggle for the emancipation of Polish Jewry was also gaining sympathizers. In Paris in 1833, under the leadership of General Marie-Joseph Lafayette, the Philanthropic Society for the Advancement of Jewish Emancipation throughout the World (known as the Lafayette Committee) was established, with the secret involvement of James de Rothschild and Crémieux, to further the Polish Jewish struggle. A concern for French Jews who were refused the right of residence in Switzerland, thereby being prevented from conducting business, eventually grew into vocal support for the emancipation of Swiss Jewry.[1]

The Damascus Affair, perhaps more than any other single event, reveals the commitment of French Jewish leaders to the concept of peoplehood and solidarity. In February 1840, after Father Thomas, a Capucin friar, disappeared, the Jewish community of Damascus was accused of committing ritual murder; many community members were arrested, imprisoned, and tortured. Spearheading a movement on behalf of the beleagured Jews of Damascus was Adolphe Crémieux. He defended them in the French press, denouncing the absurdity of the accusation, and with the support of the Central Consistory, he and Sir Moses Montefiore mounted an international effort seeking the support of England, France, and Austria. Dramatically, in the summer of 1840 a Jewish delegation led by Crémieux and Montefiore travelled to Egypt and achieved its goal: the accused were freed, and their innocence was publicly proclaimed. The courageous and effective response to the crisis in Damascus served as a powerful impetus for the continuing intervention of Paris leaders on behalf of Jews in Tsarist Russia, the Papal States, and North Africa. In time there emerged the myth attributing vast power to the Paris elite, a myth bolstered by the commitment of the Rothschild family, through its almoner Albert Cohn, to the Jews of Egypt and the Ottoman Empire. The Rothschild fortune established schools and hospitals in numerous communities, including Constantinople and Jerusalem. Cautiously, the Central Consistory supported some, though not all, of these causes and initiatives, sensing that it should act with the approval of the French government.[2] Whatever the level of involvement, the Franco-Jewish leadership viewed its commitment to world Jewry as consistent with the ideology of emancipation.

Complicating the search for a new identity was the reaction of various sectors within French society to Jewish social integration. Despite significant successes in socio-economic modernization, as well as modest achievements in French cultural and political life, at midcentury the Jews witnessed not the dissipation of hostility but its intensification. The two principal sources of hostility were missionary activity and the intensification of Catholic and Socialist Jew-hatred. Despite marked differences in form and objective, each of these phenomena challenged the place of Jews in France as equal members of society. Jewish leaders and intellectuals appear to have been unprepared for the reemergence of virulent anti-Jewish sentiment. The various forms of rejection forced intellectuals to reassess the meaning of Jewish existence and the previously formulated ideology of emancipation. In examining this phenomenon, a whole spectrum of factors—historical, political, social, and religious—must be taken into account in order to understand the impact that the legacy of anti-Jewish contempt exerted on Jewish identity.

Missionary efforts were directed at the Jewish population of France with unprecedented vigor in the 1840s and 1850s. In the forefront of this activity stood several Jewish apostates, such as Alphonse and Théodore Ratisbonne, sons of Strasbourg Consistory leader Auguste Ratisbonne, and David Drach, the converted rabbi and former director of the Jewish primary school in Paris. In 1843 the Ratisbonne brothers founded the *Notre Dame de Sion*, a convent school in Paris that was dedicated to converting Jewish youth. By 1845 this institution counted amoung its students twenty Jewish girls belonging to poor families. Among the methods used to attract Jews to the institution, in addition to the obvious material benefits of food and clothing, was a deceptively traditional observance of the Jewish Sabbath, including Friday night and Saturday afternoon Sabbath meals. Other attempts to convert Jewish children were made in hospitals and almshouses where the physically sick, the dying, and the mentally ill were approached by Catholic chaplains who lived in these institutions. In one instance a Jewish girl who had been classified by the police as an "imbecile" was baptized. Catholic journals such as the *Univers religieux* and *La Quotidienne* applauded such cases, hoping to magnify their significance in the public's mind. Seeking to alert the Jewish community to the dangers of missionary activity, the Jewish press publicized various incidents. For example, the *Archives israélites* reported that a man who claimed to have been sent by Abbé Ratisbonne visited the Paris synagogue one Saturday morning, attempting to persuade the choir children to come to *Notre Dame de Sion* for religious instruction. After a complaint was made, the man was arrested by the police.[3] In an entirely different manner, although the objective was the same, some sought to convince the Jews that Judaism was irretrievably flawed. David Drach, for example, accused Adolphe Franck of being a pantheist, since the latter had published a work on Kabbalah. The superiority of Catholicism over Judaism was the theme of several of Drach's works, particularly *L'harmonie entre le synagogue et l'eglise*.[4]

Efforts to convert the Jews were not limited to the Catholic sphere. One organization, the *Société des amis d'Israël*, was founded in Toulouse in 1831, with the conversion of the Jews to Protestantism its avowed objective. This *société* was one of several similar groups in Europe: the London Society for Promoting Christianity among the Jews (1808), a society in Frankfurt am Main (1820), and one in Berlin (1822). By 1841 the *société* of Toulouse had already published ninety-two titles, totalling 468,000 copies, containing general appeals for conversion, sermons, and biographies of converts. The *société* failed, however, to make serious inroads in the Jewish community of Toulouse, let alone of France.[5] In the early 1850s Abraham Pétavel, the Swiss Protestant theologian, directed his evangelical message to the Jews. In general, however, Protestants were much less aggressive than Catholics. All told, whatever inroads were made by missionaries were predominantly in the realm of conversion to Catholicism.

One family's conversion to Catholicism, ending with the forced baptism of the father, provides both a sense of the lure of missionary activity and an illustration of the reaction it evoked within the Jewish community. The story concerns the family of Lazare Terquem of Metz, a physician and brother of Olry, author of the *Lettres Tsarphatiques*. Lazare's wife, unfamiliar with the fundamentals of the Jewish religion and drawn to the writings of Pascal, Chateaubriand, and Lamennais, became involved with a coterie of Metz missionaries. She embraced Catholicism in 1837 or 1838 and arranged for the baptism of her eldest daughter. Lazare and his wife subsequently came to an agreement that she would have custody over their four girls and he over their son. Embarrassment over the situation finally led Terquem and his son to leave Metz for Paris in 1844; the same year his wife and daughters also moved to Paris, where they came under the influence of Abbé Ratisbonne. At the *Notre Dame de Sion* he administered baptism to the other three daughters. Nor was the son free from conversionist overtures. Terquem's brother-in-law, a convert to Catholicism, tried to influence the boy, though unsuccessfully. Lazare, in the meantime, took ill and upon his death in 1845 was converted *in extremis* by Ratisbonne and buried in a Catholic cemetery. Ratisbonne claimed that he had acted in strict accordance with the request made by the deceased shortly before he died. Olry Terquem insisted that this could not have been true, as his brother remained, throughout his family's conversions, unsympathetic to Christianity. Whatever the true story, although all indications point to a forced conversion, the incident was regarded by Jews as scandalous. Olry Terquem appears to have been moved to reassess his liberal view of Christianity and his radical reform program for Judaism. According to Isidore Cahen, author of Terquem's obituary, the affair was a turning point in the reformer's life, as it accounted for a more intensely Jewish conscience.[6] We may assume that his was not an uncommon reaction to the phenomenon of conversion.

Intensification of activity in the sphere of Jewish education was, from all indications, a direct response to the missionary threat. Many felt that the very perpetuation of Jews and Judaism was at stake, and that Jewish youth should therefore be assured of a distinctively Jewish education. One *régénérateur*, Hypolyte Lévy, observed that in Paris religious instruction for most Jewish children was almost nonexistent. He insisted that the few notions taught several months before the confirmation ceremony were inadequate "if we want our children to grow up to know they are Jewish."[7] Activity subsequently centered on the formation of special classes for public school students and evening classes for adults. The fear of proselytism may have also encouraged the creation of *salles d'asiles* (nursery schools–day care centers) to accommodate children of working class families. The first one was founded in Metz in 1842. Activity also focussed on the production of textbooks dealing with religious subjects. In 1845 the *Comité de bienfaisance des dames israélites de Bordeaux* sponsored a competition to encourage the composition of books on piety, dogma, or religious education in general. A similar competition was sponsored by the Strasbourg Consistory in 1847. A new journal, *L'ami des israélites,* proposed the formation of a *société de bons livres* to help fill the need for new textbooks and thereby raise Jewish education to the level of religious instruction offered in Christian schools.[8]

New concern for the religious education of girls was undoubtedly related to the fear that they had been designated as easy targets by the missionary movement. In its response to the Terquem Affair, the *Archives israélites* reminded heads of households that Jewish education alone could protect their daughters from this kind of seduction. No less important, the journal stressed the critical position of women in forming and maintaining the family's religious identity. While Saturday classes in moral and religious instruction were fairly widespread, separate schools and special classes for Jewish girls dated from 1844. The first girls' school was established in Strasbourg, with fifty students. Finally, new textbooks intended for girls also began to appear at this time.[9]

The composition of textbooks assigning greater prominence to Jewish particularity may also be seen as a response to the onslaught on Judaism. One history text, *Tholdoth Jeschurune* (1841), by Mayer Cahun, was careful to stress traditional Jewish values. In his introduction the author lamented the decline of Torah study in favor of *ḥokhma,* secular studies. His own contribution to the promotion of traditional learning was in the realm of Hebrew language instruction. Cahun viewed the fates of Torah and Hebrew as intertwined and therefore urged that much greater emphasis be placed on the proper instruction of Hebrew language and grammar.[10] This, he argued, would restore the crown of the Torah to its rightful place. Another book, *La source de la vie* (1845) by Rabbi Samson Lévy, school director in Sierentz, was a source reader based on the Talmud. The book's emphasis on the morality of the Talmud was praised by the *Archives israélites* as a potent weapon in resisting missionary efforts and an antidote to those who upheld the superior moral content of the Gospels. Though virtually absent from modern school curricula and texts, the Talmud seems to have reappeared in the educational literature when the distinctiveness of Judaism was emphasized anew in the 1840s. Commenting on a reissuing of *La Source de la vie* six years later, Samuel Cahen declared that "in the presence of incessant efforts of *convertisseurs*, it has become the duty of every *israélite* to block the road by familiarizing himself with the opinions of the Talmudists and with the elevated morality which sparkles in their works." In 1849, *Gan Raveh*, a catechism stressing biblical and Talmudic sources, made its appearance in Paris. Written by Lipmann Sauphar, a veteran educator, the volume warned against the dangers of assimilation, reminding students that "this land was given to them [the French nation], while we are in a land not our own; a sojourner ought not resemble a permanent resident."[11]

These remarks point to an unapologetic posture, reflected in efforts to confront Christian attacks by stressing the nobility of Jewish mores and tradition. Taking exception to the militancy of Christian attacks on Judaism, Jewish scholars such as Joseph Derenbourg strove to expose the inaccuracies of Christian polemics. The time had come, according to Derenbourg, to address charges of the Jewish religion's inferiority, particularly the accusation that in Judaism women are neglected by God—a charge made by missionaries on the basis of the alleged permissibility of polygamy and the general low esteem for women in Judaism—whereas Christianity was portrayed as according women a rank of dignity and importance. Derenbourg argued that biblical Judaism, though it did not formally prohibit polygamy, was not well disposed to it; furthermore, those Jewish communities that were not subject to Rabbenu Gershom's *takkanah* (prohibiting polygamy) did not practice it either. In spite of the inaccuracy of the Christian allegations, Derenbourg maintained that Jewish women were likely to fall victim to missionary efforts because of their general ignorance of the Jewish religion. Accordingly, he looked to religious education as an effective means of enabling individuals unschooled in the principles of Judaism to withstand the seduction of conversion; he therefore appealed to the rabbis to provide religious instruction on a regular basis. Several years later Derenbourg himself wrote a textbook, *Livre de Versets*, which emphasized classical sources. The text was subsequently adopted for use in Jewish schools.[12]

The first public response to Christian missionary activity was Joel Anspach's *Paroles d'un croyant israélite*, published in Paris in 1842. Anspach boldly asserted that though Judaism would not lower itself to the level of its adversaries, it could not afford to remain silent. Applying a careful, methodical approach to the interpretation of biblical texts, Anspach refuted Christianity's claim that the coming of Jesus was foretold by the Hebrew prophets and that Judaism had been replaced by Christianity as the religion of truth. Anspach also addressed the assertion that Jews could be saved if they gave up Jewish ritual observance. He argued that the ceremonial law enabled the Jew to preserve the monotheistic idea and that Jewish ritual observance was ongoing proof of the historicity of divine revelation. Anspach's defense of Jewish ritual practice as well as the general integrity of the Jewish religion was, nonetheless, accompanied by proposals for moderate liturgical reforms. In this regard he reiterated the general position of the *régénérateurs:* minor reforms of *la culte publique* would enhance the Jewish religion in the eyes of those Jews who had become indifferent. Anspach's *Paroles,* then, was at once a brave attempt to battle missionary efforts and an impassioned plea to his coreligionists who had abandoned Judaism to return to the faith of their fathers.[13]

In the face of aggressive missionary activity there was a new willingness to do battle with Christianity in the public arena. Joseph Derenbourg insisted that defending Judaism against Christian attacks was a matter of the utmost importance, since the very validity of the Jewish religion was questioned. Efforts to discredit Judaism would no longer permit Jews to maintain an unobtrusive posture. Defiantly, Derenbourg declared that "with gravity and dignity, we will seize each occasion where it concerns making the truth of our faith triumphant, and for that, we pay homage only to Him."[14] The critical attitude expressed by Derenbourg was by no means atypical. "We would like to believe," declared the *Archives israélites,* "that Christianity does not command hatred aga發 the Jews. But how is it that wherever it is dominant, whether it be Catholicism or Protestantism, the Jews are excluded from the *droit commun?*"[15]

Evoked by growing concern over missionary efforts, the position that emerged in the 1840s hinted at a reassessment of an earlier, more accepting attitude toward Christianity. In one instance a Jew in Lyon, Auguste Fabius, wrote a biting attack on Christianity in a work originally delivered as a sermon, *Offrande au Dieu de l'univers* (1842). Christianity was described as exemplifying the worst traits of human nature and religion: idolatry, unintelligible dogmas, persecution of nonmembers, and deception. In short, it was the antithesis of Judaism, which he portrayed as the embodiment of morality, truth, reason and peace. The Central Consistory, evidently disturbed by this public counteroffensive, sharply rebuked the author. *L'Univers,* the Catholic journal, responded to the Fabius pamphlet with great vehemence, devoting six issues to the Damascus Affair alone.[16] Another public expression of resistance to Christian propaganda was the reissuance in 1845 of an edition of Isaac Orobio's *Israel Vengé.* This work, composed by a seventeenth-century marrano who returned to Judaism upon his arrival in Amsterdam, was a refutation of the Christian interpretation of Chapter 53 of *Isaiah*. The book was published at the personal expense of Josué Perpignan, a member of the consistory of the Gironde. The *Archives israélites* commended Perpignan for his initiative, which provided "a true religious manual for the Jew in this time of struggle."[17] For some the critical attitude toward Christianity was evident in their efforts to determine the limits of religious reform. Joseph Cohen of Bordeaux warned that Christianity was an unsuitable model for reformers who sought to introduce elements fundamentally foreign to Judaism, particularly Christianity's conception of aesthetics. Nothing in Christianity was worthy of being imitated, as it was an "empty religion" no longer *en rapport* with contemporary civilization.[18]

The new posture did not, however, end with defensive measures. Leaders called on members of the Jewish community to respond in a more positive way, with a renewed dedication to the Jewish faith. Following the baptism of Dr. Terquem, for example, the *Archives israélites* made an impassioned appeal for Jewish unity: "You see that we still have adversaries to combat and enemies to repel; let us join together, then, in unison, let us show new respect for the religion of our fathers . . . with a new force; by our civic virtues and by our family obligations we will show that we are envious of no one."[19] Increasingly, a return to Jewish tradition was lauded as the most effective response to missionary activity. And typically for the *régénérateurs*, this was related fundamentally to Jewish unity.

The Revolution of 1848 set in motion significant developments in the political, intellectual, and religious climate of France, providing cause for grave concern to French Jewry. Apprehension over the new democratic election reforms was shared both by orthodox and reformist leaders, as each feared the ascendancy of the other. The most important issue, however, was the question of church–state relations. Republicans and radicals raised the possibility of a separation of church and state, and as a result it became an issue of public debate. Some supporters of the Revolution insisted that state support for religious institutions was an unjust economic imposition upon the nonreligious and therefore a violation of liberty. Fearing the potentially negative impact that separation could have on the Jewish community, Franco-Jewish leaders tended to oppose the movement for separation. According to Samuel Cahen, for example, separation would lead to a schism between orthodox and reformers. Additionally, the Central Consistory and various departmental consistories feared that in the eyes of many individual Jews the cessation of government support for state religions would signify the removal of the last vestige of legitimacy for Judaism. This would inevitably deliver a mortal blow to the communal system and deprive the community of unity and purpose.[20] Not least was the fear of the economic hardship that separation might bring on.

Another concern in the post-1848 era was the fear that the powerful Catholic Church would try to dominate state institutions and that this might very well compromise the rights of non-Catholics. The first concrete evidence of the resurgence of Catholic power was the renewed influence of the church in public education. According to new legislation written by the republican government in 1850, the church was permitted to substitute its own primary and secondary schools for those run by the state, and Catholic clergy were assigned positions on the newly constituted educational councils. Moreover, the new law, known as the *loi Falloux,* made religious instruction compulsory in state schools. These provisions, coming at a time of general apprehension over the growing militancy of the church, sparked a wave of protest from the consistory and the Jewish press. The protest succeeded in achieving two goals: first, the law was amended to include a Jewish representative on the educational councils, though it did not specify that this would be a clergyman, as in the case of the Protestants and Catholics; second, a Jewish chaplain was appointed at a Paris high school to provide religious instruction for Jewish students of the city. In the eastern provinces, where anti-Jewish sentiment was more deeply felt, some communities such as Mâcon (Bas-Rhin) in 1853 prohibited Jewish children from attending the local *lycée.* There was also concern that Catholic efforts in Paris to create *écoles libres* would endanger Jewish children. "We must not furnish the *convertisseurs* with the occasion to attract the child of the Jewish poor," the *Archives israélites* warned. Protestants, on the other hand, favored separation of church and state and showed more tolerance toward the Jews.[21]

Through several cases of anti-Jewish activity, the Catholic Church underlined its growing influence in public affairs. The most celebrated case occurred in 1849, and involved Isidore Cahen, the first Jew to be appointed to teach philosophy at the *lycée Napoléon-Vendée.* The bishop, supported by the extremist Catholic press, objected to the idea of a Jew teaching philosophy to Christians and pressured the Minister of Public Instruction to withdraw the appointment. The minister relented, offering Cahen a lower position at Tours. Efforts by the consistory to have him reinstated failed, and Cahen susequently entered the field of journalism. Similar denials and revocations of faculty appointments occurred in Alsace. I. Weill, a teacher of mathematics, was refused a position in the Haguenau *lycée* in 1849, and in the following year Jérôme Aron, who had been appointed to the chair of history at the *lycée* in Strasbourg was dismissed from his post.[22]

By 1850 blatant attacks against the Jews were routinely featured in the French Catholic press. Perhaps the greatest menace was the emergence of a militant Catholic movement that posed a threat both to the principles of French liberalism and to the participation of French Jews in public life. Most prominent was the ultramonist journal *l'Univers catholique*, led by editor Louis François Veuillot (1813–1880). Drawing on the long history of Jew-hatred, Veuillot accused the Jews of various crimes, including ritual murder and attempts to seize control of the government, the economy, and the press. They were, in his mind, foreign bodies, with a social deficiency traceable to the Talmud, the very "source of this unsociable spirit that invincibly separates Jews from Christians and the rest of men." Others called on France to expel the Jews to a distant land. Still others, such as poet Alfred de Vigny, expressed concern over the disproportionate success of the Jews within French society and culture.[23]

The image of the Jew as foreigner was further exacerbated by the identification of Judaism with the evils of capitalism. Beginning in the 1830s, critics of Louis Philippe's bourgeois monarchy assailed commercial activity as the source of society's problems. Following in the steps of Marx, many French socialists viewed the Jews as the incarnation of commerce, claiming that they were responsible for its devastating effects on society. Charles Fourier (1772–1837) remained throughout his writings transfixed on the Alsatian Jewish stereotype, which colored his view of the Jews in Paris and elsewhere. In his view, because of Jewish failings, emancipation had been premature. The only remaining solution was for the government to intervene by educating the Jews to the value of productive labor and by forcing them to engage in either agriculture or industry. Only in this manner could France solve the Jewish problem and thereby protect itself from contamination by Jewish vices. Alphonse Toussenel (1803–1885), a disciple of Fourier, not only repeated his mentor's socialist indictment of the Jews, but added criticisms drawn from the legacy of Christian anti-Judaism. His principal focus, however, was on Jewish bankers of Paris rather than on the petty traders in the northeast. In his *Les Juifs, rois de l'époque* (1845), Toussenel attacked the role of Jewish capitalists such as Rothschild and Fould in the building of the railroad. Perhaps more significant, he attacked the Jews for their anti-Christian behavior. They could not yet be exonerated for the crime of deicide, as proven by their continuing exploitation of Christian society through usury and parasitism.[24] In Toussenel theology and economics were united, reaching identical conclusions and providing mutual corroboration.

It is difficult to determine precisely the motivation in linking anti-capitalism with Christian anti-Judaism. Many of the themes were undeniably shared and, in some instances, interchangeable. Socialists may have hoped to attract greater numbers to socialism by appealing to popular anti-Jewish fears; at the same time, it is not unlikely that they themselves were influenced by the mounting criticism of Jews as foreigners to the "Christian" state and society. In some instances the paths of Catholic extremists and "secular" socialists actually converged. Toussenel, for example, had worked with Veuillot before turning his attention to the Jews.[25]

Paradoxically, Ernst Renan, a Christian who was severely critical of his own religion, may have contributed most to the widening split between Judaism and Christianity in France. The views of Renan, professor of Hebrew at the Collège de France, were the product of the dialectic that characterized the attitude of liberals toward religion. Renan's book, *La Vie de Jésus*, sought to revise the historical portrait of Jesus and, in its reinterpretation of the essence of Christianity, contributed to the formulation of a seemingly universalist-rationalist religion. Renan was an outspoken critic of religious ritual and clericalism, and his conception of the Christian faith as a religion of pure spirituality, liberated from the shackles of clericalism and accessible to all peoples, might have forsworn anti-Jewish contempt. However, in comparing Christianity with Judaism, Renan found the latter to be an outworn system of "narrow legalism" that he termed *Pharisaism*, an obsession with ritual, and thinly veiled hostility toward strangers. Worse yet, the execution of Jesus was a crime for which the entire Jewish nation shares responsibility. Moreover, Renan's characterization of the Semites, appearing in a linguistics study published fifteen years before *La Vie de Jésus*, portrayed them as an inferior race. They lacked the ability to think abstractly, to be creative in the arts, and possessed only a primitive socio-political ethos. The identification of Semites with contemporary French Jews, though not explicit (and indeed denied by Renan), nevertheless was obvious.[26] In advancing these allegations, Renan was following the line of thinking that had led the French government and the Catholic Church to treat the Jews as a separate, distinct nation.

For Jewish intellectuals the definition of the Jews that emerged from the ranks of their detractors would clarify their sense of Jewish peoplehood; in some cases, it would even inspire them to identify, perhaps for the first time, with the Jewish community. The cumulative effect of the onslaught of anti-Judaism emanating from various quarters stimulated Jews to reassess their religion's historical mission and to reconsider its role in Western civilization. It will be recalled that Salomon Munk and Adolphe Franck asserted that the Jewish people had made a critical contribution to humankind by introducing the idea of monotheism and that they had been entrusted with the mission of preserving that idea and the ethical truths associated with it until the dawn of the messianic era. In the course of public discussions concerning the utopian vision, a considerable number of Jewish intellectuals found themselves unable to accept the view that Christianity was the correct faith for humankind. Some asserted that Christianity had endured for eighteen centuries only because it "rested on the solid foundations of Judaism." Others proudly concluded that Judaism, not Christianity, could be identified with republicanism, and would ultimately be the religion of the future.[27]

Beyond the uncertainty concerning the character of the messianic era was the question of the nature and function of Judaism in what was widely regarded as the penultimate period. Though expressed in universalistic terms, in accordance with the teachings of the ancient prophets, the *régénérateurs'* interpretation of messianism hardly eschewed the value of continued ritual observance. The messianic era, according to Munk, was "the *final* victory of religious and moral ideas [and] . . . until that time we must keep intact the *dépôt* which has been entrusted to us."[28] The *dépôt* to which Munk referred was the corpus of Jewish ceremonial laws, not including those "abuses" that could be, according to the *régénérateurs*, legitimately abolished. Adherence to the law was regarded as essential inasmuch as it represented the very content of the Jewish religion and was therefore indispensable if Judaism was to execute its mission in the history of humankind. Moreover, it is clear that although Munk and others spoke of the mission of the Jewish *religion*, the idea required a *people* to embody its ideals and propel them forward. The ceremonial law, in serving as symbols of Jewish unity and cohesion, was thus understood to be crucial for the realization of the messianic era. In defining this special role for religious ceremonies, Munk's position bore distinct traces of the Mendelssohnian legacy.[29]

Unity had become, by 1850, a goal in and of itself. Rabbis frequently extolled the virtues of unity in their sermons. Lazare Wogue, for example, addressing himself to the question why Balaam referred to the tents of Jacob as "goodly" (Numbers 24:5), explained that it was because the ancient Israelites were as one, "united in their faith, in their mutual affection," with "one heart and one soul." The *Archives israélites* dedicated itself to the promotion of Jewish unity, calling it the "most assured protection against the enemy on the outside." Consolidation, the journal declared, was the necessity of the hour.[30] It is especially significant that "unity" became an argument for religious conservatism for those who had earlier advocated religious reform. Referring to the potentially devastating effects of missionary activity and the lure of French culture as "the enemy at the door," Samuel Cahen cautioned his readers against becoming embroiled in religious disputes: "We must all become *conservateurs*, not in the sense of the ghetto, but as understood by Maimonides, Ibn Ezra, and Mendelssohn." The time was ill-chosen, he declared, for reforming the religion: "to work against the missionaries, it is necessary to retreat in order to better advance."[31]

Evidence of retreat can be seen in the comments of Isidore Cahen on liturgical reform. Despite the growing numbers of Jews who were unable to understand the prayers, the *Archives israélites* maintained its strong attachment to Hebrew. Taking issue with those who would employ French prayers only, Cahen referred to the suppression of Hebrew as "the moral mutilation of Judaism." It is significant that his case for retaining Hebrew in the service was made in even stronger terms than before. First, in reiterating its function as a language common to all Jews, he referred to Hebrew as "un symbole de nationalité. . . . un lien de confraternité religieuse." Beyond this, Cahen revealed a greater awareness of its role in the consciousness of the people. Hebrew, he insisted, "represents a multitude of dear memories, a host of agreeable or unhappy sensations; it becomes, in a way, a part of us, and the words are born in us [even] before the ideas themselves." Finally, Cahen asserted that its incomprehensibility to most Jews was, ironically, a powerful argument for its retention. Prayers in Hebrew assumed an aura of mystery and majesty, not unlike the Catholic Church's Latin liturgy.[32]

This attitude toward Hebrew signifies a growing dissatisfaction with the assimilatory ideal. Cahen himself lamented the dissolution of the ancient social bonds, a process that led invariably to the abandonment of individuals to themselves. "Love of one's fellow man" (l'amour vague du prochain) was no replacement for the love of one's coreligionist.[33] The conservatism of the *régénérateurs* is thus reflected in their appreciation for the concept of Jewish peoplehood and, in particular, for the unity of French Jewry. This entailed a certain reverence for religious tradition, even if as no more than a unifying agent. *Régénération* thus came to be understood as an ideology whose chief objective was no longer social integration or patriotic loyalty. The primary focus of *régénération* was an inner-directed cohesiveness. Emphasis was thereupon placed on issues around which there was broad consensus: synagogue decorum, sermons, encouragement of religious instruction and manual labor, and the end to injustices suffered by Jews in France and abroad.[34]

All Jews did not agree on how to respond to Catholic attacks and provocations. Within the consistory there was an unmistakable hesitation to protest or answer anti-Jewish accusations. The Central Consistory had requested that the Minister of Cultes prosecute Veuillot. However, since the government refused to become involved, the consistory decided, after consulting attorneys, that it might be better to withdraw from the case. Furthermore, the Central Consistory decided not to publish a refutation of Veuillot's article, thus leaving the matter to private initiative. In similar fashion, the Paris Consistory refused to take action against Eugène de Mirecourt for a pamphlet containing anti-Jewish slurs. Greater latitude was felt by essayists and publicists, revealing a reassessment of the previously held attitude toward Christianity. These divisions would narrow before the end of the decade. In 1858 a six-year-old Jewish boy, Edgar Mortara, was abducted from his family in Bologna by Vatican guards who claimed that he had been secretly baptized as an infant by a Christian domestic servant. Both the consistory and the Jewish press expressed indignation. The Central Consistory in particular actively sought the assistance of Napoleon III and endeavored to coordinate its effort with English Jewry.[35]

To some younger activists, however, the consistory's record of responding to threats against Jews abroad appeared to be inadequate. Young men who had become aware of the various shortcomings of legal emancipation, such as Jules Carvallo, Eugène Manuel, Narcisse Leven, Isidore Cahen, and Charles Netter, were joined by the older Adolphe Crémieux and Elie Astruc in an entirely new venture. Efforts to create an organization that would "defend the Jewish name wherever it is attacked" came to fruition in 1860 with the founding of the *Alliance Israélite Universelle*. The first institution of its kind, the *Alliance* dedicated itself to work everywhere for the emancipation and moral progress of the Jews and to support those who suffer because they are Jews. Recently, Michael Graetz has written that the establishment of the *Alliance* was an expression of a Jewish collective consciousness produced by the revolutionary crisis of 1848. According to his analysis, the founders of the *Alliance* were members of a "periphery" that had become alienated from the "center" of the Jewish community. Growing politicization of the Jewish community only widened the gap between center and periphery: although the consistorial leadership was loyal to Louis Napoleon, Jewish members of the liberal professions were supporters of the Republic. Experience on the periphery exposed its members more directly to anti-Jewish hostility and discrimination and brought them to an awareness that their dream of full social integration would never be realized. Largely as a result of the post-1848 political and social debates, a Jewish collective consciousness crystallized. In challenging the views of Renan concerning the preeminence of Christianity in the future of humankind, they defended Judaism and came to portray the Jewish people as an essential element of history. Paradoxically, the same men who formerly viewed Judaism in universal terms and who fought for social integration now advanced arguments stressing the philosophical distinctiveness of Judaism and the social separateness of the Jewish people.[36]

This valuable explanation of the establishment of the *Alliance* does, however, require some qualification. First, most of the founders of the organization were indisputably involved in Jewish communal life and hardly represent "peripheral" figures, with the possible exception of Eugène Manuel. They had long been outspoken in their support of Jewish interests and were active in various regenerative projects. Second, in the ideological sense, the objectives of the *Alliance* were not new; numerous efforts in support of world Jewry had been conducted during the July Monarchy. The difference, however, was decisive. The involvement of French Jews in support of their foreign coreligionists in the earlier period came at a time of new-found stability and security. After 1848, when French Jews were themselves subjected to assorted ignominies and flagrant attacks, there emerged a sense of shared destiny, a commonality between the French and foreign conditions. The aggravated situation at home and abroad alerted leaders to the importance of an institution devoted entirely to defending Jewish interests. The founding of the *Alliance* was an expression of dissatisfaction with the way the consistory responded to the various incidents and represented a bold, more independent Jewish conscience.[37]

Do these manifestations of solidarity and collective consciousness constitute a return to authentic, traditional norms? It appears that Crémieux and other activists justified their activity on behalf of Jewish rights in France and abroad on the basis of their interpretation of French values. Recently referred to as models of the "emancipationist style of politics," Franco-Jewish intervention during the Damascus Affair and the creation of the *Alliance* were both the product of a symbiosis of Judaism and Frenchness. Their resulting conception of *le judaïsme français* was understood to be the union of secular French civilization and Jewish tradition. Infused with the French national spirit, Judaism was viewed as a vehicle for the expression of patriotic devotion. France, for its part, would enable the Jewish people to realize its historical destiny. Although certain sectors of French Jewry preserved their ties to Eretz Israel, the traditional relationship to the Holy Land was significantly transformed. As never before, Jews were able to provide assistance to the *yishuv* and to contribute to its revitalization.[38]

Ongoing support for the *yishuv* by Alsatian Jewry, the rabbinate, and the Rothschild family was an important expression of continuity with the past but must not overshadow a development that would prove more powerful. For most Jews, the Revolution slowly put an end to the long exile. More than simply a political haven of refuge, France had become *notre patrie,* having extended an unprecedented invitation to the Jews to participate fully in its social, cultural, and political life. If circumstances in France appeared to preclude the Jews' unqualified participation in society—a development that reflected the identification of French civilization with Christianity—these were viewed as signifying a temporary setback traceable to the persistence of stubborn prejudices. They also served to strengthen, and in some instances stimulate, an awareness of the importance of a distinctive Jewish identity. Through it all, French Jewish thinkers remained steadfast in their faith that what had been achieved in France was the cross-fertilization of two civilizations. At midcentury, the relative weight of each of the two components constituting Jewish identity in France was still undetermined and would remain a much-debated issue to this day. Nevertheless, French Jewish thinkers of various persuasions were convinced that French Judaism was uniquely endowed with both the capacity and the responsibility to serve as a model for world Jewry.[39]

12

Conclusion

NINETEENTH-CENTURY FRENCH JEWRY offers a portrait of a community struggling to meet the challenges of emancipation and modernity. With its origins in the founding of the French nation, this struggle constitutes the core of modern French Jewish identity. Before 1789 the Jews were a distinct social unit, defined both by the general society's imposition of numerous legal restrictions and by the desire of the Jews themselves for social exclusiveness. Rooted in a conception of history that envisioned the long-awaited messianic redemption as the ultimate realization of the nation's destiny, religious symbols and rites stressed the uniqueness of the Jewish faith and the special mission of the Jewish people. With the Revolution came the collapse of the social, political, and philosophical foundations of exclusiveness, forcing French society and the Jews to come to terms with the meaning of emancipation. Public debate on the Jewish question throughout the first quarter of the nineteenth century defined the terms of emancipation in greater detail, and raised the theoretical possibility of limitations on, or retraction of, legal equality if the Jews failed to comply with the conditions of their enfranchisement. Those Jewish leaders who participated in or responded to these discussions acknowledged the compelling nature of the criticisms levelled against the Jews and quickly advanced proposals for socio-economic and cultural improvement. Vocational training and primary education were, initially, the two major areas of regenerative activity.

In the 1830s a more comprehensive ideology of *régénération* emerged through the efforts of younger Jewish scholars and intellectuals. Adjustments in the demographic and socio-economic profile of French Jewry were accompanied by transformations in the consciousness of Jews who attended universities and had come under the influence of general intellectual life. Many Jewish intellectuals came to the realization that traditional concepts that had previously explained the Jewish experience were no longer viable; in light of French Jewry's transformed political status, it appeared that neither *exile* nor *redemption* were still intelligible. The new conception of *"régénération"* was a response to the social and religious implications of emancipation. In addition to its continued commitment to socio-economic transformation, *régénération* was characterized by the demand for the elimination of rituals that violated French conceptions of *civilisation* and social integration; a drive for greater centralization, represented by the emergence of Paris as the center of French Jewry; and the quest for inter-communal and ethnic unity, symbolized by the fusion of the Ashkenazic-Sephardic liturgies. Together, these elements formed a distinct ideology of emancipation that was designed to mediate Jewish interaction with French society and culture. Developed and articulated over the course of nearly a century, this ideology remained synonymous with *régénération*, and thus linked semantically, if not thematically, to the events of 1789. Throughout the long struggle to shape a modern Franco-Jewish consciousness, leaders were thereby able to invoke the ethos of the Revolution, despite dramatic developments that transformed the social and political life of French Jewry. By the 1860s the ideology of emancipation was fully formulated, though its objectives were only partly realized. The socio-economic condition of French Jewry, while improved, had progressed slowly. Poverty was still an unresolved problem in most communities, and the hope for significant occupational restructuring was only partly satisfied. Greater success *was* achieved in the administrative centralization of the consistories, particularly after midcentury, though Paris was not to achieve its preeminent role in French Jewish life until after the loss of Alsace-Lorraine. Socio-cultural differences between Ashkenazim and Sephardim diminished only in the latter part of the century, and even then, ethnic distinctiveness persisted. Finally, although the ideology of religious reform was, by midcentury, well developed and widely publicized, and several of its major proposals were formally endorsed by the 1856 rabbinical conference, actual changes lagged behind. Progress was exceedingly slow in all phases of *régénération*, but the stage was set for the modifications that would eventually follow.

The absence of a movement promoting radical reform and assimilation can be explained by a host of social and political factors unique to France. Ironically, in addressing the issues raised by emancipation and modernization, the leadership of French Jewry looked beyond the borders of France, and concluded that the German Haskalah was ideally suited to the needs of an emancipated population. Its balanced critique of Jewish life, and the accompanying proposals for change, were viewed as identical with the goals of *régénération*. Indeed, of all the Jewish intellectuals in the West, the *régénérateurs* evinced the greatest continuity with the Haskalah. In Germany the concern for socio-economic change was ultimately replaced by the impulse for religious reform and *Wissenschaft des Judentums*. These two movements, fuelled by the abysmal failure of emancipation, were largely the product of traumatic discontinuity. In the case of France, however, proponents of *régénération* consistently regarded their efforts on behalf of educational reform, vocational retraining, and modern scholarship as continuous with the Mendelssohnian legacy. Not without great irony, the French proved themselves to be the most faithful heirs to the Haskalah tradition. The Revolution, the Sanhedrin, and the reign of law all confirmed, in the view of community leaders, the validity of Haskalah. According to their reading of recent history, Haskalah, by virtue of its commitment to modest, well-reasoned change, could promote the modernization of French Jewry while reducing the dangers of communal schism and alienation from Judaism.

Almost all sectors of French Jewry were committed to the program of *régénération* that limited itself to socio-economic modernization and educational reform; at issue was the question of religion. Reformers strove to include ritual innovation within the program of *régénération*, convinced that religion ought to undergo modernization much as the community had. Traditionalists argued for the separation of the two realms: *régénération*, in their estimation, was an ideology that was limited to social and economic matters. Despite the inroads made by secularization in France, religion continued to be the chief component of Jewish identity for most of the century. As a result of modernization, Jewishness came to be expressed in rather diverse forms, often departing from the norms of the classical Jewish tradition. Although communities continued to be organized principally for the facilitation of religious services, Judaism as a religion had lost its attraction for many. Nevertheless, no formal ideology was substituted in its place. For most of the century religion remained the singular frame of reference for all discussions of Jewish identity.

With no perceptible link between religious reform and civic status, French *régénérateurs* did not feel the same compulsion to introduce far-reaching modifications as did the German reformers. Other factors played a role in the argument for religious reform. The distinction between essence and form, the primacy of reason, and the aesthetic ideal were among the values that influenced the *régénérateurs'* evaluation of Jewish rituals. Forms of public prayer, burial rites, and the circumcision ceremony are examples of practices that were found to be unsatisfactory when measured by contemporary standards of civility, as were *halakhic* regulations that appeared to restrict social relations with non-Jews and to preclude certain improvements in the synagogues. However, the theoretical distinction between the essence of Judaism and its exterior forms was applied to the public *culte* only, and not to either private rituals or articles of faith.

The preoccupation with religious reform in nineteenth century France was, in many ways, a reflection of the larger question of what ought to be the essence of the new Franco-Jewish identity. For the Jewish intellectual elite, both rabbinic and lay, the question of what to retain and what to excise from Judaism's cultural heritage remained at the center of the struggle to define this identity. The 1856 rabbinical conference was divided over what constituted the true Franco-Jewish *rite*. Traditionalists felt that modern French Judaism ought to draw exclusively on its medieval Ashkenazic heritage, and they therefore insisted that the liturgy remain fully intact. In their view, the retention of the *piyyutim* was imperative, while new ceremonies and prayers were to be firmly resisted. Moderates argued, in much the same way as the *régénérateurs*, that French Judaism should strive to function as an agent of unity, even if this required some departure from traditional observance. Implicitly, this would mean travelling a less doctrinaire halakhic path and would involve a greater openness to formulating a new and more distinctive *minhag Tsarfat*. Through its participation in the continuing discourse on the essence of Judaism, at times amounting to the selective application of the past to the present, Jewish critical scholarship strengthened the position shared by the *régénérateurs* and moderate rabbis.

As the century drew to a close French Jewry witnessed a dangerous intensification of anti-Jewish hostility. Whereas in the aftermath of emancipation the Jews were criticized for their failure to achieve social integration, later, especially after midcentury, a more worrisome argument was heard: that the presence of Jews in society posed a threat to France, for economic, social, and religious reasons. Ironically, French Jewry's greatest strides toward acculturation and social integration met with increasingly hostile anti-Judaism. After 1870 anti-Judaism tended to be more aggressive and more organized than before. The collapse of the *Union Générale* in 1882 precipitated new recriminations against the Rothschilds and French Jews in general. A few years later Edouard Drumont's *La France juive*, arguing that the Jews all but controlled France and bore responsibility for its major social ills, unleashed a virulent, popular anti-semitic campaign. By the time Captain Alfred Dreyfus was convicted of espionage in 1894 French Jewry was already well-versed in anti-semitism.

The modern history of French Jewry reveals the complexities inherent in emancipation and modernization. Rarely was the impact on Jewish life and thought unequivocal. Indeed, transformations resulting from emancipation did not preclude the retention of a strong sense of group consciousness and solidarity. Collective action was an idea shared by most Jews in northeastern France throughout most of the century, as evidenced by their intensive communal life. In Paris and other urban centers, many Jews in the upper echelons of banking, brokerage, and commerce, as well as those in the liberal professions, found that defending Jewish rights—whether in France or abroad—and gaining fiscal support for communal institutions were legitimate expressions of Jewish identity. Equally significant was the degree to which Jews came to regard France as their spiritual home. Throughout the nineteenth century they remained deeply loyal to the country that accorded them civic equality. Their patriotism never diminished, despite an ever-present, growing hostility within French society toward the Jews. The consistorial leadership, the rabbis, and the *régénérateurs* all shared in the belief that what had been achieved in France was an unprecedented and unequalled symbiosis of two mutually enriching civilizations. Views on precisely how the two elements ought to be balanced were fairly wide ranging. But in spite of the ominous threat posed by anti-Semitism, French Jewry's faith in the ideals of the French Revolution and in the promise of a new Jerusalem remained unshaken.

Notes

The following abbreviations have been used in the notes and bibliography:

AIF	*Archives israélites de France*
AN	*Archives Nationales*
Archives JTS	*Jewish Theological Seminary of America Archives, French Jewish documents*
Archives LBI	*Archives of the Leo Baeck Institute, New York*
CAHJP	*Central Archives of the History of the Jewish People*
CCAR	*Central Conference of American Rabbis*
HJ	*Historia Judaica*
HUC	*Hebrew Union College*
JE	*Jewish Encyclopedia. 12 vols. London, 1901–6.*
JFR	Zosa Szajkowski. *The Jews and the French Revolutions of 1789, 1830, and 1848.* New York, 1970.
JJS	*Journal of Jewish Studies*
JQR	*Jewish Quarterly Review*
JSS	*Jewish Social Studies*
LBIYB	*Leo Baeck Institute Year Book*
LI	*Le Lien d'Israël*
REJ	*Revue des études juives*
SRHJ	Salo W. Baron. *A Social and Religious History of the Jews.* 2d ed. 18 vols. to date. (New York, 1952–).
UI	*Univers israelite*

Introduction

1. On the Jews in northern France see Salo W. Baron, *SRHJ* vol. 6, and Ephraim Urbach, *Ba'ale ha-tosafot* (Jerusalem, 1955). For a comprehensive history of French Jewry,

see Simon Schwarzfuchs, *Les Juifs de France* (Paris, 1975). The most complete, though now dated, bibliographical reference work remains Bernhard Blumenkranz, *Bibliographie des Juifs en France* (Toulouse, 1974).

2. The efflorescence of Jewish culture in Provence has been brilliantly charted and assessed by Isadore Twersky, "Aspects of the Social and Cultural History of Provençal Jewry," *Journal of World History* 11 (1968), reprinted in H. H. Ben-Sasson and S. Ettinger, eds., *Jewish Society Through the Ages* (New York, 1971), pp. 185–207. For an example of the first, and hitherto unmatched, study of a major Provençal scholar, see Twersky's *Rabad of Posquières: A Twelfth Century Talmudist* (Cambridge, Mass. 1962).

3. For the history of the Portuguese, or Sephardic, Jews in southern France, see the numerous studies of Zosa Szajkowski, assembled in *JFR;* I. Révah, "Les Marranes," *REJ* 118 (1959–60): 29–77; Arthur Hertzberg, *The French Enlightenment and the Jews* (New York, 1968), [quotation p. 25.]; Frances Malino, *The Sephardic Jews of Bordeaux* (Tuscaloosa, Ala., 1978).

4. On the Jews of the northeast, see Szajkowski's studies in *JFR,* and *The Economic Status of the Jews in Alsace, Metz and Lorraine (1648–1789)* (New York, 1954); and Hertzberg, *French Enlightenment.*

5. The process of Jewish modernization in France has been the subject of several important studies. Zosa Szajkowski's numerous articles, many of which have been collected in *JFR,* provide a useful review of the archival sources. Other important works not included in this collection are, "Conflicts between Orthodox and Reformers in France" [Hebrew], *Horeb* 14–15 (1960): 253–92, and *Jewish Education in France, 1789–1939* (New York, 1980). Frances Malino's *Sephardic Jews* and Simon Schwarzfuchs's *Napoleon, the Jews, and the Sanhedrin* (London, 1979) each present a careful examination of Jewish life in the Revolutionary and Napoleonic periods, though from decidedly different perspectives. Malino emphasized the leadership role of Abraham Furtado in the struggle for emancipation. Schwarzfuchs both analyzed the decisions of the Sanhendrin and examined their reverberations in the Jewish community. Though focusing primarily on French Jewry at the time of the Dreyfus Affair, Michael Marrus's *The Politics of Assimilation* (Oxford, 1971) is actually a much broader study of Jewish identity and assimilation in the nineteeth century. The most comprehensive examination of the nineteenth-century French Jewish community is Phyllis Cohen Albert's *The Modernization of French Jewry: Consistory and Community in the Nineteenth Century* (Hanover, Mass. 1977). Albert has provided a thorough, meticulously documented account of the origins and development of the consistorial system and its role in modernizing social, economic, and religious institutions. Most recently, Michael Graetz, *From Periphery to Center* [Hebrew] (Jerusalem, 1983), in reexamining the establishment of the *Alliance Israelite Universelle,* has written an excellent and provocative study of Franco-Jewish leadership. For a summary of his argument and my critical remarks, see my review in *Zion* 51 (1986): 107–12. On terms used during the struggle for emancipation, see Jacob Katz, "The Term 'Jewish Emancipation': Its Origin and Historical Impact," in *Studies in Nineteenth Century Jewish Intellectual History,* ed. A. Altmann. (Cambridge, Mass., 1964), pp. 1–26.

6. Albert, *Modernization of French Jewry,* pp. 50–61.

7. Ibid., pp. 112–50.

8. H. J. Zimmels, *Ashkenazim and Sephardim* (London, 1958), pp. 331–32.

9. Albert, *Modernization of French Jewry,* pp. 20–22.

10. See, for example, the petitions sent by twenty-eight communities of the Haut-Rhin district to the Central Consistory, protesting the circular of 12 March 1846, in the Archives of the Leo Baeck Institute, "Alsace-Lorraine, 1808–1853," Folios 174–225. The communities were opposed to the circular because it asked aspirants for the position of

Central Consistory Grand Rabbi whether they would adopt the nine propositions for the reform of the *culte*.

11. Albert, *Modernization of French Jewry*, pp. 235, 255–56.

12. Eugen Weber, *Peasants into Frenchmen*, (Stanford, Calif., 1976), pp. 485 ff.

13. See the discussion of this same issue in Albert, *Modernization of French Jewry*, pp. 263–64.

1. The Road to Emancipation

1. Salo W. Baron, "New Approaches to Jewish Emancipation," *Diogenes* 29 (1960): 57–58.

2. Though initially not as compelling as the pressures imposed from without, forces within the Jewish community also contributed to modernization. For example, Gershom Scholem has suggested that the antinomism of the Sabbatean and Frankist movements were the first modern challenges to rabbinic authority. See Gershom Scholem, *Sabbatai Zevi, the Mystical Messiah*, trans R. J. Zwi Werblowsky (Princeton, 1973); Azriel Shoḥat has argued that the decline of traditional society had already begun in the late seventeenth century. See Shoḥat, *Beginnings of the Haskalah Among German Jewry* [Hebrew] (Jerusalem, 1960). On the emergence of the Haskalah movement, see Jacob Katz, *Tradition and Crisis* (New York, 1961), and *Out of the Ghetto* (Cambridge, Mass., 1973).

3. On the impact of the Crusades on Jewish life, see Baron, *SRHJ;* and Moses Shulvass, "Crusades, Martyrdom, and the Marranos of Ashkenaz," in *Between the Rhine and the Bosporus* (Chicago, 1964), pp. 1–14.

4. See Baron, *SRHJ*, vol. 10.

5. On the popular identification of the Jews with the devil, see Joshua Trachtenberg, *The Devil and the Jews* (New Haven, 1943), and Baron, *SRHJ*, vol. 11. On parallels between the persecution of medieval witches and Jews, see Jeffrey B. Russell, *Witchcraft in the Middle Ages* (Ithaca, N.Y., 1972) and Hugh Trevor-Roper, *The European Witch-craze of the Sixteenth and Seventeenth Centuries* (New York, 1956), pp. 182 ff.

6. Baron, *SRHJ*, vol. 2, p. 39.

7. Shmuel Ettinger, "The Beginnings of the Change in the Attitude of European Society towards the Jews," *Scripta Hierosolymitana* 7 (1961): 216.

8. Ernst Cassirer, *The Philosophy of the Enlightenment* (Boston, 1951), pp. 164–165, 275.

9. Ettinger, "The Beginnings of the Change in Attitude," 216; Hertzberg, *French Enlightenment*, pp. 21–22.

10. Ettinger, "Beginnings of the Change," pp. 16–19.

11. Condillac, *Traité des systemes*, part II, ch. 15, cited in Cassirer, *Enlightenment*, p. 20.

12. Peter Gay, *The Enlightenment: An Interpretation* (New York, 1969) vol. 2, p. 323–32, 465–70. Also see Walter M. Simon, ed., *French Liberalism: 1789–1848* (New York, 1972), p. 4.

13. Montesquieu, *L'Esprit des Lois*, cited in Cassirer, *Enlightenment*, p. 20.

14. Cassirer, *Enlightenment*, pp. 20–21, and Pierre Auberry, "Montesquieu et les Juifs," *Studies on Voltaire and the Eighteenth Century* 87 (1972): 88–89.

15. Eli F. Heckscher, *Mercantilism* (London, 1931), vol. 2, pp. 273–74, 302–3. Gustav Schmoller, *The Mercantile System and Its Historical Significance* (New York, 1895), p. 24; Hertzberg, *French Enlightenment*, pp. 22–24, 49–71. For a comprehensive treatment of the role of mercantilism in early modern Jewish history, see Jonathan Israel, *European Jewry in the Age of Mercantilism* (Oxford, 1985).

16. See Hans Rosenberg, *Bureaucracy, Aristocracy, and Autocracy: The Prussian Experi-

ence, 1660–1815 (Cambridge, Mass., 1958); and the essay by Fritz Hartung, "Enlightened Despotism," *Historical Association* 36 (1957).

17. See Jacob Katz, "The Term 'Jewish Emancipation'," pp. 1–26.

18. Christian Wilhelm Dohm, *Über die bürgerliche Verbesserung der Juden* (Berlin, 1781–1783). Translations and references from English edition, *Concerning the Amelioration of the Civil Status of the Jews*, trans. Helen Lederer (Cincinnati, 1957).

19. Honoré Gabriel Riquetti, Marquis de Mirabeau, *Sur Moses Mendelssohn, sur la réforme politique des Juifs* (London, 1787).

20. For a complete account, see Alexander Altmann, *Moses Mendelssohn: A Biographical Study* (Philadelphia, 1973), pp. 449–61; Katz, "The Term 'Jewish Emancipation'," p. 3.

21. Henri Grégoire, *Essai sur la régénération physique, morale et politique des Juifs* (Metz, 1789). On the competition in Metz see Abraham Cahen, "L'Emancipation des juifs devant la Société royale des sciences et arts de Metz et M. Roederer," *REJ* 1 (1880): 83–96; and Hertzberg: *French Enlightenment and the Jews*, pp. 328–33.

22. Dohm, *Concerning the Amelioration*, p. 1; Grégoire, *Essai*, pp. 112–20.

23. Mirabeau, *Sur Moses Mendelssohn*, p. 62.

24. See, for example, Dohm, *Concerning the Amelioration*, p. 19.

25. Ibid., pp. 14, 16–18; Grégoire, *Essai*, pp. 32–44.

26. Katz, *Out of the Ghetto*, pp. 91–92.

27. Dohm, *Concerning the Amelioration*, pp. 61, 66; Grégoire, *Essai*, p. 152.

28. On the 1787 edict and its author, Chrétien Guillaume de Lamoignin de Malesherbes, see Hertzberg, *French Enlightenment*, pp. 322–27, and Malino, *Sephardic Jews*, pp. 27–39.

29. Hertzberg, *French Enlightenment*, pp. 351, 354–56.

30. See *Encyclopedia Britannica*, Frank Manuel, "Deism." Also see Shmuel Ettinger, "Jews and Judaism as Seen by the English Deists of the Eighteenth Century" [Hebrews] *Zion* 29 (1964): 182–207; Jacob Katz, *From Prejudice to Destruction: Antisemitism, 1700–1933* (Cambridge, Mass., 1980), pp. 23–33.

31. The influence of English Deism on the French *philosophes* has been widely observed. See, for example, Cassirer, *Philosophy of the Enlightenment*, pp. 160–82; Hertzberg, *French Enlightenment*, pp. 38–39, 268–313; and Ettinger, "Jews and Judaism," 182–207.

32. Katz, *From Prejudice to Destruction*, pp. 41–42; and Hertzberg, *French Enlightenment*, pp. 253–8 and ch. 9.

33. Hertzberg, *French Enlightenment*, ch. 9, especially p. 286.

34. Jacob Katz. "Judaism and the Jews in the Eyes of Voltaire" [Hebrew]; *Molad* 5 (1973): 614–25.

35. Peter Gay, "Voltaire's Anti-Semitism," in *The Party of Humanity* (New York, 1964), pp. 97–108. It is interesting to note that the idea that Voltaire's real target was Christianity, not Judaism, was already advanced by the *Archives israélites* in the midnineteenth century. Cf. *AIF* 11 (1850): 220. A valiant defense of the Enlightenment was attempted by Hugh Trevor-Roper, in his critique of Hertzberg, "Some of My Best Friends Are Philosophes," *New York Review of Books* 11 (22 August 1968): 11–14.

36. Pierre Auberry, "Montesquieu et les Juifs," *Studies on Voltaire and the Eighteenth Century* 87 (1972): 87–99; *L'Espirit des lois*, 25, ch. 12, *Oeuvres complètes*, vol. 2, pp. 746–49. In his *Lettres Persanes* Montesquieu called Judaism the "ancient trunk which produced two branches," Christianity and Islam. Cf. *Oeuvres complètes*, vol. 1, pp. 218–19; J. Weill, "Un texte de Montesquieu sur le Judaïsme," *REJ* 49 (1904): 117–19, cited in Hertzberg, *French Enlightenment*, p. 275.

37. Henri Grégoire, *Motion en faveur des Juifs* (Paris, 1789), p. 12.

38. Dohm, *Concerning the Amelioration*, p. 18.

39. Ibid., p. 76, and Grégoire, *Motion*, p. 19. Mirabeau wrote that the Jews should be freed from the "dark phantoms of the Talmudists" (*Sur Moses Mendelssohn,*.p. 28).

40. Grégoire, Essai, pp. 176–77.

41. Ibid., 105. In an anonymous address to a member of the Société des Amis de la Constitution à Strasbourg, an advocate of Jewish emancipation wrote that it is the duty of the rabbis to purify their cult from the infinite number of superstitions and ceremonies that are incompatible with citizenship. See Anonymous, *Observations sur la possibilité et l'utilité de l'admission des Juifs en Alsace aux droits de citoyens* (n.p., 1790 [?]).

42. Grégoire considered religious reform crucial to Jewish *régénération*. According to Ruth Necheles' study, "The Abbé Grégoire and the Jews," *JSS* 33 (1971): 39, Grégoire helped congregations locate liberal rabbis who would introduce innovations.

43. The question was formulated in these terms by Dohm, for one; see *Concerning the Amelioration*, p. 56.

44. Salo W. Baron, *SRHJ*, vol. 1, p. 192, and Victor Tcherikover, *Hellenistic Civilization and the Jews* (Philadelphia, 1959), pp. 320–27.

45. This line of reasoning was used by Louis Poujol, *Quelques observations concernant les Juifs en général et plus particulièrement ceux d'Alsace* (Paris, 1806), pp. 126–29. Poujol accused the Jews of extreme idleness during nearly six months of the year.

46. Dohm, *Concerning the Amelioration*, pp. 1–16, 75–79.

47. See, for instance, ibid., p. 75. Michaelis's position on the suitability of the Jews for citizenship was articulated in his review of Dohm's book, in *Orientalische und Exegetische Bibliothek* 19 (1782).

48. Dohm, *Concerning the Amelioration*, p. 81, Grégoire, *Essai*, p. 70.

49. Dohm, *Concerning the Amelioration*, p. 80.

50. Grégoire, *Essai*, pp. 105, 171, 176–77.

2. The Emergence of the "Jewish Question"

1. Solomon V. Posener, "The Immediate Economic and Social Effects of the Emancipation of the Jews of France," *JSS* 1 (1939): 281–93; Katz, *Out of the Ghetto*, pp. 178–79.

2. Katz, *Out of the Ghetto*, pp. 178–79.

3. George Mosse, *The Culture of Western Europe* (Chicago, 1974), pp. 45–50.

4. Ibid., p. 50.

5. Ibid., p. 59.

6. Poujol, *Quelques observations*, pp. iv–vi, 40–41, 71, 152, 154–56. See Simon Schwarzfuchs, *Napoleon, the Jews and the Sanhedrin*, pp. 34–37, for the background of the pamphlet.

7. Poujol, *Quelques observations*, pp. 93, 96–109, 119, 130–35, 154–55. Poujol's assessment of the Talmud was quite standard. Others, such as Charles Bail, *Des Juifs au dix-neuvième siècle* (Paris, 1816), pp. 47–48, also emphasized the Talmud's preference for "subtleties and minutiae" over "the noble simplicity of the dogmas."

8. Schwarzfuchs, *Napoleon, the Jews and the Sanhedrin*, pp. 46–49.

9. Maurice Liber, "Napoleon," *REJ* 72 (1921): 21.

10. Schwarzfuchs, *Napoleon, the Jews, and the Sanhedrin*, p. 49.

11. Report sent by the Minister of Cultes, Portalis, cited in Schwarzfuchs, pp. 55–56.

12. *Correspondance de Napoleon Ier* (Paris, 1858–70), vol. 13, pp. 581–585, excerpts from the text of a letter to M. de Champagny, Minister of the Interior, 29 November 1806, cited in Shimon Maslin, "Napoleonic Jewry from the Sanhedrin to the Bourbon Restoration" (unpublished paper, Hebrew Union College, Cincinnati, 1957), pp. 4–5.

13. Ibid.

14. Agricole Moureau, *De l'incompatibilité entre le Judaïsme et l'exercise des droits de cité et des moyens de rendre les Juifs citoyens* (Paris, 1819), pp. 37–60.

15. Shimon J. Maslin, "Selected Documents of Napoleonic Jewry" (unpublished paper, Hebrew Union College, Cincinnati, 1957), Document I-A.

16. See Jacob Marcus, "Reform Judaism and Laity, Israel Jacobson," *CCAR* 38 (1928): 413–18.

17. Letter from Napoleon to M. Champagny, Rambouillet, 23 August 1806. Reprinted and translated in Maslin, "Selected Documents," Document I-B.

18. *Correspondance de Napoleon*, vol. 13, p. 584, cited in Maslin, "Napoleonic Jewry," p. 6.

19. Ibid., pp. 101–2, cited in Maslin, "Napoleonic Jewry," pp. 7–8.

20. For a full discussion of the decisions, see Chapter 3. Many historians feel that the members of the Sanhedrin succumbed to the wishes of Napoleon and his advisors and consequently distorted the views of the Jewish religion. See, for example, Simon Dubnow, *History of the Jews*, trans. from German (1925) ed. by Moshe Spiegel, (South Brunswick, N.J., 1967–73) vol. 4, pp. 552–55. Compare with Jacob Katz, *Exclusiveness and Tolerance* (London, 1961), pp. 182–93, where the author contends that the rabbis of the Sanhedrin were able to appease Napoleon without making any real concessions. Katz's position has recently been supported by Simon Schwarzfuchs, *Napoleon, the Jews and the Sanhedrin*, pp. 115–16.

21. Maslin, "Selected Documents," Document I-F.

22. Betting de Lancastel, *Considérations sur l'état des Juifs dans la société chrétienne et particulièrement en Alsace* (Strasbourg, 1824), p. 21; Bail, *Des Juifs*, pp. 66–67.

23. Moureau, *De l'incompatibilité*, p. 37.

24. Ibid.; Betting, *Considérations*, p. 74.

25. See, for example, Moureau, *De l'incompatibilité*, p. 24.

26. Ibid., p. 34.

27. Ibid., p. 25.

28. See Ibid., pp. 37–60.

29. Ibid., pp. 26–27.

30. Ibid., p. 34. For a similar formulation, see Bail, *Des Juifs*, p. 112.

31. Jacob Katz, "A State within a State—The History of an anti-Semitic Slogan, "*The Israel Academy of Sciences and Humanities Proceedings* 4 (1971): 32–58; see also, Katz, *Out of the Ghetto*, pp. 99–103.

32. Moureau, *De l'incompatibilité*, pp. 22–27 for examples. See, for example, Grégoire, *Essai*, p. 110, and Bail, *Des Juifs*, p. 74.

33. The definition is according to the Abbé Girard, *Synonymes français* (1780 edition), cited in Lucien Febvre, "Civilization: Evolution of a Word and a Group of Ideas," in *A New Kind of History: From the Writings of Febvre*, ed. Peter Burke (New York, 1973), p. 225.

34. Ibid., pp. 225, 231–32.

35. Ibid., p. 233.

36. Ibid., p. 238.

37. François Guizot, *La Civilisation en Europe* (Paris, 1828), pp. 12–15, 18.

38. Febvre, "Civilization," pp. 241, 247.

39. This formulation has been advanced by John Murray Cuddihy, *The Ordeal of Civility: Freud, Marx, Levi-Strauss and the Jewish Struggle with Modernity.* (New York, 1974), pp. 20–21.

40. "Programme," *Journal de la Société des Sciences, Agriculture et Arts, du département du Bas-Rhin.* 1 (1824): 114–15. On the history of learned societies in France and their

contributions to public life, see Robert de Lasteyrie. *Bibliographie générale des travaux historiques et archéologiques publié par les sociétés savants de la France* (Paris, 1885), vol. 2, p. 567.

41. Ibid.
42. Ibid.
43. Ibid.
44. Michel Berr, *Lettre au rédacteur de l'Argus* (Paris, 1824), pp. 4–5.
45. *Journal de la Société* . . . 1(1824): 114-15.
46. Ibid., vol. 2 (1825), p. 299, "Rapport de la Commission chargée d'examiner les mémoires qui ont concouru pour le prix proposé en 1824, par la Société des sciences, agriculture et arts du département du Bas-Rhin."
47. On M. le marquis de Lattier, see M.D., "Sur la régénération civile, politique et morale des Israélites français, et sur la décret du 17 mars 1808," *L'Israélite français* 1 (1817): 358–69. For an example of an opposing view of the 1808 decree, see A.N. C 2738, n° 72, "Consultation sur le Décret du 17 mars 1808 concernant les Juifs," Paris, 3 January 1816, cited in *Documents modernes sur les Juifs*, ed. Bernhard Blumenkranz (Paris, 1979), p. 254.
48. *Journal de la Société* . . . 2 (1825): 312. The quotations in the text are taken from a passage of the *mémoire* submitted by Arthur Beugnot. Although this prize-winning essay was never published, a number of passages from the original text have been preserved in the commission's report, as well as an extensive summary of the arguments.
49. Ibid.
50. Moureau, *De l'incompatibilité*, pp. 60–62, 81.
51. Betting de Lancastel, *Considérations*, p. 82, see also p. vi. The tone and substance of the arguments on behalf of exceptional legislation, expressing both punitive and rehabilitative motives, is perhaps best represented by the following passage, excerpted from Moureau, *De l'incompatibilité*, pp. 73–74: "Tâchons de les ramener à l'humanité, à la société universelle; si nos efforts sont inutiles pour faire des citoyens de la plupart d'entre eux, prenons contre ceux-ci les mesures voulues par la raison, pour que nos citoyens n'en soient par les victimes; mais si l'on devait les reduire à l'impossibilité de vivre honnêtement, il vaudrait mieux les renvoyer de nos états, et ce renvoi, qui serait alors l'effet d'une cause créée par nous, ne serait-il pas un attentat aux droits imprescriptibles de l'humanité? persuadons, s'il nous est possible; surveillons, ceux que nous ne pourrons ramener à l'exercise des devoirs sociaux, mais au nom de Dieu, ne chassons plus, ne brûlons plus personne."
52. *Journal de la Société*. . .2 (1825): 309–12.
53. The question of how extensive was the economic or occupational diversification of French Jewry in the postemancipation period is of tremendous significance, though the subject is outside the scope of this study. For studies focussing on local communities, see François Delpech, "La Seconde communauté juive de Lyon," *Cahiers d'histoire* 12 (1968): 51–66, and Christine Piette, *Les Juifs de Paris (1808–1840)* (Quebec, 1983). For a general overview, see S. Posener, "The Immediate Economic and Social Effects of the Emancipation of the Jews in France," *JSS* 1 (1939): 271–326.
54. Amédée Tourette. *Discours sur les Juifs d'Alsace* (Strasbourg, 1825), pp. 15–16.
55. On the origins of the *monte di pieta*, see Cecil Roth, *History of the Jews of Italy*. (Philadelphia, 1946), pp. 104–17.
56. Betting de Lancastel, *Considérations*, p. 130.
57. Tourette, *Discours*, p. 17. Arthur Beugnot made a similar proposal for the creation of a government controlled credit institution; cf. *Journal de la Société* . . . 2 (1825): 318–19.
58. Arthur Beugnot, *Les Juifs d'Occident* (Paris, 1824), pp. 43–44.

59. Ibid., part 3, pp. 278–83. Betting was even sharper in his criticism. He claimed that the Karaites are superior to the "Talmudists" with respect to morality, thus "proving" just how evil the Talmud is; cf. pp. 2, 12, 19.

60. *Journal de la Société* . . . 2(1825): 312–15.

61. Strasbourg had been proposed by the Bas-Rhin Consistory in 1816 as one site for the establishment of a central rabbinical seminary. Cf. LBI, Alsace-Lorraine Collection, Box III, Folios 891–92.

62. *Journal de la Société* . . . 2 (1825): 311, 316–17.

63. Ibid., pp. 317–18.

64. Tourette, *Discours*, p. 37; *Journal de la Société* . . . 2 (1825): 317–18, 305–6.

3. *French* Maskilim *and the Paris Sanhedrin*

1. With the exception of Zosa Szajkowski, historians have ignored the French version of Haskalah. Szajkowski has established in several of his articles that there were French *maskilim* and counted among them the figures treated in the present chapter. See, for example, his "Conflicts Between the Orthodox and Reformers in France," [Hebrew], 253–92.

2. Katz, *Tradition and Crisis* (Glencoe, Ill., 1961), pp. 246–47, 253–59; Katz, *Out of the Ghetto*, pp. 20–21.

3. Hertzberg, *French Enlightenment*, pp. 133–35.

4. Ibid., pp. 141–58.

5. Ibid., pp. 158–61. Concerning the religious posture and identity of the Sephardim, I think it is important to raise the following questions: (1) Can the sources Arthur Hertzberg has consulted provide reliable information concerning religiosity? It would seem that Hayyim Joseph David Azulai's *Ma'agal Tov*, David Gradis' writings, and the Bordeaux communal register may each have had agendas of their own that could very well impinge on the objectivity of these sources. Azulai, an outstanding halakhic scholar and kabalist from Jerusalem, spent most of his active years travelling abroad as an emissary of the Ḥebron yeshivah. A person of great stature and piety, he may have been unprepared for the deviations from tradional norms that he observed, and it is not unlikely that his protestations were exaggerated. It is not clear how representative were the views of David Gradis, a very unusual man, to say the least. One can also question how heavily one should rely on the reporting of public infractions of Jewish law in the communal register. (2) Even if we grant that the views expressed in these sources provide an accurate portrayal of the social and religious reality, they may be accurate only insofar as they describe the Sephardic elite. To what extent may we attribute the views and behavior of the elite to the rank and file? (3) As other students of modernization have asked, Is what we have here a conscious program of nonobservance, governed by an accompanying ideology or simply an evolving decline in religious observance and a resulting ex post facto ideological justification? Noting a decline in rabbinical authority, the exclusion of Talmud study in the local school, and the absence of "indications of a profound religiosity and spirituality in the life of the *nation*" (p. 25). Frances Malino has concluded that the Sephardim "*conscientiously* [emphasis mine] excluded any study of the Talmud" and consciously "rejected" the Talmud and Midrash as sources of divine truth. In my opinion, more evidence is needed before it can be proven that the Sephardim acted in conformity with a clear ideology. For the state of current scholarship on these matters, see Arthur Hertzberg, *French Enlightenment*, pp. 157–63, and Frances Malino, *Sephardic Jews*, pp. 23–26, 33, 56.

6. Malino, *Sephardic Jews*, pp. 24–25.

7. Ibid., p. 26. Malino notes the lack of a serious confrontation with Judaism in the writings of enlightened Sephardic Jews of Bordeaux. For a similar appraisal see Jonathan Helfand, "The Symbiotic Relationship Between French and German Jewry in the Age of Emancipation," *LBIYB* 29 (1984): 331–50.

8. Hertzberg, *French Enlightenment*, pp. 121–32.

9. Ibid., pp. 175–76. Also see Szajkowski, "Conflicts," pp. 256–58.

10. In addition to Ensheim's poems, entitled *Al ha-Va'ad Ha-Gadol asher be-Medinat Zarefat (Ha-Me'assef* [1790]: 33–37), and *La-Menaze'ah Shir* sung in the Metz synagogue to the tune of the "Marseillaise," he wrote a satire against billiards and card games, "Shalosh Ḥidot," *Ha-Me'assef* (1789): 69–72. Following his stay in Berlin at the home of Mendelssohn, Ensheim returned to Metz in 1785 where he gave private lessons in mathematics, since he was refused, as a Jew, a teaching position at the *école centrale* in the city. Ensheim spent his last years in Bayonne as a private tutor in the home of Abraham Furtado. Of additional significance is the fact that Ensheim was the tutor and later the friend of Olry Terquem (see chapter 5). For other details of Ensheim's life and activities, see *Encyclopedia Judaica*, J.H. Schirmann, "Ensheim, Moses." On the relationship between Ensheim and Terquem, see *AIF* 6 (1845): 72, and E. Prouhet, "Notice sur la vie et les travaux d'Olry Terquem," *Bulletin de biographie, d'histoire et de bibliographie mathématiques* (1862): 81–90. I am indebted to Richard Menkis for bringing the latter reference to my attention; cf., Richard Menkis, "Les Frères Elie, Olry, et Lazare Terquem," *Archives juives* 15, no. 3 (1979): 58–61.

11. Meyer Waxman, *A History of Jewish Literature*, 5 vols. (New York, 1936) vol. 3, pp. 138–39.

12. Moshe Katan, "La Famille Halévy," *Evidences* (March, 1955): 7–8. Halévy also left an unpublished manuscript, a commentary on Ecclesiastes and Proverbs. For a discussion of its major points, see *La Bible, traduction nouvelle*, Samuel Cahen, ed. (Paris, 1831–51), vol. 16, pp. xxxviii–xliii.

13. See Frances Malino, "Zalkind Hourwitz, Juif Polonais," *Dix Huitième Siecle* 13 (1981): 79.

14. *JE*, Isaac Broyde, "Zalkind Hourwitz."

15. Zalkind Hourwitz, *Apologie des Juifs* (Paris, 1789).

16. Malino, "Hourwitz," pp. 82–83.

17. Hourwitz, *Apologie*, p. 5.

18. Ibid., p. 34.

19. Ibid., pp. 36–38.

20. Malino, "Hourwitz," p. 84. In his rejection of the moral superiority of the Enlightenment, Hourwitz went well beyond Dohm and Grégoire.

21. Hourwitz, *Apologie*, pp. 48–49.

22. Ibid., pp. 49–50; see also pp. 17–18. Although Hourwitz's arguments in defense of Jewish moral conduct are in themselves not especially unique, his focus on these issues implies that these were the major objections to ameliorating the legal status of the Jews. Hourwitz was responding to a secularized form of Jew-hatred with many of the old arguments. However, once having refuted the charges, Hourwitz admitted that the Jews themselves were not exempt from criticism. The combination of apologetics and self-criticism is what distinguishes Hourwitz from earlier apologetic literature.

23. This argument, which had been used by Dohm in his *Über die bürgerliche Verbesserung der Juden*, received much greater substantiation in Hourwitz' presentation.

24. Hourwitz, *Apologie*, pp. 53–56.

25. Ibid., pp. 54–56. Efforts to demonstrate Judaism's tolerance of the non-Jew who

observes the principles of natural law became prevalent in the eighteenth century, particularly in the writings of Mendelssohn and the *maskilim* of Berlin.

26. Ibid., p. 56. Interestingly, Hourwitz wrote that the Jews could pardon Voltaire because of all that he had contributed in the struggle agaist fanaticism.

27. Ibid., p. 65. Hourwitz's remarks on the political laws of Judaism are similar to Spinoza's position in his *Theologico-Political Treatise.* It is clear that Hourwitz, the enlightened Jew living in Paris, read Spinoza and was familiar with his philosophy.

28. Ibid., pp. 56, 60–62. This was a frequent argument, advanced for example by Simone Luzzatto in his *Discorso circa il stato de gl'Hebrei et in particolar dimoranti nell'inclita città di Venetia* (Venice, 1638), trans. into Hebrew by Dan Lattes, *Ma'amar al Yehudei Venetziah* (Jerusalem, 1950).

29. For a full analysis, see Katz, *Exclusiveness and Tolerance,* pp. 106–13.

30. Hourwitz, *Apologie,* pp. 50–56.

31. Interpretations of the intention and scope of Jewish law, traditionally called *ta'amei ha-miẓvot,* has long been a preoccupation in rabbinic writings. The modern period witnessed a new type of *ta'amei ha-miẓvot* literature written by reformers who sought to determine, on the basis of research, whether a particular law or custom should continue to be practiced, abolished, or modified. This tendency represents one of several methods employed by early reformers in Germany and by the *régénérateurs* in France. For the most thorough account of the history of this literature, see Isaak Heinemann, *Ta'amei Ha-Mitzvot in the Literature of Israel* [Hebrew] 2 vols. (Jerusalem, 1955–56), especially vol. 2, pp. 9–60. Also see Moshe Pelli, "The Methodology Employed by the Hebrew Reformers in the First Temple Controversy (1818–1819)," in *Studies in Jewish Bibliography, History, and Literature in Honor of I. Edward Kiev,* ed. Charles Berlin (New York, 1971), pp. 381–97.

32. In the course of deliberations on the question of intermarriage, one delegate stated: "Great stress has been laid on the domestic inconveniences which would result from such marriages [between Jews and Christians]; but has a word been said of the great political advantages they would produce? If both should be put into the scale, could the superiority of the last be doubted? Certainly not . . ." Cf. Diogene Tama, *Transactions of the Parisian Sanhedrin* (London, 1807), p. 146.

33. See pp. 79–80.

34. See Isaiah Berr Bing's comments on the use of the Yiddish language, *Lettre du Sr. I.B.B. Juif de Metz, à l'auteur anonyme d'un écrit intitulé: "Le cri d'un citoyen contre les Juifs de Metz,"* (Metz, 1787), in *La Révolution française et l'émancipation des Juifs* (Paris, 1968), vol. 8, p. 41.

35. Hourwitz, *Apologie,* p. 37.

36. Ibid., pp. 38–39.

37. Ibid., p. 38. Hourwitz reported that the community of Metz had not had a rabbi for a period of two years but had a man sufficiently educated to answer "the everyday questions which come up in the kitchen by the mixture of milk with meat." This man was paid 1200 francs per year as compared to the usual salary for a rabbi of approximately 10,000 *livres.* Implicit in the relation of this information is the author's opinion that the institution of the rabbinate should be thoroughly transformed inasmuch as it had been reduced to answering questions of minor importance. In his criticism of the rabbinate, Hourwitz echoed the prevailing anticlericalism of the *philosophes* and *maskilim* in Germany. It would appear, though, that in certain respects Hourwitz was even more critical than the *maskilim* of Berlin. Referring, for example, to the "homicidal custom" of immediate burial, Hourwitz attributed its origin to a rabbi who had wanted to conceal his crime of murder by poisoning (see p. 72).

38. Ibid., pp. 39–40. Hourwitz' demand for government controls on Jewish economic activities was a radical position generally espoused by gentile critics.

39. Malino, "Hourwitz," pp. 86–87.

40. Ibid.

41. Unfortunately, very little is known about the life of Isaiah Berr Bing aside from his literary activities. For a more complete list of his publications and biographical data, see "Notices Biographiques," *Revue Orientale* 2 (1842): 337–38; and *Encyclopedia Judaica*, Moshe Catane, "Isaiah Berr-Bing."

42. Isaiah Berr Bing, *Lettre*.

43. Foissac [Jean Baptiste Annibal Aubert-Dubayet?], *Le cri du citoyen contre les juifs de Metz, par un capitaine d'infanterie* (Lausanne, Metz, 1786).

44. Ibid., p. 19, cited in Hertzberg, *French Enlightenment*, pp. 289–90.

45. *Le cri du citoyen*, p. 26, cited in Hertzberg, *French Enlightenment*, p. 290.

46. *Le cri du citoyen*, p. 2, cited in Hertzberg, *French Enlightenment*, p. 289.

47. See Hertzberg, *French Enlightenment*, p. 289, note 52. I assume that Aubert-Dubayet's work was well-known since the pamphlet was undoubtedly the subject of some controversy due to efforts to suppress it.

48. Bing, *Lettre*, pp. 8–9.

49. Ibid., p. 18.

50. Ibid., p. 19.

51. The Assembly of Jewish Notables insisted that the word *usure* (usury) was an incorrect translation of the Hebrew terms *neshekh* and *tarbit;* it means interest of any kind. See Diogene Tama, *Transactions*, pp. 197–98. The standard work on the history of Jewish attitudes toward lending on interest is Judah Rosenthal, "Interest from the Non-Jew," *Talpiot* 5 (1952): 475–92, 6 (1953): 130, reprinted in the author's collection of articles, *Meḥkarim u-Mekorot* (Jerusalem, 1967), vol. 2, pp. 253–323.

52. Bing, *Lettre*, p. 12.

53. Tama, *Transactions*, p. 198.

54. Bing, *Lettre*, pp. 19–29.

55. Ibid., p. 30.

56. Ibid., p. 32.

57. Ibid., p. 54–55.

58. Ibid., p. 41.

59. The translation was entitled *Instructions Salutaires adressées aux communautés juives de l'empire* (Paris, 1782). On Berr Isaac Berr, see *Encyclopedia Judaica*, Moshe Catane, "Berr Isaac Berr de Turique"; Szajkowski, "Occupational Problems of Jewish Emancipation in France, 1789–1800," *Historia Judaica* (1959), reprinted in *JFR*, p. 516.

60. Anne-Louis Henry de la Fare, *Opinion de M. L'Evêque de Nancy, député de Lorraine, sur l'admissibilité des Juifs à la plénitude de l'état civil et des droits de citoyens actifs* (Paris, 1790).

61. Berr Isaac Berr, *Lettre du Sr. Berr-Isaac-Berr, négociant à Nancy, Juif naturalisé en vertu des Lettres Patentes du Roi, à Monsieur l'Evêque de Nancy, Deputé à l'Assemblée National* (1790).

62. De la Fare argued that the Jews were aliens in French society primarily because of their religious and moral constitution. He asserted that Jewish religious observance made it impossible for Jews to fulfill the duties of citizenship, nor could they fill a position in the magistrate or municipality; see *Opinion de M. L'Evêque de Nancy*, pp. 3–4.

63. Berr Isaac Berr, *Lettre du Sr. Berr-Isaac-Berr*, pp. 18–19.

64. Ibid., pp. 19–20.

65. Hertzberg, *French Enlightenment*, pp. 344, 347–48; Szajkowski, "Jewish Auton-

omy Debated and Attacked during the French Revolution," in *JFR*, p. 580, and "Conflicts Between Orthodox and Reformers," pp. 255–56.

66. Comte Stanislas de Clermont-Tonnerre, *Opinion relativement aux persecutions qui menacent les Juifs d'Alsace* (Versailles 1789).

67. Berr Isaac Berr, *Lettre d'un citoyen, membre de la ci-devant communauté des Juifs de Lorraine, à ses confrères, à l'occasion du droit de citoyen actif, rendu aux Juifs par le décrit du 28 Septembre 1791,* (Nancy, 1791), published in Tama, *Transactions*, pp. 11–29.

68. Ibid., p. 12.

69. Ibid., pp. 12–13. Berr's words are somewhat reminiscent of the *Lefikhakh* prayer that precedes the recitation of *Hallel*. Note the similar use of religious imagery by Gerson-Lévy, *Orgue et Pioutim* (Paris 1859), p. 108: "Ce serait méconnaître les vues de la Providence, . . . de s'aveugler sur ce miracle, véritable doigt de Dieu, qui nous a fait passer, dans notre heureuse France de l'esclavage à la liberté, de la tristesse à la joie, du deuil à la fête, des ténèbres à la lumière."

70. Berr, *Lettre d'un citoyen*, p. 13.

71. Ibid., pp. 14–15.

72. Ibid., pp. 15–16.

73. Ibid., p. 16.

74. Ibid., p. 17.

75. Ibid.

76. Ibid., pp. 25–28.

77. Ibid., pp. 18–19.

78. See Chapter 8.

79. Berr, *Lettre d'un citoyen*, pp. 19–21. The project did not come to fruition until much later, under the direction of Samuel Cahen.

80. Ibid., pp. 22–23. See below, chapter 6.

81. Ibid., p. 23.

82. Ibid., p. 24.

83. Berr Isaac Berr, *Réflexions sur la régénération complète des Juifs en France* (Paris, 1806).

84. An illustration of the impact that the pressures of the convocation exerted upon the delegates is the choice by some to violate the Sabbath publicly by riding from the hotel to the synagogue, though the latter was only a few blocks away.

85. David Philipson, *The Reform Movement in Judaism* (New York, 1931), pp. 149–63. Zionist thinkers, by contrast, condemned the Sanhedrin for the same reasons that the latter was praised by the Reform movement. Peretz Smolenskin, for example, attacked the ideological premise of Emancipation that demanded the renunciation of the idea of Jewish peoplehood as well as the dream of collective restoration in the Land of Israel. Proponents of Zionism claimed that the process set in motion by the Berlin Haskalah and the Sanhedrin had failed disastrously because it had denied the essense of Jewish history. See Peretz Smolenskin, "The Haskalah in Berlin" in Arthur Hertzberg, *The Zionist Idea* (Philadelphia, 1959), pp. 154–57. Significantly, in a recent history of Zionism and Israel, Howard A. Sachar, *The History of Israel* (New York, 1979), the author opens with the Paris Sanhedrin.

86. Most notable among historians who have concluded that the Sanhedrin's decisions stayed, for the most part, within the limits of Jewish law are Jacob Katz, *Exclusiveness and Tolerance*, pp. 182–93, and Simon Schwarzfuchs, *Napoleon, the Jews, and the Sanhedrin,* pp. 115–16.

87. Berr Isaac Berr was one of the most influential members of the Assembly; his son, Michel Berr, secretary of the Sanhedrin, identified with the *régénération* movement and

made several contributions in the realm of religious instruction. Zalkind Hourẃitz, though not at the deliberations of the Assembly, consulted regularly with members, and according to Robert Anchel (*Napoléon et les Juifs* [Paris, 1928] p. 181), he even advised Champagny. For a full discussion of the durability of the communal leadership in general and with particular reference to the Sanhedrin, see Michael Graetz, *Periphery*, pp. 25–26.

88. From *Correspondence* of Napoleon, vol. 12 (Paris, 1863), pp. 700–11, no. 10537, cited in Schwarzfuchs, *Napoleon, the Jews, and the Sanhedrin*, p. 55.

89. Tama, *Transactions*, pp. 133–34.

90. Katz, *Exclusiveness and Tolerance*, p. 193.

91. Tama, *Transactions*, p. 152.

92. Ibid., pp. 154–56.

93. Katz, *Exclusiveness and Tolerance*, pp. 24–36, 106–28.

94. Tama, *Transactions*, pp. 76–80.

95. See Schwarzfuchs's note on the dissatisfaction of the commissioners with this answer (*Napoleon, the Jews, and the Sanhedrin*, p. 206, n. 3).

96. Tama, *Transactions*, pp. 194–96.

97. Ibid., pp. 199–200.

98. Katz, *Exclusiveness and Tolerance*, pp. 182–193.

99. Tama, *Transactions*, p. 200.

100. Ibid., pp. 199–200.

101. It is extremely noteworthy that Rabbi Moses Sofer, nineteenth-century champion of Hungarian orthodoxy and uncompromising opponent of religious reform, lauded Sintzheim for having succeeded in maintaining halakhic standards in the answers; see Schwarzfuchs, *Napoleon, the Jews, and the Sanhedrin*, pp. 115–16. Sintzheim himself, in a letter to Baruch Jeiteles, chief rabbi of Prague, wrote that he had succeeded in preventing any deviations from Jewish law; see N. M. Gelber, "La police autrichienne et le Sanhédrin de Napoléon," *REJ* 83 (1927): 138–40.

102. Graetz, *Periphery*, pp. 31–34.

4. The Jewish Community: Continuity and Change

1. Zosa Szajkowski, "Jewish Autonomy Debated and Attacked," *HJ* 19 (1957): 23–28.

2. Berr-Isaac-Berr, *Réflexions*, pp. 6–8.

3. Ibid., pp. 13–15.

4. Ibid., pp. 17–18, 21.

5. Ibid., pp. 22–24.

6. Ibid., pp. 9, 24–26; Zosa Szajkowski, "Jewish Religious Observance during the French Revolution of 1789," in *JFR*, 785–95; Uri Phoebus Cahen, *Halakhah Berurah* (Metz, 1793), introduction.

7. Berr, *Réflexions*, pp. 26–27. S. Posener concluded that before the Revolution the French rabbis had already lost most of their authority and influence, and were replaced by lay communal leaders in the administration of Jewish communities. See S. Posener, "The Social Life of the Jewish Communities in France in the Eighteenth Century," *JSS* 7 (1945): 195–232.

8. Berr, *Réflexions*, pp. 26–27.

9. Ibid.

10. Preaching in Yiddish and German is attested to throughout the pages of the *Archives israélites*. The fact that the journal reported without comment on the pronouncement of a eulogy in German in 1846 suggests that this was not an uncommon occurrence;

see *AIF* 7 (1846): 99. On the German translation of the *Précis élémentaire*, see *L'Ami des israélites* (1847): 211.

11. See Paula Hyman, "Jewish Fertility in Nineteenth Century France," in *Modern Jewish Fertility*, ed. Paul Ritterband (Leiden, 1981), pp. 78–93.

12. Zosa Szajkowski, "The Demographic Aspects of Jewish Emancipation in France during the French Revolution," *HJ* 21 (1959), reprinted in *JFR*, pp. 45–74.

13. CAHJP zf 483.

14. CAHJP zf 728, zf 683, zf 739. On difficulties in determining the precise occupational status of Jews, see Szajkowski, "Notes on the Occupational Status of French Jews, 1800–1880," *American Academy of Jewish Research, Jubilee Volume*, eds: S. Baron and I. Barzilay (Jerusalem, 1980), 545–48.

15. David Cohen, *La promotion des Juifs en France à l'époque du Second Empire (1852–1870)*, vol. 2, (Aix en Provence, 1980), p. 357.

16. CAHJP zf 739.

17. Albert, *Modernization of French Jewry*, 115.

18. Szajkowski, "Notes on the Occupational Status," p. 544.

19. Rodolphe Reuss, "Quelques documents nouveaux sur l'antisémitisme dans le Bas-Rhin de 1794 à 1799," *REJ* 59 (1910): 248–76, and Zosa Szajkowski, "Riots in Alsace during the Revolutions of 1789, 1830, and 1848," [Hebrew], *Zion* 20 (1955): 82–102.

20. Relatively little research has been done on the history of the eighteenth century French rabbinate. For valuable information, see M. Ginsburger, "Les Mémoriaux alsaciens," *REJ* 41 (1900): 118–43; Abraham Cahen, "Le Rabbinat de Metz," *REJ* 7 (1883): 103–16, 204–26; *REJ* 8 (1884): 255–74; *REJ* 12 (1886): 283–97; *REJ* 13 (1886): 105–14; and numerous other studies concentrating on individual figures, published throughout the pages of the *REJ*. On the careers of French rabbis who served in Frankfurt, see Markus Horovitz, *Frankfurter Rabbiner* (Jerusalem, 1969). On Reischer, also see Shohat, *Beginnings of Haskalah*, pp. 73, 95, 170, 190, 193. Abundant rabbinic writings still awaiting critical examination will undoubtedly shed new light on the rabbinate and Jewish religious life in the *ancien regime*. For the vast manuscript literature, consult the catalogue of the Institute of Microfilmed Hebrew Manuscripts, Jerusalem.

21. Alexis Blum, "Sinzheim: Le Porte-Parole des Ashkenazim," in *Le Grand Sanhédrin de Napoléon*, Bernhard Blumenkranz and Albert Soboul, eds., (Toulouse, 1979), pp. 119–131; P.L.B. [David] Drach, *De l'Harmonie entre l'église et la synagogue* (Paris, 1844), vol. 1, pp. 37–39; Freddy Raphaël and R. Weyl, eds., *Régards nouveaux sur les Juifs d'Alsace* (Strasbourg, 1980), pp. 133–144. Since 1974 the Makhon Yerushalayim has published several of Sintzheim's works including *Yad David* on tractates *Berakhot*, *Sanhedrin*, *Baba Kama*, *Gittin*, and *Kiddushin*. Thanks to the Institute, *Minḥat Ani* has appeared for the first time (2 vols., Jerusalem, 1975, ed. S. A. Schessinger).

22. On Katzenellenbogen, See JE.

23. Abraham Cahen, "Le Rabbinat de Metz," 13 (1886): 105–14, and Arthur Hertzberg, *French Enlightenment*, pp. 164–70. On Uri Phoebus Cahen, see his introduction to *Halakhah Berurah* (Metz, 1793).

24. Cahen, "Rabbinat de Metz," 13 (1886): 114–26.

25. CAHJP HM 2/4169, *Extrait du Registre des Délibérations du Consistoire israélite de la circonscription de Wintzenheim*, 21 June 1822.

26. *AIF* 3 (1842): 57, and *AIF* 11 (1850): 291–92.

27. On Worms, see Cahen, "Le Rabbinat de Metz," 13 (1886): 118–24; Naḥum Brill, "Ner la-Maor," *Oẓar ha-Sifrut* 1 (1887): 20–31; Moshe Catane, "Ha-Rav Aaron Worms and his Student Eliakim Carmoly," *Areshet* 2 (1960): 190–98. For an illustration of Worms's attitude toward Isserles, see *Me'ore Or*, vol. 5, p. 51a. Worms left numerous works

in manuscript, including commentaries on several books of the Bible, on *Seder Eliahu Rabbah*, and on the prayerbook. These manuscripts are the property of the Library of the Alliance Israélite Universelle, Paris, nos. 286.1–286.4, 287–8, and can be viewed at the Institute for Microfilmed Hebrew Manuscripts, Jersualem. The Munius manuscripts are preserved at the *école rabbinique*, Paris, nos. 135–7, and are available for viewing at the Institute for Microfilmed Hebrew Manuscripts.

28. Examples of rabbinic publications include Lion-Mayer Lambert, *Abrégé de la grammaire hébraïque* (Metz, 1820), *Catéchisme du culte judaïque* (Metz, 1818), *Elémens de psychologie* (Paris, 1827) and *Précis de l'histoire des Hébreux* (Metz, 1840); Marchand Ennery, *Dictionnaire hébreu-français* (Nancy, 1827) and *Dictionnaire général de géographie universelle ancienne et moderne historique, politique, littéraire et commerciale* (Strasbourg, 1839–41); Samuel Dreyfus, *Abrégé de la grammaire hébraïque* (Mulhouse, 1839); Salomon Ulmann, *Catéchisme ou éléments d'instruction religieuse et morale à l'usage de jeunes israélites* (Paris, 1843). Among Salomon Klein's published works are *Nouvelle grammaire hébraïque, raisonnée et comparée* (Mulhouse, 1846), *Le Judaïsme ou la vérité sur le Talmud* (Mulhouse, 1859), and an annotated French translation of David b. Bilia's *Sefer Yesodot ha-Maskil*. On scholarship in the latter part of the century, see Jonathan Helfand, "French Jewry during the Second Republic and Second Empire (1848–1870)" (unpublished diss., Yeshiva University, 1979), pp. 266–67.

29. Salomon Klein, "Lettre Pastorale, March 1861," reprinted in his *Recueil de lettres pastorales* (Colmar, 1863).

30. See, for example, Michel Gerson, *Citolège hébraïque* (Metz, 1850).

31. See examples from the correspondence of the administrative commission of the *séminaire israélite*, CAHJP 1077/1, Letter 280, 30 October 1866.

32. Archives LBI, "Alsace-Lorraine," Box 6, Folio 2546; *AIF* 12 (1851): 43–44. *LI* (July, 1855), no. 2; *AIF* 10 (1849): 392, 427.

33. Albert, *Modernization of French Jewry*, pp. 50–58.

34. Ibid., pp. 121 ff.

35. Ibid., pp. 122–25.

36. Ibid., pp. 196–221.

37. Ibid., pp. 180–83.

38. *AIF* 2 (1841): 266–68.

39. David Singer, *Des Consistoires israélites de France*, (Paris, 1820), pp. 37–38; *La Régénération* 2 (1837): 107–10; Archives JTS, Box 18, pt. 1; *AIF* 4 (1843): 213–17.

40. Archives JTS, Box 18, pt. 2, "Strasbourg, 1831."

41. Archives JTS, Box 18, pt. 2, "Consistoire de Strasbourg, 1831."

42. Ibid.

43. Ibid.

44. CAHJP zf 296; zf 311, 312; zf 300; Albert, *Modernization of French Jewry* p. 233.

45. Albert, *Modernization of French Jewry*, 140–43; see report of Strasbourg Consistorial Commission, Archives JTS, Box 18, pt. 2, "Strasbourg, 1831"; *La Régénération* 1 (1836): 24–28.

46. *AIF* 4 (1843): 614–15; *AIF* 5 (1844): 543–44.

47. *AIF* 5 (1844): 410–12.

48. Letter to the editor of *l'Alsace* (19 May 1840), reprinted in *AIF* 1 (1840): 315–17.

49. *AIF* 5 (1844): 409–10.

50. *AIF* 6 (1845): 384; *AIF* 7 (1846): 372–73; *AIF* 12 (1851): 230–31.

51. *La Régénération:* 1 (1836), 10–14, 165–71; *Lettre Pastorale* (21 July 1834).

52. Extrait des registres des déliberations du Consistoire israélite du Bas-Rhin, séance du 24 novembre 1842," *AIF* 4 (1843): 50–52; "Compte rendu, 1845," *AIF* 7 (1846): 191–92.

53. *AIF* 1 (1840): 159–64; *La Régénération:* 1 (1836), 10–11.

54. *AIF* 3 (1842): 353–54; *AIF* 6 (1845): 90; *AIF* 12 (1851): 172; "Compte rendu, 1845," *AIF* 7 (1846): 192; "Compte rendu, 1851, 1852," *AIF* 13 (1852): 206; "Compte rendu, 1852," *AIF* 14 (1853): 233.

55. *La Régénération* 2 (1837), 6, 41–42: *AIF* 3 (1842): 267–70; *AIF* 6 (1845): 390.

56. *AIF* 4 (1843): 226–27; *AIF* 6 (1845): 390.

57. Théophile Hallez, *Des Juifs en France. De leur état moral et politique depuis les premiers temps de la monarchie jusqu'à nos jours* (Paris, 1845), p. 257.

58. *L'Industriel alsacien* (23 April 1843); *AIF* 5 (1844): 401.

59. *AIF* 12 (1851): 543–44; *AIF* 17 (1856): 517.

60. *AIF* 5 (1844): 865.

61. *AIF* 2 (1841): 240.

62. *AIF* 5 (1844): 543–44.

63. *AIF* 11 (1850): 669–70; Szajkowski, "Conflicts between Orthodox and Reformers in France," pp. 263–66. The Colmar vocational school was closed on 1 January 1857, according to the *proces verbal* of Colmar Consistory, 19 October 1857, in AN F[19] 11037.

64. Archives JTS, Box 18, pt. 1, "Colmar 1842–44."

65. Cited in Albert, *Modernization of French Jewry,* pp. 118–19.

66. *AIF* 11 (1850): 291–92.

67. CAHJP zf 311, Letter from S. Weill, *commissaire surveillant* and *president du comité d'administration,* to Strasbourg Consistory (9 September 1833).

68. Graetz, *Periphery,* pp. 69–70.

69. "Report of the *Sociéte . . . Bas-Rhin,* Compte rendu of 1845," *AIF* 7 (1846): 192.

70. "Report of Metz *Société.*" *AIF* 2 (1841): 240.

5. The Flight from Traditional Identity

1. Milton Gordon, *Assimilation in American Life: The Role of Race, Religion, and National Origins* (New York, 1964), pp. 62–81.

2. Robert E. Park, "Assimilation, Social," *Encyclopedia of Social Sciences,* eds. E. Seligmann and A. Johnson (New York, 1930), vol. 2; Jonathan Helfand, "French Jewry," pp. 196–197.

3. Christine Piette, *Les Juifs de Paris (1808–1840): la marche vers l'assimilation* (Quebec, 1983), pp. 74–76.

4. P. L. B. [David] Drach, *Lettre d'un rabbin converti, aux israélites ses frères, sur les motifs de sa conversion* (Paris, 1825), pp. 47–48.

5. Report of the director of the Paris police (6 June 1806), cited in Ḥanoch Reinhold, "Joseph Salvador: His Life and Opinions" [Hebrew], *Zion* 9 (1944): 113.

6. Piette, *Les Juifs de Paris,* pp. 71–73.

7. Jacob Katz, "Religion as a Uniting and Dividing Force in Modern Jewish History," in *The Role of Religion in Modern Jewish History,* ed. Jacob Katz (Cambridge, Mass., 1974).

8. Léon Halévy, *Resumé de l'histoire des Juifs modernes* (Paris, 1828), p. 326.

9. Léon Kahn, *Les professions manuelles et les institutions de patronage* (Paris, 1885), p. 73.

10. Ratisbonne's *mémoire* is not extant, but excerpts appeared in *Journal de la Société des Sciences, Agriculture, et Arts, du département du Bas-Rhin* 3 (1826): 376–77.

11. Piette, *Les Juifs de Paris,* pp. 150–51.

12. This description is based on Jacob Katz, "Religion as a Uniting and Dividing Force," pp. 6–9. The conversion of Alphonse Ratisbonne was treated from a psychological

perspective by William James, *The Varieties of Religious Experience* (New York, 1929), pp. 219–22. For additional bibliographical material on the Ratisbonnes, see Katz, "Religion as a Uniting and Dividing Force."

13. Drach, *De l'Harmonie entre l'église et la synagogue* vol. 1, p. 251.

14. Léon Kahn, *Histoire des écoles communales et consistoriales israélites de Paris (1809–1884)*, (Paris, 1884), pp. 8, 10, 31–32. Jacob Katz, "Judaism and Christianity against the Background of Modern Secularism," *Judaism* 17 (1968): 302–4. Drach's autobiography, *Lettre d'un rabbin converti*, describes the process of and reason for his conversion. For a full bibliography of his writings, see the *Dictionnaire de biographie française* (Paris, 1967), vol 11, pp. 723–24. On Simon Deutz, see Zosa Szajkowski, "Simon Deutz: Traitor or French Patriot." *JJS* 16 (1965), reprinted in *JFR*, pp. 1043–57.

15. Frank E. Manuel, *The New World of Henri Saint-Simon* (Cambridge, Mass., 1956), pp. 122–29, 348–63.

16. Ibid., pp. 344–47; Graetz, *Periphery,* pp. 129–30, 127–28; Zosa Szajkowski, "The Jewish Saint-Simonians and Socialist Anti-Semites in France," *JFR,* pp. 1090–1118.

17. Archives JTS, Box 18, pt.1, "Consistoire Central 1821."

18. See *AIF* 23 (1862): 313–17, and above, Chapter 3, note 10. The first nine *Lettres Tsarphatiques* were published as pamphlets, appearing in the following manner: Tsarphati [Olry Terquem], *Première (–Neuvième) lettre d'un Israélite français à ses coreligionnaires* (Paris, 1821–1837). The remaining eighteen letters appeared as letters to the editor of *le Courrier de la Moselle,* 1838–1841. Although no full biography of Terquem has yet been published, important information on his life has been assembled by Richard Menkis, "Les Frères Elie, Olry et Lazare Terquem," *Archives Juives* 15, no. 3 (1979): 58–61.

19. See Albert, *Modernization of French Jewry,* p. 231.

20. Tsarphati, *Lettre 12* (24 March 1839), in *le Courrier de la Moselle. Lettres* 9–27 have been collected in the Fondswiener, Musée Lorrain, Nancy.

21. Tsarphati, *Lettre 20* (15 December 1839), in *le Courrier de la Moselle,* Fondswiener, no. 16948.

22. Ibid.

23. Tsarphati, *Lettre 12* (24 March 1839), in *le Courrier de la Moselle,* Fondswiener, no. 16948.

24. Tsarphati, *Lettre 15* (May 1839), in *le Courrier de la Moselle,* Fondswiener, no. 16948.

25. Tsarphati, Lettre 16 (June 1839) in *le Courrier de la Moselle,* Fondswiener, no. 16948.

26. Ibid.

27. Tsarphati, *Première lettre,* pp. 5–7.

28. Ibid., p. 5.

29. Ibid., pp. 9–10.

30. Tsarphati, letter to the editor of *le Courrier de la Moselle,* letter dated February 1839, Fondswiener, no. 16948.

31. Tsarphati, letter to the editor of *le Courrier de la Moselle,* letter dated December 1838, Fondswiener, no. 16948.

32. Ibid.

33. Terquem also insisted that ritual observance not be permitted to interfere in the training of Jewish craftsmen. He attacked attempts by the Orthodox to force the young apprentices of the *Société d'encouragement pour les arts et métiers* of Paris to recite prayers, wear the *Talit* and *Tephilin,* and observe Sabbath and holiday laws. He attributed the demise of the *Société* (1834) to the inability of the apprentices to harmonize the demands of

labor with the unjustified religious restrictions (*Lettre 18* to the editor of *le Courrier de la Moselle*, 11 August 1839), Fondswiener, no. 16948.

34. Tsarphati, *Première lettre*, pp. 9–11.

35. Ibid., pp. 11–13, and also in the *Troisième Lettre* (Paris, 1822), p. 19. In addition to the pragmatic argument explained earlier, Terquem endeavored to justify the transfer of the Sabbath by means of an investigation into the original meaning of the law. This method, a modified form of *ta'amei ha-miẓvot*, is characteristic of reform literature in general. Traditionally, research into *ta'amei ha-miẓvot* was conducted for the purpose of furthering one's understanding of the commandments and, as a result, enhancing one's performance. The modern, reformist version was employed to find reasons why a particular practice was either no longer applicable or was limited in its application. Terquem's conclusion, based on the ambiguity of the biblical text and his own interpretation of the meaning of the Sabbath, was that the essence of the Sabbath lay in its concretization of the idea of Creation and not in its commemoration of any particular day. Terquem added that man is empowered, since the time of Moses, to legislate time in accordance with the progress of his astronomical knowledge and in deference to economic needs (*Troisième Lettre*, pp. 9–12).

36. צ [Tsarphati], "Réponse aux critiques de M. Salomon Munk," *AIF* 2 (1841): 231–36.

37. *Ordonnance du roi portant règlement pour l'organisation du culte israélite, du 25 mai 1844,* Article 63, published in Albert, *Modernization of French Jewry,* p. 377.

38. צ [Tsarphati] "Sur l'ordonnance d'organisation du 25 mai 1844," *AIF* 5 (1844): 453–57. Fear that Terquem would demand the celebration of the Sabbath on Sunday, based on Article 63, was expressed by Rabbi Samuel Dreyfus of Mulhouse in a letter to the *Archives*. Cf. *AIF* 5 (1844): 589–91.

39. The *Kol Nidre* prayer, recited on the night of Yom Kippur, was an annulment of vows between a Jew and the Almighty. The prayer had often served as a pretext used by governments to assert that the Jews themselves considered their oaths worthless. Reformers viewed the prayer derisively, and the Reform movement of Germany removed it from the liturgy on the grounds that it served as a source for Christian accusations of Jewish untrustworthiness. See Terquem, letter to the editor of *le Courrier de la Moselle* (18 July 1838), Fondswiener, no. 16948.

40. *Shefokh Ḥamatkha* appears in the *Haggadah* of Passover. The text entreats God to "cast Your wrath upon the nations who do not know You" Terquem argued that this passage reflected a negative attitude toward non-Jews, therefore provoking anti-Jewish sentiments, and so should be deleted. See Terquem, *Lettre 23* to *le Courrier de la Moselle* (16 April 1840), Fondswiener, no. 16948.

41. Terquem, letter to the editor of *le Courrier de la Moselle* (December 1838), Fondswiener, no. 16948.

42. Terquem, *Lettre 13* to the editor of *le Courrier de la Moselle* (April 1839), Fondswiener, no. 16948.

43. Terquem, *Lettre 15* to the editor of *le Courrier de la Moselle* (May 1839), Fondswiener, no. 16948.

44. On Crémieux, see S. Posener, *Adolphe Crémieux* (Philadelphia, 1940), and André Chouraqui, *L'Alliance Israélite Universelle et la Renaissance Juive Contemporaine (1800–1900)* (Paris, 1965). On the *more judaico,* see Phyllis Cohen Albert "The Jewish Oath in Nineteenth-century France," *Spiegel Lectures in European Jewish History* (Tel Aviv, 1982). The quote by Katz is taken from Jacob Katz, "Emancipation and Jewish Studies," *Commentary* 62 (1974): 60–65.

6. Le Mouvement Régénérateur

1. See quote by Samuel Cahen, *AIF* 3 (1842): 3.

2. Szajkowski, "French Jews during the Revolution of 1830 and July Monarchy," *JRF,* pp. 1026–37.

3. I have found the expression *"le mouvement régénérateur"* used by several individuals, including Samuel Cahen, *AIF* 7 (1847): 465; and Gerson-Lévy, *Orgue et Pioutim,* p. 2. R. Salomon Ulmann used the expression on several occasions. See, for example, Archives JTS, "Ulmann Letters," letter to Marchand Ennery (23 June 1846), and *Lettre Pastorale* (11 December 1853).

4. Consistoire Central, *Procès Verbaux,* 1B3 (7 June 1830 and 4 July 1830), pp. 303, 317–18. See also, M. Thiel, "Notice sur la vie de M. Gerson-Lévy," *Extrait du mémoires de l'Académie de Metz* (Metz, 1864–1865).

5. Consistoire Central, *Procès Verbaux,* 1B3 (4 July 1830), p. 318. *AIF* 23 (1862), 61–87. Samuel Cahen's ties to the *Wissenschaft des Judentums* movement are illustrated by his translation of Zunz' *Die Gottesdienstlichen Vortige der Juden.* On Isidore Cahen, see André Chouraqui, *L'Alliance Israélite Universelle et la Renaissance Juive Contemporaire (1800–1900)* (Paris, 1965), pp. 31–32.

6. Jacques Kahn, "Charles Oulif"; Isaac Broyde, "Michel Berr." Also see Zosa Szajkowski, "Michel Berr," *JSS* 14 (1963), reprinted in *JFR,* pp. 1077–90. Berr's translation of *Shirei Tifferet* appeared in Paris in 1815. He also translated into French Kargeau's *Shir Mizmor,* a Hebrew poem celebrating the coronation of Napoleon in 1805.

7. Henry Samuel Morais, *Eminent Israelites of the Nineteenth Century* (Cincinnati, 1879), p.78. Among his many activities, a collaborative venture with Abbé Jean Baptiste Glaire may reveal an ecumenical attitude. The two collaborated on a French translation of the Pentateuch with philological notes, under the title *Torat Moshe* (Paris, 1835–1837).

8. Moïse Schwab, *Salomon Munk: sa vie et ses oeuvres* (Paris, 1900).

9. *JE,* Hartwig Derenbourg, "Joseph Derenbourg."

10. *JE,* Isidore Singer, "Albert Cohn"; and Isidore Loeb, *Biographie d'Albert Cohn* (Paris, 1878).

11. There appears to have been greater affinity and loyalty to the basic ideals of Mendelssohn and Wessely in France than among the reformers in Germany. See, for example, the remarks by Michel Berr, *Appel à la justice des nations et des rois* (Strasbourg, 1801), pp. 60–64, and Gerson-Lévy, *La Régénération* 1 (1836): 226–31. Gerson-Lévy, for one, viewed Wessely's *Divre Shalom ve-Emet* (Berlin, 1782), as a model for Jewish educational reform in France; cf. *La Régénération* 2 (1837): 5. For an example of orthodox admiration for Mendelssohn, see Rabbi Salomon Klein's remarks in *UI* 18 (1862): 459.

12. Gerson-Lévy, "Sur la necessité d'une régénération dans le Judaïsme," *La Régénération* 1 (1836): 272–77.

13. Charles Didier, "Le Maroc," *La Revue des Deux Mondes,* series 4, VIII (1 November 1836), 267, 268–269. A reply submitted by Samuel Cahen was not accepted for insertion in the journal, but was published in *La Régénération* 1 (October–November 1836): 326–29.

14. These observations, as well as the quotation from *Le Courrier du Haut-Rhin,* appeared in L. Werth, "Acception du mot 'Juif' en Alsace," *AIF* 3 (1842): 101–4.

15. On Lamennais, see Arnold Ages, "Lamennais and the Jews," *JQR* 63 (1972–1973): 158–70.

16. See Leon Poliakov, *The History of Anti-Semitism from Voltaire to Wagner,* trans. Miriam Kochan, 4 vols. (London, 1975), vol. 3, p. 351–55. On the myth of the Wandering Jew, see *Encyclopedia Judaica,* Yvonne Glikson, "Wandering Jew."

17. Poliakov, *The History of Anti-Semitism,* pp. 356–64. Cf. Charles Lehrmann, *The Jewish Element in French Literature,* trans. George Klin (Cranbury, N.J., 1971).

18. Jacob Katz, *From Prejudice to Destruction,* pp. 115–16.

19. Simon Bloch, "Sur l'esprit et la tendance de ce recueil," *La Régénération* 1 (1836): 65–67.

20. Ibid., pp. 69–70.

21. Ibid., p. 70.

22. Ibid.

23. Jacob Lazare, *Réponse à un écrit intitulé: Première lettre d'un Israélite français* (Paris, 1821); Calman de Metz, *Au pseudonyme Tzarphati malgré lui* (Paris, 1824); Godechaux Baruch-Weil, *Réflexions d'un jeune Israélite français* (Paris, 1821).

24. Albert Cohn, "Réflexions d'un Israélite allemand sur la huitième Lettre d'un Israélite français," *La Régénération* 1 (1836): 348.

25. Salomon Munk, letter to the editor, *La Régénération* 1 (1836): 330–31. As an illustration of how Terquem's views served as an impetus for the crystallization of moderate reformist thinking, see Munk's extensive review of Moïse Biding, *La Vengeance d'Israël* (Metz, 1840) in *AIF* 1 (1840): 325–32.

26. Samuel Cahen, letter to the editor of *du Courrier de la Moselle* (Paris, 1839): 5–7.

27. Albert, *Modernization of French Jewry,* p. 198.

28. Cohn, "Réflexions," 347–48; Munk, letter to the editor, p. 331; Cahen, letter to the editor, pp. 5–8, 12–13.

29. Simon Bloch, "Sur l'esprit," p. 73.

30. With slightly different emphasis, one author of an early catechism (Elie Halévy, *Instruction religieuse et morale à l'usage de la jeunesse israélite* [Metz, 1820]) stated that the function of his work was to instill "in the young hearts the piety that is at the base of each precept" (p. 7). The "spirit of the religion," he explained, is the "morality and piety that flows from its totality and that is its goal and principles" (pp. 10–11).

31. For a full treatment of the teleological role of mitzvot in Maimonides' philosophy of law, see Isadore Twersky, *Introduction to the Code of Maimonides (Mishneh Torah)* (New Haven, Conn., 1980), pp. 374–447, especially pp. 418–30.

32. Gerson-Lévy, in *Revue orientale* 1 (Brussels, 1841): 460 ff., excerpted in *AIF* 2 (1841): 531 ff., translated by W. Gunther Plaut in *The Rise of Reform Judaism* (New York, 1963), pp. 104–5.

33. Ibid.

34. See Paul Robert, *Le Petit Robert* 1: *Dictionnaire alphabétique et analogique de la langue française* (Paris, 1984).

35. On the idea of progress, see Morris Ginsberg, "Progress in the Modern Era," *Dictionary of the History of Ideas* (New York, 1973), vol 3, pp. 633–50; Harry Elmer Barnes, *A History of Historical Writing* (New York, 1963), pp. 174–80; and J. Bury, *The Idea of Progress* (London, 1920).

36. *La Bible, traduction nouvelle,* vol. 9, preface; *AIF* 1 (1840): 66–67.

37. For examples of rabbinic publications, see chapter 4, n. 28. Grand Rabbi Salomon Klein of Colmar, the most vocal French critic of *Wissenschaft,* characterized the new trend with the following: "There have arisen in the land a new group of men who do not trust in the truth of faith, but have followed the desires of their hearts. They have vented their disgusting spirit upon the Torah, which they have not accepted as from Moses, and now will do the same to the Talmud," in Klein, *Mippnei Koshet* (Frankfurt am Main, 1861), p. 14. Cf. Salomon Klein, *Ha-Emet ve-Hashalom Ehavu* (Frankfurt am Main, 1861). For examples of lay scholars whose first publications were Hebrew grammars, see

Samuel Cahen, *Cours de lecture hébraïque* (Paris, 1824), Adolphe Franck, *Meliẓ Leshon Ivrit* (Paris, 1833), and Moïse Biding, *Em la-Mikra* (Metz, 1816).

On Christian Hebraists, see Mireille Hadas-Lebel, "Les études hébraïques en France au XVIIIe siècle et la création de la première chaire d'Ecriture sainte en Sorbonne," *REJ* 144 (1985): 93–126. For data on Jewish membership in the *société asiatique*, see the minutes of the *société* published in the *Journal asiatique*. A perusal of the minutes between 1824 and 1830 reveals that no new Jewish members were admitted, and that the few who had joined earlier were entirely inactive. For evidence of Jewish-Christian collaboration, see Silvestre de Sacy, "Extrait du *Sefer Taḥkemoni*," *Journal asiatique* (October, 1833): 309; abundant examples in the *société's* minutes, beginning with 1831; and the French translation of the Pentateuch, with notes, published by abbé Jean Baptiste Glaire and Adolphe Franck, *Torat Moshe* (Paris, 1835–1837).

38. *La Bible, traduction nouvelle*, Samuel Cahen, ed., 18 vols. (Paris, 1831–51). On the fate of liberalism, see Frederick Artz, *France under the Bourbon Restoration, 1814–1830* (New York, 1963), pp. 158–63, 170–76.

39. Ibid., vol. 9, pp. vii–ix; and vol. 11. Cahen's projected work on rabbinic vocabulary, *Secher le-Miriame*, never came to fruition. For an analysis of the *Biur*, see Alexander Altmann, *Moses Mendelssohn*, pp. 368–420. See also Peretz Sandler, *Ha-Biur le Torah shel Moshe Mendelssohn ve-Siato* (Jerusalem, 1940).

40. See, for example, David Eichhorn, *Einleitung in das alte Testament* (Gottingen, 1824); Heinrich Ewald, *Die Poetischen des alten Bundes* (Gottingen, 1837); Wilhelm De Wette, *Commentar uber die Psalmer* (Heidelberg, 1811); Friedrich Heinrich Wilhelm Gesenius, *Hebräische Grammatik* (Halle, 1813); C.E.K. Rosenmüller, *Scholia in vetus Testamentum Salomonis regis et sapientis quoe perhibentur scripta* (Leipsig, 1819). In explaining the absence of biblical studies among German Jews of the early nineteenth century, most scholars follow Max Wiener, "The Ideology of the Founders of Jewish Scientific Research," *YIVO Annual of Jewish Social Science* 5 (1950): 184–96. On the relationship between scholarship and religious reform in Germany, see Michael A. Meyer, "Jewish Religious Reform and Wissenschaft des Judentums: The Positions of Zunz, Geiger and Frankel," *LBIYB* 16 (1971): 19–41.

41. Salomon Munk, *Palestine. Description géographique, historique, et archéologique* (Paris, 1845), pp. 132 ff.

42. *La Bible, traduction nouvelle*, vol. 1, pp. xi–xii.

43. In addition to the factors already cited, difficulties in earning a living undoubtedly impelled several German Jewish scholars, aside from the well-known emigres, to participate in the French Bible project. One important example is Leopold Dukes (1810–91). Among his most significant works was *Rabbinische Blumenlese* (Leipsig, 1844), a volume devoted to rabbinic proverbs and wisdom. For the French Bible project, Dukes collaborated on several volumes and wrote scholarly introductions to Proverbs, vol. 14 (1847), and the Five Megillot, vol. 16 (1848). It may be worth investigating whether the apparent geographical differentiation between Dukes's rabbinic and biblical studies was motivated by political and/or economic circumstances.

44. On the Sephardic bias, see Ismar Schorsch, "The Emergence of Historical Consciousness in Modern Judaism," *LBIYB* 28 (1983): 436; and Ivan G. Marcus, "Beyond the Sephardic Mystique," *Orim* 1 (1985): 35–36. For the Cahen quote, and for one of the earliest expressions of the desire to move the *école rabbinique* to Paris, see *La Bible, traduction nouvelle*, vol. 9, pp. xiv–xv.

45. On the pioneering contributions made by Jewish scholars in the field of Islamic studies, see Bernard Lewis, *Islam in History: Ideas, Men and Events in the Middle East* (New York, 1973), especially pp. 20–21 and 123–37. Munk originally based his translation of

the *Guide of the Perplexed* on the two Judeo-Arabic manuscripts at the *Bibliothèque royale*, and subsequently consulted the Oxford manuscripts. The first segment of the translation appeared in 1833 in *La Bible, traduction nouvelle*, vol. 4, pp. 80–89, and was finally published in its entirety as *Le Guide des égarés par Moïse ben Maimon*, 3 vols. (Paris, 1856–66). Also in *La Bible, trauduction nouvelle*, vol. 4, pp. 1–56, he published an extensive study entitled "Réflexions sur le culte des anciens Hébreux dans ses rapports avec les autres cultes de l'antiquité." In volume 9 (1838), pp. 76–101, Munk published a biographical essay on Saadia, notes on Saadia's Arabic version of Isaiah (pp. 101–34), and notes on a Persian manuscript of Isaiah (pp. 134–59). Although his plan to publish an Arabic-Rabbinic chrestomathy was abandoned, masterful studies such as *Mélanges de philosophie juive et arabe* (Paris, 1859) far exceeded other works in the field. Included in the *Mélanges* was a French translation of *Fons Vitae*, appearing as *La Source de la vie*, accompanied by scholarly notes and analysis; an extensive essay on the principal medieval Arabic philosophers; and an historical survey of medieval Jewish philosophy.

46. Graetz, *Periphery*, pp. 63–65.

47. Lion-Mayer Lambert, *Précis de l'histoire des Hébreux*.

48. *AIF* 2 (1841): 383–85; Munk, *Palestine*, p. 99.

49. *AIF* 2 (1841): 385.

50. *AIF* 1 (1840): 513–14.

51. The relatively moderate character of *régénération* is reflected in the acknowledgement that the ultimate decision to introduce ritual modifications rested with rabbinic authorities. See, for example, the comments made by Samuel Cahen, *AIF* 3 (1842): 584–88. Typical of the *régénérateurs'* attempts to work with the system, in addition to their activities in conjunction with the *école rabbinique* (chapter 9), was their solicitation of the opinions of rabbis on specific *halakhic* questions. See, for example, the query addressed to Grand Rabbi Salomon Ulmann of Nancy, and his opinion on the permissibility of introducing an organ in the synagogue, *AIF* 5 (1844): 377–79. The expression *Réforme graduée* appeared in *La Bible, traduction nouvelle*, vol. 9, p. ix.

52. On the Paris school controversy, see Leon Kahn, *Histoire des écoles*, p. 36. For an example of a text where the Ashkenazic pronunciation was presumed, see Michel Gerson, *Citolège hébraïque* (Metz, 1850).

53. *UI* 9 (1852): 336.

54. Gerson-Lévy, *Culte israélite* (Metz, 1841).

55. See Theodore Zeldin, *France, 1848–1945: Politics and Anger* (New York, 1982), introduction.

56. Renée Neher-Bernheim, "Sephardim et Ashkenazim à Paris au milieu du XIXe siècle: un essai avorté de fusion des rites," in *Les juifs au regard de l'histoire: Mélanges en l'honneur de Bernhard Blumenkranz*, ed. Gilbert Dahan (Paris, 1985), pp. 369–82. For the liturgical details of the proposal for fusion, see the deliberations of the consistorial commission, "Travaux de la commission de fusion des rites, 1865–66," Brandeis University, Franco-Judaica Archives. It is interesting to note that of the members of the commission, Joseph Derenbourg alone was unreconciled to the idea of fusion. He felt that in an era when religious sentiments were declining, it was inopportune to establish a new rite that would not correspond to the memories of anyone's youth. Klein's opinion was solicited by Simon Bloch, and was published in *UI* 20 (1864): 304 ff.

57. Neher-Bernheim, "Sephardim et Ashkenazim"; *UI* 20 (1864): 271–72. The proposal for a cantorial school in Bordeaux was made in 1853; *Extrait du registre des délibérations*, (15 November 1853), Bordeaux Consistory, in HUC, Archives, "Sephardic Jews of France," 4/1 (1852–1853).

7. Schools and Schoolmen

1. Zosa Szajkowski, "Jewish Religious Observance during the French Revolution of 1789," *YIVO* 12 (1958–1959): 222–23, in *JFR*, 796–97.

2. Zosa Szajkowski, "Secular versus Religious Jewish Life in France," in *The Role of Religion in Modern Jewish History*, ed. Jacob Katz (Cambridge, Mass., 1975), p. 111.

3. Cited in S. Posener, "The Immediate Economic and Social Effects of the Emancipation of the Jews of France," *JSS* 1 (1939): 308.

4. Ibid., pp. 308–10.

5. Ibid., p. 310.

6. Ibid., p. 311.

7. Ibid., pp. 308–9.

8. Henri Grégoire, *Observations Nouvelles sur les Juifs et spécialement ceux d'Allemagne* (Paris, 1806), p. 8, cited in Posener, "Immediate Effects," p. 312.

9. Posener, "Immediate Effects," p. 312.

10. Ibid.

11. *L'Israélite français* 1 (1817): 249.

12. *Distribution des prix faite aux élèves des écoles israélites de Metz* (1 October 1819).

13. *Distribution des prix . . . Metz* (1 October 1821). Also see the remarks by Noé Noé of Bordeaux, *AIF* 4 (1843): 213–17. On schools as agents of socialization, see the discussion in Weber, *Peasants into Frenchmen*, pp. 332 ff.

14. In addition to the Paris school, a secondary school was established in Dieulefit in 1819 and an *école normale* for girls in Saint-Foy in 1818. The Protestant *Société pour l'encouragement de l'instruction primaire* later created a full-fledged *école normale* in Courbevoie (1844) and Boissy Saint-Leber (1846). By 1840 there were 677 Protestant schools. For a full discussion, see Raoul Stephan, *Histoire du Protestantisme Français* (Paris, 1961).

15. *L'Israélite français* 1 (1817): 252.

16. S. Mayer Dalmbert, "Institute Israélite," *L'Israélite français* 1 (1817): 86–93. On Dalmbert, see *AIF* 1 (1840): 243–47.

17. Léon Kahn, *Histoire des écoles*, pp. 6–9.

18. In the preliminary report of the commission (17 January 1819), the words "and over which the grand rabbis will preside" were crossed out. David Drach, however, in his curriculum prospectus, stated that the grand rabbis would inspect all matters related to religion at least once a month. Archives JTS, Box 1, "Institution Académique."

19. Abraham Cologna, "De l'éducation," *L'Israélite français* 1 (1817): 9–13.

20. Preliminary report of the commission of instruction, (17 January 1819), in Archives of Paris Consistory, B7 liasse 3, "Ecoles et Instruction."

21. Ibid.

22. Ibid.

23. Ibid.

24. Ibid.

25. Deliberation of the administrative council of the *Société pour l'encouragement de l'instruction élémentaire dans le département de la Moselle*, meeting of 20 April 1818; reprinted by the Metz Consistory in a letter to the editor, *L'Israélite français* 2 (1818): 97–98.

26. Ibid., pp. 101–3.

27. Ibid., pp. 103–5.

28. Ibid., p. 105.

29. Ibid., pp. 102, 105.

30. Ibid., p. 100.

31. "Fondation d'une école élémentaire israélite à Metz," a circular sent by the Metz Consistory to Jews of the *département* (30 June 1818); reprinted in *L'Israélite français* 2 (1818): 97–98. On Worm's involvement, see *La Régénération* 2 (1837): 5.

32. *AIF* 2 (1841): 539.

33. The twelve schools were distributed as follows: Paris (1), Marseille (1), Bordeaux (1), Nancy (1), Metz (3), Strasbourg (2), and Wintzenheim (3). Archives JTS, "Consistory Correspondence," 1813–1820.

34. See John Moody, *French Education since Napoleon* (Syracuse, N.Y., 1978), pp. 21–31; and H. C. Barnard, *Education and the French Revolution* (Cambridge, Mass., 1969), pp. 224–25.

35. Szajkowski, *Jewish Education in France, 1789–1939* (New York, 1980), p. 6.

36. A.N. F^{17} 12514, "Projet de règlement concernant les comités primaires israélites" (17 April 1832).

37. Kahn, *Histoire des écoles*, pp. 47–48.

38. Ibid.

30. The rector of the *Académie* of Bordeaux submitted a request for 600 francs to the Minister of Public Instruction and Cults, arguing that this would enable the Jewish school there to admit an additional fifty students. AN F^{17} 12514, letter (29 August 1830).

40. AN F^{17} 12514, letter from the president of the Strasbourg Consistory to the rector of the *Académie* of Strasbourg (20 December 1831). The Strasbourg school was then receiving 600 francs from the municipal council.

41. AN F^{17} 12514, letter (8 June 1831).

42. AN F^{17} 12514, letter (4 October 1832).

43. The salaries of the schoolmaster and his assistant in the Paris school had been paid, since 1830, by the city of Paris. AN F^{17} 12514, report by an inspector of the *Académie* of Paris, *Université de France* (5 September 1832). The Marseille school also obtained an allocation from the city. See AN F^{17} 12514.

44. See Brandeis University Archives, Franco-Judaica Collection, IV 2a, Letter from Paris Consistory to M. le Comte de Rambuteau (17 July 1843). For details on the "arrangement" between the Consistory and the Municipal Council, see Kahn, *Histoire des écoles*, pp. 56–58.

45. See AN F^{17} 12514 for the report of the Minister of Public Instruction and the Cultes (20 September 1831); letter from the Prefecture de la Gironde to the Minister of Public Instruction and the Cultes (17 September 1830); letter from the rector of the *Académie* of Bordeaux to Minister of Public Instruction and the Cultes (29 August 1830).

46. Victor Treschan, "The Struggle for Integration: The Jewish Community of Strasbourg, 1818–1850" (unpublished diss. University of Wisconsin–Madison, 1978), p. 94. Cottard took an active interest in Jewish curricular matters as well. Convinced that the life of Moses Mendelssohn ought to be studied by Jewish children in France, he composed *Souvenirs de Moïse Mendelssohn* (Strasbourg, 1832), and arranged for its introduction into the Jewish schools of the Bas-Rhin.

47. AN F^{17} 12514, letter to the Minister of Public Instruction (19 March 1831).

48. Ibid.

49. AN F^{17} 12514, letter from Cottard to the Minister of Public Instruction (19 March 1831). The schools were located in Strasbourg, Bischeim, Haguenau, Wissembourg, Marmontier, Soultz-sous-Forêts, Schlestadt, and Quatzenheim. There were approximately three hundred children in these schools.

50. Béatrice Phillippe, *Les Archives israélites de France, 1840–1848* (Paris, 1978), p. 62.

51. Aron's report was published in *AIF* 4 (1843): 278–89.

52. Based on the figures cited by Aron, the average salary was approximately 750 francs. This compared favorably with salaries for teachers in the French public schools, where the salaries were approximately 646 francs. See Peter Meyers, "Professionalization and Societal Change: Rural Teachers in Nineteenth Century France," *Journal of Social History* 9 (1976): 542–58.

53. Théophile Hallez, *Des Juifs en France*, p. 257; *Souvenir et Science* 5 (July): 4.

54. *La Régénération* 1 (1836): 20–21.

55. Letter from the mayor of Schlestadt to Cottard (2 June 1834), cited in Treschan, "The Struggle for Integration," pp. 99–100.

56. See *AIF* 3 (1842): 475–76.

57. *AIF* 4 (1843): 470.

58. Ibid., p. 473.

59. *La Régénération* 1 (1836): 20–21.

60. *AIF* 5 (1844): 75.

61. AN F^{17} 12514, letter from Cottard to the Minister of Public Instruction (12 October 1829).

62. AN F^{17} 12514, letter from Cottard to the Minister of Public Instruction (19 March 1831).

63. Treschan, "The Struggle for Integration," pp. 94–95.

64. Ibid., pp. 90–91.

65. M. Cheuvreusse, "Observations sur les écoles israélites du département de la Moselle," an inspection report submitted to the *comité supérieur de Metz*, and published in *AIF* 4 (1843): 76–88, 466–75.

66. *La Régénération* 1 (1836): 20.

67. Ibid., pp. 20–21.

68. Cheuvreusse, "Observations sur les écoles israélites."

69. AN F^{17} 12514, letter from Cottard to the Minister of Public Instruction (19 March 1831).

70. In a letter to the editor, *AIF* 5 (1844): 81–83, dated 10 December 1843, Sigisbert Spire, a member of the Nancy Consistory, explained that a daily class would be offered separately to boys and girls under the direction of the grand rabbi. The decision was reversed by 1845. Cf. *AIF* 6 (1845): 217–19.

71. Samuel Cahen, "Souvenirs d'un voyage en Alsace," *AIF* 5 (1844): 469.

72. *AIF* 1 (1840): 449–50.

73. *AIF* 7 (1846): 593–96.

74. Kahn, *Histoire des écoles*, pp. 39–40.

75. Report of the commission (28 December 1826), cited in Kahn, *Histoire des écoles*, p. 40, n. 1.

76. The Paris Consistory, nonetheless, attempted to provide higher education to indigent students judged worthy of continued instruction. Samuel Cahen taught an evening class for these students, but it was discontinued after six months. See Kahn, *Histoire des écoles*, p. 41.

77. For a full treatment of the subject, see Harvey Chisick, *The Limits of Reform in the Enlightenment: Attitudes toward the Education of the Lower Classes in Eighteenth Century France*, (Princeton, N.J., 1981).

78. *AIF* 11 (1850): 49–50.

79. David Singer, *Des Consistoires israélites de France*, pp. 37–38; Archives JTS, Box 18,

pt. 1; *AIF* 4 (1843): 213–17; *AIF* 4 (1843): 279–80. On the use of the expression *émancipation intérieure,* see *AIF* 4 (1843): 3.

80. The discussion that follows benefited enormously from Peter Meyers, "Professionalization," pp. 542–58.

81. Archives JTS, Box 18, pt. 1, "Consistoire Central, 1821."

82. Archives JTS, Box 1, "Institution Académique."

83. Meyers, "Professionalization," pp. 544–46.

84. "Rapport presenté au Consistoire Israélite de Strasbourg par M. Arnaud Aron, Grand Rabbin," *AIF* 4 (1843): 279–90.

85. CAHJP zf 469. According to the figures compiled by Meyers, it was quite routine for teachers to serve as *chantre* at Sunday Mass. Meyers, "Professionalization," pp. 547–48.

86. *La Pure Vérité* 2 (23 July 1847): 31.

87. Based on the figures cited by Aron, the average salary was approximately 750 francs. This compared favorably with salaries for teachers in the French rural schools where according to Meyers ("Professionalization," p. 548), salaries were approximately 500 francs.

88. *AIF* 5 (1844): 611.

89. Kullmann, "Histoire de la vie de Ben Tsaroth," *La Pure Vérité* 2 (23 July 1847): 31; *AIF* 5 (1844): 545.

90. *AIF* 5 (1844): 545.

91. *La Régénération* 2 (1837): 2–5; on the *arrêté* of the Haut-Rhin Consistory, see *AIF* 12 (1851): 349; *AIF* 4 (1843): 91; *AIF* 5 (1844): 545; Archives HUC, "Sephardic Jews of France," 4/1 (1852–1855), letter from Consistoire Central to Consistoire de St. Esprit (23 July 1855).

92. *AIF* 3 (1842): 390, letter by S. Ullmann (teacher from Dornach) in *La Pure Vérité* 2 (23 July 1847): 32, also see p. 30.

93. *AIF* 11 (1850): 109, 171.

94. *AIF* 5 (1844): 737; see also S. Ullman's letter in *La Pure Vérité* 2 (23 July 1847): 30.

95. Szajkowski, *Jewish Education in France,* p. 14.

96. JTS Archives, "Correspondence of Rabbi Salomon Ulmann," Letter to Lévy (8 July 1846).

97. Brandeis University Archives, Franco-Judaica Collection, Box A; *AIF* 7 (1846): 207-9. See the response of S. Lévy, *ministre officiant.* in Blamont, *AIF* 7, (1846): 330-31.

98. *AIF* 13 (1852): 18.

99. *AIF* 7 (1846): 208.

100. *L'ami des israélites* (1847): 182.

101. *AIF* 2 (1841): 344; *AIF* 7 (1846): 587. The newspaper was the *Messages du nord.*

102. On the educational activities of several rabbis, see *AIF* 5 (1844): 547; *AIF* 4 (1843): 188; *AIF* 5 (1844): 459–60; *AIF* 4 (1843): 272.

103. The list of signatories is in the F[19] 11015. There the name of the head teacher in most communities with Jewish schools appears among the petitioners.

8. The Ideology of Educational Reform

1. See Paul Levy, *Histoire Linguistique d'Alsace et de Lorraine* (Paris, 1929), Vol. 3, p. 38.

2. Kahn, *Histoire des écoles,* p. 12.

3. Cited in Treschan, "The Struggle for Integration," p. 71.

4. *AIF* 4 (1843): 81.

5. See, for example, Naphtali Herz Wessely, *Divre Shalom ve-Emet* second letter, pp. 42–44; see also Isaiah Berr Bing's comments, *Lettre,* p. 41.

6. *Distribution des prix . . . Metz* (11 October 1820), pp. 18–19.

7. According to the "Plan d'Etudes de l'école communale israélite de Strasbourg" (18 September 1837), cited in Treschan, "The Struggle for Integration," pp. 179–84.

8. Michel Berr, *Abrégé de la Bible et choix de morceaux de piété et de morale à l'usage des israélites de France* (Paris, 1819).

9. *Distribution des prix . . . Metz* (11 October 1820), pp. 19–20.

10. Berr, *Abrégé de la Bible,* pp. v–ix.

11. D. Masse, review of *Le Sentier d'Israël, AIF* 8 (1847): 65–67.

12. On the efforts of Israel Jacobson and fellow reformers to introduce prayers in the vernacular in the synagogue, see, for example, Michael Meyer, *The Origins of the Modern Jew* (Detroit, 1967), pp. 132–36.

13. Anspach's translation. *Rituel des Prières Journalières à l'usage des Israélites* (Metz, 1820), was preceded by a translation by M. Venture of the Sephardic rite, *Prières journalières à l'usage des Juifs portugaises ou espagnols,* (Nice, 1772–73).

14. *Distribution des prix . . . Metz* (October 1820), p. 3. Anspach originally underscored the educational function of his translation in a letter to the members of the *Commission d'administration des écoles israélites à Paris,* Archives of Paris Consistory, series F1 (8 November 1819).

15. Anspach, *Rituel des prières,* pp. i, ii. Anspach referred to Venture as having been "the first to nationalize our prayers" (*qui le premier nationalisa nos prières*). For a similar assessment of the significance of prayer book translation, see Schwarzfuchs, *Napoleon, the Jews and the Sanhedrin,* p. 20.

16. This incident was recalled by Samuel Cahen, *AIF* 11 (1850): 658.

17. Concerning the Haskalah's emphasis on Hebrew language, see, for example, Wessely, *Divre Shalom ve-Emet,* pp. 22–25. On the Cahen volume, see Archives JTS, "Central Consistory Correspondence, no. 3, 1831–1837," letter to Cahen. A special edition of the text was proposed for the *école centrale rabbinique,* but it is unknown whether it was ever used.

18. See "Daily Curriculum of the Jewish Elementary School for Boys in Strasbourg," in Treschan, "Struggle for Integration," pp. 179–84.

19. *AIF* 13 (1852): 19–21.

20. Mayer Cahun, *Ḥinukh Sefat Eber* (Metz, 1842) and *Tholdoth Jeschurune* (Strasbourg, 1841).

21. Examples, in addition to Cahun's books, include H. Kullmann, *Le première livre de lecture hebraïque* (Mulhouse, 1848) and *Le second livre de lecture et de traduction hébraïque* (Mulhouse, 1849).

22. Samuel Cahen, for instance, asserted that "it is certain that the veritable religious instruction is based on knowledge of Hebrew," *AIF* 12 (1851): 308.

23. Cahun, *Tholdoth Jeschurune,* pp. iii–vi.

24. Kahn, *Histoire des écoles,* p. 12.

25. *Distribution des prix . . . Metz* (11 October 1820), p. 22.

26. Kahn, *Histoire des écoles,* p. 35.

27. In the Bordeaux schools, where Hebrew instruction was not intensive, historical studies occupied a prominent position; cf. *AIF* 7 (1846): 28–30. Singing was introduced in the Paris school curriculum in 1834; see Kahn, *Histoire des écoles,* p. 52.

28. AN F^{19} 11028 (6 November 1821), cited in Treschan, "The Struggle for Integration," p. 77.

29. AN F^{17} 12514, report by the inspector of the Académie de Paris (5 September 1832).

30. According to a report in the *Progrès,* reprinted in *AIF* 8 (1847): 72–73, Jewish schools in the northeast were flourishing, particularly those of Colmar, Mulhouse, and Sierentz. The inspector of primary schools of the *Moselle,* in a letter to the president of the Metz Consistory (13 May 1846), similarly commended the Jewish schools in the *arrondissement* of Sarreguemines. This letter appeared in the *AIF* 7 (1846): 418–20. The chief inspector of the department of Haut-Rhin called the Jewish communal school of Hegenheim "the flower of Alsatian schools" (cited in *AIF* 5 (1844): 610). These citations, of which there are many other examples, illustrate the relative quality of instruction in the Jewish schools and the recognition it achieved among French educators.

31. Quoted in *Distribution des prix . . . Metz* (1 October 1821), p. 13.

32. "Instruction Publique. Ecole municipale Israélite de Metz," *AIF* 2 (1841): 538–41.

33. *L'Industriel alsacien* (23 April 1843); cf. *AIF* 7 (1843): 226–27.

34. Jakob J. Petuchowski, "Manuals and Catechisms of the Jewish Religion in the Early Period of Emancipation," in *Studies in Nineteenth-Century Jewish Intellectual History,* pp. 47–48.

35. Jacob Katz, *Tradition and Crisis,* p. 190.

36. *Divre Shalom ve-Emet* (Berlin, 1782).

37. Ibid., pp. 4–6.

38. Ibid., pp. 5–6.

39. Although we can only speculate on the reasons for the lack of opposition to Wessely's views in France, it is difficult to accept Hertzberg's suggestion (p. 187) that there the ground was better prepared for such ideas than elsewhere. The evidence points in the opposite direction. The appearance of the French translation certainly made Wessely's views no more accessible to the rabbinic establishment of Alsace.

40. Wessely, *Divre Shalom ve-Emet,* pp. 34–35; second letter, p. 59. The influence of Philanthropinism on the Berlin maskilim has been carefully examined by Ernst Simon, "Pedagogical Philanthropinism and Jewish Education" [Hebrew], *Mordechai Kaplan Jubilee Volume* (New York, 1953), pp. 149–87.

41. Jacob Katz, *Out of the Ghetto,* pp. 128–30.

42. Wessely, *Divre Shalom ve-Emet,* pp. 34–35.

43. See Mordechai Eliav, *Jewish Education in Germany in the Period of Enlightenment and Emancipation* [Hebrew] (Jerusalem, 1960).

44. Douglas Johnson, *Guizot: Aspects of French History 1787–1874* (London, 1963), p. 99; John Moody, *French Education since Napoleon,* pp. 21–30.

45. Moody, *French Education since Napoleon,* pp. 21–30.

46. *Distribution des prix . . . Metz* (1 October 1819), p. 24.

47. *Règlement* of the Paris school, article 24, cited in David Singer, *Des Consistoires israélites de France,* p. 71.

48. "Plan d'études de l'école communale israélite de Strasbourg" (18 September 1837), cited in Treschan, "Struggle for Integration," pp. 179–85.

49. Treschan, "Struggle for Integration," pp. 90–91.

50. *AIF* 3 (1842): 135.

51. *AIF* 5 (1844): 78–79.

52. *Distribution des prix . . . Metz* (1 October 1819).

53. Petuchowski, "Manuals and Catechisms," p. 58.

54. Jacob Katz, "Jewry and Judaism in the Nineteenth Century," *Journal of World History* 4 (1958): 894.

55. *La Régénération* 2 (1837): 4–5, 155.

56. Salomon Ulmann, *Catéchisme ou éléments d'instruction religieuse et morale* (1843).

57. Salomon Ulmann, *Catéchisme ou éléments d'instruction religieuse et morale à l'usage des jeunes israélites* (Paris, 1860), preface, p. 6.

58. *L'Israélite français* 1 (1817): 181.

59. Ibid.

60. Samuel Cahen, *Précis élémentaire d'instruction religieuse et morale pour les jeunes français israélites* (Paris, 1820).

61. Ibid., p. 12.

62. Ibid., pp. 25–26.

63. Elie Halévy, *Instruction religieuse et morale à l'usage de la jeunesse israélite* pp. 99–101.

64. Johnson, *Guizot,* p. 99.

65. *Distribution des prix . . . Metz* (11 October 1820), p. 23.

66. Ibid., pp. 23–24.

67. *La Régénération* 1 (1836): 43.

68. Ibid., p. 124.

69. Ibid., pp. 45–49.

70. Ibid., pp. 46–50, 119.

71. Ibid., pp. 120–22.

72. Ibid., pp. 122–23.

73. Ibid., 123. For a similar view of the role of Bible study in moral education, see the review of J. Ennery's *Le Sentier d'Israël* by M. Mas and S. Munk, *AIF* 5 (1844): 652.

74. See Petuchowski, "Manuels and Catechisms," pp. 63–64, for the formulation which he quotes from Eduard Kley's catechism.

75. AN F[19] 11028, "Examen fait par le Consistoire Central, d'après les ordres de son Excellence le Ministre des Cultes, de l'ouvrage manuscrit, intitulé, *Principes de la Religion Moïse, pour servir à l'instruction des jeunes gens,* par J. Johlson" (28 May 1813).

76. AN F[19] 11028, *Rudiments d'instruction religieuse et morale pour les jeunes français israélites.*

77. AN F[19] 11028, Central Consistory, "Rapport à son Excellence le Ministre de l'Intérieur sur l'ouvrage de M. Berr" (18 July 1820).

78. Samuel Cahen, "La Pâque," *AIF* 1 (1840): 235–37.

79. Michel Berr, *Nouveau précis élémentaire d'instruction religieuse et morale, à l'usage de la jeumesse français israélite à l'usage de la jeunesse français israélite* (Nancy, 1839).

81. Ibid., p. 62.

82. The notion of the contemporary relevance of the holidays is best represented by the Talmudic statement, which appears in the present day Haggadah: "In every generation a man is obligated to see himself as if he left Egypt." Toward the end of the nineteenth century Rabbi Zadoc Kahn of Nîmes referred to the Revolution as "our flight from Egypt . . . , our modern Passover," in Benjamin Mossé, *La Révolution français et le rabbinat français* (Paris, 1890), cited in Michael Marrus, *The Politics of Assimilation,* p. 9.

83. Ibid.

84. Berr, *Nouveau précis élémentaire,* p. 70. For a provocative discussion of aspects of Jewish historical memory, see Yosef Yerushalmi, *Zakhor: Jewish History and Jewish Memory* (Philadelphia, 1982).

85. "Letter to the editor," (from Lorraine, 12 July 1841), *AIF* 2 (1841): 463.

9. The Modernization of Rabbinic Training

1. David Singer, *Des Consistoires* (Paris, 1820) pp. 39–40. For biographical information on Singer, see *AIF* 7 (1846): 100–2. Singer's proposal that there be four lay members and one rabbi (instead of two lay members and three rabbis) was eventually implemented.

2. Ibid., pp. 32–34.

3. The transformation of the French rabbinate in the period following the Revolution has yet to be examined systematically. For the official opinion of the Assembly of Jewish Notables, see *Transactions of the Paris Sanhedrin*, pp. 194–96.

4. *Règlement*, 1806, article 21, published in Albert, *Modernization of French Jewry*, pp. 346–47.

5. See Alexander Altmann, "The New Style of Preaching in Nineteenth-Century Germany," in *Studies in Nineteenth-Century Jewish Intellectual History*, pp. 65–116.

6. *AIF* 1 (1840): 234.

7. *AIF* 5 (1844): 673.

8. See, for example, *AIF* 3 (1842): 130–31.

9. The persistent use of Yiddish and German in preaching is clearly indicated by the need to issue a prohibition against preaching in any language other than French by the consistorial temple in Metz in 1846. *AIF* 7 (1846): 641. The infrequency of preaching in Alsace was the subject of repeated criticism. See for example Gerson-Lévy, "Le Rabbinat français," *AIF* 7 (1846): 337–47.

10. Szajkowski, "Simon Deutz: Traitor or French Patriot," in *JFR*, pp. 1050–51.

11. Schwarzfuchs, *Napoleon, the Jews, and the Sanhedrin*, pp. 41–43.

12. Albert, *Modernization of French Jewry*, pp. 242–43. For the proposed regulations, see "Projet de Règlement additional à celui de 1806, Archives. JTS, Box 18, pt. 1, "Consistoire Central 1821."

13. See, for example, the remarks by Singer, *Des Consistoires*, pp. 34–35.

14. Albert, *Modernization of French Jewry*, p. 244. On parallel developments in Germany, see Michael Meyer, "Differences of Opinion on Modern Rabbinic Training in Nineteenth Century Germany" [Hebrew], *Proceedings of the Sixth World Congress of Jewish Studies* (Jerusalem, 1973), vol. 2, pp. 195–200.

15. Albert, *Modernization of French Jewry*, p. 244.

16. As proof, the Central Consistory cited Article 49 of the *ordonnance royale* of 17 February 1819.

17. AN F[19] 11025, "Ecole Centrale Rabbinique: Organisation de cette école," letter from the Central Consistory to the Minister of the Interior (12 September 1828).

18. Ibid. *Phaedon* was translated into Hebrew by Isaiah Berr Bing, in 1786.

19. AN F[19] 11052, letter from the Central Consistory to the Minister of Justice and Cultes (19 November 1837), in reference to the Minister's letter of 7 October 1837.

20. AN F[19] 11052, letter from members of the Metz Consistory and the *comité cantonnal des écoles* to the Minister Secretary of State in the Department of the Interior (10 February 1822).

21. AN F[19] 11052, letter from the Central Consistory to the Minister of the Interior (21 April 1822).

22. AN F[19] 11052, letter from the Central Consistory to the Minister of Justice and Cults (11 February 1838).

23. AN F[19] 11052. The signatories of the letter from the *comité cantonnal* to the Minister Secretary of State included in addition to Rabbi J. Wittersheim, the following

leading *régénérateurs:* Jacob Goudchaux Beer, C. Bing, J. Anspach, L. Terquem, C. Oulif, Gerson-Lévy, and E. Terquem.

24. AN F[19] 11052.

25. AN F[19] 11052, letter to the Minister Secretary of State in the Department of Justice and Cults from a group of *régénérateurs* in Metz (9 August 1837).

26. AN F[19] 11052, "Rapport presenté au consistoire israélite de Metz par la commission administrative de l'Ecole Centrale Rabbinique de France, sur la situation financière et morale de cette école pendant l'année 1840" (20 January 1841).

27. Ibid.

28. Franck's views on the *école rabbinique* were first published in the February issue of the *AIF,* 1841, and later restated in an expanded form in *AIF* 4 (1843): 714 ff.

29. Ibid., p. 718.

30. AN F[19] 11052, note appended to the report of the administrative commission of the école rabbinique, by the Minister of Justice and Cults (30 June 1841).

31. Albert, *Modernization of French Jewry,* p. 247.

32. "Projet de Règlement pour l'école centrale rabbinique de Metz," *AIF* 8 (1847): 523–31.

33. This would be approximately equivalent to a level of achievement attained by a high school graduate today.

34. "Projet de Règlement pour l'école centrale rabbinique de Metz," Section II, *AIF* 7 (1847): 524–57.

35. CAHJP zf 1077/1, *commission administrative* to director, letter 13 (22 January 1860).

36. *AIF* 7 (1847): 77–78.

37. Albert, *Modernization of French Jewry,* p. 247; *AIF* 13 (1852): 72.

38. Graetz, *Periphery,* pp. 52–53.

39. CAHJP zf 1077/1, to director, letter no. 408 (20 June 1873).

40. Ibid., to Paris Consistory, letter no. 494 (24 December 1877).

41. Ibid., to members of the administrative commission, letters nos. 119, 120, 164, 200, 225, 253, 274, 275; letter no. 233, to Paris Consistory (15 November 1864).

42. Ibid. letter no. 441 (25 January 1875).

43. Ibid., to director, letter no. 479 (14 March 1877).

44. Ibid., to Paris Consistory, letter no. 523 (14 July 1879).

45. Albert, *Modernization of French Jewry,* pp. 250–53.

10. The Struggle over Religious Reform

1. "Rapport présenté au Consistoire Israélite de Paris, par l'ancien Comité de Secours et d'Encouragement de la même ville," (July 1838), in *AIF* 2 (1841): 126.

2. Gerson-Lévy, "Sur la necessité d'une régénération dans le Judaïsme," *La Régéneration* 1 (1836): 273. Also see the report of the Comité de Secours et d'Encouragement, *AIF* 2 (1841): 130.

3. See Phyllis Cohen Albert, "Nonorthodox Attitudes in Nineteenth Century French Judaism," in *Essays in Modern Jewish History: A Tribute to Ben Halpern.* (East Brunswick, N.J., 1982), pp. 121–141, and Albert, *Modernization of French Jewry,* pp. 231–36.

4. *AIF* 8 (1847): 9.

5. Gerson-Lévy, *Culte israelite,* pp. 5, 8–9.

6. Ibid.

7. Ibid., p. 7; *AIF* 5 (1844): 237–39; Gerson-Lévy, *Culte israélite,* p. 5.

8. Terquem, for one, criticized the project. See *Lettre 27* (24 August 1841), in Fondsweiner, no. 16948; *AIF* 5 (1844): 230–31.

9. Gerson-Lévy, *Culte israélite*, p. 6; Letter form thirty-one heads of households in Nancy to Metz Consistory, reprinted in *AIF* 2 (1841): 469; *AIF* 5 (1844): 231, 234–35.

10. *AIF* 7 (1846): 538–39.

11. Baruch Mevorach, "The Belief in the Messiah in the Early Reform Polemics" [Hebrew]. *Zion* 24 (1969): 189–218.

12. *Die Deutsche Synagoge oder Ordnung des Gottestdienstes fur die Sabbath-und Festtage des ganzen Jahre, zum Gebrauche der Gemeinden, die sich der deutschen Gebete bediene*, Hrsg, von Dr. E. Kley und Dr. E. S. Günsberg (Berlin, 1817). Mevorach, ibid., 190–94. David Philipson, *The Reform Movement in Judaism*, p. 152.

13. Anspach's translation, *Rituel des Prières journalières à l'usage des Israélites* was preceded by M. Venture's translation of the Sephardic rite, *Prières journalières à l'usage des Juifs portugaises ou espagnols*. Anspach, *Rituel*, pp. vii–viii. For a similar formulation of the messianic doctrine, see Anspach, *Paroles d'un croyant israélite* (Metz, 1842); and for its employment in textbooks, see Michel Berr, *Nouveau précis élémentaire*, pp. 45–47.

14. See, for example, Berr, *Nouveau Précis élementaire*, pp. 45–47.

15. *AIF* 6 (1845): 642–43.

16. *AIF* 6 (1845): 859–63.

17. *AIF* 5 (1844): 602–8. For a discussion of the *Reformfreunde's* position on religious reform, see Robert Liberles, *Religious Conflict in Social Context: The Resurgence of Orthodox Judaism in Frankfurt am Main, 1838–1877* (Westport, Conn., 1985), pp. 52–61.

18. *AIF* 7 (1846): 566–67. Cf. Baruch Mevorach, "The Belief in the Messiah," pp. 189–218. Michael Meyer, *German Political Pressure and Jewish Religious Response in the Nineteenth Century* (New York, 1981), pp. 11–14, has challenged the idea that religious reform was a strategy employed to strengthen the case for emancipation.

19. Archives JTS, Box 18, pt. 1, "Consistoire Central, 1839." Albert, *Modernization of French Jewry*, pp. 74–75.

20. Albert, *Modernization of French Jewry*, pp. 82–83, 280–81; Archives HUC, "Sephardic Jews of France," 4/1 (1852–55); David Cohen, *La Promotion des Juifs*, vol. 2, pp. 130–31.

21. Albert, *Modernization of French Jewry*, pp. 82–83.

22. AN F^{19} 11015, "Adhésions de 82 communes du Bas-Rhin à la petition de la communauté israélite de Strasbourg."

23. *AIF* 2 (1841): 405–6.

24. Archives JTS, Box 18, Folio 405–7.

25. Albert, *Modernization of French Jewry*, p. 74.

26. Article 10, *"ordonnance, 1844,"* cited in Albert, *Modernization of French Jewry*, p. 369; Article 24, *"Projet d'ordonnance 1839,"* cited in Albert, *Modernization of French Jewry*, p. 360.

27. Article 38, *"ordonnance, 1844,"* cited in Albert, *Modernization of French Jewry*, p. 374. This was a restatement of Article 12 of "ordonnance, 1823." Article 23, *"projet d'ordonnance, 1839,"* cited in Albert, *Modernization of French Jewry*, p. 360. Article 12, *"ordonnance, 1844,"* cited in Albert, *Modernization of French Jewry*, pp. 385–86.

28. For the full text of the circular, see Albert, *Modernization of French Jewry*, pp. 385–86.

29. Jonathan Helfand, "The Election of the Grand Rabbi of France (1842–1846)," in *Proceedings of the Eighth World Congress of Jewish Studies* (Jerusalem, 1982), vol. 2, 142. The following responses to the 1846 questionnaire by candidates for the position of Central Consistory Grand Rabbi are extant: Samuel Dreyfus (Mulhouse) and Mahir Charleville

(Dijon) in Archives JTS, Box 18; Marchand Ennery (Paris), Leopold Lehmann (Belfort), Isaac Weil (Blotzheim), and Dittisheim (Wintzenheim), in Archives LBI.

30. For the text of the manifesto, see *AIF* 7 (1846): 281–82, and *Allegemeine Zeitung des Judentums* 10 (1846): 290–91, cited in Philipson, *The Reform Movement in Judaism*, p. 460, n. 63. See Albert, *Modernization of French Jewry*, pp. 296–97 for Lambert's reply to the consistory's criticism of the manifesto. The Goudchaux-Lambert letter was the subject of an extended exchange, including a biting criticism of their position authored by Baruch Zeitlin, *Ḥazut Kashah* (Paris, 1846), and a defense of traditionalist orthodoxy, by Salomon Klein, *Ma'aneh Rakh* (Mulhouse, 1846).

31. *UI* 2 (1846): 69–79. For a critical report on the Colmar meeting, see *AIF* 7 (1846): 287–88.

32. Nearly all of the petitions are at the Archives of the Leo Baeck Institute, "Alsace-Lorraine, 1808–1853," Folios 174–225.

33. On the introduction of the organ, preaching, and funeral reforms and on the elimination of the sale of honors, see Albert, *Modernization of French Jewry*, pp. 233–39. See for example *AIF* 4 (1843), 410.

34. *JE*, Jacques Kahn, "Salomon Ulmann"; *AIF* 26 (1865): 418–29.

35. *AIF* 5 (1844): 796.

36. *AIF* 3 (1842): 655–57.

37. For an example of the ceremony's proceedings, see *AIF* 8 (1847): 465-69; *AIF* 5 (1844): 505.

38. *AIF* 7 (1846): 389.

39. *AIF* 10 (1849): 392, 427.

40. *AIF* 14 (1853): 5.

41. *AIF* 12 (1851): 250, 301–2.

42. Michel Aron Gerson, *Citolège hebraïque.*

43. P. Meyer-Siat, "L'orgue dans les synagogues d'Alsace," *Archives juives* 8, no. 1 (1971–72). On Marseille, see *AIF* 2 (1841): 646–48; on developments elsewhere, see *AIF* 5 (1844): 659; *AIF* 6 (1845): 535–36, 692; *AIF* 7 (1846): 391.

44. *AIF* 7 (1846): 276–77. On the proliferation of organs, see *AIF* 6 (1845): 535–36, and *AIF* 7 (1846): 391.

45. *AIF* 5 (1844): 746.

46. *AIF* 5 (1844): 377–79.

47. Archives JTS, "Correspondence of Rabbi Salomon Ulmann," letter no. 12 (1844).

48. Ibid.

49. *AIF* 6 (1845): 628; *AIF* 7 (1846): 760.

50. Ibid. (1846): 746–48.

51. Archives JTS, "Correspondence of Rabbi Salomon Ulmann," letter to R. Arnaud Aron (28 December 1844).

52. Ibid., to M. Spire, letter 32 (12 August 1845).

53. See Ennery's letter to *AIF* 6 (1845): 201.

54. The views of Ulmann were fully consistent with the consensus of progressive rabbis on these matters. The 1846 responses to the questionnaire required of candidates for the position of Central Consistory Grand Rabbi uniformly endorsed the introduction of the organ, the elimination of the *piyyutim*, and supported the idea of convening a synod to resolve other ritual matters. For Ulmann's remarks on sermons, see *Lettre Pastorale* (11 December 1853).

55. *LI* 1, no. 1 (1855).

56. *UI* 1 (1844): 14–15.

57. *AIF* 6 (1845): 200–1.

58. Archives JTS, "Correspondence of Rabbi Salomon Ulmann," letter no. 22 (10 January 1844); and letter no. 28 (November 1844).

59. Ibid., letter no. 36 (December 1845).

60. *UI* 3 (1846): 63.

61. Archives JTS, "Correspondence of Rabbi Salomon Ulmann," letters of 8 May 1846 and 23 December 1846.

62. *AIF* 17 (1856): 307.

63. Dreyfus, *LI* 2, no. 2 (July 1856). Coming from a liberal rabbi who only three years earlier had appealed to Frankel to convene a European rabbinic congress [*AIF* (1853): 535], Dreyfus' conservatism is somewhat problematic. It is quite possible that he felt excluded from the the reformation process; his position also reveals disagreement on the appropriate agent of religious change. Dreyfus argued that the Paris conference had introduced the notion of the subordination of communal rabbis to the grand rabbis and claimed that such a hierarchical division was foreign to Judaism. Generally, the Mulhouse rabbi was criticized for the inconsistency in his thinking.

64. Salomon Klein, *Mippnei Koshet*, pp. 2–5. On the reaction of Hirsch and others in Central Europe, see Noah Rosenbloom, *Tradition in an Age of Reform: The Religious Philosophy of Samson Raphael Hirsch* (Philadelphia, 1976), pp. 107–8, and p. 405 for bibliography. For a brief biography of Klein, see Paul Klein (Catane), "Schlôme Wolf Klein," *Bulletin de nos communautés* 10 (1954): nos. 10–12.

65. Klein, *Mippnei Koshet*, pp. 11, 16–17.

66. Ibid., pp. 29–31.

67. Salomon Klein, *Lettre Pastorale* (7 October 1856); this critique of the conference was reprinted in *UI* 14 (1857): 104–17.

68. Ibid.; AN F^{19} 11037, letter from Klein to the Minister of Public Instruction and Cultes (31 December 1856). For another example of Klein's positive view of the Napoleonic Sanhedrin, see *Le Judaïsme ou la vérité sur le Talmud*, p. 86.

69. AN F^{19} 11037, letter from the Minister of Public Instruction and Cultes to Central Consistory (14 April 1857); *Procès-verbal* of meeting of Colmar Consistory (19 October 1857); letter from Central Consistory to the Minister of Public Instruction and Cultes (23 November 1857); letter from Klein to the Minister of Public Instruction and Cultes (31 December 1856). Cf. Klein's letter to Rabbi Esriel Hildesheimer, published in Simon Schwarzfuchs, "Three Documents from the Life of the Jewish Communities of Alsace-Lorraine (Lothringen)," *Michael* 4 (1976): 9–31. Albert, *Modernization of French Jewry*, pp. 295–96.

70. The most important collections of the French ritual and *piyyutim* are Simḥa b. Samuel, *Maḥzor Vitri* (n.d.), edited by S. Hurwitz (Berlin, 1893); a separate volume, *Kuntrus Hapiyyutim*, edited by H. Brody (Berlin, 1894); and Nathan b. Judah b. Azriel, *Sefer Maḥkim* (n.d.), edited by I. Freimann (Cracow, 1909). *Rishonim* were divided on the halakhic question of whether the *piyyutim* constitute an interruption in prayer. Generally, this division followed Ashkenazic-Sephardic lines, with Ashkenazic authorities favoring *piyyutim* and Sephardic authorities opposed. The major exception among Ashkenazim was Rashi, who opposed the recitation of *piyyutim*. On this question see *Tur, Oraḥ Ḥayyim,* section 68, and the *Beit Yosef* and the *Bayyit Ḥadash,* ad loc. For examples of the prevailing Ashkenazic position, see *Maḥzor Vitri*, p. 364; *Shibolei Ha-Leket*, Samuel Mirsky, ed., (New York, 1966), pp. 209–18; and *Sefer Ha-Manhig*, Laws of Prayer, section 58. On the modern controversy in Germany and England, see Jacob Petuchowski, *Prayerbook Reform in Europe: The Liturgy of European Liberal and Reform Judaism* (New York, 1968), pp. 27–29, 46–50, 190, 199.

71. See, for example, Report of 1838 Paris *comité*, *AIF* 2 (1841): 128.

72. In fact, neither Goudchaux (Colmar) nor Ennery (Paris) officially protested the use of the organ, and they modified the liturgical selections in their own districts. *LI* II (1856): 109; Helfand, "French Jewry," p. 154.

11. Unity and Solidarity

1. Zosa Szajkowski, "French Jews during the Revolution of 1830 and the July Monarchy," *JFR*, pp. 1026–37; Phyllis Cohen Albert, "Ethnicity and Jewish Solidarity in Nineteenth Century France," in *Mystics, Philosophers, and Politicians: Essays in Jewish Intellectual History in Honor of Alexander Altmann*, ed. Jehuda Reinharz and Daniel Swetchinski (Durham, NC, 1982), pp. 249–74.

2. Graetz, *Periphery*, Ch. 3; Albert, *Modernization of French Jewry*, pp. 150–69.

3. E. H., "Du Prosélytisme," *AIF* 6 (1845): 477–78, 674–75, 481–89, 845; *AIF* 4 (1843): 456.

4. *AIF* 5 (1844): 54. For Drach's principal works, see Chapter 5, notes 13 and 14.

5. Elie Szapiro, "Le Prosélytisme Chrétien et les Juifs à Toulouse au XIXe siècle," *Archives juives* 15, no. 3 (1979): 53–57.

6. Letter by Olry Terquem to Paris Consistory, reprinted in *AIF* 6 (1845): 453–59. For another example of family strife and tragedy, see Lita L. Schwartz and Natalie Isser, "Some Involuntary Conversion Techniques," *JSS* 43 (1981): 2–3. Olry Terquem's obituary appeared in *AIF* 23 (1862): 313–17; also see Richard Menkis, "Les Frères Elie, Olry, et Lazare Terquem," *Archives juives* 15, no. 3 (1979): pp. 58–61.

7. *AIF* 3 (1842): 458.

8. Szajkowski, *Jewish Education in France, 1789–1939*, p. 9; *AIF* 8 (1847): 577. Also see *L'ami des israélites* (1847): 65–67.

9. *AIF* (1845): 189. For a description of special Saturday classes in Ribeauvillé, see *AIF* 6 (1845): 91. On the Strasbourg school, see *AIF* VI (1845), 89–90. Of the textbooks intended for girls, see, for example, G. Heumann, *La Fille d'Israël* (Haguenau, 1847).

10. Cahun, *Tholedoth Jeschurune*, pp. iii–vi.

11. Samson Lévy, *La Source de la vie; AIF* 4 (1845): 687. Lipmann Sauphar, *Gan Raveh* (Paris, 1849), p. 210.

12. J. Derenbourg, "De la Monogamie parmi les Juifs," *AIF* 2 (1841): 336–41. J. Derenbourg, *Livre de Versets; AIF* 6 (1845): 597.

13. Joel Anspach, *Paroles d'un croyant israélite* pp. 33–107, 15–16.

14. *AIF* 2 (1841): 342.

15. *AIF* 6 (1845): 365.

16. August Fabius, *Offrande au Dieu de l'univers* (Lyons, 1842). On Fabius' work and the consistorial reaction to it, see *AIF* 4 (1843): 13, 257–58, 266–69.

17. The original work was entitled *Prevenciones divinas contra la vana idolatria de las Gentes* (Amsterdam, n.d.) Portions were published by Baron d'Holbach in French, under the title *Israël vengé* (London, 1770); a modified English translation by Grace Aguilar appeared in 1842. For a full discussion of various editions and translation, see Yosef Kaplan, *From Christianity to Judaism: The Life and Work of Isaac Orobio* [Hebrew] (Jerusalem, 1982), esp. Appendix 6, pp. 393–405. *AIF* 6 (1845): 902–3.

18. *AIF* 5 (1844): 10–16.

19. *AIF* 6 (1845): 189.

20. *AIF* 9 (1848): 205–210; Salo W. Baron, "Aspects of the Jewish Communal Crisis in 1848," *JSS* 14 (1952): 105–6; Helfand, "French Jewry," pp. 74–75; Szajkowski, "Internal Conflicts in French Jewry at the time of the Revolution of 1848," *JFR*, pp. 1073–74.

21. Helfand, "French Jewry," pp. 77–81; *AIF* 11 (1850): 295; Albert, *Modernization of French Jewry*, p. 155.

22. Helfand, "French Jewry," pp. 83–85; *AIF* 11 (1850): 648. See Albert, *Modernization of French Jewry*, pp. 156–57, for other examples of discrimination.

23. Helfand, "French Jewry," pp. 211–12, 217; Arnold Ages, "Veuillot and the Talmud," *JQR* 64 (1974), 229–60.

24. Katz, *From Prejudice to Destruction*,. pp. 121–25; Robert Byrnes, *Antisemitism in Modern France* (New Brunswick, N.J., 1950), pp. 118 ff.

25. Paula Hyman, *From Dreyfus to Vichy* (New York, 1979), p. 17; Byrnes, *Antisemitism*, 120.

26. Katz, *From Prejudice to Destruction*, pp. 133–37; Graetz, *Periphery*, pp. 229–35.

27. Graetz, *Periphery*, pp. 253–61. Simon Bloch, *M. Renan et le Judaïsme* (Paris, 1860).

28. *AIF* 1 (1840): 328–29.

29. See Graetz, *Periphery*, pp. 59–60, for a similar appraisal.

30. *AIF* 13 (1852): 12.

31. *AIF* 11 (1850): 343.

32. *AIF* 14 (1853): 426–30.

33. Ibid., p. 427.

34. *AIF* 12 (1851): 170–71.

35. Helfand, "French Jewry," pp. 210, 296–97; Albert, *Modernization of French Jewry*, pp. 161–65. Also see Salomon Klein, *Le Judaisme ou la verité sur le Talmud*, and Elie A. Astruc, *Les Juifs et L. Veuillot* (Paris, 1859).

36. Graetz, *Periphery*, pp. 253–70.

37. See this author's review of Graetz' book, *Zion* 51 (1986), 107–12.

38. On "emancipationist politics," see Jonathan Frankel, "Crisis as a Factor in Modern Jewish Politics, 1840 and 1881–82," in *Living with Antisemitism: Modern Jewish Responses*, ed. Jehuda Reinharz (Hanover, N.H., 1987). Work on the relationship of French Jewry to the land of Israel has been pioneered by Jonathan Helfand, "The Ties between French Jewry and Eretz Israel," *Cathedra* 36 (1985): 37–54; for the broader European context, see Israel Bartal, ". . . So Have Our Brethren Misunderstood the Liberties of France," [Hebrew], *Cathedra* 36 (1985): 58–61.

39. The idea of symbiosis was a recurrent theme among Jewish thinkers in France. One of the most articulate expressions of this idea was offered by Simon Bloch, *UI* 7 (1851): 241–46; 281–88. Representative of the patriotic views of the French rabbinate are the sermons of Rabbi Benjamin Lipman, which were collected in a biographical account written by his son, A. Lipman, *Un Grand Rabbin Français: Benjamin Lipman* (Paris, 1923), pp. 36–37, 77–83, 95–97.

Glossary

BEIT DIN — A Jewish court of law

DAYYAN — Judge

DERASHAH — A homiletical discourse

EVEN HA-EZER — A section of the *Shulḥan Arukh* that deals with family law

GEZEROT — Edicts enacted as preventive measures against the violation of biblical law

HALAKHAH — Jewish law

HAFTAROT — Selections from the Prophets, chanted on Sabbaths and holidays following the reading of the Torah

HAGGADAH — Text used at the Passover Seder to retell the story of the Israelite exodus from Egypt

ḤEDER — Traditional Jewish elementary school

ḤUMASH — Pentateuch

KINOT — Lamentations recited on Tisha B'Av

MIDOT — Rules of biblical hermeneutics

MINHAG — Custom or rite

MINYAN — Quorum of ten males needed to form public prayer meeting

MUSSAR — Exhortative or moralistic teaching

POSEK — One authorized to decide matters of Jewish law

RISHONIM — Jewish legal authorities who were active until the sixteenth century

SHEMA — The first word of the affirmation of faith: "Hear, O Israel, the Lord our God, the Lord is One." The term refers to the three paragraphs that follow.

SHOḤET — Ritual slaughterer

SELIḤOT — Penitential prayers

STAM YEINAM — Gentile wine, forbidden for Jewish consumption

YEIN NESEKH — "Wine of libation" produced by idolators and therefore forbidden for Jewish consumption or trade

ẒIẒIT — Ritual fringes worn on a four cornered garment

Selected Bibliography

I. Archival Sources

Archives Nationales, Paris

F^{17} 12514 Ecoles primaires israélites: subventions, comités consistoriaux, distribution de livres. 1816–1833.

F^{19} 11015 Projets de réforme et préparation de l'ordonnance organique du 25 mai 1844 (1837–1844).

F^{19} 11025 Ecole centrale rabbinique: organisation et réformes; rapports sur la situation morale de l'école. 1829–1859.

F^{19} 11028 Délibérations et correspondance du consistoire central au sujet de la création d'écoles primaires et autres. Secours aux écoles primaires israélites. Rapports du consistoire central sur des ouvrages d'instruction religieuse. 1809–1887.

F^{19} 11037 Conflits entre le consistoire de Colmar et le consistoire centrale (1849–1857).

F^{19} 11052 Ecole centrale rabbinique. 1829–1851.

Brandeis University. Franco-Judaica Collection

Boxes I–VIII

Central Archives for the History of the Jewish People, Jerusalem

Archival Collection

zf 296 Plainte contre le Grand Rabbin trop conservateur en ce qui concerne le service du samedi. 1831.

zf 300   Lettres de la communauté de Strasbourg au Consistoire. 1837.

zf 311   Correspondance diverse de la communauté de Strasbourg et de ses administrateurs avec le Consistoire du Bas-Rhin. 1838.

zf 312   Correspondance adressé au Consistoire du Bas-Rhin par les commissions administratives et ministres du culte. 1839.

zf 469   Recensement notables, écoles. Etat des écoles de la circonscription de Metz. 1831–1851.

zf 483   Statistique des ministres du culte et de leurs traitements dans divers consistoires. 1858.

zf 683   Etat nominatif des habitants israélites de la commune de Herlisheim. 1850.

zf 728   Repartition des frais du culte à Saverne. 1824.

zf 739   Liste des contribuables israélites les plus imposés du Haut-Rhin. 1828.

Microfilm Collection

HM 5517   Copies de lettres du comité local de surveillance pour les écoles israélites de Strasbourg. 1831–1843.

HM 5529   Registre des déliberations du comité cantonal des écoles du culte hébraïque de Strasbourg. 1821–1832.

HM 2/ 4949 Correspondence concerning Jewish religious affairs. 1808–1861.

Central Consistory Archives, Paris

1B3   Procès verbaux des séances et des délibérations du consistoire central.

Hebrew Union College, Cincinnati

"Sephardic Jews of France"

Paris Consistory Archives, Paris

AA 2   Procès verbaux, 1825–1839.

B 7   Ecoles et Instruction

F 1   Ecoles, 1812–1873

1^{cc}14   Letters from the Strasbourg consistory to the Central Consistory.

Archives of the Leo Baeck Institute, New York

Boxes 1–6 Alsace-Lorraine

Archives of the Jewish Theological Seminary of America, New York (French Jewish Documents)

Box 1   "Institution Académique"

Box 2   1681–1889

Box 18   "Nineteenth and Twentieth Century Arguments between Reform and Orthodoxy."

"Correspondence of Rabbi Salomon Ulmann."

II. Printed Primary Sources
Journals

L'Ami des Israélites. Strasbourg, 1847.
Archives israélites de France. Paris, 1840–1935.
L'Industriel alsacien. Mulhouse, 1835–1877.
L'Israélite français. Paris, 1817–1818.
Journal asiatique. Paris, 1822–
Journal de la Société des sciences, agriculture, et arts, du département du Bas-Rhin. Strasbourg, 1824–
Le Lien d'Israel. Mulhouse, 1855–1861.
La Pure Vérité. Strasbourg, 1846.
La Régénération (Wiedergeburt). Strasbourg, 1836–1837.
Revue orientale. Brussels, 1841–1844.
L'Union israélite. Paris, 1847–1848.
Univers israélite. Paris, 1844–1939.

Books, Pamphlets, and Documents

Anonymous. Observations sur la possibilité et l'utilité de l'admission des Juifs en Alsace aux droits de citoyens, adressées à un membre de la Société des Amis de la Constitution à Strasbourg, par un ami de l'homme. 1790 [?].
Anspach, Joel. Paroles d'un croyant israélite. Metz, 1842.
————. Rituel des Prières Journalières à l'usage des Israelites. Metz, 1820.
Aron, Arnaud. Prières d'un coeur israélite. Paris, 1848.
Astruc, Elie A. Les Juifs et L. Veuillot. Paris, 1859.
Bail, Charles Joseph. Des Juifs au dix-neuvième siècle. Paris, 1816.
Baruch-Weil, Godechaux. Réflexions d'un jeune Israélite français. Paris, 1821.
Berr, Berr Isaac. Lettre du Sieur Berr-Isaac-Berr, manufacturie membre du Conseil municipal de Nancy, à M. Grégoire, sénateur, à Paris. Nancy, 1806.
————. Lettre d'un citoyen, membre de la ci-devant communauté des Juifs de Lorraine à ses confrères à l'occasion du droit de citoyen actif, rendu aux Juifs par le décrit du 28 septembre 1791. Nancy, 1791. Reprinted in La Révolution française et l'émancipation des Juifs, vol. VIII: Lettres, mémoires et publications diverses, 1787–1806. Paris, 1968.
————. Lettre du Sr. Berr-Isaac-Berr, négociant à Nancy, Juif naturalisé en vertu des Lettres Patentes du Roi, a Monsieur l'Evêque de Nancy, Deputé à Assemblée Nationale. n.p., 1790.
————. Réflexions sur la régénération complète des Juifs en France. Paris, 1806.
Berr, Michel. Abrégé de la Bible et choix de morceaux de piété et de morale à l'usage des Israélites de France. Paris, 1819.
————. Appel à la justice des nations et des rois. Strasbourg, 1801.
————. Lettre au rédacteur de l'Argus. Paris, 1824.
————. Nouveau précis élementaire d'instruction religieuse et morale, à l'usage de la jeunesse français israélite. Nancy, 1839.
Betting de Lancastel. Considérations sur l'état des Juifs dans la société chrétienne et particulièrement en Alsace. Strasbourg, 1824.
Beugnot, Arthur. Les Juifs d'Occident. Paris, 1824.
La Bible, traduction nouvelle. Samuel Cahen, ed. 18 vols. Paris, 1831–1851.
Bing, Isaiah Berr. Lettre du Sr. I.B.B. Juif de Metz à l'auteur anonyme d'un écrit intitulé: "Le cri du citoyen contre les Juifs." Metz, 1787. Reprinted in La Révolution française et

l'émancipation des Juifs, vol. 8: *Lettres, mémoires et publications diverses, 1787–1806.* Paris, 1968.

Bloch, Simon. *M. Renan et le Judaisme.* Paris, 1860.

Cahen, Samuel. *Cours de lecture hebraïque.* Paris, 1824.

———. "La Pâque." *AIF* 1 (1840): 235–37.

———. *Précis élémentaire d'instruction religieuse et morale pour les jeunes français israélites.* Paris, 1820.

———. "Souvenirs d'un voyage in Alsace." *AIF* 5(1844).

Cahen, Uri Phoebus. *Halakhah Berurah.* Metz, 1793.

Cahun, Meyer. *Ḥinukh Sefat Eber.* Metz, 1842.

———. *Tholdoth Jeschurune.* Strasbourg, 1841.

Calman de Metz. *Au pseudonyme Tzarphati malgré lui.* Paris, 1824.

Clermont-Tonnerre, Comte Stanislas de. *Opinion relativement aux persecutions qui menacent les Juifs d'Alsace.* Versailles, 1789.

Cologna, Abraham. "De l'education." *L'Israélite français* 1 (1817): 9–13.

Correspondance de Napoléon Ier. 32 vols. Paris (1858–1870).

Dalmbert, S. Mayer. "Institute Israélite." *L'Israélite français* 1 (1817): 86–93.

Derenbourg, Joseph. *Livre de versets.* Paris, 1844.

Distribution des prix faite aux élèves des écoles israélites de Metz. Rapport fait au nom du Comité d'administration des écoles israélites, par M. Gerson-Lévy (1 October 1819).

Distribution des prix faite aux élèves des écoles israélites de Metz. Rapport fait au nom du Comité d'administration des écoles israélites, par M. J. Anspach (11 October 1820).

Distribution des prix faite aux élèves des écoles israélites de Metz. Rapport fait au nom du Comité d'administration des écoles israélites (1 October 1821).

Distribution des prix faite aux élèves des écoles israélites de Metz. Rapport fait au nom du Comité cantonnal des écoles israélites, par M. Ch. Bing (4 October 1824).

Dohm, Christian Wilhelm. *Über die bürgerliche Verbesserung der Juden.* Berlin, 1781–1783. English translation: *Concerning the Amelioration of the Civil Status of the Jews.* trans. Helen Lederer, Hebrew Union College Series, Ellis Rivkin, ed. Cincinnati, 1957.

Drach, P.L.B. [David]. *De l'Harmonie entre l'eglise et la synagogue,* 2 vols. Paris, 1844.

———. *Deuxième lettre d'un rabbin converti aux israelites ses freres, sur les motifs de sa conversion.* Paris, 1827.

———. *Lettre d'un rabbin converti aux israélites ses frères, sur les motifs de sa conversion.* Paris, 1825.

Dreyfus, Samuel. *Abrégé de la grammaire hébraïque à l'usage des élèves israélites des écoles primaires de Mulhouse.* Mulhouse, 1839.

Ennery, Jonas. *Le Sentier d'Israël, ou Bible des Jeunes israelites.* Paris, 1843.

Fabius, Auguste. *Offrande au Dieu du l'univers.* Lyon, 1842.

Fare, Anne-Louis Henry de la. *Opinion de M. L'Evêque de Nancy, deputé de Lorraine, sur l'admissibilité des Juifs à la plénitude de l'état civil, et des droits de citoyens actifs.* Paris, 1790.

Foissac [Jean Baptiste Annibal Aubert-Dubayet?] *Le cri du citoyen contre les Juifs de Metz, par un capitaine d'infanterie.* Laussanne, Metz, 1786.

Gerson, Michel Aron. *Citolège hebraïque.* Metz, 1850.

———. "Le rabbinat francais," *AIF* 7 (1846): 337–47.

Gerson-Lévy. *Culte israélite.* Metz, 1841.

———. *Orgue et pioutim.* Paris, 1859.

————. "Sur la necessité d'une régénération dans le Judaïsme." *La Régénération* 1 (September 1836), 272–77.

Grégoire, Henri. *Essai sur la régénération physique, morale et politique des Juifs.* Metz, 1789.

————. *Motion en faveur des Juifs.* Paris, 1789.

Guizot, François. *La Civilisation en Europe.* Paris, 1828.

Halévy, Elie. *Instruction religieuse et morale á l'usage de la jeunesse israélite.* Metz, 1820.

Halévy, Léon. *Résumé de l'histoire des Juifs modernes.* Paris, 1828.

Hallez, Théophile. *Des Juifs en France. De leur état moral et politique depuis les premiers temps de la monarchie jusqu'a nos jours.* Paris, 1845.

Heumann, G. *La Fille d'Israël.* Haguenau, 1847.

Hourwitz, Zalkind. *Apologie des Juifs.* Paris, 1789.

Kahn, Léon. *Les professions manuelles et les institutions de patronage.* Paris, 1885.

————. *Histoires des écoles communales et consistoriales israélites des Paris (1809–1884).* Paris, 1883.

Klein, Salomon W. *Le Judaïsme ou la verité sur la Talmud.* Mulhouse, 1859.

————. *Mippnei Koshet.* Frankfurt am Main, 1861.

————. *Recueil de Lettres Pastorales.* Colmar, 1863.

H. Kullmann. "Histoire de la vie de Ben Tsaroth." *La Pure Vérité* (23 July 1847): 31.

————. *Le premier livre de lecture hébraïque.* Mulhouse, 1848.

————. *Le second livre de lecture et de traduction hébraïque.* Mulhouse, 1849.

Lambert, Lion Mayer. *Catéchisme du culte judaïque.* Metz, 1818.

————. *Précis de l'histoire des Hébreux depuis le patriarche Abraham jusqu'en 1840.* Metz, 1840.

Lasteyrie, Robert de. *Bibliographie générale des Travaux Historiques et archéologiques publié par les sociétés savants de la France,* 6 vols. Paris, 1885–1918.

Lazare, Jacob. *Réponse à un écrit intitulé: Première lettre d'un Israélite français.* Paris, 1821.

Lévy, Benoît. *L'instruction morale et religieuse des Israélites.* Strasbourg, 1847.

Lévy, Samson. *La Source de la vie.* Strasbourg, 1845.

Mendelssohn, Moses. *Jerusalem oder über religiose Macht und Judentum.* Berlin, 1783. English translation: *Jerusalem and Other Jewish Writings,* trans. and ed. Alfred Jospe. New York, 1969.

Mirabeau, Honoré- Gabriel Riquetti, Marquis de. *Sur Moses Mendelssohn, sur la réforme politique des Juifs.* London, 1787.

Montesquieu, Charles Louis de Secondat. *Oeuvres complètes.* 8 vols. (includes *De l'Esprit des lois*) Basle, 1799.

Moureau, Agricole. *De l'incompatibilité entre le Judaïsme et l'exercise des droits de cité et des moyens de rendre les Juifs citoyens.* Paris, 1819.

Munk, Salomon. *Mélanges de philosophie juive et arabe.* Paris, 1859.

————. *Palestine. Description géographique, historique, et archéologique.* Paris, 1845.

Orobio, Isaac. *Prevenciones divinas contra la vana idolatria de la Gentes.* Portions published by Baron d'Holbach in French, under the title *Israël vengé ou exposition naturelle des prophéties hebraïques que les Chrétiens appliquent à Jésus, leur prétendu messie.* London, 1770.

Poujol, Louis. *Quelques observations concernant les Juifs en général et plus particulièrement ceux d'Alsace.* Paris, 1806.

Prières journalieres à l'usage des Juifs portugaises ou espagnols, trans. M. Venture. Nice, 1772–1773.

Rituel des prières journalières à l'usage des Israélites, trans. Joel Anspach. Metz, 1820.

Sauphar, Lipmann. *Gan Raveh (Jardin fertile).* Paris, 1849.

Selected Documents of Napoleonic Jewry, trans. and ed. Simeon Maslin. Cincinnati, 1957.

Singer, David. *Des Consistoires israélites de France.* Paris, 1820.

Sintzheim, Joseph David. *Minḥat Ani.* Paris, 1810 (ms) published by Makhon Yerushalayim, ed. S.A. Schlesinger. Jerusalem, 1975.

———. *Yad David.* Offenbach, 1799. New edition published by Makhon Yerushalayim. Jerusalem, 1976–1977.

Tama, Diogene. *Transactions of the Paris Sanhedrin.* London, 1807.

Tsarphati [Olry Terquem]. *Première Lettre d'un Israélite français à ses coreligionnaires.* Paris, 1821.

———. *Troisième Lettre d'un Israélite français à ses coreligionnaires.* Paris, 1822.

———. *Quatrième Lettre d'un Israélite français à ses coreligionnaires.* Paris, 1823.

———. *Cinquième Lettre d'un Israélite français à ses coreligionnaires.* Paris, 1824.

———. *Neuvième Lettre d'un Israélite français à ses coreligionnaires.* Paris, 1837.

———. *Lettres Tsarphatiques* (IX–XXVII). *Le Courrier de la Moselle.* 1838–1841. Fondswiener, no. 16948, Musée Lorrain, Nancy.

Tourette, Amédée. *Discours sur les Juifs d'Alsace.* Strasbourg, 1825.

Transactions of the Parisian Sanhedrin, ed. Diogene Tama. Paris, 1806–1807; trans. F. D. Kirwan. London, 1807.

Ulmann, Salomon. *Catéchisme ou elements d'instruction religieuse et morale à l'usage des jeunes israélites.* Paris, 1843.

Wessely, Naphtali, Herz. *Divre Shalom ve-Emet.* Berlin, 1782.

Worms, Aaron. *Me'ore Or.* Seven vols. Metz, 1789–1831.

III. Secondary Sources

Ages, Arnold. "Veuillot and the Talmud." *JQR* 64 (1974): 229–60.

———. "Lamennais and the Jews." *JQR* 63 (1972–1973): 158–70.

Albert, Phyllis Cohen. "Ethnicity and Jewish Solidarity in Nineteenth Century France." *Mystics, Philosophers and Politicians. Essays in Jewish Intellectual History in Honor of Alexander Altmann,* eds. Jehuda Reinharz and Daniel Swetchinski. Durham, N.C., 1982, pp. 249–74.

———. "The Jewish Oath in Nineteenth-Century France." *Spiegel Lectures in European Jewish History.* Tel Aviv, 1982.

———. *The Modernization of French Jewry: Consistory and Community in the Nineteenth Century.* Hanover, Mass., 1977.

———. "Nonorthodox Attitudes in Nineteenth Century French Judaism." *Essays in Modern Jewish History: A Tribute to Ben Halpern.* East Brunswick, N.J., 1982, pp. 121–41.

Altmann, Alexander. *Moses Mendelssohn: A Biographical Study.* Philadelphia, 1973.

———. "The New Style of Preaching in Nineteenth-Century Germany." In *Studies in Nineteenth-Century Jewish Intellectual History,* ed. A. Altmann. Cambridge, Mass., 1964, pp. 65–116.

Anchel, Robert. *Napoléon et les Juifs.* Paris, 1928.

Anderson, R. D. *Education in France, 1848–1870.* Oxford, 1975.

Arnold, Matthew. *The Popular Education of France.* London, 1861.

Artz, Frederick. *The Development of Technical Education in France, 1500–1850.* Cambridge, Mass., 1966

———. *France under the Bourbon Restoration, 1814–1830.* New York, 1963.

Selected Bibliography

Auberry, Pierre. "Montesquieu et les Juifs." *Studies on Voltaire and the Eighteenth Century* 87 (1972): 87–99.

Barnard, H. C. *Education and the French Revolution.* Cambridge, Mass., 1969.

Barnes, Harry Elmer. *A History of Historical Writing.* New York, 1963.

Bartal, Israel. ". . . So Have Our Brethren Misunderstood the Liberties of France" [Hebrew], *Cathedra* 36 (1985): 58–61.

Baron, Salo W. *A Social and Religious History of the Jews,* 2d ed., 18 vols. to date. New York, 1952– . [1st ed., 3 vols. New York, 1937.]

————. "Aspects of the Jewish Communal Crisis in 1848," *JSS* 14 (1952).

————. "New Approaches to Jewish Emancipation." *Diogenes* 29 (1960): 56–81.

Bauer, Jules. *L'Ecole Rabbinique de France.* Paris, 1930.

Berkovitz, Jay R. Review [Hebrew] of M. Graetz, *From Periphery to Center,* in *Zion* 51 (1986): 107–12.

Bloch, Joseph. *Historique de la Communauté Juive de Haguenau.* Haguenau, 1968.

Blum, Alexis. "Sinzheim: Le Porte-Parole des Ashkenazim." *Le Grand Sanhedrin de Napoleon.* eds. Bernhard Blumenkranz and Albert Soboul. Toulouse, 1979, pp. 119–31.

Bury, J. *The Idea of Progress.* London, 1920.

Byrnes, Robert. *Antisemitism in Modern France.* New Brunswick, N.J., 1950.

Cahen, Abraham. "L'émancipation des Juifs devant la Société royale des sciences et des arts de Metz en 1787 et M. Roederer." *REJ* 1 (1880), 83–104.

————. "Le Rabbinat de Metz." *REJ* 7 (1883): 103–16, 204–26; *REJ* 8 (1884): 225–74; *REJ* 12 (1886): 283–97; *REJ* 13 (1886): 105–26.

Carr, E. H. *What Is History?* New York, 1961.

Cassirer, Ernst. *The Philosophy of the Enlightenment.* Boston, 1951.

Catane, Moshe. "Une Oraison Funèbre de Jacob Meyer." *REJ* 124 (1965): 213–18.

Chisick, Harvey. *The Limits of Reform in the Enlightenment: Attitudes toward the Education of the Lower Classes in Eighteenth Century France.* Princeton, N.J., 1981.

Chouraqui, André. *L'Alliance Israélite Universelle et la Renaissance Juive Contemporaine (1800–1900).* Paris, 1965.

Cohen, David. *La promotion des Juifs en France a l'époque du Second Empire (1852–1870).* 2 vols. Aix-en-Provence, 1980.

Cuddihy, John M. *The Ordeal of Civility: Freud, Marx, Levi-Strauss and the Jewish Struggle with Modernity.* New York, 1974.

Delpech, François, "La Seconde Communauté Juive de Lyon." *Cahiers d'Histoire* 12 (1968): 51–66.

Dubnow, Simon. *History of the Jews,* 1925 ed., trans. from German, Moshe Spiegel, 5 vols. South Brunswick, N.J., 1967–1973.

Eliav, Mordechai. *Jewish Education in Germany in the Period of the Enlightenment and Emancipation* [Hebrew]. Jerusalem, 1960.

Ettinger, Shmuel. "The Beginnings of the Change in the Attitude of European Society towards the Jews." *Scripta Hierosolymitana* 7 (1961): 193–219.

————. "Jews and Judaism as Seen by the English Deists of the Eighteenth Century" [Hebrew]. *Zion* 29 (1964): 182–207.

Febvre, Lucien. "Civilisation: Evolution of a Word and a Group of Ideas." In *A New Kind of History: From the Writings of Lucien Febvre,* ed. Peter Burke. New York, 1973.

Frankel, Jonathan. "Crisis as a Factor in Modern Jewish Politics, 1840 and 1881–82." In *Living with Antisemitism: Modern Jewish Responses,* ed. Jehuda Reinharz. Hanover, N.H., 1987.

Gay, Peter. *The Enlightenment: An Interpretation,* 2 vols. New York, 1969, vol. 2.

—————. *The Party of Humanity.* New York, 1964.

Gelber, N. M. "La police autrichienne et le Sanhédrin de Napoleon." *REJ* 83 (1927).

Girard, Patrick. *Les Juifs de France de 1789 a 1860: De l'émancipation à l'égalité.* Paris, 1976.

Ginsberg, Morris. "Progress in the Modern Era." *Dictionary of the History of Ideas,* 5 vols. New York, 1933, vol. 3.

Ginsburger, M. "Les memoriaux alsaciens." *REJ* 40 (1899): 231–47; 41 (1900): 118–43.

Gordon, Milton M. *Assimilation in American Life: The Role of Race, Religion, and National Origins.* New York, 1964.

Graetz, Michael. *From Periphery to Center* [Hebrew]. Jerusalem, 1983.

Hadas-Lebel, Mireille. "Les études hé braïques en france au XVIIIᵉ siècle et la création de la première chaire d'Ecriture sainte en Sorbonne." *RES* 144 (1985): 93–126.

Hartung, Fritz. "Enlightened Despotism." *Historical Association* 36 (1957).

Heckscher, Eli F. *Mercantilism,* 2 vol. London, 1931, vol. 2.

Heinemann, Isaak. *Ta'amei Ha-Mitzvot in the Literature of Israel* [Hebrew], 2 vols. Jerusalem, 1955–56, vol. 2.

Helfand, Jonathan. "The Election of the Grand Rabbi of France (1842–1846)," *Proceedings of the Eighth World Congress of Jewish Studies.* Jerusalem, 1982, vol. 2, pp. 139–44.

—————. "French Jewry during the Second Republic and Second Empire (1848–1870)." Unpublished diss., Yeshiva University, 1979.

—————. "The Symbiotic Relationship Between French and German Jewry in the Age of Emancipation." *LBIYB,* 29 (1984), 331–50.

—————. "The Ties between French Jewry and Eretz Israel" [Hebrew], *Cathedra* (1985): 37–54.

Hertzberg, Arthur. *The French Enlightenment and the Jews.* New York, 1968.

—————. *The Zionist Idea.* Philadelphia, 1959.

Hyman, Paula. *From Dreyfus to Vichy.* New York. 1979.

—————. "Jewish Fertility in Nineteenth Century France." In *Modern Jewish Fertility,* ed. Paul Ritterband. Leiden, 1981, pp. 78–93.

—————. "Joseph Salvador." *JSS* 34 (1972): 1–22.

James, William. *The Varieties of Religious Experience.* New York, 1929.

Johnson, Douglas. *Guizot: Aspects of French History, 1787–1874.* London, 1963.

Kahn, Léon. *Histoire des écoles communales et consistoriales israélites de Paris.* Paris, 1884.

Kaplan, Yosef. *From Christianity to Judaism: The Life and Work of Isaac Orobio* [Hebrew]. Jerusalem, 1982.

Katan, Moshe. "La Famille Halevy." *Evidences* (March 1955).

Katz, Jacob. "Emancipation and Jewish Studies." *Commentary* 62 (1974): 60–65.

—————. *Exclusiveness and Tolerance.* London, 1961.

—————. *From Prejudice to Destruction: Antisemitism, 1700–1933.* Cambridge, Mass., 1980.

—————. "Jewry and Judaism in the Nineteenth Century." *Journal of World History* 4 (1958): 881–900. Reprinted in Jacob Katz, *Emancipation and Assimilation.* Westmead, G.B., 1972.

—————. "Judaism and Christianity against the Background of Modern Secularism." *Judaism* 17 (1968): 299–315. Reprinted in Katz, *Emancipation and Assimilation.* Westmead, G.B., 1972.

—————. "Judaism and the Jews in the Eyes of Voltaire" [Hebrew]. *Molad* 5 (1973): 614–25.

————. *Out of the Ghetto.* Cambridge, Mass., 1973.

————. "Religion as a Uniting and Dividing Force in Modern Jewish History." In *The Role of Religion in Modern Jewish History,* ed. Jacob Katz. Cambridge, Mass., 1974, pp. 1–17.

————. "A State within a State—The History of an anti-Semitic Slogan." *The Israel Academy of Sciences and Humanities Proceedings* 4 (1971): 32–58. Reprinted in Katz, *Emancipation and Assimilation.* Westmead, G.B., 1972.

————. "The Term 'Jewish Emancipation': Its Origin and Historical Impact." *Studies in Nineteenth Century Jewish Intellectual History,* ed. A. Altmann. Cambridge, Mass., 1964, pp. 1–26.

————. *Tradition and Crisis.* Glencoe, Illinois, 1961.

Lehrmann, Charles. *The Jewish Element in French Literature,* trans. George Klin. Cranbury, N.J., 1971.

Levy, Paul. *Histoire Linguistique d'Alsace et de Lorraine.* Paris, 1929.

Lewis, Bernard. *Islam in History: Ideas, Men and Events in the Middle East.* New York, 1973.

Liber, Maurice. "Napoléon et les Juifs." *REJ* 70 (1920): 127–47; *REJ* 72 (1921):1–23, 135–62.

Liberles, Robert. *Religious Conflict in Social Context: The Resurgence of Orthodox Judaism in Frankfurt am Main, 1838–1877.* Westport, Conn., 1985.

Lipman, Armand. *Un Grand Rabbin Francais: Benjamin Lipman.* Paris, 1923.

Loeb, Isadore. *Biographie d'Albert Cohn.* Paris, 1878.

Malino, Frances. *The Sephardic Jews of Bordeaux.* Tuscaloosa, Ala., 1978.

————. "Zalkind Hourwitz, Juif Polonais." *Dix Huitieme Siecle* 13 (1981): 79–89.

Manuel, Frank. *The New World of Henri Saint-Simon.* Cambridge, Mass., 1956.

Marcus, Ivan G. "Beyond the Sephardic Mystique." *Orim* 1 (1985).

Marcus, Jacob R. "Reform Judaism and Laity, Israel Jacobson." *CCAR* 38 (1928): 386–498.

Marrus, Michael R. *The Politics of Assimilation.* Oxford, 1971.

Maslin, Shimon. "Napoleonic Jewry from the Sanhedrin to the Bourbon Restoration." Unpublished paper, Hebrew Union College, Cincinnati.

————. "Selected Documents of Napoleonic Jewry." Unpublished paper, Hebrew Union College, Cincinnati, 1957.

Menkis, Richard. "Les Freres Elie, Olry et Lazare Terquem." *Archives Juives* 15, no. 3 (1979): 58–61.

Mevorach, Baruch. "The Belief in the Messiah in the Early Reform Polemics" [Hebrew]. *Zion* 24 (1969): 128–218.

Meyer, Michel A. "Differences of Opinion on Modern Rabbinic Training in Nineteenth Century Germany" [Hebrew]. *Proceedings of the Sixth World Congress of Jewish Studies.* Jerusalem, 1973, vol. 2, pp. 195–200.

————. *German Political Pressure and Jewish Religious Response in the Nineteenth Century.* New York, 1981.

————. "Jewish Religious Reform and Wissenschaft des Judentums: The Positions of Zunz, Geiger and Frankel." *LBIYB* 16 (1971), 19–41.

————. *The Origins of the Modern Jew.* Detroit, 1967.

Meyer-Siat, P. "L'orgue dans les synagogues d'Alsace." *Archives Juives* 8, no. 1 (1971–72).

Meyers, Peter V. "Professionalization and Societal Change: Rural Teachers in Nineteenth Century France." *Journal of Social History* 9 (1976): 542–58.

Moody, John. *French Education since Napoleon.* Syracuse, N.Y., 1978.

Morais, Samuel Henry. *Eminent Israelites of the Nineteenth Century.* Cincinnati, 1879.

Mosse, George. *The Culture of Western Europe.* Chicago, 1974.

Necheles, Ruth. "The Abbé Grégoire and the Jews." *JSS* 33 (1971): 120–40.

Neher-Bernheim. "Sephardim et Ashkenazim à Paris au milieu du XIXᵉ siecle: Un essai avorte de fusion des rites." In *Les Juifs au regard de l'histoire: Melanges en l'honneur de Bernhard Blumenkranz,* ed. Gilbert Dahan. Paris, 1985, pp. 369–82.

Park, Robert E. "Assimilation, Social." *Encyclopedia of the Social Sciences,* eds. Edwin R. A. Seligman and Alvin Johnson. New York, 1930, vol. 2.

Pelli, Moshe. "Intimations of Religious Reform in the German Haskalah Literature." *JSS* 32 (1970): 3–13.

———. "The Methodology Employed by the Hebrew Reformers in the First Temple Controversy (1818–1819)." In *Studies in Jewish Bibliography, History, and Literature in Honor of I. Edward Kiev,* ed. Charles Berlin. New York, 1971, pp. 381–97.

Petuchowski, Jakob J. "Manuals and Catechisms of the Jewish Religion in the Early Period of Emancipation." In *Studies in Nineteenth-Century Jewish Intellectual History,* ed. Alexander Altmann. Cambridge, Mass., 1964, pp. 47–64.

———. *Prayerbook Reform in Europe: The Liturgy of European Liberal and Reform Judaism.* New York, 1968.

Phillippe, Beatrice. *Les Archives Israelites de France, 1840–1848.* Paris, 1978.

Philipson, David. *The Reform Movement in Judaism.* New York, 1931.

Piette, Christine. *Les Juifs de Paris (1808–1840): la marche vers l'assimilation.* Quebec, 1983.

Plaut, W. Gunther. *The Rise of Reform Judaism.* New York, 1963.

Poliakov, Leon. *The History of Anti-Semitism from Voltaire to Wagner.* London, 1975.

Posener, S. *Adolphe Cremieux,* trans. Eugene Golub. Philadelphia, 1940.

———. "The Immediate Economic and Social Effects of the Emancipation of the Jews of France." *JSS* 1 (1939): 271–326.

———. "The Social Life of the Jewish Communities in France in the Eighteenth Century." *JSS* 7 (1945): 195–232.

Raphael, Freddy, and Robert Weyl eds. *Régards nouveaux sur les Juifs d'Alsace.* Strasbourg, 1980.

Ratcliffe, Barrie. "Crisis and Identity: Gustave d'Eichthal and Judaism in the Emancipation Period." *JSS* 37 (1975): 122–40.

Reinhold, Hanoch. "Joseph Salvador: His Life and Opinions" [Hebrew]. *Zion* 9 (1944): 109–25.

Revah, I. "Les Marranes." *REJ* 118 (1959–60): 29–77.

Rosenberg, Hans. *Bureaucracy, Aristocracy, and Autocracy: The Prussian Experience, 1660–1815.* Cambridge, Mass., 1958.

Rosenbloom, Noah. *Tradition in an Age of Reform: The Religious Philosophy of Samson Raphael Hirsch.* Philadelphia, 1976.

Rosenthal, Judah. "Interest from the Non-Jew" [Hebrew]. *Talpiot* 5 (1952): 475–92. Reprinted in Judah Rosenthal, *Mehkarim u-Mekorot,* 2 vols. Jerusalem, 1967, vol. 2, pp. 253–323.

Roth, Cecil. *History of the Jews of Italy.* Philadelphia, 1946.

Russell, Jeffrey B. *Witchcraft in the Middle Ages.* Ithaca, N.Y., 1972.

Sachar, Howard A. *The History of Israel.* New York, 1979.

Schmoller, Gustav. *The Mercantile System and Its Historical Significance.* New York, 1895.

Scholem, Gershom. *Sabbatai Zevi, the Mystical Messiah,* trans. R. J. Zwi Werblowski. Princeton, N.J., 1973.

Schorsch, Ismar. "The Emergence of Historical Consciousness in Modern Judaism." *LBIYB* 28 (1983).

———. "Emancipation and the Crisis of Religious Authority: The Crisis of the Modern Rabbinate." *Revolution and Evolution: 1848 in German-Jewish History.* Tubingen, 1981, pp. 205–47.

Schwartz, Lita L., and Natalie Isser. "Some Involuntary Conversion Techniques." *JSS* 43 (1981): 1–10.

Schwarzfuchs, Simon. *Les Juifs de France.* Paris, 1975.

———. *Napoleon, the Jews and the Sanhedrin.* London, 1979.

———. "Three Documents from the Life of the Jewish Communities of Alsace-Lorraine (Lothringen)." *Michael* 4 (1976): 9–31.

Shohat, Azriel. *Beginnings of the Haskalah Among German Jewry* [Hebrew]. Jerusalem, 1960.

Shulvass, Moses. "Crusades, Martyrdom, and the Marranos of Ashkenaz." *Between the Rhine and the Bosporus.* Chicago, 1964, pp. 1–14.

Simon, Ernst. "Pedagogical Philanthropinism and Jewish Education" [Hebrew]. *Mordechai Kaplan Jubilee Volume.* New York, 1953, pp. 149–87.

Simon, Walter, ed. *French Liberalism 1789–1848.* New York, 1972.

Stephan, Raoul. *Histoire du Protestantisme français.* Paris, 1961.

Szajkowski, Zosa. "Conflicts between Orthodox and Reformers in France" [Hebrew]. *Horeb* 14–15 (1960): 253–92.

———. "The Demographic Aspects of Jewish Emancipation in France during the French Revolution." *HJ* 21 (1959). Reprinted in *JFR*, pp. 45–74.

———. *The Economic Status of the Jews in Alsace, Metz and Lorraine (1648–1789).* New York, 1954.

———. "French Jews during the Revolution of 1830 and July Monarchy." *HJ* 22 (1960): 105–30. Reprinted in *JFR*, pp. 1017–42.

———. "Internal Conflicts in French Jewry at the Time of the Revolution of 1848." *JFR*, pp. 1073–74.

———. *The Jews and the French Revolutions of 1789, 1830, and 1848 (New York, 1970).*

———. "Jewish Autonomy Debated and Attacked during the French Revolution." *HJ* 19 (1957). Reprinted in *JFR*, pp. 576–91.

———. *Jewish Education in France, 1789–1939.* New York, 1980.

———. "Jewish Religious Observance during the French Revolution of 1789" *YIVO Annual* 12 (1958–1959): 211–34.

———. "The Jewish Saint-Simonians and Socialist Anti-Semites in France." *JSS* 9 (1947): 22–60. Reprinted in *JFR*, pp. 1091–1118.

———. "Michel Berr." *JSS* 14 (1963). Reprinted in *JFR*, pp. 1077–90.

———. "Notes on the Occupational Status of French Jews, 1800–1880." *American Academy of Jewish Research, Jubilee Volume,* eds. S. Baron and I. Barzilay. Jerusalem, 1980.

———. "Occupational Problems of Jewish Emancipation in France, 1789–1800," *Historia Judaica* 21 (1959).

———. "Riots in Alsace during the Revolutions of 1789, 1830, and 1848" [Hebrew], *Zion* 20 (1955): 82–102.

———. "Secular versus Religious Jewish Life in France." In *The Role of Religion in Modern Jewish History,* ed. Jacob Katz. Cambridge, Mass., 1975.

———. "Simon Deutz: Traitor or French Patriot." *JJS* 16 (1965). Reprinted in *JFR*, pp. 1043–57.

Szapiro, Elie. "Le proselytisme chrétien et les Juifs à Toulouse au XIXe siècle." *Archives Juives* 15, no. 3 (1979): 53–57.

Tcherikover, Victor. *Hellenistic Civilization and the Jews*. Philadelphia, 1959, pp. 320–27.

Thiel, M. "Notice sur la vie de M. Gerson-Lévy." *Extrait du mémoires de l'Académie de Metz*. Metz, 1864–1865.

Trachtenberg, Joshua. *The Devil and the Jews*. New Haven, 1943.

Treschan, Victor. "The Struggle for Integration: The Jewish Community of Strasbourg 1818–1850." Unpublished diss., University of Wisconsin—Madison, 1978.

Trevor-Roper, Hugh. *The European Witch-Craze of the Sixteenth and Seventeenth Centuries, and Other Essays*. New York, 1969.

———. *The European Witchcraft of the Sixteenth Centuries*. New York, 1956.

———. "Some of My Best Friends Are Philosophes." *New York Review of Books* 11 (22 August 1968): 11–14.

Twersky, Isadore. "Aspects of the Social and Cultural History of Provençal Jewry." *Journal of World History* 11 (1968). Reprinted in H.H. Ben-Sasson and S. Ettinger, *Jewish Society Through the Ages*. New York, 1971, pp. 185–207.

———. *Code of Maimonides (Mishneh Torah)*. New Haven, Conn., 1980.

———. *Rabad of Posquières: A Twelfth Century Talmudist*. Cambridge, Mass., 1962.

Urbach, Ephraim. *Ba'ale ha-tosafot*. Jerusalem, 1955.

Waxman, Meyer. *A History of Jewish Literature*, 5 vols. New York, 1936.

Weber, Eugen. *Peasants into Frenchmen*. Stanford, 1976.

Weill, J. "Un text de Montesquieu sur le Judaïsme." *REJ* 49 (1904): 117–19.

Weissbach, Lee Shai. "The Jewish Elite and the Children of the Poor: Jewish Apprenticeship Programs in Nineteenth-Century France." *AJS Review* 12 (1987): 123–42.

Wiener, Max. "The Ideology of the Founders of Jewish Scientific Research." *YIVO Annual of Jewish Social Science* 5 (1950): 184–96.

Yerushalmi, Yosef. *Zakhor: Jewish History and Jewish Memory*. Philadelphia, 1982.

Zeldin, Theodore. *France, 1848–1945: Politics and Anger*. New York, 1982.

Zimmels, H. J. *Ashkenazim and Sephardim*. London, 1958.

Index

Index